AF210031

Online Small Groups as Sites of Teaching

Dissertationes Theologicae Holmienses

Dissertations from University College Stockholm

www.ehs.se/dth

Editors:

Joel Halldorf

Jonas Ideström

Thomas Kazen

Samuel Rubenson

Susanne Wigorts Yngvesson

No. 7

Simon Hallonsten

Online Small Groups as Sites of Teaching

An Action Research Dissertation into Christian
Religious Education in the Church of Sweden

Enskilda Högskolan Stockholm
2024

Online Small Groups as Sites of Teaching: An Action Research Dissertation into Christian Religious Education in the Church of Sweden

Dissertation presented at University College Stockholm to be publicly examined in Room 219–220 at Åkeshovsvägen 29, Bromma, May 24, 2024, at 13:00, for the degree of Doctor of Philosophy in Theology (Practical Theology with Church History: Practical Theology). The examination will be held in English.

Faculty examiner: Courtney T. Goto, Associate Professor of Religious Education, Boston University.
Supervisor: Tone Stangeland Kaufman, Professor of Practical Theology, MF Norwegian School of Theology, Religion and Society.
Assistant supervisor: Heather Walton, Professor of Theology and Creative Practice, University of Glasgow.

Abstract

Centered around a reflective narrative recounting the experiences of a participatory action research project into leading online small groups for adults in the Church of Sweden Diocese of Stockholm during 2021 and 2022, the dissertation argues for the need to reconceptualize and reemphasize teaching as an important aspect in Christian religious education. Employing creative non-fiction methods, the dissertation aims to broaden the scope of the initial *Online Small Groups* project, by inviting readers to join into a "learning journey." The narrative account is complemented with more traditional forms of analysis that connect experiences from online small groups in the Church of Sweden to similar research from Anglo-Saxon countries, noting especially how notions of community diverge due to different ecclesiological understandings. Insights are then synthesized into eight teaching strategies aimed at communicating actionable knowledge to small group leaders, before noting how the study complements research on Christian religious education and, particularly, the current debate about learning and teaching in the Church of Sweden.

Digitala smågrupper som platser för undervisning: En aktionsforskningsavhandling om religionspedagogik i Svenska kyrkan

Akademisk avhandling presenterad vid Enskilda Högskolan Stockholm för disputation i sal 219–220, Åkeshovsvägen 29, Bromma, 24 maj 2024, kl. 13.00, för teologie doktorsexamen i praktisk teologi med kyrkohistoria med inriktning mot praktisk teologi. Disputationen kommer att äga rum på engelska.

Opponent:	Courtney T. Goto, Associate Professor of Religious Education, Boston University.
Handledare:	Tone Stangeland Kaufman, Professor i praktisk teologi, MF vitenskapelig høyskole.
Bitr. handledare:	Heather Walton, Professor of Theology and Creative Practice, University of Glasgow.

Sammanfattning

Avhandlingen är centrerad kring en reflekterande berättelse om erfarenheterna från ett deltagande aktionsforskningsprojekt om att leda digitala smågrupper för vuxna i Svenska kyrkans Stockholms stift under 2021 och 2022. Avhandlingen argumenterar för behovet av att rekonceptualisera och betona undervisning som en viktig aspekt i kristen religionspedagogik. Genom att använda skönlitterära metoder syftar avhandlingen till att bredda insikterna från det ursprungliga *Online Small Groups*-projektet genom att bjuda in läsarna att delta i en "läranderesa." Den narrativa berättelsen kompletteras med mer traditionella former av analys som kopplar erfarenheter från digitala smågrupper i Svenska kyrkan till liknande forskning från anglosaxiska länder, och noterar särskilt hur uppfattningar om gemenskap skiljer sig åt på grund av olika ecklesiologiska förståelser. Insikterna sammanfattas sedan i åtta undervisningsstrategier som syftar till att förmedla användbar kunskap till smågruppsledare, innan det noteras på vilka sätt studien kompletterar forskning om kristen religionspedagogik och, i synnerhet, den aktuella debatten om lärande och undervisning i Svenska kyrkan.

Enskilda Högskolan Stockholm

Enskilda Högskolan Stockholm erbjuder utbildningsprogram i mänskliga rättigheter och demokrati, samt i teologi/religionsvetenskap. Högskolan grundades 1993 genom en sammanslagning av utbildningsinstitutioner med rötter från 1866, hette tidigare Teologiska högskolan, Stockholm, och har tre avdelningar: Avdelningen för mänskliga rättigheter och demokrati, Avdelningen för religionsvetenskap och teologi, samt Avdelningen för östkyrkliga studier. Forskarutbildningen i Praktisk teologi med kyrkohistoria bedrivs inom inriktningarna Praktisk teologi respektive Kyrkohistoria. Utbildningen fokuserar på den kristna kyrkans utveckling och den kristna trons praktiska gestaltning, i ett konstruktivt samspel mellan empiriska metoder och teori. Utbildningen innefattar bland annat historiska, hermeneutiska, filosofiska, teologiska, sociologiska och etnologiska perspektiv.

University College Stockholm

University College Stockholm offers programmes in Human Rights and Democracy and in Theology / Religious Studies. The university college was founded in 1993 through a merger of educational institutions with roots dating back to 1866, is also known as Stockholm School of Theology, and has three departments: the Department of Human Rights and Democracy, the Department of Religious Studies and Theology, and the Department of Eastern Christian Studies. The doctoral programme in Practical Theology with Church History provides specialisations in Practical Theology and Church History respectively. It focuses on the development of the Christian church and practical expressions of Christian faith, in a constructive interplay between empirical methods and theory. The programme includes historical, hermeneutical, philosophical, theological, sociological, and ethnological perspectives.

© 2024 Simon Hallonsten

ISBN: 978-91-88906-25-0
Page and cover design by Carl Johan Berglund. Typeset in EB Garamond.
Printed by BoD – Books on Demand, Norderstedt, Germany.

University College Stockholm
Åkeshovsvägen 29, 168 39 Bromma, Sweden
www.ehs.se

Acknowledgements

This dissertation would not have been possible without the extensive involvement of numerous individuals. I am profoundly grateful to my co-researchers for our collaboration in the action research project and to all participants in the online small groups for their willingness to share their experiences. Without you none of this would have been possible.

Special acknowledgment is due to Sara Garpe and Andreas Holmberg, whose early recognition of the need to explore the consequences of being church in digital space during the COVID-19 pandemic was the origin of this project. I extend my gratitude to Sara Garpe and Jonas Ideström for their leadership, as well as to my colleagues at the University College Stockholm—Tone Stangeland Kaufman, Frida Mannerfelt, and Rikard Roitto—for their unwavering support and encouragement.

I owe a particular debt of gratitude to Tone Stangeland Kaufman, not only as my colleague but as my supervisor, who has shepherded me and my dissertation through years of writing and revising this dissertation. Thank you for your patience with my ever so many drafts and ideas and changes of direction. Your support and encouragement, your critiques and challenges, have not only formed this dissertation, but me as a researcher and scholar.

I am also thankful to my co-supervisor, Heather Walton, whose perspective on practical theology has profoundly influenced my own, opening up an alternative approach to scholarship.

My journey would have been markedly different without a group of companions to share the joys and sorrows of postgraduate research. I am grateful for the time we spent in the Church and Society research school at the University College Stockholm. I am indebted to our research leaders—Joel Halldorf, Sune Fahlgren, Jonas Ideström, and Tone Stangeland Kaufman—as well as to my fellow researchers: Ann-Christine Falk, Björn Asserhed, Daniel Strömner, Ellen Vingren, Elin Lockneus, Frida Mannerfelt, Hanna Alenius, Joel Appelfeldt, Pernilla Myrelid, and Torbjörn Toll. Sharing both triumphs and challenges with you all has been invaluable.

I appreciate the contributions of Elisabeth Tveito Johnsen, Knut Tveitereid, and Fredrik Saxegaard, whose critical comments helped refine my arguments. Dorte Kappelgaard's careful reading and empathetic engagement with my work have been tremendously encouraging, as have Jonas Ideström's comments and his many words of advise throughout the years.

In the final stages, David Michael played a crucial role in working with me on editing, especially the more creative aspects of this dissertation. His balanced feedback and encouragement were instrumental in bringing this project to fruition. Thanks also go to Thomas Kazen and Carl Johan Berglund for their assistance in the final preparation of the manuscript.

Lastly, the support from my spouse, Hanna, has been indispensable. Hanna, I am deeply grateful for your support. I couldn't have done this without you.

Stockholm in April 2024
Simon Hallonsten

Contents

Tables and Figures

Figures

Tables

Part I:
Groundings

1. Introduction: The Purpose and Rationale of the Research

Teaching is one of the church's fundamental callings. This is true for all churches, and it is true for the Church of Sweden, the focus of this dissertation.[1] The Church of Sweden has formalized its commitment to teaching through its Church Ordinance, identifying it as one of four primary parish functions alongside the celebration of the liturgy, the practice of diakonia, and mission work.[2] The Ordinance further clarifies the purpose of these fundamental tasks: "people come to faith in Christ and live in faith, a Christian community is created and deepened, the kingdom of God is extended and creation is restored."[3]

Yet, in recent years, the Church of Sweden's teaching ministry has been the subject of various critiques and debates.[4] Jørgen Straarup and Mayvor Ekberg, for instance, have argued that the Church of Sweden has failed to establish an adequate teaching ministry.[5] In discussions about the Church's religious education, Ann-Louise Erikson and Caroline Klintborg have noted that contemporary Swedes lack the necessary religious literacy to fully grasp sermons and key aspects of the liturgy, respectively.[6] Similarly, Jakob Wirén and Sara Fransson have

---

[1] I largely follow the *SBL Handbook of Style* recommendations for capitalization of terms. I hence capitalize "Church" when referring to a specific church, such as the Church of Sweden, and use lower case to indicate church as a theological and sociological concept. Often "Church" is short for "Church of Sweden."

[2] Svenska kyrkan, *Kyrkoordning för Svenska kyrkan* (Uppsala: Svenska kyrkan, 2023), Ch 2 § 1.

[3] Svenska kyrkan, *Kyrkoordning*, Introduction to Ch 2.

[4] See section 1.5.1.

[5] Jørgen Straarup and Mayvor Ekberg, *Den sorglöst försumliga kyrkan belyst norrifrån* (Skellefteå: Artos, 2012).

[6] Anne-Louise Eriksson, *Att predika en tradition: Om tro och teologisk literacy* (Lund: Arcus, 2012); Caroline Gustavsson [Klintborg], *Delaktighetens kris: Gudstjänstens pedagogiska utmaning* (Skellefteå: Artos, 2015).

highlighted how Sweden's evolving cultural and religious landscape demands new educational approaches from within the Church.[7]

Giving credence to these critiques, the Church of Sweden has initiated a process to refocus its educational ministry. Over the last decade, there has thus been a renewed emphasis on learning and teaching within the Church, evidenced by its *Sharing Faith, Sharing Life* program (2013–2018), and its successor, the *Program for Learning and Teaching* (2018–2022), the latter of which was designed to enhance and deepen knowledge and familiarity with the Christian faith among the broader population.[8]

Engaging with the academic debate on Christian religious education and the current educational practices of the Church of Sweden, this dissertation seeks to reorient these recent discussions, proposing that an insufficient engagement with the concept and practice of teaching has led to the neglect of large parts of the Church of Sweden's educational ministry.

1.1 The Dissertation in a Nutshell

This dissertation centers on a participatory action research project within the Church of Sweden's Diocese of Stockholm. Over the course of a year, I collaborated with two pastors and two deacons to explore, understand, and improve online small groups. In recounting our story and reflecting on our experiences, I aim to move from the initial, specific learnings the project afforded to articulating insights of significance to a broader audience.[9]

---

[7] Jakob Wirén, *Utmaningsdriven undervisning: Hur kyrkan kan dela tro och liv idag* (Stockholm: Verbum, 2017); Sara Fransson, ed., *Konfirmation i förändringens tid: En rapport om konfirmander och ledare 2007–2022* (Uppsala: Svenska kyrkan, 2023).

[8] Wirén, *Undervisning*, 54; Thomas Westerberg et al., "Utvärdering av Svenska kyrkans program för lärande och undervisning: Slutrapport," Oxford Research AB (Stockholm, 2023), 4–5. For am introduction to the *Sharing Faith, Sharing Life* program see Wirén, *Undervisning*, 52–54.

[9] This is a hallmark goal of action research dissertations. See Peter Reason and Judi Marshall, "Research as Personal Process," in *Appreciating Adults Learning: From the Learner's Perspective*, ed. David Boud and Virginia Griffin (London: Kogan Page, 1987), 112–26 at 112–13; Mary Brydon-Miller, Davydd Greenwood, and Patricia Maguire, "Why Action Research?," *Action Research* 1, no. 1 (2003): 9–28 at 25; Kathryn Herr and Gary L. Anderson, *The Action Research Dissertation: A Guide for Students and Faculty* (Thousand Oaks: SAGE Publications, 2012); David Coghlan and Patricia Gaya, "Dissertation Writing," in *The SAGE Encyclopedia of Action Research*, ed. David Coghlan and Mary Brydon-Miller (Thousand Oaks: SAGE Publications Ltd, 2014), 281–83. See also section 1.3 and 3.2.

I position this dissertation within the field of Christian religious education and, more broadly, practical theology. However, practical theology encompasses a variety of operative understandings regarding its nature and objectives, rendering it a diverse and expansive discipline.[10] More specifically, then, my dissertation resides at the intersection of two strands within white practical theology.[11]

The first strand aims to deepen the understanding of Christian religious practices and directly aid in their improvement.[12] Within this strand, I locate my work within *collaborative research designs*, specifically *theological action research*.[13] This approach to theological research emphasizes producing reliable and actionable

---

[10] For some recent Scandinavian discussions see Jonas Ideström and Tone Stangeland Kaufman, eds., *What Really Matters: Scandinavian Prspectives on Ecclesiology and Ethnography* (Eugene: Pickwick Publications, 2018); Lisbet Christoffersen, Niels Henrik Gregersen, and Karen Marie Sø Leth-Nissen, eds., *Den praktiske teologi i Danmark 1973–2018: Festskrift til Hans Raun Iversen* (Copenhagen: Eksistensen, 2019). Practical theology has also been the subject of discussion in a number of recent journal issues. See *Nordic Journal of Practical Theology* 37, no. 1 (2020), *Svensk Teologisk Kvartalskrift* 97, no. 1 (2021), and *Studia Theologica – Nordic Journal of Theology* 75, no. 1 (2021).

[11] I take the term "white practical theology" from a discussion ensuing from the chapters on Black practical theology and Asian-American practical theology in the edited volume *Opening the Field of Practical Theology*, to demonstrate that all forms of practical theology are produced from specific social and cultural locations. See Courtney T. Goto, "Asian American Practical Theologies," in *Opening the Field of Practical Theology: An Introduction*, ed. Kathleen A. Cahalan and Gordon S. Mikoski (Lanham: Rowman & Littlefield, 2014), 31–44; Tom Beaudoin and Katherine Turpin, "White Practical Theology," in *Opening the Field of Practical Theology: An Introduction*, ed. Kathleen A. Cahalan and Gordon S. Mikoski (Lanham: Rowman & Littlefield, 2014), 251–69; Courtney T. Goto, "Writing in Compliance with the Racialized 'Zoo' of Practical Theology," in *Conundrums in Practical Theology*, ed. Bonnie J. Miller-McLemore and Joyce Ann Mercer (Leiden; Boston: Brill, 2016), 110–33. See also my discussions in sections 2.8 and 6.3.3.

[12] John Swinton and Harriet Mowat, *Practical Theology and Qualitative Research*, 2nd ed. (London: SCM press, 2016).

[13] Helen Cameron and colleagues have coined the term Theological Action Research (TAR) to denote a specific way of employing action research in theology. To differentiate between the method and the field, Jonas Ideström calls the latter "Theology and Action Research" and Jason Boyd prefers to speak of his approach as Action Research in Theology (ART). Jonas Ideström, "Action Research and Theology," in *The Wiley Blackwell Companion to Theology and Qualitative Research*, ed. Pete Ward and Knut Tveiterid (Oxford: Wiley Blackwell, 2022), 425–34; Jason Boyd, *The Naked Preacher: Action Research and a Practice of Preaching* (London: SCM Press, 2018). In contrast, I use theological action research to denote the field as I find it to be the most accurate descriptor, and use the capitalized version to denote the specific method developed by Cameron et al.

knowledge, frequently through collaboration between academics and practitioners of joint action, data collection, and analysis, typically manifesting as conversations.[14]

Challenges with the representation of our collaborative research in the writing
of this dissertation steered me towards the second strand, which emphasizes integrating *creative practices* and *arts-based research* into practical theology. Drawing
inspiration from (auto)ethnography, this strand often pays special attention to the
question of representation and its consequences for both academic writing and
knowledge production.[15]

In this line of scholarship, I found resources to employ reflective writing and
narrative as alternatives to the traditional case study approach for extending initial
insights.[16] Consequently, within the larger discipline of practical theology, I position the dissertation at the intersection of theological action research, Christian

---

[14] Henk de Roest, *Collaborative Practical Theology: Engaging Practitioners in Research on
Christian Practices* (Leiden, Boston: Brill, 2020), 156–96; Cameron Harder, "Using Participatory
Action Research in Seminary Internships," *Theological Education* 42, no. 2 (2007): 127–39;
Helen Cameron et al., *Talking about God in Practice: Theological Action Research and Practical
Theology* (London: SCM Press, 2010); Clare Watkins, *Disclosing Church: An Ecclesiology Learned
from Conversations in Practice* (Abingdon: Routledge, 2020); Ideström, "Action Research."

[15] This strand of practical theology is a loose configuration rather than a coherent school.
However, scholars working within this strand all share the recognition that their personal lives
are deeply intertwined with their academic scholarship, and usually try to connect the two in
their writing. See for example Bonnie J. Miller-McLemore, *Also a Mother: Work and Family as
Theological Dilemma* (Nashville: Abingdon Press, 1994); Natalie Wigg-Stevenson, *Ethnographic
Theology: An Inquiry into the Production of Theological Knowledge* (New York: Palgrave
Macmillan, 2014); Heather Walton, *Not Eden: Spiritual Life Writing for this World* (London:
SCM Press, 2015); Pamela D. Couture, *We Are Not All Victims: Local Peacebuilding in the
Democratic Republic of Congo* (Zurich: Lit Verlag, 2016); Claire Wolfteich, *Mothering, Public
Leadership, and Women's Life Writing: Explorations in Spirituality Studies and Practical
Theology* (Leiden: Brill, 2017); Courtney T. Goto, *Taking on Practical Theology: The Idolization
of Context and the Hope of Community* (Leiden; Boston: Brill, 2018); Todd D. Whitmore,
Imitating Christ in Magwi: An Anthropological Theology (London: T&T Clark, 2019); Julian
Müller, John Eliastam, and Sheila Trahar, eds., *Unfolding Narratives of Ubuntu in Southern
Africa* (London: Routledge, 2019); Nicola Slee, *Fragments for Fractured Times: What Feminist
Practical Theology Brings to the Table* (London: SCM Press, 2020). In Scandinavia, Cecilia Nahn-
feldt is one of the scholars who works within this stream of practical theology. Cecilia Nahnfeldt,
"'Tu veux un chewing-gum?' Encounters in Hospitality and Willfulness," in *Contemporary
Christian-Cultural Values*, ed. Cecilia Nahnfeldt and Kaia S. Rønsdal (London: Routledge,
2021), 61–78.

[16] I explain this in more detail in section 3.5.2.

religious education, and theology through creative practice, as illustrated in figure 1.1.

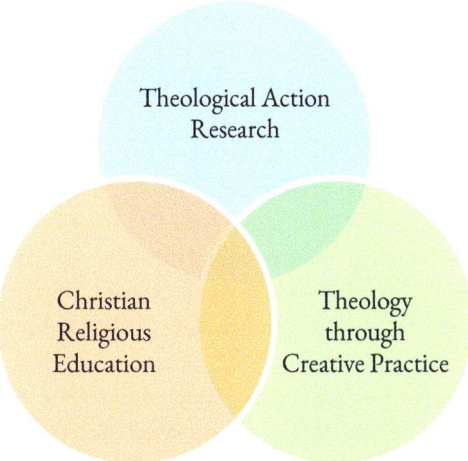

Figure 1.1 General Placement of the Dissertation

As an action research dissertation, the research question is formulated practically, facilitating the articulation of usable knowledge in part 4.

The research question is: *How can online small groups within the Church of Sweden be improved as instances of Christian religious education, and do these improvement possibilities suggest any implications for Christian religious education within the Church of Sweden more generally?*

To address my research question, I begin with a theoretical discussion on Christian religious education and define teaching as the theoretical lens through which I examine our experiences of leading online small groups.[17] I narrate our experiences from the *Online Small Groups* project, utilizing creative non-fiction techniques in part 2, a mode of analysis and reflective writing that is gaining prominence within qualitative research and holds significant promise for practical theologians.[18]

---

[17] See sections 2.2–2.3.

[18] James Clifford and George E. Marcus, *Writing Culture: The Poetics and Politics of Ethnography* (Berkeley: University of California Press, 1986); Laurel Richardson, *Writing Strategies: Reaching Diverse Audiences* (Newbury Park, Calif.: Sage Publications, 1990); Kristen

Then I connect these reflective narratives to theories and previous research on Christian religious education, online learning, and small groups, offering a complementary analysis of our online small groups in chapter 4. I explore different interpretations of community within these groups in chapter 5.[19] Then, in chapter 6, I revisit my teaching perspective to examine how leaders of online small groups may be perceived as "teachers," and the potential ramifications of such a perspective on group leadership.

The research question receives its most direct response in chapter 7, where I identify eight teaching strategies for online small groups within the Church of Sweden. Finally, in chapter 8, I delve into broader inquiries concerning learning and teaching in the Church of Sweden, returning to the initial discussion about its educational ministry briefly outlined above.[20]

The remainder of this introductory chapter is structured as follows: I provide a concise introduction to the *Online Small Groups* project, followed by an explanation of the specific form of this action research dissertation. Subsequently, I situate my work within the field of religious education and review recent literature on both Christian religious education in the Church of Sweden and online learning and small groups. Lastly, I outline the aims and research questions before articulating this dissertation's contribution.

1.2 The *Online Small Groups* Project

The *Online Small Groups* project was conducted in 2021 and 2022 as part of a larger participatory action initiative.[21] Named *Church in Digital Space*, this broader effort united the Church of Sweden Diocese of Stockholm, its national level, seven parishes within the diocese, and five researchers from the Stockholm

---

Rogheh Ghodsee, *From Notes to Narrative: Writing Ethnographies that Everyone Can Read* (Chicago: The University of Chicago Press, 2016); Laurel Richardson and Elizabeth Adams St. Pierre, "Writing: A Method of Inquiry," in *The SAGE Handbook of Qualitative Research*, ed. Norman K. Denzin and Yvonna S. Lincoln (Los Angeles: Sage Publications, 2018), 1410–44; Heather Walton, *Writing Methods in Theological Reflection* (London, England: SCM Press, 2014); Walton, *Not Eden*; Couture, *Not All Victims*; Slee, *Fragments*; Natalie Wigg-Stevenson, *Transgressive Devotion: Theology as Performance Art* (London: SCM Press, 2021). See also section 3.5.

[19] See chapters 4 and 5.

[20] For a more in-depth presentation see section 1.5.1.

[21] The original project was called *digitala samtalsgrupper* (lit. digital conversation groups). However, as I relate the project here to literature on online learning and on small groups, I opt to call the project *Online Small Groups* to demonstrate the links to these two bodies of scholarships.

School of Theology. Together, we explored ways to enhance parishes' online presence through increased interactivity, participation, and relationship building, and processed the theological and communicative questions that arise when Christian faith is shaped by and lived out in digital space.[22] *Online Small Groups* was one of four research and development tracks in this larger project. The other initiatives focused on (1) communication, mission, and language; (2) proclamation, rite, and worship; and (3) digital church rooms and virtual parishes.[23]

Online Small Groups initially derived its objectives from the overarching *Church in Digital Space* initiative. To guide our investigation, we articulated two questions: "How can we facilitate digitally mediated conversations that contribute to increased interactivity, participation, and relationship building?" and "Can digitally mediated conversations serve as a comprehensive alternative for onsite conversations, and if so, for whom and under what circumstances?"[24]

Early on, however, we realized that our online small groups were not static entities; instead, they were dynamic and evolving contexts of ministry. To address the second question, it became apparent that we needed to evaluate whether online small groups were functioning at their optimum or if it was necessary to further develop the Church's online ministry to ensure it could serve as a viable and effective alternative to traditional onsite meetings.

At the heart of the *Online Small Groups* project was the collaboration between myself and four leaders of online small groups within the Church of Sweden: two deacons and two pastors.[25] Table 1.1 provides a summary of the groups and the materials collected.

---

[22] Sara Garpe and Jonas Ideström, eds., *Kyrka i digitala rum: Ett aktionsforskningsprojekt om församlingsliv online i Svenska kyrkan* (Uppsala: Church of Sweden, 2022).

[23] Garpe and Ideström, *Kyrka i digitala rum*, 15–16.

[24] Simon Hallonsten, "Digitala samtalsgrupper för vuxna," in *Kyrka i digitala rum: Ett aktionsforskningsprojekt om församlingsliv online i Svenska kyrkan*, ed. Sara Garpe and Jonas Ideström (Uppsala: Svenska kyrkan, 2022), 82–98 at 84.

[25] The Church of Sweden has two ordained offices: deacons and pastors. Like pastors, deacons are ordained for life and generally in charge of the church's outreach ministry, pastoral care, and teaching, even as these frequently overlap with pastor's responsibilities. Pastors are responsible for preaching and leading the celebration of the liturgy. Literally translated the Church of Sweden uses the term "priest" (präst) for this function. I use "pastor" here to keep to the US distinction between Catholic priests and protestant pastors. For a discussion see Tone Stangeland Kaufman, *A New Old Spirituality? A Qualitative Study of Clergy Spirituality in the Nordic Context*, Church of Sweden Research Series, (Eugene: Pickwick Publications, 2017).

	#S:t Eskils	#Margareta	#Djursholm	#Älvsjö
Time	Aug – Oct 2021	Sep – Oct 2021	Jan – Apr 2022	Mar – Apr 2022
Type	Book Club	*Lectio Divina*	*Lectio Divina*	Bible Study
Leader	Jessica Bergqvist, Deacon & Lotta Adamsson, Librarian	Karin Andersson, Pastor	Eva Karlsson, Deacon & Simon Hallonsten	Camilla Lindström, Pastor & Simon Hallonsten
Meetings	6	3	7	7
Participants	6–8	2–6	4–5	10–11
Type	Closed	Open	Closed	Closed
Target audience	Lay parishioners	Lay parishioners	Lay parishioners	Church of Sweden pastors
Methods for Observation and Reflection	Leader Feedback forms (8), Participant Feedback forms (13), Participant Observation (1), Planning & Reflection Meetings (3)	Leader Feedback forms (3), Participant Feedback forms (6), Interviews (2), Participant Observation (1), Planning & Reflection Meetings (4)	Participant Observation (6), Group Evaluation (2)	Participant Observation (6), Group Evaluation (2), Planning & Reflection Meetings (8)

Table 1.1 Summary of Groups in the Online Small Groups Project

The original project included five groups. In addition to the groups I describe here, we also had a "churchwarden" (*kyrkvärd*) group who participated as a hybrid group, which combined online and onsite meetings through a videoconferencing system. However, the dynamics in the hybrid group differed from the pure online groups to such a degree, that I opt to only focus on the pure online groups here. The hybrid group also decided to discontinue the possibility for members to join online, opting to become a pure onsite group, as it had been before the pandemic. As I see it, hybrid meetings face particular challenges that are partially different from the challenges in pure online group and therefore deserve to be treated separately.

The four groups were based in three parishes located in the inner suburbs of Stockholm. To maintain the anonymity of research participants, I have assigned fictitious parish names to each group. Given that there was no interaction between the two groups from the same parish, I believe this approach does not affect the portrayal of the research process or the results.[26]

Engaging with action research cycles, we aimed to identify and plan potential improvements, implement these enhancements, observe the outcomes, and reflect on their implications, thereby discovering further opportunities for improvement. Consequently, the research shifted its focus towards more generalized strategies for improving the groups, progressing beyond the initial emphasis on interactivity, participation, and relationship building.[27]

Throughout the project, we pinpointed opportunities for improvement based on our observations and feedback from participants. In this dissertation, I expand upon that dialogue and present a broader argument for enhancing online small groups within the Church of Sweden.[28] Naturally, the concept of improvement is contingent upon specific criteria to assess change, thus necessitating a framework of normative assumptions, as explained in chapter 2. At its core, I connect online small groups with fundamental principles of Christian religious education, thereby exploring how online small groups can be understood and developed as sites of teaching.

1.3 An Action Research Dissertation

Action research represents a distinct approach to social inquiry, based on the principle that deep understanding is cultivated through active engagement with evolving situations. Although action research remains relatively novel within Scandinavian practical theology, it boasts a rich history, not least in the realm of education.

Tracing its origins to the early conceptualizations by Kurt Lewin and John Collier in the 1930s and 1940s, action research thrived within the progressive education movement, which sought to improve schooling, teaching, and learning, aligning with the emerging emphasis on child-centered education.[29] In the 1950s,

---

[26] For a discussion see section 3.4.2.

[27] See part 2.

[28] See section 1.3.

[29] Cher C. Hendricks, "History of Action Research in Education," in *The Wiley Handbook of Action Research in Education*, ed. Craig A. Mertler (Newark: John Wiley & Sons, 2019), 29–51 at 30–36; Knud Illeris, "An Overview of the History of Learning Theory," *European Journal of Education* 53, no. 1 (2018): 86–101 at 87–88.

Stephen Corey explicitly connected action research with education, paving the way for its expansion to the UK in the 1970s. There, the burgeoning Teacher-as-Researcher Movement posited that education research should be both testable and practical for educators.[30] As it evolved, action research in education adopted a more participatory stance, with advocates calling for learner involvement in the research process to ensure the quality of findings. Consequently, action research in education has progressively shifted towards a participatory action research model.[31]

Today, action research is well established in education research worldwide, encompassing all subjects. This includes a significant presence in the field of religious education, with studies conducted in diverse countries such as Greece,[32]

---

[30] Hendricks, "History of Action Research in Education," 41–44. To my knowledge "education research" and "educational research" are synonymous, referring both to "the scientific field of study that examines education and learning processes and the human attributes, interactions, organizations, and institutions that shape educational outcomes." "What is Education Research?," American Educational Research Association, 2023, accessed 25 Sep, 2023, *https://-www.aera.net/About-AERA/What-is-Education-Research*. See for example, "Educational Research Journal," National Foundation for Educational Research, 2023, accessed 25 Sep, 2023, *https://www.nfer.ac.uk/publications-research/educational-research-journal/*. The difference might be one between British and American English. I use there the term "education research."

[31] Hilary Bradbury, Rolla Lewis, and Dusty Columbia Embury, "Education Action Research: With and for the Next Generation," in *The Wiley Handbook of Action Research in Education*, ed. Craig A. Mertler (Newark: John Wiley & Sons, 2019), 7–28 at 10–13; Andrea C. Burrows, "US Perspectives on Action Research in Education," in *The Wiley Handbook of Action Research in Education*, ed. Craig A. Mertler (Newark: John Wiley & Sons, 2019), 75–96 at 76–77.

[32] Marios Koukounaras Liagkis, "The Socio-Pedagogical Dynamics of Religious Knowledge in Religious Education: A Participatory Action-Research in Greek Secondary Schools on Understanding Diversity," *Religions* 13, no. 5 (2022): 395–52.

Indonesia,[33] Norway,[34] Sweden,[35] Thailand,[36] the United Kingdom,[37] and the United States,[38] spanning Buddhist,[39] Jewish,[40] Muslim,[41] Christian,[42] and secular settings across various educational levels.[43]

Common to these studies is their focus on formal education, whether in kindergartens, schools, or universities, even though the distinction between school-

---

[33] Tedi Supriyadi and J. Julia, "The Problem of Students in Reading the Quran: A Reflective-Critical Treatment through Action Research," *International Journal of Instruction* 12, no. 1 (2019): 311–26; Isa Anshori, "Problem-Based Learning Remodelling Using Islamic Values Integration and Sociological Research in Madrasas," *International Journal of Instruction* 14, no. 2 (2021): 421–42.

[34] Øystein Lund Johannessen, "Negotiating and Reshaping Christian Values and Professional Identities through Action Research: Experiential Learning and Professional Development among Christian Religious Education Teachers," *Educational Action Research* 23, no. 3 (2015): 331–49; Dag Husebø, Øystein Lund Johannessen, and Geir Skeie, "Impact of Action Research in Norwegian Religious Education," *British Journal of Religious Education* (2022): 45–56.

[35] Malin Löfstedt and Katarina Westerlund, "Turning to Practice in Academic Theology and Religious Studies: Research Circles as an Example," *Studia Theologica* 75, no. 1 (2021): 79–98.

[36] Phramaha Jittipong Chanthago, Phrakrudhammapissamai Phrakrudhammapissamai, and Chayanon Jantaragaroon, "Development of a Learning School in Wat Srichan School, Khon Kaen Province: A Participatory Action Research," *International Journal of Higher Education* 9, no. 1 (2019): 11–21.

[37] Kevin O'Grady, "Researching Religious Education Pedagogy through an Action Research Community of Practice," *British Journal of Religious Education* 32, no. 2 (2010): 119–31; David Lundie et al., "A Practitioner Action Research Approach to Learning Outside the Classroom in Religious Education: Developing a Dialogical Model Through Reflection by Teachers and Faith Field Visitors," *British Journal of Religious Education* 44, no. 2 (2021): 138–48.

[38] Miriam Raider-Roth et al., "Shared Power, Risk-taking, and Innovation: Participatory Action Research in Jewish Education," *Journal of Jewish Education* 85, no. 2 (2019): 187–208; Mary K. McVey and Susan R. Poyo, "Preparing Catholic Educators to Educate and Evangelize in 21st Century Schools: Action Research of an Analysis of Educator Preparation Program Requirements Including Professional and Pedagogical, Relational, Formational and Evangelistic Education for P-16 Students (PROFEss)," *Catholic Education* 22, no. 2 (2019): 107–18.

[39] Chanthago, Phrakrudhammapissamai, and Jantaragaroon, "Development of a Learning School."

[40] Raider-Roth et al., "Shared Power."

[41] Anshori, "Problem-Based Learning Remodelling Using Islamic Values"; Supriyadi and Julia, "The Problem of Students in Reading the Quran."

[42] Johannessen, "Negotiating and Reshaping"; McVey and Poyo, "Preparing Catholic Educators."

[43] O'Grady, "Researching Religious Education"; Koukounaras Liagkis, "The Socio-Pedagogical Dynamics of Religious Knowledge"; Lundie et al., "Practitioner Action Research"; Löfstedt and Westerlund, "Research Circles."

based and church-based religious education sometimes becomes blurred, particularly in Catholic and Islamic schools.[44] Additionally, a subset of action research has explored Christian religious education within seminaries, colleges, and universities.[45]

Action research has been employed to examine Christian religious education within churches, parishes, and congregations as well. However, this branch of action research typically falls under the umbrella of theological action research rather than the broader domain of educational action research, with only a handful of references to educational action research appearing in this specific literature.[46]

Theological action research traces its origins to the United States during the 1970s and 1980s, with scholars initially applying action research methods to study

---

[44] McVey and Poyo, "Preparing Catholic Educators"; Anshori, "Problem-Based Learning Remodelling Using Islamic Values."

[45] Arch Chee Keen Wong, Cameron Harder, Mark Chapman, and Daniel P. Rhodes all report independently of each other on the benefits of using participatory action research as part of internships or field research in theological education, whether at interdenominational evangelical universities, Lutheran seminaries, or Jesuit institutions. Arch Chee Keen Wong, "Christian Faculty Teaching Reflective Practice: An Action Research Approach to Learning," *Christian Higher Education* 8, no. 3 (2009): 173–86; Arch Chee Keen Wong et al., "Learning Through Shared Christian Praxis: Reflective Practice in the Classroom," *Teaching Theology & Religion* 12, no. 4 (2009): 305–20; Arch Chee Keen Wong, "How Is the Internship Going Anyways? An Action Research Approach to Understanding the Triad Relationship between Interns, Mentors, and Field Advisors," *Educational Action Research* 19, no. 4 (2011): 517–29; Arch Chee Keen Wong, "Considering Reflection From the Student Perspective in Higher Education," *SAGE Open* 6, no. 1 (2016): 1–9; Harder, "Using Participatory Action Research"; Mark Chapman, "Changing the World without Doing Harm: Critical Pedagogy, Participatory Action Research and the Insider Student Researcher," *Religious Studies and Theology* 38, no. 1–2 (2019): 100–16; Daniel P. Rhodes, "Theology as Social Activity: Theological Action Research and Teaching the Knowledge of Christian Ethics and Practical Ministry," *Scottish Journal of Theology* 73, no. 4 (2020): 340–57.

[46] Bruce Martin, "'Living' Education: Action Research as a Practical Approach to Congregational Education," *Religious Education* 95, no. 2 (2000): 151–66; Dent Davis, "Learning our Way: Engaging Laity through Large-scale Participatory Action Research," *Journal of Adult Theological Education* 4, no. 1 (2007): 48–62; Steve Thomason, "Participatory Action Research as Trinitarian Praxis and a Pedagogical Model for the Suburban Congregation," *Religious Education* 113, no. 1 (2018): 96–108.

and develop parishes and congregations.[47] However, this research strand remained marginal, with a resurgence in publications only beginning in the early 2000s.[48]

Later, the approach took root in the United Kingdom, seemingly independent of the earlier US-American efforts. *Talking About God in Practice* by Helen Cameron and colleagues emerged as a pivotal work, igniting a fresh wave of scholarship, particularly robust in the UK.[49] Nowadays, theological action research is also making headway in Scandinavia, marking a relatively novel expansion in this region.[50]

---

[47] George Lovell, *The Church and Community Development: An Introduction* (Pinner: Grail Publications, 1972); Walter J. Hollenweger, "Efficiency and Human Values: A Theological Action-Research-Report on Co-Decision in Industry," *Expository Times* 86, no. 8 (1975): 228–32; Terence J. Lovat, "Action Research and the Praxis Model of Religious Education: A Critique," *British Journal of Religious Education* 11, no. 1 (1988): 30–37.

[48] Martin, "'Living' Education"; Paul R. Dokecki, J. R. Newbrough, and Robert T. O'Gorman, "Toward a Community-Oriented Action Research Framework for Spirituality: Community Psychological and Theological Perspectives," *Journal of Community Psychology* 29, no. 5 (2001): 497–518; John Trout et al., "Action Research on Leadership for Community Development in West Africa and North America: A Joining of Liberation Theology and Community Psychology," *Journal of Community Psychology* 31, no. 2 (2003): 129–48.

[49] Cameron et al., *Talking*; Nick Shepherd, "Action Research as Professional Development: Educating for Performative Knowledge and Enhancing Theological Capital," *Journal of Adult Theological Education* 9, no. 2 (2012): 121–38; Elaine Graham, "Is Practical Theology a Form of 'Action Research'?," *International Journal of Practical Theology* 17, no. 1 (2013): 148–78; Lynda Barley, "Towards the Development of Priest Researchers in the Church of England" (Professional Doctorate in Practical Theology, Anglia Ruskin University, 2014); Susanna Brouard, "Using Theological Action Research to Embed Catholic Social Teaching in a Catholic Development Agency: Abseiling on the Road To Emmaus" (Professional Doctorate in Practical Theology, Anglia Ruskin University, 2015); Boyd, *The Naked Preacher*; Watkins, *Disclosing Church*; James Butler, "The 'Long and Winding Road' of Faith: Learning about the Christian Life and Discipleship from two Methodist Congregations," *Practical Theology* 13, no. 3 (2020): 277–89; James Butler, "Prayer as a Research Practice? What Corporate Practices of Prayer Disclose about Theological Action Research," *Ecclesial Practices* 7, no. 2 (2020): 241–57.

[50] Jonas Ideström and Stig Linde, "Det här är någonting vi måste göra: Ett teologiskt aktionsforskningsprojekt med Svenska kyrkan i Mölndal (Uppsala: Svenska kyrkans forskningsenhet, 2017); Jonas Ideström and Stig Linde, "Welfare State Supporter and Civil Society Activist: Church of Sweden in the 'Refugee Crisis' 2015," *Social Inclusion* 7, no. 2 (2019): 4–13; Jonas Ideström, *Här får jag vara: En rapport från ett teologiskt forskningsprojekt om konfirmand- och ungdomsverksamheten i Vadstena och Dals församlingar* (Linköping: Svenska kyrkan (Linköpings stift), 2019); Jonas Ideström and Stig Linde, "'Att famna komplexiteten': Aktionsforskning, teologi och organisatoriskt lärande," in *Aktionsforskning: Möjligheter, utmaningar och variationer*, ed. Hanna Bertilsdotter Rosqvist, Magdalena Elmersjö, and Lisa Kings (Lund: Studentlitteratur, 2021), 171–99.

A handful of studies have applied theological action research within the realm of Christian religious education. Bruce Martin used action research as a framework for fostering congregational change and community development, particularly in the domains of congregational teaching and educational programming.[51] Dent C. Davis outlines a similar participatory action research endeavor aimed at transforming his congregation's educational ministry. [52] Additionally, Steve Thomason conducted a participatory action research project with suburban congregations within the Evangelical Lutheran Church in America, experimenting with various educational activities focused on spirituality and spiritual formation.[53]

Despite these contributions, theological action research remains relatively nascent within the broader spectrum of theological studies. One consequence is that while existing studies explore the approach, there remains a notable scarcity of methodological literature. *Talking About God in Practice* stands as the most thorough articulation of this approach to date. However, it primarily outlines Theological Action Research as a specific method, leaving many methodological

---

Action research in practical theology is also increasingly used by other scholars. Notable is Dorte Kappelgaard's dissertation, and work by Caroline Gustavsson [Klintborg], and Katharina Westerlund, as well as the *Church in Digital Space* project of which this dissertation project was a part. Caroline Gustavsson [Klintborg], *En process på riktigt: Lärande och undervisning i Västerås pastorat 2018: Redovisning av ett forskningsprojekt* (Västerås: Västerås pastorat, 2019); Dorte Kappelgaard, "Kirke i bevægelse: At understøtte lokal udvikling af kontekstuelle kirkelige praksisser" (PhD, Københavns Universitet, 2021); Löfstedt and Westerlund, "Research Circles"; Garpe and Ideström, *Kyrka i digitala rum.*

To my knowledge mine is the first theological action research dissertation in practical theology in Sweden.

[51] Bruce Martin, "Transforming a Local Church Congregation through Action Research," *Educational Action Research* 9, no. 2 (2001): 261–78. Martin, "'Living' Education."

[52] Davis, "Learning."

[53] Thomason, "Participatory Action Research as Trinitarian Praxis."

nuances unaddressed.[54] Consequently, I refer to the broader corpus of action research literature for a more detailed methodological discourse.[55]

In section 3.2, I outline three core characteristics of action research. First, a prevalent view among action researchers is that the genesis of knowledge is optimally conducted at the local level. They typically caution against the separation of data collection and analysis, advocating for these processes to be integrated and grounded in the immediate context.[56] Second, action researchers often actively engage in the environments they examine, motivated by the belief that knowledge stems from active involvement geared toward positive change.[57]

Third, within the framework of participatory action research, like the *Online Small Groups* project, the creation of knowledge is a collaborative endeavor between academic and practitioner researchers. Academic researchers do not produce knowledge *on* or *about* participants. Instead, knowledge is generated *by* participants or academic researchers in cooperation *with* participants.[58] Thus, in chapter 3, I describe action research as an orientation towards inquiry that attempts to

---

[54] This does not mean that there is no methodological reflection. Cameron and colleagues clearly reflect methodologically on theological action research, as do John Todd and Jason Boyd. However, methodological reflections are often presented in connection with ongoing projects and there is less methodological reflection that attempts to formulate learnings from concluded projects. Clare Watkins's *Disclosing Church* is an exception, but Watkins focuses again more on the method of Theological Action Research then the underlying methodology. Cameron et al., *Talking*; Andrew John Todd, "The Talk, Dynamics and Theological Practice of Bible-Study Groups: A Qualitative Empirical Investigation" (PhD, Cardiff University, 2009); Boyd, *The Naked Preacher*; Watkins, *Disclosing Church*.

[55] See also section 3.2.

[56] Brydon-Miller, Greenwood, and Maguire, "Why Action Research?"; Hilary Bradbury Huang, "What is Good Action Research? Why the Resurgent Interest?," *Action Research* 8, no. 1 (2010): 93–109 at 98.

[57] Peter Reason and William Torbert, "The Action Turn: Toward a Transformational Social Science," *Concepts and Transformation: International Journal of Action Research and Organizational Renewal* 6, no. 1 (2001): 1–37 at 6–10; Patricia Gayá Wicks, Peter Reason, and Hilary Bradbury, "Living Inquiry: Personal, Political and Philosophical Groundings for Action Research Practice," in *The SAGE Handbook of Action Research: Participative Inquiry and Practice*, ed. Peter Reason and Hilary Bradbury (London: SAGE Publications, 2008), 15–30 at 19; Andrew Townsend, *Action Research: The Challenges of Understanding and Changing Practice* (New York: Open University Press, 2013), 34–35.

[58] Brydon-Miller, Greenwood, and Maguire, "Why Action Research?," 16–20; Herr and Anderson, *Action Research Dissertation*, 4; Jacques Chevalier and Daniel Buckles, *Participatory Action Research: Theory and Methods for Engaged Inquiry*, 2nd ed. (Milton: Routledge, 2019), 24–30.

generate public knowledge through structured reflection on present action at the local level by or with people "owning" the situation in which such action occurs.[59]

Building on the previous point, the principle in action research that knowledge is collaboratively produced at the local level with participants holds significant weight. According to this principle, the *Online Small Groups* project yielded insights and understandings separate from the writing of this dissertation.[60] Substantial knowledge emerges then directly from the action research activity, and not merely from analyzing data post-process.

However, the insights gained from action research are initially "local," meant "for me" and "for us" who were directly involved.[61] Mary Brydon-Miller, Davydd Greenwood, and Patricia Maguire have pointed out that the inherent local focus of action research could be seen as a limitation, as it might instigate change within a specific setting without being able to extend its impact further.[62]

Highlighting the necessity of broadening local insights, Coghlan and Gaya emphasize the crucial role of action research dissertations in overcoming this hurdle.[63] Addressing this challenge constitutes, consequently, a major purpose of this dissertation. In essence, the dissertation serves as a form of "narrative," detailing the "story" of the *Online Small Groups* project in such a way that others in similar contexts may be able to learn from our experiences.[64]

As people can absorb insights from all kinds of texts, the goal of producing a narrative from which others can derive knowledge might seem redundant or obvious. However, as I contend in section 3.5, not all texts facilitate learning with equal ease. Following Laurel Richardson's perspective, I argue that reflective narrative enables the communication of insights particularly well.[65]

This process of extrapolating learnings to a broader context prompts reflection on the relationship between this dissertation and the original *Online Small Groups*

---

[59] For a more detailed introduction to action research see section 3.2.

[60] In action research there is a close relationship between experiential learning and knowledge production. I use the terms learnings and knowings to denote practical knowledge as opposed to propositional knowledge. Reason and Torbert, "The Action Turn," 13–28. See also section 3.2.3.

[61] Reason and Marshall, "Research as Personal Process," 112–13; Reason and Marshall, "Research as Personal Process," 112–13.

[62] Brydon-Miller, Greenwood, and Maguire, "Why Action Research?," 25.

[63] Coghlan and Gaya, "Dissertation Writing," 5.

[64] The other purpose is reflection on our experience in a way that contributes to the general discussion of learning and teaching in the Church of Sweden. Narration is thus one part of the overall purpose. See section 1.6.

[65] Richardson, *Writing Strategies*; Richardson and Adams St. Pierre, "Writing."

project. In participatory action research dissertations like this one, typically authored by an individual, a challenge arises in aligning the knowledge production for the dissertation with the collaborative knowledge production that occurred during the project. This issue of representation is not unique to action research.[66] Yet, the common assertion among action researchers that they conduct research *with*, rather than *on*, their co-researchers demands particular attention to how representation is managed.[67]

I have explored three distinct approaches authors have adopted to navigate this challenge. Frida Mannerfelt's dissertation on preaching in a digital culture and age utilizes action research to collect the empirical material for a case study on co-preaching. Conversely, Dorte Kappelgaard's work scrutinizes the action research process in her examination of how church organizations might foster contextual church practices with a strong emphasis on volunteer participation.[68] Therefore, while Mannerfelt employs action research primarily as a method for data collection, Kappelgaard positions action research itself as the central subject of her analysis.

Jason Boyd's dissertation represents a third approach: extending the original project through additional layers of analysis and reflection.[69] This means that for Boyd, there is a closer relationship between the action research project and his dissertation than is the case for Mannerfelt and Kappelgaard. These three approaches vary in their treatment of action research and the collaborative knowledge production it involves, categorizing it either as a method for data collection, the focus of the research, or an integral part of the research process itself.

In this dissertation, I adopt the third approach, advancing the learning journey initiated in the *Online Small Groups* project. Consequently, I maintain the emphasis on improvement that characterized the *Online Small Groups* project.

---

[66] Natalie Wigg-Stevenson, "What's Really Going On: Ethnographic Theology and the Production of Theological Knowledge," *Cultural Studies ↔ Critical Methodologies* 18, no. 6 (2018): 423–29; Kristy Nabhan-Warren and Natalie Wigg-Stevenson, "Situating the 'Crisis of Representation' in Ethnographic Approaches to Theology and Working Toward Community-Centered, Dialogic Approaches," *Ecclesial Practices* 8, no. 2 (2021): 123–28; Janna L. Hunter-Bowman, "Representation and Intersectionality," in *The Wiley Blackwell Companion to Theology and Qualitative Research*, ed. Pete Ward and Knut Tveitereid (Oxford: Wiley Blackwell, 2022), 141–50.

[67] Peter Reason and Hilary Bradbury, eds., *The SAGE Handbook of Action Research: Participative Inquiry and Practice*, 2nd ed. (London: SAGE Publications, 2008), 3–4.

[68] Kappelgaard, "Kirke i bevægelse," 4, 220.

[69] Boyd, *The Naked Preacher*, 10–25.

Consequently, I see this dissertation as a further instantiation of the knowledge produced in the *Online Small Groups* project.[70] Engaging theory and previous research, my interpretation of our experiences in the *Online Small Groups* has continued to develop after the original project was concluded and it is these developments I present here. It is with this perspective that I designate this work as an action research dissertation.

This dissertation navigates a middle path between constructive and empirical research. Mirroring the approach of constructive theology, my reflections aim to articulate a comprehensive argument for teaching within the Church of Sweden, adopting a prescriptive-constructive approach.[71] Consequently, the goal of my reflections is not simply to describe and comprehend online small groups, but to produce insights that can enrich the Church's teaching ministry.

Nevertheless, my discussion is consistently informed by the tangible experiences derived from the *Online Small Groups* project. Therefore, the dissertation does not align with a purely theoretical framework as defined by religious education researcher Geir Afdal, who characterizes theoretical approaches as those that do "not use empirical material to describe and analyze the practice of religious education or other relevant material."[72] Consequently, I perceive this dissertation as bridging constructive and empirical approaches, akin to the integration demonstrated by scholars such as Serene Jones, Clare Watkins, and Natalie Wigg-Stevenson.[73]

1.4 Placement in Religious Education

As mentioned, this dissertation is positioned within the field of religious education broadly, and Christian religious education specifically. However, the definition of religious education, both as a term and a research field, is not straightforward, with terminology differing within and between languages. Thus, Stephen G. Parker

---

[70] Karin Knorr Cetina, "Objectual Practice," in *The Practice Turn in Contemporary Theory*, ed. Karin Knorr Cetina, Theodore R. Schatzki, and Eike von Savigny (London: Routledge, 2001), 175–88 at 181–83.

[71] Jason A. Wyman Jr., *Constructing Constructive Theology: An Introductory Sketch* (Minneapolis: Fortress Press, 2017), xxvii-xxxiv. See especially section 3.4.3.

[72] Geir Afdal, *Researching Religious Education as Social Practice* (Münster: Waxmann Verlag GmbH, 2010), 16.

[73] Serene Jones, *Feminist Theory and Christian Theology: Cartographies of Grace* (Minneapolis: Augsburg Fortress, 2000); Watkins, *Disclosing Church*; Wigg-Stevenson, *Transgressive Devotion*.

demonstrates how religious education is interpreted in a variety of often disputed ways and Caroline Klintborg notes, "using a certain term is no guarantee that you are talking about the same thing and in a Swedish context it has been shown that despite the use of different concepts people sometimes still talked about the same thing."[74]

Similarly, clarifying various approaches to religious education, Geir Afdal emphasizes the significance of distinguishing between the practice of research and the practice of religious education.[75] Beginning with the latter, I differentiate between confessional and non-confessional approaches to religious education, each with distinct objectives.

Confessional religious education aims for learners to increasingly identify with the religion, cultivating deeper religiosity. In contrast, non-confessional education focuses on imparting knowledge *about* and insights *from* various religions, without urging students to adopt the specific beliefs, values, and practices of any religion in their personal lives.[76]

In European scholarship, a clear distinction is made between religious education ("RE"), representing non-confessional state education, and religious instruction or Christian education, denoting confessional church education. Conversely, in the United States, the term religious education or Christian religious education commonly describes the confessional approach.[77] Additionally, theological education has occasionally been used to describe the confessional approach, although it

---

[74] Caroline Gustavsson [Klintborg], "Religionspedagogik: Ett forskningsfält i tiden," *Nordic Journal of Practical Theology* 37, no. 1 (2020): 78–89 at 79; Stephen G. Parker, "Religion and Education: Framing and Mapping the Field," *Religion and Education* 1, no. 1 (2019): 6–16 at 12.

[75] Afdal, *Researching*, 9.

[76] Parker, "Religion and Education," 12–16. Raymond Holley, "Learning Religion," in *Critical Perspectives on Christian Education: A Reader on the Aims, Principles and Philosophy of Christian Education*, ed. Jeff Astley and Leslie J. Francis (Herefordshire: Gracewing, 1994), 76–84 at 83. John Sealey, "Education as a Second-Order Form of Experience and its Relation to Religion," in *Critical Perspectives on Christian Education: A Reader on the Aims, Principles and Philosophy of Christian Education*, ed. Jeff Astley and Leslie J. Francis (Herefordshire: Gracewing, 1994), 91–94; Jeff Astley, "Definitions, Aims and Approaches: An Overview," in *Critical Perspectives on Christian Education: A Reader on the Aims, Principles and Philosophy of Christian Education*, ed. Jeff Astley and Leslie J. Francis (Herefordshire: Gracewing, 1994), 3–12 at 3.

[77] Astley, "Definitions," 3–4.

typically signifies advanced theological studies at seminaries, colleges, and univer-sities.[78]

Terminology use further diversifies with religious educators like John Wester-hoff using catechesis to refer to the confessional method.[79] Thomas Groome, how-ever, assigns catechesis specifically to oral instruction, while John A. Berntsen links catechesis more directly with the development of religious emotions and affec-tions.[80]

In Sweden, the term for the school subject is religious education (*religionskun-skap*, literally "knowledge of religion"), while education in churches, parishes, and congregations may be referred to either as religious education (*religionspedagogik*, literally "religious pedagogy") or as parish education (*församlingspedagogik*, liter-ally "congregational pedagogy" or "parish pedagogy").[81]

Terminology usage thus varies significantly. Here, I adopt Thomas Groome's compounded term "Christian religious education" to refer to confessional reli-gious education, aiming for clarity and comprehension among both European and North American audiences.[82] My usage of "Christian religious education" encom-passes both *religionspedagogik* and *församlingspedagogik*.

---

[78] Jeff Astley and Colin Crowder, "Theological Perspectives on Christian Education: An Overview," in *Theological Perspectives on Christian Formation: A Reader on Theology and Christian Education*, ed. Jeff Astley, Leslie J. Francis, and Colin Crowder (Herefordshire: Gracewing, 1996), x–xix at xi; Maria Liu Wong, *On Becoming Wise Together: Learning and Leading in the City* (Grand Rapids: Wm. B. Eerdmans Publishing Company, 2023).

[79] John Westerhoff, "Formation, Education, Instruction," in *Critical Perspectives on Christian Education: A Reader on the Aims, Principles and Philosophy of Christian Education*, ed. Jeff Astley and Leslie J. Francis (Herefordshire: Gracewing, 1994), 61–72 at 62–63.

[80] Thomas H. Groome, *Christian Religious Education: Sharing Our Story and Vision* (San Francisco: Jossey-Bass, 1980), 26–27; John A. Berntsen, "Christian Affections and the Catechumenate," in *Theological Perspectives on Christian Formation: A Reader on Theology and Christian Education*, ed. Jeff Astley, Leslie J. Francis, and Colin Crowder (Herefordshire: Gracewing, 1996), 229–43 at 229.

[81] The Swedish term *församling* translates variably as either parish or congregation. In the context of the Church of Sweden and its parochial system I have opted for the term parish edu-cation, whereas the term congregational education might make more sense in the context of other churches. Caroline Klintborg, *Vägen är allt: En introduktion till religionspedagogik för den kristna församlingen* (Varberg: Argument, 2021); Rune Larsson, *Församlingspedagogik: en kyrka som undervisar genom hela sitt liv* (Stockholm, Sverige: Books on demand, 2018).

[82] Groome adopts the terminology of Christian Religious Education as the specific Christian variant of religious education that attends to the transcendent dimension of life from within the Christian tradition. Groome, *Christian Religious Education*, 22–25.

Regarding the practice of Christian religious education research, I distinguish between prescriptive and non-prescriptive approaches based on their conceptualization of research objectives. Prescriptive research aligns its goals with those inherent to the practice of religious education itself, aiming to directly influence or improve educational practices. In contrast, non-prescriptive research sets its objectives independently of the practical goals of practitioners, focusing instead on generating knowledge for its own sake or broader analytical purposes.[83]

Differentiating between confessional and non-confessional forms of religious education, along with prescriptive and non-prescriptive research approaches, enables the identification of four distinct research trajectories within the field. These pathways are illustrated in figure 1.2, providing a structured framework for understanding the diverse approaches to studying religious education.[84]

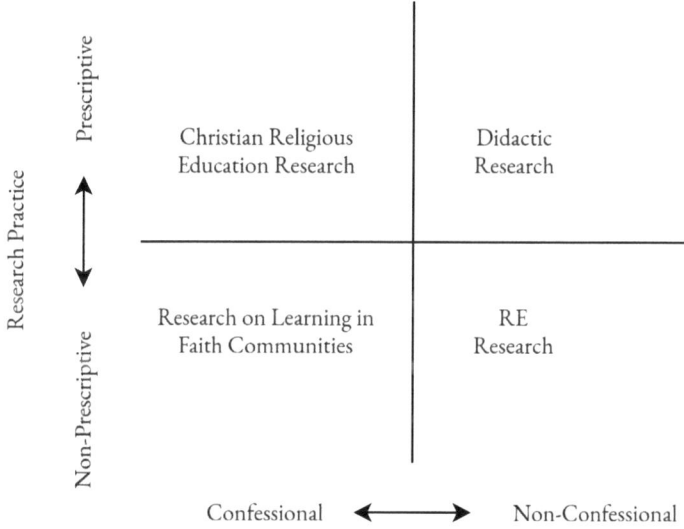

Figure 1.2 Research Streams in Religious Education

[83] Afdal, *Researching*, 68–77.

[84] The prescriptive research practice studying confessional religious education could also be called "confessional religious education," of which Christian religious education would be a subtype. I use Christian religious education in figure 1.2 to make it easier to locate my approach in the figure.

Although my presentation initially implies two binary distinctions, it is more accurate to perceive both the confessional—non-confessional and the prescriptive—non-prescriptive dimensions as continuums. This perspective allows for the placement of individual research projects within a spectrum of research approaches, conceptualizing them as clusters of studies with similar orientations, rather than fitting strictly into one of four separate categories. Consequently, it is not always straightforward to precisely categorize a given study or to conclusively delineate the boundaries between these four approaches.

In Sweden, religious education (RE) research predominantly focuses on formal, non-confessional education, exploring the interplay between schools, religions, diversity, and identity formation.[85] This emphasis is particularly evident in discussions of teaching or didactics, where the didactics of religious education are frequently synonymous with formal education in Sweden.[86] This concentration

---

[85] Gustavsson [Klintborg], "Religionspedagogik," 82–85; Jenny Berglund, "State-Funded Faith-Based Schooling for Muslims in the North," *Religion & Education* 46, no. 2 (2019): 210–33; Carina Holmqvist Lidh, "Representera och bli representerad: Elever med religiös positionering talar om skolans religionskunskapsundervisning" (Licentiate thesis, Karlstads universitet, 2016); Thérèse Halvarson Britton, "Studiebesök i religionskunskapsundervisningen: Elevers tal om islam före, under och efter ett moskébesök" (Licentiate thesis, Karlstads universitet, 2014); Anders Sjöborg, "Religious Education and Intercultural Understanding: Examining the Role of Religiosity for Upper Secondary Students' Attitudes Towards RE," *British Journal of Religious Education* 35, no. 1 (2013): 36–54. Skeie argues that the same trend can be observed in Norway, Denmark, and Finland. Geir Skeie, "Mangfoldets utfordringer og muligheter sett gjennom religionsdidaktisk forskning. Et nordisk overblikk," *Acta Didactica Norden* 11, no. 3 (2017): 1–23.

[86] Emma Hall and Bodil Liljefors Persson, eds., *Religionsdidaktik: I teori och praktik* (Malmö: Föreningen lärare i religionskunskap, 2010); Malin Löfstedt, *Religionsdidaktik: Mångfald, livsfrågor och etik i skolan* (Lund: Studentlitteratur, 2011); Carl Eber Olivestam, *Religionsdidaktik: Om teori, perspektiv och praktik i religionsundervisningen* (Stockholm: Remus, 2012); Torsten Löfstedt and Roland Hallgren, eds., *Religionsdidaktiska studier* (Växjö: Linnaeus University Press, 2015); Sören Dalevi and Kristian Niemi, "RE Didactics in Sweden: Defined by the national curriculum? Discussing Didactics of RE in a Swedish context," *Usuteaduslik Ajakiri* 69, no. 1 (2016): 62–78. However, Karin Osbeck uses the term more generally as also applicable to nonformal learning, and Caroline Klintborg argues that both didactics and pedagogy are part of the larger field of religious education. Christina Osbeck, *Att förstå livet: Religionsdidaktik och lärande i diskursiva praktiker* (Uppsala: Church of Sweden, 2009); Gustavsson [Klintborg], "Religionspedagogik."

on schooling results in a predominance of studies centered on children and youth, leading to a notable lack of research on adult religious education.[87]

The distinction between "RE research" and "didactic research" is not always straightforward. However, didactic research tends to more closely align with the practices of non-confessional religious education, especially in terms of its practical research implications. The action research studies previously mentioned serve as prime examples of this research trend, as does the volume *Didactic Classroom Studies*, edited by Christina Osbeck, Åke Ingerman, and Silwa Claesson.

In their introduction, Osbeck, Ingerman, and Claesson define didactics as the intersection of academic theory and practical application, emphasizing that the outcomes of didactic classroom studies play a crucial role in refining educational practices.[88] Osbeck further observes that in Sweden, didactic research often focuses on deliberate teaching rather than on learning processes per se, which may contribute to the prescriptive character of this research domain.[89]

Conversely, research focusing on learning within faith communities highlights non-prescriptive studies of confessional education.[90] A notable example of this direction is the surge of empirical studies on non-formal religious education in Norway, spurred by the Faith Education Reform in 2003.[91] The Learning and Knowledge Trajectories in Congregations project exemplifies this trend.[92]

---

[87] Löfstedt and Hallgren, *Religionsdidaktiska studier*; Sören Dalevi and Christina Osbeck, *Kyrkopedagogik i Munkfors: En utvärdering av ett samarbetsprojekt skola-kyrka* (Karlstad: Karlstad University Press, 2012); Sven Hartman and Tullie Torstenson-Ed, *Barns tankar om livet* (Stockholm: Natur & Kultur, 2007). This also means that confirmation has been a privileged area for investigation in Sweden. See for example Jonas Eek, *Stanna i vattnet: Kateketikens syfte och sammanhang* (Stockholm: Verbum, 2011); Elisabeth Porath Sjöö, "Konfirmandernas bildningsresa: Ungdomars berättelser om sitt deltagande i konfirmandundervisningen" (PhD, Lunds Universitet, 2008).

[88] Christina Osbeck, Åke Ingerman, and Silwa Claesson, "An Introduction to Didactic Classroom Studies," in *Didactic Classroom Studies: A Potential Research Direction*, ed. Christina Osbeck, Åke Ingerman, and Silwa Claesson (Lund: Nordic Academic Press, 2018), 9–20 at 9–10.

[89] Osbeck, *Förstå livet*, 17; Osbeck, Ingerman, and Claesson, "Introduction" 11–13.

[90] For a discussion of the relationship between normativity and prescriptivity see section 3.3.4.

[91] Heid Leganger-Krogstad, "The Characteristics of Non-Formal Religious Education in a Folk Church: The Norwegian Education Reform," in *Researching Non-Formal Religious Education in Europe*, ed. Friedrich Schweitzer, Wolfgang Ilg, and Peter Schreiner (Münster: Waxmann, 2019), 51–70.

[92] Leganger-Krogstad, "Non-Formal Religious Education"; Elisabeth Tveito Johnsen and Geir Afdal, "Practice Theory in Empirical Practical Theological Research: The Scientific Contribution of LETRA," *Nordic Journal of Practical Theology* 37, no. 2 (2020): 58–76.

Elisabeth Tveito Johnsen's research into the religious learning experiences of children within two Church of Norway congregations and Morten Holmqvist's examination of learning in confirmation classes and camps serve as key instances of this research focus.[93]

Germany presents another instance where empirical research on non-formal Christian religious education is gaining momentum. This burgeoning interest is showcased in the edited collection *Researching Non-Formal Religious Education in Europe* which gathers both theoretical explorations and empirical investigations of non-formal Christian religious education. This volume spans a variety of contexts, including kindergarten, Sunday school, First Communion preparation, confirmation work, and activities involving young volunteers, highlighting the diverse settings in which non-formal religious education occurs.[94]

Research within Christian religious education typically adopts a prescriptive approach, closely aligning its focus with the practice of Christian religious education.[95] This dissertation is situated within this particular trajectory. Notable contributions to this field include the works of Mary Elisabeth Moore, Jane Regan,

---

[93] Elisabeth Tveito Johnsen, "Hvordan medierer undervisningspreget trosopplæring kristen tro og tradisjon? En Vygotskij-inspirert analyse av læringssituasjoner i Den norske kirkes trosopplæring," *Teologisk tidsskrift* 1, no. 2 (2012): 138–65; Elisabeth Tveito Johnsen, "Læring inn i den kristne religionen: Mediering og subjektivering," *Prismet* 64, no. 3 (2013): 173–201; Elisabeth Tveito Johnsen, "Gudstjenestelæring gjennom deltagelse," in *Gudstjeneste på ny*, ed. Geir Hellemo (Oslo: Universitetsforlaget, 2014), 151–77; Elisabeth Tveito Johnsen, "Religiøs læring i sosiale praksiser: En etnografisk studie av mediering, identifisering og forhandlingsprosesser i Den norske kirkes trosopplæring" (PhD, Oslo University, 2014); Morten Holmqvist, "Learning Religion: Exploring Young People's Participation Through Timespace and Mediation at Confirmation Camp," *Mind, Culture, and Activity* 22, no. 3 (2015): 201–16; Morten Holmqvist, "The Material Logics of Confirmation," *International Journal of Actor-Network Theory and Technological Innovation* 6, no. 4 (2014): 26–37.

[94] Friedrich Schweitzer, Wolfgang Ilg, and Peter Schreiner, eds., *Researching Non-Formal Religious Education in Europe* (Münster: Waxmann, 2019).

[95] I use the term Christian religious education both to denote the Christian confessional religious education practice, and the field of prescriptive research that aligns its aims with that practice. Where necessary I distinguish between them by referring to the research practice and the educational practice, respectively.

Norma Everist Cook, Courtney Goto, and Maria Liu Wong, among others.[96] I return to this trajectory and its implications for the dissertation below.[97]

Despite the distinct nature of the four streams of religious education research, there is significant methodological and thematic overlap among them. While situated in the Christian religious education stream, my dissertation shares commonalities with didactic classroom studies, which primarily aim to improve teaching and learning in formal education settings, adopting a comparable prescriptive stance.[98] Similarly, it connects with non-prescriptive research on learning within faith communities, dedicated to exploring and understanding the mechanisms of non-formal religious education.[99]

The primary difference between my dissertation and didactic research lies in the educational setting. Didactic classroom studies are generally centered on formal education, whereas my work delves into non-formal education within Church of Sweden parishes, significantly impacting the objectives and intentions of education and, by extension, the goals teaching aims to achieve. When compared to research on learning in faith communities, notable differences emerge in both the perceived purpose of the studies—illustrating the divide between prescriptive and non-prescriptive research—and their focal points. Research on learning within faith communities typically emphasizes the learning process, while studies in Christian religious education more frequently address the broader scope of educational practice.[100]

---

[96] Jane E. Regan, *Toward an Adult Church: A Vision of Faith Formation* (Chicago: Loyola Press, 2002); Mary Elizabeth Mullino Moore, *Teaching as a Sacramental Act* (Cleveland: The Pilgrim Press, 2004); Norma Cook Everist, *The Church as Learning Community: A Comprehensive Guide to Christian Education* (Nashville: Abingdon Press, 2011); Jane E. Regan, *Where Two or Three Are Gathered: Transforming the Parish through Communities of Practice* (New York: Paulist Press, 2016); Courtney T. Goto, *The Grace of Playing: Pedagogies for Leaning into God's New Creation* (Eugene: Pickwick, 2016); Liu Wong, *Becoming Wise.* The choice of examples is influenced by my discussion of a predominant white and male bias. See section 6.3.3.

[97] For a general introduction to this trajectory see section 2.2–2.5. For a discussion of Christian religious education in relation to the Church of Sweden see section 1.5.1.

[98] Christina Osbeck, Åke Ingerman, and Silwa Claesson, eds., *Didactic Classroom Studies: A Potential Research Direction* (Lund: Nordic Academic Press, 2018).

[99] Elisabeth Tveito Johnsen and Geir Afdal, "Learning and Knowledge Trajectories in Congregations," *Praktische Theologie* 55, no. 2 (2020): 70–75.

[100] Groome, *Christian Religious Education*, 23–26; Gert Biesta, "Freeing Teaching from Learning: Opening Up Existential Possibilities in Educational Relationships," *Studies in Philosophy and Education* 34 (2015): 229–43. See also the discussion in section 2.1–2.3.

1.5 Literature Review

As I situate the dissertation within the realm of Christian religious education and relate it to the ongoing discussion about learning and teaching in the Church of Sweden, I primarily engage previous research related to the Church of Sweden within the Christian religious education strand. Additionally, I consider studies that address the context of online small groups, including research on online learning and studies on small groups. I review each in sequence, emphasizing the former.

1.5.1 Previous Research on Christian Religious Education in the Church of Sweden

In my review of the literature on learning and teaching related to the Church of Sweden, I encountered challenges in determining which publications should be classified as research—in the academic sense—and, hence, be included in this review, and which publications do not live up to the standards of academic research and should therefore be excluded.[101]

Beyond standard textbooks, there exists a variety of popular introductions to Christian religious education targeted not only at university students but also at religious educators within Swedish churches.[102] These resources typically provide an overview of Christian religious education by outlining its role and objectives, methods, and foundational pedagogical and didactic theories. Although not considered research in the strict sense, these publications nonetheless contribute to the broader ecosystem of Christian religious education in Sweden.

Similarly, there is a distinct category of publications collecting reflections by religious educators. These works feature personal insights on Christian religious education at large or delve into specific practices within the field, to inspire

---

[101] I have searched for literature using Lund University's search function LubSearch in February 2024 using the search teams "Religionspedagogik AND Svenska kyrkan" (religious education AND Church of Sweden), "Religionspedagogik" (religious education), "Kateketik" (Catechesis), "Kristendomsundervisning" (Christian education), and "Svenska kyrkan" (Church of Sweden). I limited the search to publications since the year 2000 when the Church of Sweden was fully and finally separated from the Swedish state. While all search terms were in Swedish, the search also picked up publications in other languages (English and German).

[102] Anders Hedman, *Undervisa i kristen tro* (Varberg: Argument, 2015); Rune Larsson, *Medvandrare: Vägmärken i religionspedagogiken* (Stockholm: BoD – Books on Demand, 2019); Klintborg, *Vägen är allt*; Rune Larsson, *Samtal vid brunnar: Introduktion till religionspedagogikens teori och didaktik* (Lund: Arcus, 2009).

educators and enrich their commitment to their educational practices.[103] Although these contributions engage with the broader discourse on learning and teaching within the Church of Sweden, they typically do not intersect with the academic discussion.

For this review, I have chosen to exclude both of these types of publications and to focus more narrowly on research within Christian religious education. This research is characterized by publications that actively engage with the ongoing academic debate, as evidenced by the standard inclusion of academic references.[104]

Framing the Broader Situation

The current debate about Christian religious education within the Church of Sweden needs to be understood against a broader discussion about the Church's identity and role in Swedish society.

For centuries, the Church of Sweden held the status of the Swedish state church, holding authority over the nation's religious matters. This began to change in the latter half of the 18th century as other Christian denominations gained official recognition. This shift gradually led to the Church of Sweden being reimagined not as a state church but as a national or folk church—a church for the Swedish people.[105]

An initial decline in membership attributed to the emergence of religious diversity was quickly surpassed by a more significant loss due to secularization and disaffiliation trends in the second half of the 20th century.[106] Consequently, the Church of Sweden has transitioned from a central to a more peripheral role,

---

[103] Björn Wiedel, *Att se är att lära* (Älvsjö: Studieförbundet Bilda, 2010); Maria Store, *Kyrkan lär i förändring* (Stockholm: Verbum, 2017); Björn Wiedel, *Orden och Jorden: Om trons pedagogik och teologi* (Stockholm: Proprius, 2020); Gita Andersson, *Bättre än vi trodde: Att förvandlas som människa och kyrka* (Stockholm: Libris, 2022); Fredrik Beverhjelm, *Guide till det strategiska konfirmandarbetet* (Stockholm: Verbum, 2023).

[104] I make an exception to this rule in section 2.3, when I briefly discuss Anders Hedman's textbook *Undervisa i kristen tro* in relation to the concept of teaching.

[105] Martin Berntson, Bertil Nilsson, and Cecilia Wejryd, *Kyrka i Sverige: Introduktion till svensk kyrkohistoria* (Stockholm: Skellefteå, 2012).

[106] Kirsten Donskov Felter, Ninna Edgardh, and Tron Fagermoen, "The Scandinavian Ecclesial Context," in *What Really Matters: Scandinavian Perspectives on Ecclesiology and Ethnography*, ed. Jonas Ideström and Tone Stangeland Kaufman (Eugene: Pickwick Publications, 2018), 7–14 at 5–11.

prompting increasingly prevalent descriptions of Sweden as a post-Christian society.[107]

This shift has prompted a thorough examination of the Church of Sweden's identity and purpose. Part of the broader discourse seeks to chart and comprehend changes in Sweden's religious fabric, illustrating both a widespread departure from organized religion and the continued significance of spirituality and religious traditions within Swedish society and culture.[108] Another aspect of the debate focuses specifically on the evolving relationship between Swedish society and the Church, aiming to discern how the Church might adjust to these changes.[109] This includes discussions of Swedish folk church theology and reevaluations of its mission.[110]

Research on Christian religious education within the Church of Sweden forms a part of this wider discourse. Sara Fransson, a researcher for the Church of Sweden, highlights this in a recent report on confirmation training: "Over the past few decades, Europe has undergone religious transformation. Secularization and migration are changing the religious landscape in which churches operate," underscoring the need to comprehend how churches engage young people in times of religious change.[111]

---

[107] Jan Eckerdal, *Kyrka i mission: Att gestalta kristen tro i en efterkristen tid* (Stockholm: Verbum, 2017); Wirén, *Undervisning*; Sven Thidevall, ed., *Mindre folk – mer kyrka? Möjligheter för Svenska kyrkan i en postkristen tid: Rapport 2 från projektet 'Folkkyrka i minoritet'* (Skellefteå: Artos, 2021).

[108] Anders Bäckström, Ninna Edgardh, and Per Pettersson, *Religiös förändring i norra Europa: En studie av Sverige* (Uppsala: Diakonivetenskapliga institutet, 2004); David Thurfjell, *Det gudlösa folket: De postkristna svenskarna och religionen* (Stockholm: Molin & Sorgenfrei, 2015); David Thurfjell, *Granskogsfolk: Hur naturen blev svenskarnas religion* (Stockholm: Norstedts, 2020).

[109] Sven Thidevall, *När kartan inte längre stämmer: Svenska kyrkans församlingar i ett samtidshistoriskt perspektiv* (Uppsala: Diakonivetenskapliga institutet, 2003); Elisabeth Arborelius, "Finns det en klyfta mellan kyrkan och folket? Intervjuer med församlingsbor och präster i Stockholmsområdet" (Acta Universitatis Upsaliensis, 2009); Marie Rosenius, *Svenska kyrkan samma kyrka? Ecklesiologi före och efter relationsförändringen mellan kyrka och stat* (Skellefteå: Artos, 2015); Kristina Helgesson Kjellin, *En bra plats att vara på: En antropologisk studie av mångfaldsarbete och identitetsskapande inom Svenska kyrkan* (Skellefteå: Artos & Norma, 2016); Andreas Holmberg, *Kyrka i nytt landskap: En studie av levd ecklesiologi i Svenska kyrkan* (Skellefteå: Artos Academic, 2019).

[110] Jonas Ideström, *Folkkyrkotanken: Innehåll och utmaningar: En översikt av studier under 2000-talet* (Uppsala: Svenska kyrkan, 2012); Thidevall, *Mindre folk – mer kyrka? Möjligheter för Svenska kyrkan i en postkristen tid: Rapport 2 från projektet 'Folkkyrka i minoritet'*; Eckerdal, *Kyrka i mission*.

[111] Fransson, *Konfirmation*, 9.

Similarly, as previously noted, Jørgen Straarup and Mayvor Ekberg contend that, as state school education grew more secular throughout the 20th century, the leadership of the Church of Sweden failed to respond effectively. Straarup and Ekberg maintain that this oversight has led not only to the absence of a comprehensive program for church education but also to an increasing number of individuals lacking religious language, which in turn results in a diminished interest in church activities, particularly the liturgy.[112] Thus, Straarup and Ekberg's critique aligns with broader discussions on the evolving role and function of the Church of Sweden within the country's shifting religious context.

To provide a balanced view, it is important to note that Straarup and Ekberg's assertion is not backed by empirical evidence, a limitation they acknowledge themselves.[113] Consequently, it remains uncertain whether the problem was a lack of response. Marie Rosenius and Thomas Girmalm have critiqued this argument, suggesting that to attribute educational neglect to the Church's leadership oversimplifies the issue, despite agreeing with the fundamental problem identified.[114] Nevertheless, there is a consensus among many scholars in religious education that contemporary Swedes face a significant barrier in accessing religious language, a situation often described as religious illiteracy.

Anne-Louise Eriksson's work, *Att predika en tradition* (To Preach a Tradition), serves as a poignant example, linking the prevalent lack of knowledge about Christianity and the faith of the Church of Sweden to a broader inability to grasp the Christian tradition. Eriksson posits that religious illiteracy hampers individuals' capacity to experience and comprehend encounters with the divine within the context of Christian traditions, resulting in a form of religiosity today that often appears ineffective and aimless.[115]

Caroline Klintborg similarly contends that contemporary Swedes struggle to grasp the significance of religious symbols present in the Church of Sweden's liturgy. This risks making the liturgy more of an alienating experience rather than an inviting one.[116] Klintborg further discusses changes in religious socialization,

---

[112] Straarup and Ekberg, *Försumliga kyrkan.*

[113] Straarup and Ekberg, *Försumliga kyrkan,* 10.

[114] Marie Rosenius and Thomas Girmalm, "Från folkbildning till fortbildning: Synen på lärande och kyrka i Luleå stifts herdabrev," *Svensk Teologisk Kvartalskrift* 95, no. 1 (2019): 17–32.

[115] Eriksson, *Predika,* 8. I introduce the text in more detail below.

[116] Gustavsson [Klintborg], *Delaktighetens kris,* 224–28. I introduce the text in more detail below.

highlighting that numerous young people today do not receive education about Christianity either at home or at school.[117]

Therefore, it is not unusual to depict a rather grim outlook for the Church of Sweden. The forces of pluralization and secularization are gradually sidelining the Church, compounded by shifts in religious socialization that impede effective communication with people. It is in this context that Christian religious education emerges as a potential tool to confront, and possibly reverse, these trends. To tackle these challenges, previous research on Christian religious education in the Church of Sweden has concentrated on three main areas: theoretical exploration of learning and teaching within the Church, the integration of Christian religious education with liturgical practices, and a special emphasis on confirmation and youth engagement.

Conceptualizing Learning and Teaching in the Church

Several studies specifically address learning and teaching within the Church of Sweden, frequently blending an examination of Sweden's shifting sociocultural landscape with a consideration of the implications or potential impacts of these changes on Christian religious education.

Henry Cöster's work, *...bedriva undervisning...* (...to teach...) offers a conceptual exploration of Christian religious education, depicting tradition, education, and teaching as deeply interconnected.[118] Cöster contends that the task of teaching is to reveal the gift bestowed upon both educator and learner: the tradition that is seen as a divine endowment.[119]

Cöster posits this form of teaching as related to the being of the church and maintains that teaching is actualized in everything the church does. Still, it is possible to differentiate between proclamation, wherein a Christian way of life, courage, and faith are made manifest and articulated, and general education (*folkbildning*), which encompasses a duty towards fostering religious literacy.[120] Learning, therefore, happens both in structured "lessons" and through social practices, demanding from those in teaching roles a deep comprehension of the learning

---

[117] Caroline Gustavsson [Klintborg], "Mellan verklighet och vision: En diskursanalys av Riktlinjer för Svenska kyrkans konfirmandarbete," *Prismet* 67, no. 3 (2016): 201–14 at 201; Gustavsson [Klintborg], *En process på riktigt*, 41.

[118] Svenska kyrkan, *Kyrkoordning*, Introduction to Ch 2.

[119] Henry Cöster, *"... bedriva undervisning ..."*: Om kyrkans didaskalia (Uppsala: Church of Sweden, 2009), 1–10.

[120] Cöster, *bedriva undervisning*, 11–23.

process.[121] Cöster specifically posits that effective teaching demands linguistic proficiency, historical awareness, a critical mindset, and deliberate contemplation of the church's theological heritage—skills underpinned by a hermeneutical didactic expertise.[122]

...bedriva undervisning... is one of two publications commissioned and partly funded by the Church of Sweden's Department for Church Life and Social Responsibility, with Christina Osbeck's *Att förstå livet* (To Understand Life) being the other.[123] Given their similarities, I discuss them concurrently.

Like Cöster, Osbeck engages in a theoretical exploration of learning and teaching, examining how discursive practices offer individuals opportunities to interact with distinct worldviews or conceptions of life—a practical understanding of life's mechanics, its valuable principles, and the essence of meaning.[124] Osbeck begins by distinguishing between intentional and unintentional learning, advocating for recognition of the inadvertent learning occurring in all learning situations (the implicit curriculum).

This leads to her assertion that educators must comprehend how learning transpires.[125] She further argues that all educational efforts should be mindful of external contexts, as these significantly shape learning modalities.[126] Teaching within the Church of Sweden should then consider the pedagogical approaches used in schools, recognizing that formal educational methods greatly influence the learning strategies that individuals bring also to non-formal church education settings.

Osbeck additionally argues that the church, as an institution, has a dual responsibility: to safeguard tradition (a particular discourse) and to critically evaluate how alternative discourses might skew the intended process of meaning-making. To achieve this, she advises educators within the Church to foster agreement on objectives, undertake "external monitoring" (*omvärldsbevakning*), and critically examine the discourses present in specific contexts.[127] This approach aims to

---

[121] Cöster, *bedriva undervisning*, 41–45.

[122] Cöster, *bedriva undervisning*, 51–63.

[123] Cöster, *bedriva undervisning*, 5; Osbeck, *Förstå livet*.

[124] Osbeck, *Förstå livet*, 21.

[125] Osbeck, *Förstå livet*, 21–24.

[126] Osbeck, *Förstå livet*, 25.

[127] Osbeck, *Förstå livet*, 51–58. The Swedish "omvärldsbevakning" is a broad concept referring to the collection of information about events and changes in the outside world that affect an organization, here, the Church of Sweden.

ensure that the educational activities of the Church remain aligned with its core values while being responsive to broader societal and cultural shifts.[128]

Osbeck concludes by emphasizing the significance of structuring teaching activities in such a way that they facilitate discussions on "language about life" and "language about religions." This approach, which blends interpretive and descriptive elements, aims to enrich religious education by providing learners with the tools to engage deeply with both their own life experiences and the broader religious context. This methodology echoes Cöster's distinction between proclamation and general education.[129]

There are notable parallels in the way Cöster and Osbeck approach the concepts of learning and teaching. First, both frame the objective of education as either an understanding of life (Osbeck) or a courage for life (Cöster), indicating a broad conceptualization of learning and teaching within Christian religious education that extends beyond narrower Christian doctrines like discipleship or conversion.[130] Second, they agree that learning and teaching transpire through discursive practices, underscoring the critical role of language and the necessity for an understanding of how discourses can evolve or be misconstrued. This consensus on the dynamics of discourse leads both to emphasize the importance of educators being cognizant of learning processes.[131]

Jakob Wirén provides an alternative perspective on teaching and learning within the Church of Sweden, starting from the post-Christian and secular context described earlier. He examines how Churches in other countries facing similar post-Christian conditions approach education and mission. By analyzing these examples, Wirén seeks to identify practices and insights that could be applicable or beneficial to the Church of Sweden's own educational and missionary endeavors.[132]

Wirén specifically identifies four key challenges: (1) a diminishing understanding of Christian faith overall, (2) a shortage of volunteers participating in teaching and missionary activities, (3) the necessity of redefining the church's identity in the

---

[128] Osbeck, *Förstå livet*, 51–58.

[129] Osbeck, *Förstå livet*, 51–57. Even though Osbeck doesn't make the connection, I think that a fruitful way to understand the distinction is through Anna Sfard's two metaphors of learning as either acquisition (language about religions) or participation (language about life). See Anna Sfard, "On Two Metaphors for Learning and the Danger of Choosing Just One," *Educational Researcher* 27, no. 2 (1998): 4–13.

[130] For a discussion see section 2.2.

[131] I return to this in section 8.3.

[132] Wirén, *Undervisning*, 11–17.

wake of its history as a state church within a multicultural society, and (4) the imperative to reconsider the concept of mission in an environment marked by diverse religious beliefs.[133]

Wirén explores the faith education reform of the Church of Norway, the Church of England's initiatives with lay ministers and the *Mission Shaped Church*, and the Evangelical Lutheran Church in America's focus on fostering community through various Bible study groups, assessing their potential applicability to the Church of Sweden.[134] From his analysis, Wirén suggests the potential benefits of developing a national church curriculum, increasing engagement with lay volunteers, and transitioning from a national folk church model to one centered on more distinctly defined local communities.[135]

Particularly relevant to my dissertation is how Wirén links the concept of teaching with mission, diverging from Cöster and Osbeck's emphasis on life courage and understanding. This approach introduces more traditionally Christian concepts into the discourse on teaching. I return to this point in section 8.1.2.

Christian Religious Education and the Liturgy

A notable focus within Christian religious education in the Church of Sweden pertains to the interplay between learning, teaching, and the liturgy. Caroline Klintborg, for example, studied the experiences of adult choir members (aged 11–40) regarding their active involvement in the Church of Sweden's Sunday liturgy, adopting a sociocultural lens. Through interviews with pastors, church musicians, and choir members, Klintborg reveals that choir members' participation in the liturgy is not always *active* or *engaged*.[136] She notes that adult choir members often struggle to grasp the meanings intended by the Church through artifacts like pulpits and vestments, resulting in a sense of alienation rather than inclusion. Klintborg identifies a critical challenge for the Church of Sweden: reestablishing a collective understanding against which the liturgy can function. She argues that to

---

[133] Wirén, *Undervisning*, 11–18.

[134] Wirén, *Undervisning*.

[135] Wirén, *Undervisning*, 201–42.

[136] Gustavsson [Klintborg], *Delaktighetens kris*. Klintborg introduces the difference between *deltagande* and *delaktighet*, which is difficult to render into English. *Deltagande* (participation) denotes the physical presence in an activity, whereas *delaktighet* (active participation) is defined as "the jointly defined activity is at the heart of participation in worship. The context and questions of power constitute a kind of condition. In addition, both people's active participation is both formal and informal participation, interaction, security, autonomy, commitment, and identity." Gustavsson [Klintborg], *Delaktighetens kris*, 224.

address these educational challenges effectively, the liturgy needs to transcend its role as a "catechetical act" and evolve into a "living meeting space" for communal engagement.[137]

Anne-Louise Eriksson research, mentioned earlier, also falls into this category. Eriksson explores the role of learning within the liturgy by analyzing forty-three sermons delivered on Easter Sunday and the Fifth Sunday in Lent. Her study focuses on how these sermons craft and convey the "faith of the Church of Sweden" as a form of traditioning, linking her findings to the broader conversation on religious literacy. Eriksson concludes that a substantial amount of knowledge is required for listeners to fully comprehend a sermon, enabling sermons to act as "caregivers of tradition." This necessary knowledge encompasses understanding the Bible, the fundamentals of Christianity, and the Church's traditions.[138]

Karin Rubenson presents research on the experiences of children (aged 7–13) engaging with the Church of Sweden's liturgy, shedding light on how these young participants perceive their learning processes. Although Rubenson's study is not primarily framed around learning and teaching, it unveils noteworthy insights into children's perspectives on learning, juxtaposing them against adult expectations.[139]

Rubenson observes that while adults tend to highlight the liturgy's experiential aspects, the children in her study are more inclined towards "theoretical knowledge," particularly regarding the readings, sermons, and Sunday school activities. The interviewed children see knowledge as essential for their active participation in the liturgy, subtly reinforcing Anne-Louise Eriksson's earlier observations.[140]

Marie Rosenius also contributes significantly to this discussion with her theoretical exploration of educational strategies aimed at enhancing children's involvement in the liturgy. She identifies teaching, simplification, and socialization as three primary methods adults employ to encourage active participation among children. Rosenius's analysis provides a deeper understanding of how these strategies are applied within the context of the liturgy to make religious practices more accessible and engaging for younger members of the congregation.[141]

---

[137] Gustavsson [Klintborg], *Delaktighetens kris*, 226.

[138] Eriksson, *Predika*.

[139] Karin Rubenson, "Karnevalesk gudstjänst: Barns plats i kyrkans liturgi" (PhD, Uppsala University, 2021), 111–32.

[140] Rubenson, "Karnevalesk gudstjänst," 131–32.

[141] Marie Rosenius, *Delaktig i vilken mening?: En teologisk analys av delaktighetsstrategier i svenskkyrkligt gudstjänstliv* (Skellefteå: Artos, 2021).

This area of research presents two distinct inquiries. The first revolves around the nature of the learning that occurs within the liturgy, examining children's learning experiences (as highlighted by Rubenson) and the efforts by parishes to instruct children on engaging with the liturgy (as discussed by Rosenius).

The second inquiry centers on religious literacy's role in liturgy, church communication, and sermon delivery. Eriksson and Klintborg delve into the knowledge necessary for individuals to comprehend and access the intended religious meaning. They underscore that the absence of a broad interpretive framework complicates the understanding of traditional Christian symbols and rituals, prompting a deeper investigation into how individuals can gain the requisite understanding of Christian tradition and the Church's teachings.

A Focus on Confirmation and Young People

One of the most extensively studied facets of Christian religious education within the Church of Sweden concerns confirmation and youth education. Caroline Klintborg identifies twenty studies conducted between 2008 and 2023 in this area.[142] For this review, I will focus specifically on studies that have direct implications for the broader practices of teaching and learning within the Church of Sweden.

Jonas Eek delves into the teaching and learning experiences of confirmands within the Church of Sweden, offering insights into ecclesiology, theological anthropology, the historical context of confirmation, and providing statistical data on participants and the confirmation process itself. This comprehensive approach aims to sketch a detailed portrait of confirmation practices.[143] Particularly relevant to this discussion, Eek conceptualizes teaching as a structured process and emphasizes the need for clear objectives prior to the planning and execution of educational activities.[144] He advocates for a narrative pedagogy, underscoring the significance of storytelling, attentive listening, and compelling, authentic narration in the learning experience.[145]

Eek wraps up his analysis by outlining three key strategies for enhancing confirmation practices: prioritizing, focusing, and optimizing confirmation efforts. He emphasizes the need for the Church to treat confirmation as a priority. The

---

[142] Caroline Klintborg, *Var är Jesus? Ungas röster om konfirmandundervisning* (Stockholm: Verbum, 2023), 141–49.

[143] Eek, *Stanna i vattnet.*

[144] Eek, *Stanna i vattnet*, 135.

[145] Eek, *Stanna i vattnet*, 141–49.

focus should be directed toward confirmation camps, liturgical practices, the physical church space, and rites, with a suggestion to extend the confirmation process over several years. The optimization of confirmation involves acknowledging the role of music, addressing the needs of confirmands with special requirements, leveraging local expertise, and fostering cooperation driven by pastoral care.[146]

Caroline Klintborg's latest empirical research focuses on the experiences of youth undergoing confirmation training within the Church of Sweden. Utilizing twenty-eight interviews and employing Gert Biesta's framework of good teaching, Klintborg explores how confirmation training facilitates youths' journey towards selfhood (subjectification) and integration into the confirmation group (socialization). However, she notes a gap in equipping them with the skills necessary for living as Christians (qualification).[147]

Briefly, qualification, as defined by Biesta, involves the capacity to perform or act in a certain way, here, embodying Christian life. Klintborg observes that this critical component of comprehensive education is somewhat lacking in the Church of Sweden's approach to confirmation training.[148]

In collaboration with Sara Fransson, Klintborg has emphasized the significance of selecting suitable teaching methodologies. Their investigation, employing a mixed-methods research design, suggests that dissatisfaction among confirmands regarding their learning about specific subjects like God and Jesus may be attributed to the teaching strategies employed by confirmation leaders.[149] Through cluster analysis, Klintborg and Fransson categorize leaders into two groups: "narrow spectrum users," who utilize a limited set of methods primarily focused on games, play, and music, and "broad spectrum users," who incorporate a more diverse array of techniques, including games, play, music, as well as discussions,

---

[146] Eek, *Stanna i vattnet*, 11–170.

[147] Klintborg, *Var är Jesus?*, 91–111. For a brief introduction see Gert Biesta, "What is Education For? On Good Education, Teacher Judgement, and Educational Professionalism," *European Journal of Education* 50, no. 1 (2015): 75–87.

[148] Klintborg, *Var är Jesus?*, 111–23.

[149] The study mixes methods as it combines Fransson's data from a large scale random stratified survey (777 confirmands and 421 leaders) from 2022 with Klintborg's deep interviews with 22 confirmands, the same material she also draws on in *Klintborg, Var är Jesus?* See Caroline Klintborg and Sara Fransson, "Metodernas (icke-) betydelse? Ett religionspedagogiskt perspektiv," in *Konfirmation i förändringens tid*, ed. Sara Fransson (Uppsala: Church of Sweden, 2023), 77–93; Fransson, *Konfirmation*, 11–11.

storytelling, dramatization, and role-playing. This distinction highlights the impact of varied teaching approaches on confirmands' learning experiences.[150]

Klintborg and Fransson contend that employing a wider variety of teaching methods enhances young people's satisfaction with their learning about God and Jesus. This observation implies that reliance solely on games, play, and music might hinder youths' understanding of these theological concepts, compared to a more diversified pedagogical approach. Despite "narrow spectrum users" and "broad spectrum users" sharing similar educational goals, the breadth of methodologies used significantly influences the effectiveness of teaching about God and Jesus, pointing to the importance of methodological diversity in religious education.[151]

For my project, the aspects that stand out include Jonas Eek's exploration of diverse strategies for confirmation training and Caroline Klintborg's insights into what constitutes a good education. Additionally, the issue of identifying suitable teaching methods, as discussed by Klintborg and Sara Fransson, is particularly relevant and is a topic I revisit in sections 8.2–8.3. These discussions contribute valuable perspectives to the broader examination of Christian religious education, especially in the context of the Church of Sweden.

Teaching and Theologizing

I aim to succinctly examine two additional studies that are pertinent to this project but do not align directly with the previously outlined themes. Caroline Klintborg conducted a formative evaluation (*följeforskning*) within the parish of Västerås throughout 2018, aimed at assessing and accompanying the development of a new Pastoral for Christian religious education. In her publication, *En Process på riktig* (A Genuine Process), Klintborg shares her reflective observations from this endeavor, many of which are relevant to the current study.

In her evaluation, Klintborg initially expresses reservations about how Västerås Parish adopted a sociocultural learning perspective without a comprehensive understanding of its implications. She acknowledges the value of the sociocultural perspective but cautions against granting any single learning theory unchecked predominance.[152] Furthermore, Klintborg observes that the notion of teaching in Västerås Parish seems ambiguous and prone to being oversimplified into discussions about effective teaching methods, at the expense of broader pedagogical

---

[150] Klintborg and Fransson, "Metodernas," 81–85.
[151] Klintborg and Fransson, "Metodernas," 81–90.
[152] Gustavsson [Klintborg], *En process på riktigt*, 34.

considerations. This situation, she warns, may lead to expectations on religious educators "to contribute to and create a positive atmosphere without any real [teaching] content." Consequently, Klintborg underscores the necessity of integrating the substance of teaching (*what*) with pedagogical strategies (*how*) in Christian religious education, to ensure depth and richness in the learning experience.[153]

Jonas Ideström introduces a compelling perspective that serves as a critical counterpart to my concept of teaching, through his development of the concept of theologizing. Although Ideström's work is not centered explicitly on Christian religious education, he conceives theologizing as an integrated form of learning, crucial to the parish and church's exploration of God, the world, and their mission.[154]

In my interpretation, theologizing emerges as a unique approach to learning, wherein individuals engage with the Christian tradition—through narratives, artifacts, and practices—and contemporary life experiences. This process not only fosters a deeper self-understanding and comprehension of our lives but also contributes to the ongoing shaping and reshaping of the Christian tradition itself.[155]

For Ideström, learning through theologizing is a continuous activity occurring within parishes and churches, initiated by creating spaces for open conversation and dialogue. This process is significantly influenced by its environmental context and the material artifacts involved, suggesting that theologizing is deeply rooted in both the physical and the communal aspects of church life.[156]

Ideström posits that while theologizing cannot be strictly engineered through specific methodologies or strategies, there are numerous approaches that can facilitate more conducive environments for its occurrence. This perspective underscores the organic nature of theologizing, highlighting the importance of fostering conditions that encourage this form of learning.[157] The nuances distinguishing teaching from theologizing will be further explored in the concluding chapter of this dissertation.[158]

In conclusion, the body of previous research on Christian religious education within the Church of Sweden must be contextualized within the larger discourse

---

[153] Gustavsson [Klintborg], *En process på riktigt*, 31–39. *What* and *how* are two of the didactic questions that are often used in Sweden to discuss Christian religious education. See section 2.6.

[154] Jonas Ideström, *Ikoniska kartor: Att göra teologi i kyrkans vardag* (Stockholm: Verbum, 2021), 18.

[155] Ideström, *Ikoniska kartor*.

[156] Ideström, *Ikoniska kartor*, 121–48.

[157] Ideström, *Ikoniska kartor*, 179.

[158] See section 8.2.1.

surrounding Sweden's evolving religious landscape, which is frequently viewed as a force that could marginalize the Church. Against this backdrop, numerous researchers in Christian religious education have contended that shifts in religious socialization and a rise in religious illiteracy present significant challenges for the Church's capacity to engage with contemporary people. These issues, in turn, complicate the Church's teaching responsibilities, highlighting the need for innovative approaches to religious education that can bridge the growing gap between traditional church teachings and the lived experiences of today's Swedes.

The literature addresses this challenge by emphasizing theoretical explorations of learning and teaching, aiming to delineate the essential prerequisites for effective religious instruction. Additionally, it involves examining the practices of other Churches that could offer valuable insights and direction. This approach not only seeks to understand the foundational requirements for teaching within the religious context but also to identify successful strategies and innovations from broader ecclesial settings that could be adapted to address the specific challenges faced by the Church of Sweden.

Furthermore, significant attention has been given to Christian religious education within the context of the liturgy and with a particular focus on confirmation and the education of young people. However, there remains a persistent need to engage with other modalities of Christian religious education and to reevaluate our approaches to understanding and framing teaching within this domain. Through this dissertation, I aspire to enrich the ongoing dialogue on Christian religious education in the Church of Sweden, offering new perspectives and insights into its evolving challenges and opportunities.

1.5.2 Previous Research on Online Learning in Christian Religious Education

The body of literature on online learning is vast and expanding. A search conducted in April 2024 using Lund University's LubSearch for the subject terms "online learning," "e-learning," and "distance learning" yielded 104,447 entries.[159] Furthermore, publications such as the *Journal of Online Learning Research*, the *Journal of Computer Assisted Learning*, the *Journal of Online Learning and Teaching*, and the *International Journal of Web-Based Learning and Teaching Technologies* are dedicated to disseminating both theoretical and empirical research in the field of online learning. However, a cursory review of these sources reveals a

---

[159] In comparison, searching for the subject terms "Christian religious education" and "Christian education" returned only 22,621 entries.

predominant focus on formal educational settings, particularly involving children, adolescents, and post-secondary students.[160]

The online learning literature is distinguished by its focus on practical and pragmatic issues. This research is predominantly action-oriented, targeting the enhancement of specific learning and teaching methodologies over establishing a theoretical basis for online versus traditional, in-person learning. Martha F. Cleveland-Innes and Randy Garrison, for instance, employ the term "online learning theory" not to denote a singular, unified theory but to describe an approach that emphasizes collaboration, community, and quality assurance.[161] Consequently, online learning is not viewed as a separate theoretical perspective but as the adaptation of established pedagogical frameworks to the context of online education.[162]

Particularly relevant to my dissertation is research underscoring the significance of community within online learning. Carole Chapman, Leonie Ramondt, and Glenn Smiley have framed online learning within a social and cooperative context, making a distinction between mere information exchange and the formation of online communities. They argue that intentionally fostering communities plays a pivotal role in enhancing learning outcomes.[163] This aspect is revisited in chapter 5, where I explore the concept of community in relation to our online small groups and examine the strategies for the improvement of online learning as proposed by Jane E. Brindley, Kerstin M. Blaschke, and Christine Walti, based on their research

---

[160] For a systematic review of research on online teaching and learning from 2009 to 2018 see Florence Martin, Ting Sun, and Carl D. Westine, "A Systematic Review of Research on Online Teaching and Learning from 2009 to 2018," *Computers & Education* 159 (2020): 1–17.

[161] Martha F. Cleveland-Innes and D. Randy Garrison, "Teaching, Learning, and Beyond," in *An Introduction to Distance Education: Understanding Teaching and Learning in a New Era*, ed. Martha F. Cleveland-Innes and D. Randy Garrison (Milton: Taylor and Francis, 2020), 191–201.

[162] Janette R. Hill, Liyan Song, and Richard E. West, "Social Learning Theory and Web-Based Learning Environments: A Review of Research and Discussion of Implications," *American Journal of Distance Education* 23, no. 2 (2009): 88–103; Europe Singh, "Learning Theory and Online Technologies," *Open Learning* 29, no. 1 (2014): 89–92; Kathleen Pierce-Friedman and Laurie Wellner, "Faculty Professional Development in Creating Significant Teaching and Learning Experiences Online," in *Handbook of Research on Creating Meaningful Experiences in Online Courses*, ed. Lydia Kyei-Blankson, Esther Ntuli, and Joseph Blankson (Hershey: IGI Global, 2020), 1–13 at 5.

[163] Carole Chapman, Leonie Ramondt, and Glenn Smiley, "Strong Community, Deep Learning: Exploring the Link," *Innovations in Education and Teaching International* 42, no. 3 (2005): 217–30.

into the impact of small, conversation-driven collaborative learning groups in online settings.[164]

The literature concerning online learning within religious education reflects the broader themes prevalent in the general online learning discourse. This similarity is observed in both confessional and non-confessional educational contexts, with a shared emphasis on identifying suitable teaching methods and instructional principles applicable to tertiary education.[165] Discussions often extend to the integration of various technologies designed to facilitate online learning and teaching.[166] Additionally, the shift towards online education, prompted by the COVID-19 pandemic, has been the subject of multiple studies, typically underlining the obstacles and opportunities associated with implementing online learning frameworks in religious and theological education.[167]

Distinctive to the body of work on online Christian religious education is the emphasis on formation, regarded as a crucial element in theological education and

---

[164] Jane E. Brindley, Lisa M. Blaschke, and Christine Walti, "Creating Effective Collaborative Learning Groups in an Online Environment," *International Review of Research in Open and Distance Learning* 10, no. 3 (2009): 1–18.

[165] Andrew T. Babyak, "A Teaching Strategy for a Christian Virtual Environment," *Journal of Research on Christian Education* 24, no. 1 (2015): 63–77; Beverley McGuire, "Principles for Effective Asynchronous Online Instruction in Religious Studies: Asynchronous Online Instruction," *Teaching Theology and Religion* 20, no. 1 (2017): 28–45; Brian H. Smith, "Teaching Religion Online to Nontraditional Adult Learners," *Teaching Theology & Religion* 25, no. 2–3 (2022): 61–71; Peter Mudge, "'In the Land of the Blind, the One-Eyed Is King': Some Pedagogical Foundations for Deep, Practical Online Student Learning," *Journal of Adult Theological Education* 12, no. 2 (2015): 106–20.

[166] Alison Le Cornu, "Teaching Practical Theology Using Reusable Electronic Learning Objects: Practical, Educational and Theological Challenges," *Journal of Adult Theological Education* 5, no. 1 (2008): 71–85; James Dalziel, "Learning Design, Lams, and Christian Education," *Journal of Christian Education* os-54, no. 1 (2011): 39–56; Eric C. Smith, "Makeshifting the LMS: Strategies and Tactics in the Digital Classroom," *Theological Education* 52, no. 2 (2019): 25–42.

[167] Jones H. Mawerenga and Johannes J. Knoetze, "Theological Education and the COVID-19 Pandemic in Sub-Saharan Africa: A Malawian Perspective," *In die Skriflig* 56, no. 1 (2022): 1–10; Mualla Selçuk et al., "The Online Learning Experience of Theology Students in Turkey during the COVID-19 Pandemic: A New Disposition for RE?," *Religious Education* 116, no. 1 (2021): 74–90; M. Giunco Kierstin et al., "Lessons From the Field: Catholic School Educators and COVID-19," *Journal of Catholic education* 23, no. 1 (2020): 243–67; Johannes J. Knoetze, "Online Theological Education within the South African Context," *HTS Teologiese Studies / Theological Studies* 78, no. 1 (2022): 1–7.

ministerial training.[168] Thus, Christian religious education transcends mere content acquisition to encompass personal development and integration into a community. This process ensures that the learner assimilates and reflects the community's beliefs, values, and practices. G. Brooke Lester succinctly encapsulates this concept, describing formation as a "transformation towards community."[169]

Initial studies in the realm of online formation concentrated on proving that formative processes could indeed occur within digital environments.[170] Subsequent research shifted towards identifying elements that facilitate online formation. Lester emphasizes the critical need to maintain a strong connection between learning and formation, while Barbara Blodgett advocates for the creation of close-knit communities to reduce the sense of distance inherent in online settings.[171] Pamela C. Moore underscores the significance of online communities and further stresses the need to equip learners with effective virtual communication skills.[172] J. David Stark, on the other hand, points out the necessity of focusing on formation as a process of acquiring specific linguistic capabilities.[173] This progression of research highlights a broadening understanding of online formation, acknowledging its complexities and the various factors that can enhance or impede it.

The studies mentioned largely concentrate on Christian religious education within formal educational contexts. Indeed, research on online learning in nonformal Christian religious settings is notably scarcer. Kara Sevensma and colleagues' large-scale review of publications from 1970 to 2016 illustrates that the majority of research at the nexus of Christian religious education and online learning

---

[168] Deborah H. C. Gin, Lester G. Brooke, and Barbara Blodgett, "Forum on Seminary Teaching and Formation Online," *Teaching Theology & Religion* 22, no. 1 (2019): 73–87 at 71–77.

[169] Gin, Brooke, and Blodgett, "Formation Online," 78.

[170] Roger White, "Promoting Spiritual Formation in Distance Education," *Christian Education Journal* 3, no. 2 (2006): 303–15; Mark A. Maddix and James R. Estep, "Spiritual Formation in Online Higher Education Communities: Nurturing Spirituality in Christian Higher Education Online Degree Programs," *Christian Education Journal* 7, no. 2 (2010): 423–34; Diane Hockridge, "What's the Problem? Spiritual Formation in Distance and Online Theological Education," *Journal of Christian Education* os-54, no. 1 (2011): 25–38.

[171] Gin, Brooke, and Blodgett, "Formation Online."

[172] Pamela C. Moore, "Instructional Designers and Online Theological Education: May We Help You?," *Theological Education* 52, no. 2 (2019): 13–24.

[173] J. David Stark, "Gaming the System: Online Spiritual Formation in Christian Higher Education," *Theological Education* 52, no. 2 (2019): 43–54.

targets formal education.[174] My own search through Lund University's LubSearch corroborated this trend, revealing just a single empirical study addressing online Christian religious education in non-formal contexts. This study, "Godly Play Went Home" by Cheryl V. Minor and Hannah Sutton-Adams, investigates the adaptation of Godly Play practitioners to online formats during the COVID-19 pandemic when onsite gatherings were not feasible.[175] Consequently, the area concerning online learning for adult small groups within a Christian religious framework is significantly under-researched, indicating a gap in the literature and a potential avenue for future inquiry.

In my exploration of online learning within Christian religious education, I primarily focus on the critical role of community in online educational.[176] Given that the *Online Small Groups* project was initially aimed at enhancing online small group interactions, the works of Mark Nichols and Mark A. Maddix, which examine the attributes of online communities, are particularly pertinent.[177] These studies offer insights more directly applicable to my research objectives than those like Travis S. Hines and his colleagues or Angela A. Deulen, who mainly emphasize the general significance of collaborative learning. This distinction guides my review toward literature that specifically addresses the dynamics and potential of community building in online religious education environments.[178]

---

[174] Kara Sevensma et al., "Seeking a Scholarship of Pedagogy, Technology, and Faith: A Literature Survey," *International Journal of Christianity & Education* 22, no. 3 (2018): 252–73.

[175] Cheryl V. Minor and Hannah Sutton-Adams, "Godly Play Went Home: An Exploratory Study of the Experience of Godly Play in Homes during the Covid-19 Pandemic through the Lens of Caregivers," *Religious Education* 117, no. 4 (2022): 313–23.

[176] Angela A. Deulen, "Social Constructivism and Online Learning Environments: Toward a Theological Model for Christian Educators," *Christian Education Journal* 10, no. 1 (2013): 90–98; Mark A. Maddix, "Developing Online Learning Communities," *Christian Education Journal* 10, no. 1 (2013): 139–48; Michael Porterfield and E. Paulette Isaac-Savage, "The Formation of Online Wisdom Communities amongst Ministerial Students," *Journal of Adult Theological Education* 10, no. 2 (2013): 116–31; Porterfield and Isaac-Savage, "Online Wisdom"; Mark Nichols, "The Akadameia as Paradigm for Online Community in Theological Distance Education," *Journal of Christian Education* 54, no. 1 (2011): 5–23; Travis S. Hines et al., "Online Theological Education: A Case Study of Trinity School for Ministry," *Christian Higher Education* 8, no. 1 (2008): 32–41.

[177] Nichols, "Akadameia as Paradigm"; Maddix, "Online Learning."

[178] Hines et al., "Online Theological Education"; Deulen, "Social Constructivism."

1.5.3 Previous Research on Small Groups

Despite their widespread presence, Harley Atkinson and Joshua Rose highlight a notable scarcity of empirical research on small groups that extends beyond anecdotal observations.[179] Among the limited studies available, Robert Wuthnow's seminal research on small groups in the United States during the 1990s stands out prominently. Utilizing a comprehensive mixed-methods approach that includes in-person surveys, detailed interviews, and participant observation, Wuthnow does more than merely chart the landscape of 1990s' small groups; he examines the small-group movement in the context of evolving concepts of community and spirituality.[180]

Sharing the Journey serves a dual purpose: it not only details the dynamics of small groups but also contributes to the broader sociological discourse on community dynamics and shifts in US-American spirituality, resonating with the work of Robert N. Bellah and colleagues in *Habits of the Heart* and Robert Putnam and Lewis Feldstein in *Better Together*.[181]

Wuthnow's primary focus is on the macro-level societal impacts of the small-group movement, rather than directly aiming to enhance the functioning of these groups. Nevertheless, Wuthnow's analysis of the small group movement is fundamentally positive, crediting it with the potential to mitigate the fragmentation of US-American society during the 1990s.[182] Wuthnow's research further demonstrates how church-based small groups are typically reported to enable participants to deepen their faith and foster a closer connection to God.[183]

However, Wuthnow also identifies a critical crossroads for the small-group movement. While these groups offer a sense of community, the stability of this community is fragile, often predicated on a self-interested "what's in it for me" mindset. This attitude can lead individuals to leave groups that do not meet their expectations in favor of others that might. Wuthnow argues that for small groups to cultivate a durable sense of community, they must achieve a higher level of

---

[179] Harley Atkinson and Joshua Rose, "The Small-Group Ministry Movement of the Last Four Decades," *Christian Education Journal* 17, no. 3 (2020): 547–59 at 553.

[180] Robert Wuthnow, *Sharing the Journey: Support Groups and America's New Quest for Community* (New York: The Free Press, 1994).

[181] Robert Neely Bellah, *Habits of the Heart: Individualism and Commitment in American Life* (Berkeley: University of California Press, 1996); Lewis M. Feldstein and Robert D. Putnam, *Better Together: Restoring the American Community* (New York: Simon & Schuster, 2003).

[182] Wuthnow, *Sharing the Journey*, 21–25.

[183] Wuthnow, *Sharing the Journey*, 231–39.

interpersonal engagement. He makes several recommendations to attain this, which I explore in chapter 7.[184]

Subsequent research on church-based small groups has sought to confirm, expand upon, and refine Wuthnow's insights. For example, Roger Walton researched small groups in the United Kingdom between 2010 and 2011. His findings resonate with those of Wuthnow's research. Walton observed that in the North of England, small groups are primarily focused on personal growth and mutual support, rather than on mission and evangelization. Furthermore, he notes that within these groups, maturity is perceived more as a matter of individual development rather than as engagement in Christian practices like witnessing, ministry, or outreach.[185]

Other research aims to delineate effective practices for small groups' optimal operation, much like the objectives of this project. Theresa Latini builds upon Wuthnow's work, focusing on well-developed small groups as exemplars of best practices that embody Wuthnow's recommendations, including leadership training, crafting of purpose statements, and deliberate organizational strategies.[186] Studying four groups within the Presbyterian Church and two in the Reformed Church in America, Latini proposes a small group theology centered on multidimensional *koinonia*—fellowship that spans the relationship between believers and God, amongst believers themselves, and between believers and the broader world.

Latini outlines four pivotal strategies for small groups to overcome community challenges effectively: (1) development of small-group mission statements, (2) comprehensive training for small-group leaders, (3) strategic integration of small groups into the wider congregational ministries, and (4) regular evaluation of small groups' growth and impact.[187] I return to these strategies in section 7.2.

Ian Hussey's research on small groups in Australia, characterized by high participation rates, reveals that a welcoming culture and structured organization significantly boost involvement.[188] Further empirical studies on adult small groups

---

[184] Wuthnow, *Sharing the Journey*, 361–66.

[185] Roger Walton, "Disciples Together: The Small Group as a Vehicle for Discipleship Formation," *Journal of Adult Theological Education* 8, no. 2 (2011): 99–114.

[186] Theresa F. Latini, *The Church and the Crisis of Community: A Practical Theology of Small-Group Ministry* (Grand Rapids: William B. Eerdmans, 2011), 41–47.

[187] Latini, *Crisis of Community*, 141–79.

[188] Ian Hussey, "Investigating High Levels of Small Group Participation in Churches: Case Study Research from Australia," *Practical Theology* (2019): 1–13.

have looked into essential factors like participant motivation and leader recruitment strategies.[189]

Research also examines the impact groups have on learning. Findings consistently show that participation in small groups fosters substantial personal and spiritual development,[190] better prepares individuals to tackle situational challenges,[191] and enhances ministerial education.[192] These insights highlight the multifaceted benefits of small group participation in fostering deeper engagement and growth within religious contexts.

Also in the landscape of literature on small groups, there exists a category that straddles the line between popular guides and scholarly research. Works such as Ed Stetzer and Eric Geiger's *Transformational Groups*, Jim Egli and Dwight Marable's *Big Impact*, Joel Comiskey and Jim Egli's *Groups that Thrive*, and Harley Atkinson's *The Power of Small Groups in Christian Formation* concentrate on identifying best practices or strategies for church-based small groups.[193]

While these publications present findings from research, transparency regarding the reliability of their results is often lacking due to insufficiently detailed research methodologies. Additionally, none of these works have been published by academic presses, which does not necessarily undermine their value as insightful resources. However, it is important to note that theoretical engagement tends to

---

[189] Alice W. Mambo, "The Rationale Motive of Adult Christians' Participation in Education Programs among Episcopal Churches in Southern California," *Christian Education Journal* 16, no. 1 (2019): 7–25; David R. Dunaetz et al., "Barriers to Leading Small Groups among Generation Z and Younger Millennials: An Exploratory Factor Analysis and Implications for Recruitment and Training," *Christian Education Journal* 19, no. 1 (2022): 152–69.

[190] Rune Larsson, Carl Eber Olivestam, and Björn Wiedel, *Livsnära: Teori och praktik kring kyrkans bibelundervisning* (Umeå: Institutionen för religionsvetenskap, Univ., 1995), 162; James A. Lang and David J. Bochman, "Positive Outcomes of a Discipleship Process," *Journal of Spiritual Formation and Soul Care* 10, no. 1 (2017): 51–72.

[191] Selena D. Headley, "A Praxis-Based Approach to Theological Training in Cape Town," *HTS Teologiese Studies/Theological Studies* 74, no. 3 (2018): 1–7.

[192] Peter Gubi, "An Exploration of the Impact of Small Reflexive Groups on Personal and Spiritual Development," *Practical Theology* 4, no. 1 (2011): 49–66.

[193] Ed Stetzer and Eric Geiger, *Transformational Groups: Creating a New Scorecard for Groups* (Nashville: B&H Books, 2014); Jim Egli and Dwight Marable, *Big Impact: Connecting People to God and One Another in Thriving Groups* (Apple Valley: ChurchSmart Resources, 2011); Jim Egli and Joel Comiskey, *Groups that Thrive: 8 Surprising Discoveries About Life-giving Small Groups* (Moreno Valley: CCS Publishing, 2018); Harley Atkinson, *The Power of Small Groups in Christian Formation* (Eugene: Resource Publications, 2018).

be minimal in these texts, positioning them closer to the genre of how-to manuals than to academic discourse.

I relate to this literature when discussing how small groups are conceptualized, but not in relation to the academic discussion I develop. I hence treat these more akin to material for analysis than as conversation partners.

Two significant aspects emerge from the literature. First, studies, particularly from the USA, emphasize the crucial role of community in small group settings. Here, community is viewed not just as an instrument for collaborative learning but also as a valuable goal in its own right. Second, there is a consistent focus on how church-based small groups interact with the larger congregation, parish, or church framework. These small groups are often seen as mission-focused initiatives that serve as gateways into the church community, aiming to enhance church membership. This dual focus on community as both a method and objective, along with the strategic role of small groups in church growth, underscores the multifaceted impact of small groups within religious organizations.[194] I return to these aspects in chapters 4 and 5, where I compare and contrast insights from our groups with the findings in this literature.

1.6 Aim and Research Question

The dissertation pursues two primary objectives. First, it aims to develop the "local" insights gained from the *Online Small Groups* project into a more widely accessible resource. In other words, my goal is to narrate the experiences garnered from the *Online Small Groups* project in a way that encourages individuals, who did not participate in the project, to learn from our experiences.[195]

The second objective is to present my reflections on our "story." These reflections are intended to identify specific strategies for improving online small groups and to articulate a broader discussion on teaching within the Church of Sweden. I aspire for these insights to significantly contribute to the ongoing academic discourse previously outlined.[196]

---

[194] Wuthnow, *Sharing the Journey*, 341–52; Latini, *Crisis of Community*, 101–08; Hussey, "High Levels," 2. Note that Latini is critical of the idea that small groups are expected to grow church membership numerically. Still, her discussion shows that this is a common expectation of small group leaders.

[195] See section 3.5.

[196] See chapters 7 and 8.

Accordingly, I pose the central research question: *How can online small groups within the Church of Sweden be improved as instances of Christian religious education, and do these improvement possibilities suggest any implications for Christian religious education within the Church of Sweden more generally?*

To comprehensively address the primary research question, I explore several sub-questions:

1. What does it entail to conceptualize online small groups as instances of Christian religious education?
2. To what extent and in what ways do group leaders teach in online small groups?
3. How can adopting a teaching perspective contribute to the improvement of online small groups?

1.7 Contribution

Since David Tracy's examination in *The Analogical Imagination*, it has become commonplace that theological research addresses three distinct audiences: wider society, the academic community, and the church.[197] Although theological studies often engage all three, it is typical for a specific study to prioritize one audience. This dissertation primarily engages with the church, with a particular focus on the Church of Sweden, aiming to provide a practical contribution.

The core of my contribution lies in sharing and reflecting on the *Online Small Groups* project, thereby enabling individuals in comparable contexts to benefit from our insights. Through this, I aim to offer actionable knowledge that can contribute to strengthen the Church of Sweden's educational ministry.

However, my work also makes an academic contribution. Specifically, it adds conceptual tools to the debate about learning and teaching in the Church of Sweden, that can aid future research in expanding the scholarly engagement with non-formal Christian religious education. By presenting a worked example and linking it to creative non-fiction writing techniques and issues of representation, this dissertation also substantially enriches the methodological discourse surrounding theological action research.

---

[197] David Tracy, *The Analogical Imagination: Christian Theology and the Culture of Pluralism* (New York: Crossroad, 1981), 5.

1.8 Disposition

Just as action research is a unique approach to social inquiry, action research dissertations form a distinct category within academic writing.[198] David Coghlan and Patricia Gaya, in their contribution to the *SAGE Encyclopedia of Action Research* on dissertation writing, propose that such dissertations should contain:

> the purpose and rationale of the research, the context, the methodology and method of inquiry, the story and outcomes, self-reflection and learning of the action researcher, reflection on the story in the light of the experience and the theory, and extrapolation to a broader context and articulation of usable knowledge.[199]

This comprehensive structure ensures that action research dissertations not only present findings but also deeply engage with their practical implications and theoretical underpinnings.

While Coghlan and Gaya emphasize the importance of incorporating discussions on specified topics over adhering strictly to their sequence as chapter headings, I have chosen to closely align my dissertation's structure with their recommended framework. This decision is based on two reasons: first, I believe that their outlined structure offers a robust framework that aids in clearly presenting and organizing the content of this action research dissertation, particularly in facilitating the communication of the project's processes and findings. Second, adhering closely to Coghlan and Gaya's recommendations serves as a bridge to established best practices within the action research community, a connection I find crucial given that, to the best of my knowledge, this work is the first action research dissertation in practical theology in Sweden.

I thus outlined the purpose and rationale of this research in this introductory chapter, where I also touched upon the societal, ecclesial, local, and academic contexts framing this dissertation. I slightly diverge from Coghlan and Gaya's suggested structure by incorporating a chapter dedicated to my theoretical perspectives. In chapter 2, I thus elucidate my views on Christian religious education (2.2) and develop an understanding of teaching (2.3). Additionally, I formulate a

---

[198] See for example Brouard, "Using Theological Action Research"; Jason Boyd, "Action Research as a Way of Doing Theology (ART): Transforming My Practice of Preaching the Bible with My Congregation" (PhD, University of Chester, 2015); David Elias Weekley, "Exploring Transgender Spirituality Within a Retreat Setting: Theological Action Research" (Doctor of Ministry, Boston University, 2016); Peter Babington, "Ageing Well: Using Action Research in a Parish Church Setting" (Doctor of Practical Theology, University of Birmingham, 2017); Kappelgaard, "Kirke i bevægelse."

[199] Coghlan and Gaya, "Dissertation Writing," 2.

taxonomy of models of Christian religious education (2.4), which later informs the discussion of our online small groups in chapter 7. Consequently, chapter 2 transcends a mere review of existing theories and analytical frameworks (2.5–2.6); it operationalizes a specific viewpoint, directly addressing my initial sub-question: *What does it entail to conceptualize online small groups as instances of Christian religious education?* Furthermore, in my summary and reflections, I turn to the question of how this project is an expression of white practical theology (2.8).

In chapter 3, I delve into the methodologies and methods that guide this inquiry, offering a detailed exploration of action research (3.2), and specifically the prescriptive-constructive approach utilized in this dissertation (3.3). The chapter also narrates the project's inception and progression, showcasing how methods were applied and complementing the reflective narrative presented in part 2 (3.4). Furthermore, I explain the use of creative non-fiction writing techniques (3.5), discussing their relevance to representation and the imperative of broadening the context. This approach not only elucidates the methodological underpinnings of my work but also enhances the communicative and interpretative richness of the dissertation.

Part 2 is dedicated to sharing the reflective narrative of our project, underscoring that every recounting inherently involves interpretation, as noted by Coghlan and Gaya.[200] This section aims to enable readers to glean insights and draw conclusions from our experiences. It serves to address the sub-question: *To what extent and in what ways do group leaders teach in online small groups?*

Part 3 presents my reflections, analyzing the project's narrative against the backdrop of both previous research and theory. Chapter 4 engages with literature on small groups (4.1), offering a nuanced view of our online small groups through the lens of the didactic relations model (4.2), thus presenting a different, and complementary, perspective on these groups. In chapter 5, the focus shifts to community within online learning, juxtaposing our approach to community formation against broader concepts found in both small group and online learning literature (5.1–5.2). This comparison highlights the unique aspects of small groups within the Church of Sweden compared to those in Anglo-Saxon contexts (5.3).

Chapter 6 centers on the notion of leadership within small groups as a form of teaching (6.1–6.2) and addresses potential objections to this view (6.3). This section also responds to the sub-questions: *To what extent and in what ways do group*

---

[200] Coghlan and Gaya, "Dissertation Writing," 4. I discuss this point in section 3.5.

leaders teach in online small groups? and *How can adopting a teaching perspective contribute to the improvement of online small groups?*

In part 4, the focus shifts towards broadening the scope of the project's insights and delineating actionable knowledge. Chapter 7 commences this exploration by articulating eight teaching strategies for online small groups (7.1), scrutinizing these strategies against existing research (7.2), and evaluating their practical application (7.4–7.5). Through this examination, the chapter aspires to offer valuable insights that contribute to the enhancement of online small groups, underpinning the dissertation's aim to provide practical, applicable knowledge for the improvement of Christian religious education in the Church of Sweden. This chapter thus directly addresses the first part of the overarching research question: *How can online small groups within the Church of Sweden be improved as instances of Christian religious education?*

Chapter 8 synthesizes the dissertation's diverse insights, advocating for the significance of a teaching-focused approach within Christian religious education in the Church of Sweden (8.1). It connects the dots between the dissertation's arguments and the scholarly work outlined in earlier sections (8.2), evaluating how research on Christian religious education can pragmatically benefit its practice (8.3–8.4). By exploring the broader implications of suggested improvements for Christian religious education, this chapter responds to the overarching research question's latter portion: *Do these improvement possibilities suggest any implications for Christian religious education within the Church of Sweden more generally?* Through this comprehensive analysis, chapter 8 aims to contribute constructively to the ongoing academic and practical discourse on Christian religious education, emphasizing the transformative potential of a teaching perspective.

Coghlan and Gaya note that the self-reflection and learning of the action researcher is an important aspect in which action research dissertations differ from more traditional dissertation designs.[201] However, in my attempt to communicate public knowledge, I found it difficult to find an appropriate place for these more personal reflections. I therefore turn to these in the epilogue.

---

[201] Coghlan and Gaya, "Dissertation Writing," 4.

2. Theoretical Perspective(s)

In this chapter, I explore the theoretical frameworks that inform my analysis of online small groups and highlight the teleological nature of Christian religious education. This examination is important in light of my focus on the improvement of online small groups. As stated in chapter 1, the notion of improvement hinges not only on observing changes but encompasses evaluative judgments regarding the value of these changes. To be transparent, such judgments require a set of evaluative criteria, which are influenced, in turn, by the theoretical lenses one adopts. It consequently makes a difference whether one aims to improve online small groups as instances of Christian religious education, as gathering places, or as communities of trust and fellowship.

Christian religious education thus serves not only as the field within which this dissertation is situated but also as the theoretical vantage point from which I examine our online small groups. The objective of this chapter is to delineate this perspective, addressing my first sub-question: *What does it entail to conceptualize online small groups as instances of Christian religious education?*

I begin with a brief reflection on my use of theoretical perspectives (2.1) and proceed to discuss Christian religious education as a theoretical framework (2.2). I then engage in a conceptual discussion of teaching and, to a lesser extent, learning (2.3). Moving forward, I develop several models of Christian religious education that function as analytical tools in chapter 7 (2.4) and relate these models to the concept of constructive alignment as a teaching design (2.5). I introduce the didactic relations model, which I employ as an analytical tool in chapter 4 (2.6), before wrapping up with a discussion on teaching strategies (2.7), laying the theoretical groundwork for chapter 7. In my summary and reflections, I revisit the concept of white practical theology and note how it relates to the theoretical perspectives I present here (2.8).

2.1 A Toolkit Approach

Instead of adhering to a singular theoretical perspective, I adopt what Davide Nicolini has termed "programmatic eclecticism," or more succinctly, a "toolkit approach."[1]

Discussing the study of social practices through the use of practice theories, Nicolini recognizes that many practice theories exhibit significant similarities, even as they shed light on different aspects of social practices. Furthermore, each practice theory has its distinct advantages and limitations, suggesting that they can complement one another effectively. Consequently, Nicolini advocates employing practice theories in various combinations rather than committing exclusively to any single one.[2]

Analogous reasoning leads me to embrace a toolkit approach. Just as there is no unified theory of social practice, so too is there no single, comprehensive theory of teaching, or learning. Instead, the field hosts a multitude of competing and complementary theories, each with its strengths and limitations, each capable of highlighting certain facets of teaching and learning.[3] Committing to any single theory, or even a specific school of theories, thus risks neglecting important aspects of teaching and learning, even as it reveals others. I thus found that a variety of theories elucidate the dynamics within our online small groups, each adding a piece of the puzzle, without for that reason establishing a complete picture.[4]

In Nicolini's perspective, two considerations guide the effective utilization of a toolkit approach. First, Nicolini emphasizes the importance of maintaining an internally coherent toolbox. He therefore contends that the theories and methods comprising the toolkit should align in their ontological assumptions and methodological choices.[5] Second, according to Nicolini, an effective theoretical package must accomplish three objectives: (1) it should accurately describe social reality as it pertains to the phenomenon under investigation, (2) enable the representation of this phenomenon in textual form, and (3) furnish resources that deepen the understanding of the said phenomenon.[6] Applied to learning, this implies that a

---

[1] Davide Nicolini, *Practice Theory, Work, and Organization: An Introduction* (Oxford: Oxford University Press, 2013), 213.

[2] Nicolini, *Practice Theory*, 211–39.

[3] See for example Knud Illeris, ed., *Contemporary Theories of Learning: Learning Theorists… in Their Own Words*, 2nd ed. (Oxon: Routledge, 2018).

[4] See chapter 7.

[5] Nicolini, *Practice Theory*, 217.

[6] Nicolini, *Practice Theory*, 218.

toolkit approach must possess the capacity to identify human activities as teaching or learning, articulate these activities in written form, and provide a deepened understanding of teaching and learning practices.

Although I am confident that the theoretical resources utilized in this dissertation accomplish the three objectives set forth by Nicolini, I did not commence the *Online Small Groups* project with a comprehensive toolkit. Rather, my use of theories and theoretical perspectives evolved and expanded throughout the research process, with several theoretical perspectives emerging only during or after the *Online Small Groups* project, as detailed in section 3.3.

Consequently, my toolkit comprises a diverse array of tools. More specifically, I draw upon resources from Christian religious education, learning theories, teaching designs, and action research, and while I do not perceive any fundamental disparities among these, which would make it impossible to employ them in a single toolkit, I am also not convinced that they share the same ontological and methodological foundations, neither do I delved into each with the depth required to affirm their ontological and methodological compatibility.

This might represent the most significant limitation of my application of the toolkit approach. Employing a variety of theoretical perspectives without delving deeply into each carries the risk of misinterpreting the theories, potentially leading to their superficial application and undermining their efficacy as analytical tools. I acknowledge this as a legitimate concern.

Nonetheless, this dissertation does not aim to definitively explain teaching or learning but rather explores ways in which teaching can be comprehended and improved. Therefore, I believe the advantage lies in the ability to see various facets of teaching and learning in online small groups, rather than in conducting a detailed analysis of teaching through the lens of a single theory.

An additional limitation of the toolkit approach becomes apparent when I forego selecting a distinct theoretical perspective for engaging with teaching and learning. This choice complicates the task of linking the tangible outcomes of my analysis to broader theoretical conversations. The diversity of theoretical resources I utilize leads to a variety of seemingly unrelated results, formulated in terms of teaching strategies in chapter 7, which can appear unconnected.

Diversity in perspectives thus hampers my ability to integrate these findings into existing theoretical discussions, potentially limiting my contribution to the development of theory. However, I believe this issue is mitigated by how my discussion contributes to the current discourse on learning and teaching within the Church of Sweden.[7]

2.2 Christian Religious Education as an Intentional Activity

In this dissertation, I adopt Jeff Astley's definition of Christian religious education, which he identifies as "intentional activity by a teacher or educator that results in the facilitation of Christian learning."[8] I find further support in defining education as broader than learning in the work of educational theorist Gert Biesta.[9]

Critiquing the prevailing emphasis on learning within education research, Biesta contends that learning is inherently specific and asserts that "the point of education is that students learn *something*, that they learn it for a *reason*, and that they learn it from *someone*."[10] Education is thus with necessity teleological, requiring education research to extend beyond the mere act of learning, to consider the aims and quality of education, including what constitutes a *good* education.[11]

---

[7] See chapter 8.

[8] Jeff Astley, "Aims and Approaches in Christian Education," in *Learning in the Way: Research and Reflection on Adult Christian Education*, ed. Jeff Astley (Herefordshire: Gracewing, 2000), 1–32 at 3. This is a generally accepted understanding of Christian religious education. See for example Craig R. Dykstra, *Growing in the Life of Faith: Education and Christian Practices* (Louisville: Geneva Press, 1999); Mullino Moore, *Teaching*; Hedman, *Undervisa*.

[9] Gert Biesta, *The Rediscovery of Teaching* (New York: Routledge, 2017). In Scandinavian, and particularly Norwegian, religious education research in the learning in faith communities trajectory (see section 1.4), it is common to understand learning as the overarching concept. Much attention has therefore been given to learning and learning theories also in relation to discussions of teaching. See for example Tveito Johnsen, "Religiøs læring." Teaching as a theoretical concept has however received less attention. Geir Afdal notes that teaching is a social practice, but does not elaborate on the practice nor on the relationship between learning and teaching. Geir Afdal, *Religion som bevegelse: Læring, kunnskap og mediering* (Oslo: Universitetsforlaget, 2013), 41–49.

[10] Biesta, "What is Education For?," 76 Emphasis in original.

[11] Biesta, "What is Education For?," 71–77; Biesta, "Freeing Teaching," 231–35. Critics might be quick to point out that Biesta operates with a highly reductionist concept of learning. His criticism of learning might thus be more due to the way in which he constructs learning as comprehension, rather than problems inherent in the concept of learning itself. While I agree that Biesta's criticism of learning is not entirely convincing, I still deem his overall argument to be important. Learning is a specific activity and as such it is always a learning of *something* and

Biesta's reflections on education are valuable, against the backdrop of the prevailing learning paradigm.[12] He proposes an alternative that reorients attention from the learner and their activities towards the responsibilities and possibilities of teachers and educators.[13] His perspective on education research aligns, furthermore, with research in Christian religious education, a field that does not center primarily on learning within congregations but rather explores how Christian religious educators educate and teach. Consequently, it examines how congregations, parishes, and churches serve both as educational settings and as active participants in the educational process.[14] Lastly, Biesta points to the teleological nature of education, emphasizing the importance of understanding Christian religious education in relation to its final purpose.

In discussing purpose, I follow Thomas Groome and distinguish between purpose and metapurpose. Christian religious education aims to introduce individuals to the foundational beliefs of the Christian faith, impart religious language and literacy, present Christian and biblical narratives, nurture a connection with the divine, and encourage Christian living in the world, among other objectives.[15]

---

education research needs to attend to how this *something* is constructed and how it functions in promoting education.

[12] Biesta, "Freeing Teaching," 230.

[13] Biesta, *Rediscovery*, 96–98. This is comparable to didactic classroom studies which focuses on the role of the teacher. See Osbeck, Ingerman, and Claesson, *Didactic Classroom Studies*, 15; Christina Osbeck, "Questions and Speech Genres in Social Studies Classrooms: Comparisons of Communication Patterns," in *Didactic Classroom Studies: A Potential Research Direction*, ed. Christina Osbeck, Åke Ingerman, and Silwa Claesson (Lund: Nordic Academic Press, 2018), 23–45; Angelika Kullberg and Christina Skodras, "Systematic Variation in Examples in Mathematics Teaching," in *Didactic Classroom Studies: A Potential Research Direction*, ed. Christina Osbeck, Åke Ingerman, and Silwa Claesson (Lund: Nordic Academic Press, 2018), 47–65.

[14] Groome, *Christian Religious Education*; Thomas H. Groome, *Sharing Faith: A Comprehensive Approach to Religious Education and Pastoral Ministry: The Way of Shared Praxis* (Eugene: Wipf and Stock, 1998); Jeff Astley, ed., *Learning in the Way: Research and Reflection on Adult Christian Education* (Herefordshire: Gracewing, 2000); Mullino Moore, *Teaching*; Cook Everist, *Learning Community*; Jeff Astley, "Discipleship Learning," *Rural Theology* 13, no. 1 (2015): 1–3; Regan, *Two or Three*; Liu Wong, *Becoming Wise*; Goto, *Playing*.

[15] Groome, *Christian Religious Education*; Astley, "The Place of Understanding in Christian Education and Education about Christianity"; Holley, "Learning Religion"; Michael Warren, "Religious Formation in the Context of Social Formation," in *Critical Perspectives on Christian Education: A Reader on the Aims, Principles and Philosophy of Christian Education*, ed. Jeff Astley and Leslie J. Francis (Herefordshire: Gracewing, 1994), 202–14; Dean M. Martin, "Learning to Become a Christian," in *Critical Perspectives on Christian Education: A Reader on*

Despite these distinct goals, Groome identifies a more profound, underlying purpose—a metapurpose—which he interprets as the kingdom or reign of God.[16]

For Groome, the Kingdom denotes "God's own vision and intention for all
people and creation."

> In summary, the Kingdom of God is God's intention for creation. It is the central theme
> and purpose in the preaching and life of Jesus, the Christ. Therefore, when an educa-
> tional activity is intended to sponsor people toward Christian faith, the overarching pur-
> pose (the ultimate, or metapurpose) of such education is the Kingdom of God in Jesus
> Christ.[17]

In *Sharing Faith*, Groome distances himself from the expression "kingdom of
God," noting its patriarchal implications and suggesting that "'reign' is a more accurate translation of the Hebrew *malkuth Yahweh* and the Greek *basileia tou
theou*."[18] Despite this terminological shift, the concept of the reign of God serves
the same purpose in *Sharing Faith* as the kingdom of God does in *Christian Religious Education*.

Courtney Goto makes a similar analysis of the Kingdom, highlighting its patriarchal overtones.[19] Consequently, Goto prefers the term "God's new creation,"
a concept eluding strict definitions, which she intentionally leaves open-ended.[20]
However, Goto interprets the new creation as a call to action for "Christians to be,
to be with others, and to behave in new ways, including those that might challenge
habitual ways of being. In this sense, the image of leaning into God's new creation
is one of resistance to the status quo and change from old to new."[21] Within the
context of this discussion, Goto's concept of God's new creation can be understood to serve a similar role as the Kingdom. God's new creation describes the

---

the *Aims, Principles and Philosophy of Christian Education*, ed. Jeff Astley and Leslie J. Francis
(Herefordshire: Gracewing, 1994), 184–201; Jeff Astley, "The Role of Worship in Christian
Learning," in *Theological Perspectives on Christian Formation: A Reader on Theology and
Christian Education*, ed. Jeff Astley, Leslie J. Francis, and Colin Crowder (Herefordshire:
Gracewing, 1996), 244–51; Stanley Hauerwas, "The Gesture of a Truthful Story," in *Theological
Perspectives on Christian Formation: A Reader on Theology and Christian Education*, ed. Jeff
Astley, Leslie J. Francis, and Colin Crowder (Herefordshire: Gracewing, 1996), 97–105; Dykstra,
Life of Faith; Cook Everist, *Learning Community*.

[16] Groome, *Christian Religious Education*, 31–55; Groome, *Sharing Faith*, 11–17.

[17] Groome, *Christian Religious Education*, 49.

[18] Groome, *Sharing Faith*, 14.

[19] Goto, *Playing*, 33–34.

[20] Goto, *Playing*, 32.

[21] Goto, *Playing*, 12.

metapurpose of Christian religious education, guiding its more concrete aims and practices.

Also, Maria Liu Wong articulates a metapurpose in her discussion of theological education. Liu Wong understands the ultimate goal, or telos, of Christian religious education as "the flourishing of God's people and world, the reconciliation of brokenness, and glimpses of grace and wholeness in families, churches, and communities across the world."[22]

Although neither Goto nor Liu Wong explicitly refer to their visions for Christian religious education as a metapurpose, their descriptions align with such an idea. I contend that their perspectives on the purpose of Christian religious education can indeed be interpreted as embodying a metapurpose, indicating that diverse scholars within the field might concur on the existence of an overarching goal for Christian religious education.

An advantage of both the Kingdom and God's new creation is that they serve as prominent symbols for the metapurpose of Christian religious education. I employ the concept of the "kingdom of God" because it closely aligns with the Church of Sweden's own interpretation of its mission, as delineated in the Church Ordinance.[23]

In comparison to the term "reign of God," I believe the term more effectively captures the idea of a specific state of being rather than a process or activity. Additionally, I am not entirely persuaded by Groome's assertion that "reign" offers a less patriarchal alternative to "Kingdom."

I also find that Groome's exploration of the Kingdom provides a more concise articulation of Christian religious education's ultimate goal compared to Goto's more open-ended examination of God's new creation. While I acknowledge and share Goto's concerns, as well as her emphasis on the ongoing revelation of God's new creation, I therefore choose to adhere to the concept of the Kingdom for the purposes of this discussion.[24]

In Groome's interpretation, the concept of the Kingdom is deeply intertwined with a teleological perspective on existence itself, representing a state of "peace and justice, love and freedom, wholeness and fullness of life for all, and for the well-

---

[22] Liu Wong, *Becoming Wise*, 132.

[23] Svenska kyrkan, *Kyrkoordning*, Ch 2 § 1. See also chapter 1 and the discussion in section 6.3.1.

[24] Goto notes that the Kingdom resonates with her concept of God's new creation. Likewise, I do not understand these concepts to be in opposition. Goto, *Playing*, 33.

being of creation (shalom)."[25] The Kingdom symbolizes the right ordering of relationships among God, humans, and the entirety of creation.

However, as an eschatological notion, the Kingdom exists in a state of being both "already" present and "not yet" fulfilled. Initiated by Jesus, its ultimate realization lies only at the end of time.[26] Consequently, the Kingdom's presence is dynamic, capable of both expanding and withering away.

Here, Groome establishes the link between Christian religious education and the concept of the Kingdom, underscoring the necessity for *metanoia* or conversion—an ongoing call to reevaluate and realign our relationships. Connecting the kingdom of God, as proclaimed by Jesus the Christ to the "love commandment as the supreme law of the Kingdom," Groome asserts that the Kingdom demands "not 'love of God *and* love of neighbor,' but 'love of God *by* love of neighbor,' with no limits to 'neighbor.'"[27] The Kingdom invites individuals into an ongoing journey of reorientation, encouraging a turning "outward toward God in our neighbor." This transformative endeavor is identified as the fundamental purpose of Christian religious education.[28]

2.3 Learning and Teaching in Christian Religious Education

In contrast to learning, teaching has received comparably little recent conceptual articulation. A recent overview of learning theories comprises no fewer than seventeen chapters dedicated to understanding and conceptualizing learning, yet there seems to be no equivalent body of literature focused on dissecting the nature of teaching.[29] Indeed, many Christian religious educators tend to link Christian

---

[25] Groome, *Sharing Faith*, 16.

[26] Groome, *Sharing Faith*, 16.

[27] Groome, *Christian Religious Education*, 41. Emphasis in original.

[28] Groome, *Christian Religious Education*, 35.

[29] Illeris, *Contemporary Theories*.

Reviewing literature on teaching in the spring of 2023 using Lund University's search engine LubSearch, I was surprised how little discussion I found about the concept of teaching as such. As I understand it, there has been a shift in the analytical philosophy of education since the 1980s which led educational philosophers to abandon more analytic questions (what is teaching?) in favor of more pragmatic questions (how do we improve teaching?), with the effect that the philosophy of education is today less interested in defining basic concepts. See Randall Curren,

religious education directly with teaching, without delving into a nuanced conceptual exploration of teaching itself.[30]

What is more, the conceptual discussions on teaching that I have come across occasionally lack a certain depth. For example, Mary Elizabeth Moore characterizes teaching as

> an act of walking with, sharing with, acting with, remembering with, and constructing meaning with people in a learning community. Teaching is what Thomas Groome describes as "sharing faith"; teachers are wise companions on the journey,[31]

a definition that lacks the sophistication often present in theoretical perspectives on learning, that generally describe the learning process in detail, including a description of *who* learns *what* from *whom* and *how* this learning is accomplished.[32]

Similarly, Anders Hedman observes that teaching is a multivariant concept, linking a teacher's preparation (past), the act of teaching (present), and the outcomes of teaching (future), alongside students' experiences, situations, and future aspirations, as well as the interactions between teachers and learners.[33] However, Hedman does not delve deeper into the "many factors that influence teaching and thus learning," leaving the discussion of teaching at this surface level.[34]

2.3.1 Conceptualizing Teaching

One notable conceptual exploration I have engaged with is Gert Biesta's analysis of teaching and its interplay with learning. Biesta begins by asserting that, although teaching and learning are interconnected, they ought to be distinguished. This

---

Emily Robertson, and Paul Hager, "The Analytical Movement," in *A Companion to the Philosophy of Education* (2003), 176–91.

The only conceptual analysis I found was Biesta's and a discussion by Paul H. Hirst, one of the prominent philosophers of education in the 20th century. This does of course not mean that Biesta and Hirst are the only ones who have written about the nature of teaching, as Biesta's reference to Gary D. Fenstermacher below makes clear. However, I content that it remains true that teaching has received much less theoretical attention than learning.

[30] Most literature on Christian religious education contains ideas about teaching without offering a conceptual analysis of the term. See for example Groome, *Christian Religious Education*; Groome, *Sharing Faith*; Dykstra, *Life of Faith*; Astley, *Learning in the Way*; Cook Everist, *Learning Community*. I note the same tendency in didactic classroom studies. See Osbeck, Ingerman, and Claesson, *Didactic Classroom Studies*.

[31] Mullino Moore, *Teaching*, 13.

[32] See Illeris, *Contemporary Theories*.

[33] Hedman, *Undervisa*, 21–29.

[34] Hedman, *Undervisa*, 21–33.

distinction ensures that teaching is not mistakenly perceived as the direct *cause* of learning and acknowledges that there is no *conceptual* necessity for teaching to result in learning.[35]

Highlighting the confusion arising when "learning" is used to refer both to an activity and its outcome, Biesta contends that the objective of teaching is not directly focused on learning. Instead, it targets "studenting," a term borrowed from Gary D. Fenstermacher, who defines "studenting" as

> instructing the learner on the procedures and demands of the studenting role, selecting the material to be learned, adapting that material so that it is appropriate to the level of the learner, constructing the most appropriate opportunities for the learner to gain access to the content (...), monitoring and appraising the student's progress, and serving the learner as one of the primary sources of knowledge and skill.[36]

Biesta acknowledges, however, that studenting can lead to learning. From my perspective, the question then revolves around whether learning serves as the immediate or final goal of teaching, rather than maintaining a rigid separation between teaching and learning.

The same conclusion can be drawn from Paul H. Hirst's conceptual exploration of teaching, another significant discussion I have engaged with.[37] Hirst initiates his examination by stating that for any activity to constitute teaching it must be intentional. Although learners may learn from unintentional activities, such instances typically fall outside the realm of teaching. Yet, intentionality alone does not suffice.

Hirst emphasizes that for an activity to qualify as teaching, it must be reasonable to anticipate that the activity will enable learners to grasp what the teacher aimed to convey. For instance, teaching differential equations through lectures on WWII, regardless of intention, would not meet this criterion.

---

[35] Biesta, "Freeing Teaching," 231. For Biesta's more political critique of learning see for example Gert Biesta, "Interrupting the Politics of Learning," in *Contemporary Theories of Learning: Learning Theorists... in Their Own Words*, ed. Knud Illeris (Oxon: Routledge, 2018), 243–59.

[36] Gary D. Fenstermacher, "Philosophy of Research on Teaching: Three Aspects," in *Handbook of Research on Teaching*, ed. Merlin C. Wittrock (New York: MacMillan, 1986), 37–49 at 31–40. cited in Biesta, "Freeing Teaching," 233.

[37] For an introduction to Hirst's thinking and work see the special issue *A Celebration of the Writing and Professional Work of Paul H. Hirst* of the Journal of Philosophy of Education (Volume 57, Issue 1, February 2023).

Therefore, teaching is an activity characterized by both intentionality and a focus on specific objectives, meaning it is always specific.[38] To elaborate, effective teaching links the teacher with the learner and a defined learning outcome. In Hirst's more formal terminology, "A cannot simply teach, she must be teaching B, and she must be teaching B, X."[39] This implies that teaching must be tailored to accommodate the unique circumstances and needs of learners, as well as the learning objectives, for it to truly qualify as teaching.[40]

Teaching is then necessarily connected to the capacity for learning. However, as contemporary learning theorists have pointed out, not all learning requires teaching; thus, teaching should not be seen as an essential prerequisite for learning.[41] Similarly, teaching does not rely on learning, even though it is anticipated to facilitate learning at least occasionally.[42] The relationship between teaching and learning is thus characterized by empirical regularity rather than by an indispensable conceptual link or causality.

I see common ground between Hirst and Biesta on several critical points: (1) teaching is an intentional or teleological activity, (2) teaching is not the direct cause of learning, (3) learning can occur without teaching, and (4) the ultimate aim of teaching is to facilitate learning. The primary distinction lies in Hirst's stance that an activity must at least occasionally lead to learning to be considered teaching—a perspective I share and find absent in Biesta's argument. Embracing Hirst's viewpoint implies that educators must understand and incorporate the ways in which human beings learn.

Peter Jarvis's theory on adult learning significantly enriches Hirst's framework. Jarvis posits that individuals are inherently social beings, and as such, learning invariably occurs within and through social situations.[43] Acknowledging the social

---

[38] Paul H. Hirst, *Knowledge and the Curriculum: A Collection of Philosophical Papers* (London: Routledge, 1974), 84.

[39] Hirst, *Knowledge*, 84.

[40] Hirst, *Knowledge*, 81–85.

[41] See Christina Osbeck's distinction between intentional and unintentional learning I mentioned in section 1.5.1. For an introduction to contemporary learning theories see: Illeris, *Contemporary Theories*.

[42] Nel Noddings, "Is Teaching a Practice?," *Journal of Philosophy of Education* 37, no. 2 (2003): 241–51 at 241–43.

[43] Peter Jarvis, *Adult Learning in the Social Context* (Oxon: Routledge, 1987).#31–85 The insight that learning is necessarily social is in no way unique for Jarvis. The same point is for example made in socio-cultural and socio material learning theories. See Illeris, *Contemporary Theories*. I argue below for why I chose to engage with Jarvis for the present purpose.

dimension of learning suggests that A not only teaches B, X, but that A teaches B, X in the social situation C, likely involving the participation of others. This underscores the necessity for teaching approaches to account for the social aspects of learning.

Pulling all this together, I define teaching as the deliberate creation of specific potential learning situations, that is, situations in which teachers, learners, content, and activities are brought together in a way that makes it possible and likely that learners learn the intended learning outcomes, under the specific conditions dictated by the situation.

I refer to the goal of teaching as the creation of a learning situation rather than learning itself, aligning with the idea that teaching enhances the possibility and likelihood of learning without guaranteeing it. The term "potential" is employed to emphasize that learning cannot be controlled by teachers, and "specific" is used to indicate that these learning situations are designed around certain desired learning outcomes and conditions.

Some may argue that this broad definition of teaching dilutes the concept. Yet, as I argue more comprehensively in section 6.2.4, learning itself is widely recognized as a broad concept. This recognition suggests that the breadth of concepts is not inherently problematic, and it implies that teaching, by nature, shares in the expansiveness of learning.

2.3.2 Use of Learning Theories

To bridge teaching with learning, I engage with various learning theories. However, choosing appropriate learning theories is not a straightforward task. Currently, scholars in the field of (Christian) religious education explore a wide array of both competing and complementary learning theories, indicating the absence of a single, universally accepted learning theory to rely upon.[44]

My choice of learning theories is informed by the specific characteristics of the learners we encountered, the objectives we defined for our groups, and the distinct online context. Given that all participants in our groups were adults, my focus leans towards adult learning theories rather than those centered on young children

---

[44] See Illeris, "Overview"; Illeris, *Contemporary Theories*; Staffan Larsson, *Vuxendidaktik: Fjorton tankelinjer i forskningen om vuxnas lärande* (Stockholm: Natur & Kultur, 2013); Afdal, *Religion som bevegelse*; Roger Säljö, *Lärande: En introduktion till perspektiv och metaforer*, 2nd ed. (Malmö: Gleerups, 2022).

or mental and cognitive development stages.[45] Nonetheless, my approach in choosing these theories remains both pragmatic and eclectic; I rely on learning theories that have proven effective in interpreting and organizing our experiences with online small groups.[46]

Specifically, I draw upon three theories of adult learning: Peter Jarvis's theory of adult learning in the social context, Paulo Freire's critical pedagogy, and Malcolm S. Knowles's model of adult education. Each theory offers insights into adult learning processes, enriching the discussion on teaching as the creation of specific potential learning situations, that is, situations in which learning is both possible and likely. I introduce these theories when discussing our experiences with online small groups in chapters 6 and 7.

2.4 Models of Christian Religious Education

The types of specific potential learning situations religious educators should create largely depend on how they integrate the purpose, content, and method of Christian religious education. In other words, if the kingdom of God represents the metapurpose of Christian religious education, there are various approaches that Christian religious educators might adopt to realize this goal. These approaches involve determining the more immediate purpose, content, and method of Christian religious education.

In this section, I explore various approaches and formulate a series of teaching models or ideal types.[47] These models serve as a taxonomy or heuristic device,

---

[45] Two influential traditions in learning theories are based on Jean Piaget and Lev Vigotsky, respectively. Piaget and Vigotsky were both interested in the mental and cognitive development of children and conceptualized learning in relation to children. Orlando Lourenço, "Piaget, Jean," in *Encyclopedia of Educational Theory and Philosophy*, ed. Denis C. Phillips (Thousand Oaks: SAGE Publications, 2014), 624–28; Anton Yasnitsky, "Vygotsky, Lev," in *Encyclopedia of Educational Theory and Philosophy*, ed. Denis C. Phillips (Thousand Oaks: SAGE Publications, 2014), 844–46. Of course, this doesn't mean that these traditions are unsuitable to explain adult learning. I argue, however, that one should be mindful of their original intent when using the original theories.

[46] See chapters 6 and 7.

[47] Today, there are several models of Christian religious education in use each with its particular orientation and purpose. See for example Astley, "Aims and Approaches"; Harold W. Burgess, *Models of Religious Education: Theory and Practice in Historical and Contemporary Perspective* (Nappanee: Evangel Publishing House, 2001); John Elias, "Models of Theological Education for the Laity," *Journal of Adult Theological Education* 3, no. 2 (2006): 179–93; John

providing a framework through which different educational activities can be analyzed, particularly in relation to the concept of constructive alignment, which I
introduce below. This is how I utilize the models in chapter 7.

2.4.1 Purpose

A prevalent interpretation of the more immediate purpose of Christian religious
education is fostering growth in faith. This is the position Thomas Groome takes,
defining the purpose as "to sponsor people toward maturity in Christian faith as a
lived reality."[48] Likewise, Craig Dykstra conceptualizes the aim of Christian religious education as "to help one another understand our experience of [the divine]
Mystery in its breadth and depth and in its implications for ourselves and for the
world."[49] Dykstra further clarifies that such understanding involves acquiring specific information and grasping it both intellectually and emotionally. Through this
process of understanding, individuals are enabled to discern the "inner character
and hidden nature of things," involving activities like "investigation, criticism, interpretation, and care," so that "education in faith" may deepen their experience
of the divine Mystery.[50]

Drawing from a Swedish perspective, Anders Hedman identifies the objective
of Christian religious education as the cultivation of specific attitudes—hope,

---

Collier, "Models of Christian Education," *TEACH Journal of Christian Education* 7, no. 1 (2013):
4–7; Klintborg, *Vägen är allt*, 111–26. Caroline Klintborg bases her models on the models developed by Rune Larsson. See Larsson, *Församlingspedagogik*.

Collier's model presents different target audiences and Elias's model four different teaching
methods. These models are thus less comprehensive and do not engage the nature and purpose
of Christian religious education in the way the other models do. A difference between my models
and Burgess's is that Burgess derives his models historically, while I establish them conceptually.

While my models share many similarities with Astley's, I expand on his models by differentiating between a praxis and practice model and focusing on worship rather than spiritual development. Klintborg and I differ in terms of the models we present, even if there is substantial
overlap. Thus, I develop a practice and a community model, whereas Klintborg includes a growth
and a dialogical model.

[48] Groome, *Christian Religious Education*, 73.
[49] Dykstra, *Life of Faith*, xii.
[50] Dykstra, *Life of Faith*, xiii.

trust, and confidence.[51] These attitudes describe the act of believing, thereby directly connecting to faith.[52]

Although the interpretations of Christian religious education's purpose by Groome, Dykstra, and, Hedman differ, they share a common foundation. Both Groome and Hedman emphasize faith as the central aim of Christian religious education. Also, Dykstra's perspective aligns with this focus, envisioning the immediate goal as an "education in faith."[53]

Faith encompasses, however, multiple dimensions. Thomas Groome categorizes faith into three key aspects: believing, trusting, and doing. The first dimension, believing, pertains to the doctrinal beliefs of Christianity. Traditionally, this has been referred to as *fides quae*, signifying the faith that is believed. The second dimension, trust, involves a deeper, affective commitment beyond mere cognitive acceptance of Christian teachings, traditionally known as *fides qua*— the faith by which one believes. This dimension signifies entering into a personal relationship with the divine, characterized by love, reverence, and worship. The final aspect, doing, reflects the practical consequences of faith, embodying Groome's view that faith necessitates love of God and neighbor, manifesting in various forms of worship and acts of kindness and care towards humanity and the environment.[54]

Most Christian educators and practical theologians align with Groome's perspective, albeit framing the dimensions of faith in slightly different terms. Mary McClintock Fulkerson echoes Groome's view that faith transcends mere adherence to scriptural and traditional propositions, and instead incorporates practices emerging within a faith community's specific context.[55] Ann Christie, in discussing Christology, defines faith as encompassing "ideas/concepts, feelings/experien-

---

[51] Hedman uses the expression "hopp, tillit och livsmod," which is difficult to render in English. "Hopp" translates as hope and is unproblematic. However, "tillit," which literally means trust, is often used in the discourse of the Church of Sweden in which Hedman is a pastor to refer to the act of trusting in God and could therefore also be translated as faith. Lastly, the Swedish "livsmod" translates directly as "courage for live" or "courage to live." It refers to an optimistic outlook on live in general, a willingness to embrace live and to trust in the future. Hedman, *Undervisa*, 51.

[52] Hedman, *Undervisa*, 11–21.

[53] Dykstra, *Life of Faith*, xii.

[54] Groome, *Christian Religious Education*, 51–66.

[55] Mary McClintock Fulkerson, *Places of Redemption: Theology for a Worldly Church* (Oxford: Oxford University Press, 2007), 1–11.

ces and actions. It is a cognitive, affective and conative ('lifestyle') affair."[56] Similarly, Zoë Bennett and her colleagues recognize faith as encompassing belief, trust, and action, further introducing the dimension of belonging, akin to McClintock Fulkerson's interpretation.[57] I concur with Bennett and her colleagues and see faith as containing believing, trusting, doing, and belonging.

However, while these dimensions are widely recognized, Christian educators usually place different emphases on these in their approaches. Thomas Groome situates his approach within the liberation or praxis tradition, underscoring the significance of doing.[58] Craig Dykstra, on the other hand, stresses the importance of believing, understanding, and acknowledging God's love.[59] Anders Hedman highlights the affective dimension of faith, prioritizing trust, above all.[60]

Despite these differences, Christian educators largely concur that faith represents the immediate goal of Christian religious education. However, the focal points they choose have profound effects on the chosen content and pedagogical methods, shaping the direction and implementation of Christian religious education. The four dimensions can hence be understood as distinct approaches within Christian religious education, as illustrated in figure 2.1.

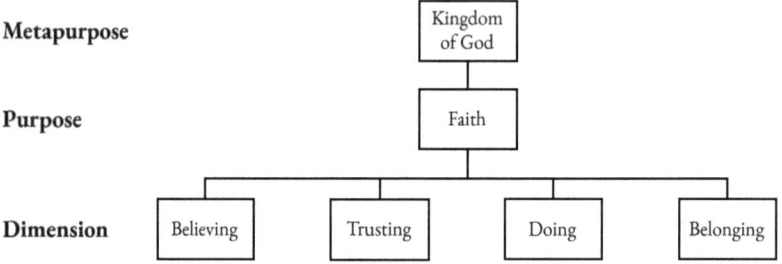

Figure 2.1 Metapurpose, Purpose, and Faith Dimensions

---

[56] Ann Christie, *Ordinary Christology: Who Do You Say I Am? Answers from the Pews* (Farnham: Ashgate, 2012), 7.

[57] Zoë Bennett et al., *Invitation to Research in Practical Theology* (London: Routledge, 2018), 71.

[58] Groome, *Christian Religious Education*, 31–51.

[59] Dykstra, *Life of Faith*, 11–19.

[60] Hedman, *Undervisa*, 18.

2.4.2 Content

Raymond Holley identifies five key elements that constitute the content of Christian religious education: information, understanding, skills, attitudes, and knowing God.[61] One dimension of content is thus information on the fundamental beliefs and practices of Christianity. That is, Christian religious education aims to furnish individuals with the knowledge necessary for living as Christians. Evelina Orteza y Miranda underscores this point, arguing that it is implausible for anyone to identify as a Christian without possessing any knowledge of the Christian faith and practices.[62]

Information becomes truly impactful only when it is understood. Thus, Christian religious education seeks not only to disseminate basic information but also to facilitate a comprehensive understanding of it. Jeff Astley emphasizes that this understanding transcends mere cognitive grasp; it must encompass an affective dimension as well.[63] The distinction lies between cognitively understanding the Christian belief that Jesus died for humanity's salvation as a fact and feeling a personal connection to the idea that Jesus died for one's salvation. It is this deeper, affective understanding that engages the learner on a more profound level, potentially leading to religious commitment.[64]

Beyond imparting information and fostering understanding, religious education endeavors to cultivate particular skills and attitudes in learners. Through engagement with the Christian faith, individuals practice specific skills, including how to pray and celebrate religious festivals. Attitudes fostered through this education might encompass a reverence for the divine, obedience to religious teachings, and love for God and fellow human beings. The ultimate goal of these varied educational efforts is to facilitate the development of a personal relationship between the believer and the divine.[65]

Although all five elements typically feature in Christian religious education, the specific focus of each program can lead educators to prioritize certain content elements over others. Hence, information primarily supports the dimension of

---

[61] Holley, "Learning Religion."

[62] Evelina Orteza y Miranda, "Some Problems with the Expression 'Christian Education'," in *Critical Perspectives on Christian Education: A Reader on the Aims, Principles and Philosophy of Christian Education*, ed. Jeff Astley and Leslie J. Francis (Herefordshire: Gracewing, 1994), 16–28 at 20.

[63] Astley, "Place of Understanding," 111–11.

[64] Holley, "Learning Religion," 78–79.

[65] Holley, "Learning Religion," 71–81.

belief, while understanding bridges belief and trust. Skills are closely aligned with actions and a sense of belonging, attitudes foster trust and belonging, and knowing God intersects with all four dimensions. It's crucial to recognize that these associations are not rigid. Information plays a critical role across all content areas, influencing every faith dimension. Similarly, practices like prayer or worship contribute to the development of trust, among other aspects. However, prioritizing one faith dimension over others has consequences for the content appropriate in any given approach to Christian religious education, illustrating the interconnectedness of content and the multifaceted nature of faith.

2.4.3 Method

The interplay between the purpose (*why*) and content (*what*) of Christian religious education inevitably influences the selection of teaching methods (*who* and *how*). The most traditional approach within Christian religious education is didactic instruction, wherein a teacher directly imparts information to students. Yet, modern practices in Christian religious education have largely moved away from a strictly instructional or schooling model, favoring more interactive and participatory methods.

One category of methods in Christian religious education is characterized by its dialectical nature. Douglas E. Wingeier introduces a faith translation model that emphasizes the crucial interplay between learners' personal experiences and the Christian belief system.[66] Similarly, Groome's praxis approach utilizes a dialogic method to connect learners' experiences with the Christian story, aiming to foster collective action.[67] In line with Groome's ideas, other liberation-oriented strategies in Christian religious education, like those proposed by Paulo Freire, advocate for conscientization—a process designed to spur liberating action.[68] These dialectical methods engage learners in critical dialogue with both the teachings of the Christian faith and their personal life experiences, focusing on critical understanding and appropriation of the Christian faith and the pursuit of emancipatory actions.

---

[66] Douglas E. Wingeier, "Christian Education as Faith Translation," in *Critical Perspectives on Christian Education: A Reader on the Aims, Principles and Philosophy of Christian Education*, ed. Jeff Astley and Leslie J. Francis (Herefordshire: Gracewing, 1994), 238–50 at 238.

[67] Groome, *Christian Religious Education*, 181–94.

[68] Paulo Freire, "Education, Liberation and the church," in *Theological Perspectives on Christian Formation: A Reader on Theology and Christian Education*, ed. Jeff Astley, Leslie J. Francis, and Colin Crowder (Herefordshire: Gracewing, 1996), 169–86.

The second cluster of methodologies within Christian religious education places a stronger emphasis on the formative aspects fostered by the faith community. Through examining socialization processes, Michael Warren advocates for a model of Christian formation that presents Christianity as a counterculture.[69] Dean M. Martin introduces an enculturation approach, where acquiring a Christian language readies the learner to adopt the Christian faith.[70] Stanley Hauerwas suggests a narrative model that immerses individuals in God's story, while Craig Dykstra promotes engaging in formative Christian practices.[71] Additionally, Norma Cook Everist presents a learning community model where every member of a parish, as a bearer of the Word, plays a role in both learning and teaching processes.[72] These approaches can collectively be described as participatory, as they underscore the significance of engaging with the faith community's activities and practices in fostering a comprehensive embrace of the Christian faith.

The final set of methodologies underscores the critical roles of affection and spirituality in Christian religious education. John A. Berntsen anchors his approach within the catechumenate tradition, emphasizing the cultivation of affections and religious experiences.[73] Likewise, Jeff Astley explores the transformative impact of worship in Christian religious education, identifying it as a key context where religious experiences, attitudes, and beliefs converge.[74] The essence of these methods can be described as spiritual, focusing on nurturing particular emotions and outlooks that support and enhance religious experiences.

It's important to recognize that numerous Christian educators advocate for a multifaceted approach to Christian religious education, rather than adhering strictly to a single method. For instance, John Westerhoff's model encompasses instruction, education, and formation. These elements collectively cover the transmission of knowledge and skills, critical reflection on religious experiences, and the cultivation of believers within the faith community.[75] Similarly, Thomas Groome's praxis model incorporates aspects of socialization and emphasizes the significance of worship in the educational journey.[76] Jeff Astley, in turn, highlights worship as a critical juncture where emotions and understandings merge, further

---

[69] Warren, "Religious Formation," 201–10.
[70] Martin, "Learning to Become," 181–87.
[71] Hauerwas, "The Gesture of a Truthful Story," 103; Dykstra, *Life of Faith*, 51–78.
[72] Cook Everist, *Learning Community*, 21–59.
[73] Berntsen, "Christian Affections."
[74] Astley, "Role of Worship."
[75] Westerhoff, "Formation, Education, Instruction," 63.
[76] Groome, *Christian Religious Education*.

illustrating the complexity and diversity of methodologies in Christian religious education.[77]

2.4.4 The Models

To systematize the assortment of approaches in Christian religious education, I construct six distinct models. These models serve as ideal types, which seldom manifest in their pure form within specific educational activities. As previously mentioned, most religious educators employ a spectrum of approaches, often integrating elements from multiple models to suit their educational goals and contexts.[78]

Model	Schooling	Critical	Spiritual	Praxis	Practice	Community
Dimension	Believing	Believing	Trusting	Doing	Doing	Belonging
Content	Beliefs	Beliefs	Attitudes	Beliefs	Skills	Attitudes
Method	Instruction	Correlation	Worship	Conscientization	Participation	Incorporation

Table 2.1 Models of Christian Religious Education

In the traditional schooling model, the objective of Christian religious education is for the learner to acquire accurate knowledge about the Christian faith, delivered from a "teacher" to a "student" via direct instruction. This model emphasizes the transfer of information, placing the teacher in an authoritative role. Consequently, education within this framework operates as a unidirectional flow from the teacher to the student, with the content of the Christian faith typically perceived as static and unchanging.

The critical education model places its emphasis on understanding. While it shares the goal of instilling Christian beliefs with the instruction model, the critical model prioritizes the learners' critical engagement with the Christian belief system. In this approach, the teacher acts more as an interpreter rather than an instructor,

---

[77] Astley, "Role of Worship."

[78] The six models are inspired by the models proposed by Rune Larsson in 1995 and the various ways in which Jeff Astley as classified different approaches to Christian religious education. See Rune Larsson, "Modeller för undervisning," in *Livsnära: Teori och praktik kring kyrkans bibelundervisning*, ed. Carl Eber Olivestam (Umeå: Umeå University, 1995), 38–62 at 41–60; Astley, "Definitions"; Astley and Crowder, "Theological Perspectives"; Astley, "Aims and Approaches."

aiding learners in interpreting their lives through the lens of Christian tradition and integrating the tradition into their personal narratives. This model aligns with more liberal theological approaches, valuing the believers' ability to independently interpret and internalize faith through a dialectical interaction between personal experiences and the tenets of Christianity.[79]

The praxis model shares similarities with the critical model, particularly in its use of a dialectical method that relates experiences to the faith tradition. However, the primary aim of the praxis model is not understanding but rather action, frequently conceptualized as praxis—the integration of critical reflection and action.[80] In this model, the teacher acts as a facilitator rather than an interpreter, striving to connect an understanding of the Christian tradition with tangible actions. While the content of the faith tradition is typically seen as stable in both the critical and praxis models, similar to the traditional schooling model, this content serves merely as one aspect of the dialectic. Given that individual experiences can differ greatly across various contexts, the outcomes derived from the critical and praxis models tend to be more dynamic compared to those of the traditional schooling model.

The spiritual model shifts the focus away from information and understanding to deeply engage with the faith's affective aspects. In this model, the teacher is perceived as a spiritual guide, pastor, or preacher who aids learners in their spiritual development. Educational activities include worship, prayer, and spiritual practices like *Lectio Divina* and retreats. The overarching aim of the spiritual approach is to facilitate the development of a personal relationship between learners and the divine. Consequently, the content in this model tends to be non-cognitive, emphasizing the learners' personal religious experiences and emotional responses.

The practice approach to Christian religious education posits that knowledge of God emerges from engaging in specific Christian practices, which cultivate particular understandings and attitudes through active participation.[81] Thus, practices are viewed as epistemic, encompassing not just actions but also cognitive and affective insights.[82] Craig Dykstra identifies activities such as narrating the Christian story, worship, giving thanks, prayer, confession, and forgiveness as Christian

---

[79] Wingeier, "Christian Education."

[80] Paulo Freire, *Pedagogy of the Oppressed*, trans. Myra Bergman Ramos (New York: Penguin Random House, 2017), 39–40.

[81] Dykstra, *Life of Faith*, 61–82.

[82] Bennett et al., *Invitation to Research*, 58–59.

practices.[83] In this model, the teacher acts akin to a coach, guiding, instructing, and facilitating learners' involvement in these practices. The emphasis on content within the practice model centers on the skills necessary for engaging in Christian practices, making the content both static and adaptable simultaneously. While Christian practices are seen as established by tradition and therefore fixed, the practice approach also acknowledges the inherent fluidity and dynamism of these practices, recognizing their continuous evolution.[84]

The community model, akin to the practice model, places a significant emphasis on participation. Yet, it diverges by centering less on the specific practices of the community and more on integrating learners into the community itself. The central goal of the community model is fostering a sense of belonging. In this framework, the teacher functions as a community leader or organizer, charged with the task of shaping a learning community in which everyone assumes the roles of both teacher and student. Among the six models, the community model stands out as the most conceptually broad, with belonging encompassing not just the development of specific attitudes but also the acquisition of particular skills and understandings. Engagement with the entire life of the community constitutes a comprehensive educational experience. However, given its strong ties with Christian religious education approaches that emphasize enculturation or socialization, the community model primarily aims to impart a distinct Christian language and culture, aligning closely with the cultivation of attitudes.[85]

Integrating these insights, the models of Christian religious education represent varied and complementary strategies for linking the overarching goal of Christian religious education with specific content and method, as illustrated in figure 2.2.

---

[83] Craig R. Dykstra, "No Longer Strangers: The Church and its Educational Ministry," in *Theological Perspectives on Christian Formation: A Reader on Theology and Christian Education*, ed. Jeff Astley, Leslie J. Francis, and Colin Crowder (Herefordshire: Gracewing, 1996), 106–18 at 111–15.

[84] Dykstra, *Life of Faith*, 61–70.

[85] Martin, "Learning to Become."

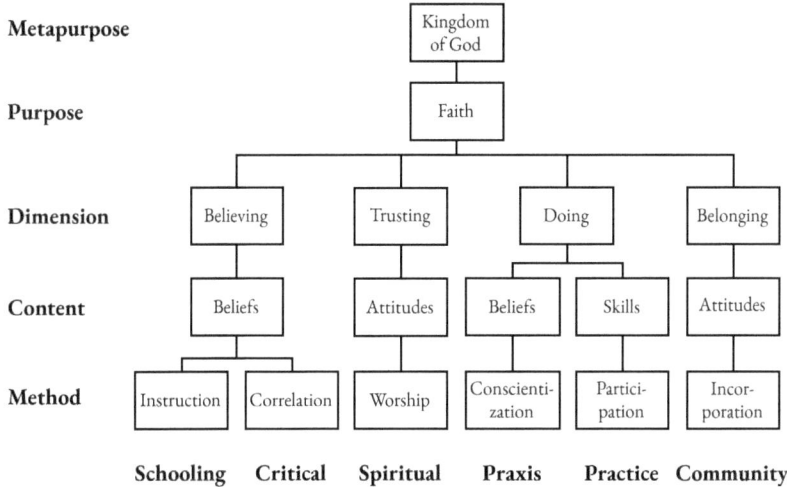

Figure 2.2 Models and Dimensions of Christian Religious Education

It is important to remember that the models outlined are ideal types, meaning they serve more as conceptual tools than exhaustive categories. Consequently, not all approaches to Christian religious education will conform to these models and their implied categorization. This is evident in the work of Courtney Goto, whose focus on playing and revelatory experiencing in Christian religious education does not fit neatly into any one category.[86] While playing might align with the practice model due to its skill-based nature, revelatory experiencing spans across multiple models, touching upon aspects of worship, praxis, and community engagement. Furthermore, Goto's interpretation of revelatory experiencing diverges from my depiction of "faith," and her emphasis on aesthetics introduces an element not explicitly accounted for in these models, suggesting a significant expansion of the typology.[87]

The complexity and diversity of approaches to Christian religious education are further highlighted by Maria Liu Wong's research. Liu Wong illustrates how Christian religious education unfolds within formal, non-formal, and informal settings, influenced by the unique contributions of communities like families,

---

[86] Goto, *Playing.*
[87] Goto, *Playing*, 83–113.

neighborhoods, and cities, along with their historical contexts.[88] Therefore, the primary utility of these models lies not in their capacity to encapsulate the full range of educational practices but in offering a framework for critically examining and reflecting upon those practices.[89]

2.5 Constructive Alignment

To bridge the models of Christian religious education with my conceptualization of teaching, I introduce the concept of *constructive alignment*. This framework, devised by John Biggs and Catherine Tang, is aimed at enhancing the quality of both teaching and learning within the context of university education. It serves as a structured approach to align educational objectives with teaching methods and assessment strategies, ensuring that all components work cohesively to support effective learning outcomes.[90]

Biggs and Tang argue that the essence of effective teaching lies in its capacity to aid learners in achieving the learning outcomes predetermined by their teachers. This premise leads them to conclude that the teaching process should commence with the careful determination of appropriate learning outcomes. These outcomes should then guide the development of teaching and learning activities, assessment tasks, and grading criteria, promoting congruency among them.[91] This alignment significantly enhances the effectiveness of teaching.[92]

Constructive alignment thus highlights the importance of understanding the learning objectives set by teachers and how teaching and learning activities are designed to facilitate the achievement of these objectives. According to Biggs and Tang, constructive alignment "provides a conceptual framework for reflecting on the questions that need to be answered at crucial stages of teaching in general.

---

[88] Liu Wong, *Becoming Wise*.

[89] Here my typology functions analogous to Goto's theoretical perspectives. Goto, *Playing*, 121.

[90] John Biggs and Catherine Tang, *Teaching for Quality Learning at University: What The Student Does*, ed. Catherine Tang, 4th ed. (Maidenhead: Society for Research into Higher Education, 2011).

[91] Biggs and Tang, *Teaching*, 91–100. Constructive alignment can also be used for lesson planning. See Glory Tobiason, "Going Small, Going Carefully, With a Friend: Helping Faculty Adopt Lesson-Level Constructive Alignment through Non-Evaluative Peer Observation," *Active Learning in Higher Education* 25, no. 1: 53–66.

[92] Biggs and Tang, *Teaching*, 99. I agree with Gert Biesta that education research cannot stop at the question of effective education but needs to include the question of *good* education. However, I do not think that the latter excludes considerations of effectiveness. See Biesta, "What is Education For?," 75.

Those questions are:

1. What do I want my students to learn?
2. What is the best way in my circumstances and within available resources of getting them to learn it?
3. How can I know when or how well they have learned it?"[93]

Constructive alignment encourages strategic reflection on the educational process, ensuring that teaching methods are effectively aligned with learning goals and assessment strategies.

Therefore, constructive alignment serves as a valuable tool for both the planning and design of teaching, as well as for evaluating teaching effectiveness. By centering on the intended learning outcomes and examining the extent of their alignment with the teaching and learning activities, educators can ensure that their instructional strategies are structured to meet educational objectives.

To make constructive alignment possible, intended learning outcomes ought to articulate the anticipated state of student knowledge following their participation in an educational activity. According to Biggs and Tang, effective intended learning outcomes should specify the type of knowledge being targeted, detail the content of this knowledge, and clarify the expected level of understanding.[94] The benefit of well-defined intended learning outcomes is that they empower teachers to create teaching and learning activities tailored to facilitate the achievement of these outcomes by learners.

Constructive alignment intersects with the models of Christian religious education at the juncture of purpose, content, and method. Each model represents a coherent blend of these elements. Consequently, adherence to a singular model is likely to enhance teaching effectiveness, while combining models without careful alignment could potentially diminish it. In chapter 7, I apply the models in this manner, focusing on the congruence of educational activities within our online small groups. Specifically, I examine how closely teaching and learning activities in our groups align with or diverge from the various models and the impact of such alignment or mixing on the effectiveness of teaching.

Just as with the selection of learning theories discussed above, my approach to choosing a theoretical framework here is pragmatic. I employ constructive alignment to illuminate the interplay between purpose, content, and method within Christian religious education, specifically in the context of our online small

---

[93] Biggs and Tang, *Teaching*, 49.
[94] Biggs and Tang, *Teaching*, 121–24.

groups. Although constructive alignment was originally devised for formal education settings, its utility is not necessarily limited by this context. Contrarily, I contend that constructive alignment can enhance teaching effectiveness across various
educational formats, including non-formal education, albeit with necessary adjustments to the framework. This argument is further elaborated upon in section
6.3.2.

2.6 Didactic Relations Model

In Swedish Christian religious education, I have observed a prevalent focus on
what is known as the "didactic questions": *why, who, whom, what,* and *how.*[95] This
approach systematically addresses the fundamental aspects of education. A parallel
perspective exists in Norway, referred to as the "didactic relations model." This
model integrates several components of the educational process, including the
abilities of the learner (*whom*), the learning processes (*how*), the objectives of education (*why*), the content being taught (*what*), frame factors (*who*), and the methods of assessment.[96] These frameworks collectively emphasize that Christian religious education must comprehensively address the questions of *who* is teaching,
whom they are teaching, *what* is being taught, *how* it is being taught, and *why* teaching is structured in this way.

I perceive a notable advantage in the didactic relations model, particularly in
its ability to more distinctly showcase the interconnectedness of teaching's various
components compared to the didactic questions approach. Consequently, I opt
to utilize the didactic relations model over the didactic questions for my analysis
and discussion of our online small groups.[97]

---

[95] Klintborg, *Vägen är allt*, 11–14. The number of didactic questions varies slightly. Jakob
Wirén restricts the questions to *what, how,* and *why,* Henry Cöster omits *who,* Anders Hedman
adds *when,* and Christina Osbeck adds both *when* and *where.* Wirén, *Undervisning*, 252; Cöster,
bedriva undervisning, 11–15; Hedman, *Undervisa*, 11; Osbeck, *Förstå livet*, 19; Klintborg, *Var är
Jesus?*

[96] Bjarne Bjørndal and Sigmund Lieberg, *Nye veier i didaktikken? En innføring i didaktiske
emner og begreper* (Oslo: Aschehoug, 1978); Trond Eiliv Hauge, *Å planlegge og designe undervisning* (Oslo: Capelen Damm, 2018); Hilde Hiim and Else Marie Hippe, *Undervisningsplanlegging for yrkesfaglærere*, 4th ed. (Copenhagen: Gyldendal, 2021).

[97] Neither the didactic relations model nor constructive alignment are full fletched explanatory theories in the sense of connecting cause and effect. However, I use them here as theoretical
perspectives on teaching and hence include them as part of my "theories."

The didactic relations model, introduced by Bjarne Bjørndal and Sigmund Lieberg in 1978, illustrates that learning and teaching emerge from several interacting factors. Initially, the model included categories such as student and teacher conditions, goals, frame factors, methods, content, and assessment.[98]

The didactic relations model has significantly influenced teacher education and education research in Norway, undergoing minor adaptations and developments over time.[99] Hilde Hiim and Else Hippe have expanded the model to include six dimensions: learning abilities, learning processes, goals, content, frame factors, and assessment.[100]

Trond Eiliv Hauge refined the model by dividing the learning process into tools and methods, resulting in seven dimensions: student experience/characteristics, teaching tools, teaching methods, goals, content, teaching frames, and assessment.[101] However, Hiim and Hippe emphasize that the specific labels assigned to these dimensions are of only secondary importance. The core purpose of the model is to highlight that teaching is a multifaceted activity shaped by interrelated dimensions.[102] It is important to note, though, that while the didactic relations model acknowledges the interaction among these dimensions within the teaching process, it does not delve into the specifics of how each dimension influences and is influenced by the others.

What makes the didactic relations model particularly valuable for my analysis is its utility as an analytical framework.[103] The model delineates various dimensions that can be used to assess a given specific potential learning situation. It is in this way I apply the model in chapter 4.

2.7 Teaching Strategies

I employ the concept of teaching strategies as a theoretical perspective to structure the presentation of usable knowledge in chapter 7. The formulation of teaching

---

[98] Bjørndal and Lieberg, *Nye veier.*

[99] Hauge, *Å planlegge,* 31.

[100] In the Norwegian original: *læreforutsetninger, læreprosessen, mål, innhold, rammefaktorer* and *vurdering.* Hiim and Hippe, *Undervisningsplanlegging,* 40.

[101] In the Norwegian original: *elevens erfaring/forutsetninger, arbeidsredskaper, arbeidsmåter, mål, lærestoff, vurdering,* and *rammer for undervisningen.* Hauge, *Å planlegge,* 31–32.

[102] Hiim and Hippe, *Undervisningsplanlegging,* 41–21.

[103] Hiim and Hippe, *Undervisningsplanlegging,* 141–57.

strategies is a widespread practice in the field of education research.[104] Yet, despite its common usage, the term often lacks a precise definition, leading to ambiguity about its exact meaning. This vagueness complicates understanding whether different authors are discussing the same idea when they refer to teaching strategies. This issue is compounded by the unclear distinctions between related terms such as teaching principles or teaching approaches.[105]

The concept of teaching strategies not only frequently goes undefined, but scholars who discuss it have not reached a consensus on its precise meaning. For instance, Roy Killen views teaching strategies as intermediaries between the curriculum and teaching techniques, which he sees as straightforward educational tools like providing clear explanations.[106] Killen identifies practices such as direct instruction, discussion, small-group work, and case studies as strategies, though some may regard these more as teaching methods.[107]

On the other hand, R. Douglas Greer defines strategies as "verbally mediated practices that determine the possible source or locus of variability in behavior,

---

[104] For some examples see Graham Gibbs, Trevor Habeshaw, and Mantz Yorke, "Institutional Learning and Teaching Strategies in English Higher Education," *Higher Education* 40, no. 3 (2000): 351–72; Jaap Schuitema, Geert ten Dam, and Wiel Veugelers, "Teaching Strategies for Moral Education: A Review," *Journal of Curriculum Studies* 40, no. 1 (2008): 69–89; S. Senthamarai, "Interactive Teaching Strategies," 3, no. Suppl. 1 (2018): S36–S38; Karin Flensner, "Dealing With and Teaching Controversial Issues: Teachers' Pedagogical Approaches to Controversial Issues in Religious Education and Social Studies," *Acta Didactica Norden* 14, no. 4 (2020): 1–21; Tina J. Herring and M. Lynn Woolsey, "Three Suggested Teaching Strategies for Students Who are Deaf or Hard of Hearing," *Support for Learning* 35, no. 3 (2020): 346–58; Luis Moisés Peña-Lévano and Grace Melo, "Adaptation of Teaching Strategies during the COVID-19 Pandemic," *Applied Economics Teaching Resources* 4, no. 1 (2022): 12–33; Eek, *Stanna i vattnet*; Rosenius, *Delaktig i vilken mening?*

[105] See for example Rikke Alberg Peters and Hildegunn Juulsgaard Johannesen, "What is Actually True? Approaches to Teaching Conspiracy Theories and Alternative Narratives in History Lessons," *Acta Didactica Norge* 14, no. 4 (2020); Mehdi Farashahi and Mahdi Tajeddin, "Effectiveness of Teaching Methods in Business Education: A Comparison Study on the Learning Outcomes of Lectures, Case Studies and Simulations," *The International Journal of Management Education* 16, no. 1 (2018): 131–42.

[106] Roy Killen, *Teaching Strategies for Quality Teaching and Learning* (Claremont: Juta, 2010), 35.

[107] Killen, *Teaching Strategies*. Mehdi Farashahi and Mahdi Tajeddin understand lecture, case study, and simulation as teaching methods, rather than strategies, as does Inna Popil. Farashahi and Tajeddin, "Effectiveness"; Inna Popil, "Promotion of Critical Thinking by Using Case Studies as Teaching Method," *Nurse Education Today* 31, no. 2 (2011): 204–07.

learning problems, or instructional difficulties."[108] For Greer, strategies are observable and teachable repertoires of behaviors designed to prompt specific responses from learners.[109] To illustrate, knowing when to lecture is a teaching strategy, and not the act of lecturing itself.

Similarly, Enikő Szőke-Milinte, influenced by Gyula Ferenczi and László Fodor, characterizes strategies as

> well-defined means of activity orientating the process of learning which, due to their internal logic, allow for the selection and construction of methods, tools, processes and organizational forms while representing a fundamental pedagogical approach.[110]

My understanding of strategies aligns with Greer's and Szőke-Milinte's interpretations of strategies as generalized plans for teaching that empower educators to select suitable activities, thereby creating specific potential learning situations. Strategies, therefore, offer broad behavioral guidelines and conceptual approaches that are instrumental in the design and facilitation of educational activities, such as online small groups. Thus, strategies act as a bridge between theoretical underpinnings and their practical application in teaching, embodying the "theory" actualized in the practice of teaching.[111]

Like Greer, I perceive strategies as "verbally mediated" and, hence, teachable, signifying that strategies can be acquired through communication and not only through personal experiences. The utility of strategies lies in their capacity to abstract, facilitating the transfer of behavioral guidelines across various contexts and teaching situations. In essence, strategies enhance teaching by enabling educators to incorporate insights gleaned from the experiences of others. Therefore, teaching strategies offer a systematic framework to address the first segment of my overarching research question: *How can online small groups within the Church of Sweden be improved as instances of Christian religious education?*

---

[108] R. Douglas Greer, *Designing Teaching Strategies: An Applied Behavior Analysis Systems Approach* (New York: Academic Press, 2002), 343.

[109] Greer, *Designing Teaching*, 56–59.

[110] Enikő Szőke-Milinte, "Didactic Teaching Strategies for Successful Learning," *PedActa* 3, no. 2 (2013): 49–58.

[111] For a further discussion of the possibilities and difficulties with implementing these strategies see chapter 7.

2.8 Summary and Reflections

In this chapter, I have delineated my theoretical perspectives, addressing my first sub-question: *What does it entail to conceptualize online small groups as instances of Christian religious education?*

My argument posits that conceptualizing online small groups as instances of Christian religious education involves perceiving these groups as inherently goal-directed, with their ultimate orientation towards the kingdom of God as the metapurpose of Christian religious education. It is important to clarify that this perspective is theoretical and "etic," serving as a basis for the examination of our online small groups as sites of teaching in chapter 6, rather than an "emic" perspective reflecting our explicit understanding as group leaders as expressed in part 2.[112]

To clarify, I am not implying that online small groups must inherently be associated with Christian religious education. On the contrary, as I explore in chapter 4, it is often the case that small groups are perceived primarily as meeting spaces or as communities built on trust and support, without a direct link to education.[113] However, I posit that viewing small groups through the lens of Christian religious education offers a valuable and, potentially, highly beneficial perspective, as I discuss in chapters 6 to 8.

Considering online small groups as instances of Christian religious education opens avenues for their possible improvement. In this discussion, I have linked the overarching goal of Christian religious education with the immediate aim of fostering faith, encapsulated in the dimensions of knowledge, belief, trust, action, and belonging. By integrating these with various perspectives on the content and methods of Christian religious education, I created a set of models. Linking the typology to the principle of constructive alignment, I have argued for the potential to enhance teaching effectiveness by maintaining coherence across these different aspects. This approach enables an evaluative look at teaching practices, thereby identifying opportunities for enhancement. Furthermore, in this chapter, I have presented the didactic relations model as a tool for reflecting on our engagement with online small groups. Lastly, I have proposed the concept of teaching strategies as a framework for structuring practical, applicable insights, thereby proposing a way

---

[112] A neat distinction between "etic" and "emic" perspectives is troubled by my involvement in the *Online Small Groups* project, suggesting that I articulate both emic and etic views. My point here is to indicate that the conceptualization of teaching is based on theoretical considerations rather than the concrete experiences we made when leading our groups.

[113] See section 4.1.

to address the overarching research question regarding the improvement of online small groups in the Church of Sweden as an instance of Christian religious education.

Before delving into the specifics of my research design and methodology, I find it pertinent to briefly consider the specific standpoint from which my theoretical perspectives are derived. As mentioned in the introduction, this project is positioned within *white* practical theology, a designation not yet broadly used. The term originates from the discussion sparked by Courtney Goto's critical examination of how Asian American and other racial or ethnic perspectives are marginalized within practical theology, in the edited collection *Opening the Field of Practical Theology*.[114]

Invited to write a chapter on Asian American practical theology, Goto highlighted the frequent expectation for scholars of color to validate their viewpoints and assume the mantle of "experts" on racial issues, a process that essentializes and homogenizes racial and ethnic contributions. Goto critiques the presumption that her chapter should offer a definitive or objective analysis of Asian American practical theology, underscoring the problematic nature of such expectations. These assumptions overlook the rich diversity of experiences, perspectives, and opinions that exist within the Asian American community.[115]

In her reflections, Goto observes that white scholars often celebrate the richness and diversity within practical theology by dedicating chapters to key approaches, like contextual, empirical, and postmodern practical theology.[116] Moreover, these scholars are usually not asked to label their approach to practical theology as *white*, suggesting that all key approaches to practical theology are white, effectively othering ethnic and racial perspectives.[117]

Goto identifies the issue as stemming more from the unconscious marginalization of scholars of color than from deliberate racism. Nevertheless, this unconscious bias does not absolve white scholars of the responsibility to become aware of their own biases and the underlying assumptions they may hold. Goto further elaborates on this in "The Ubiquity of Ignorance," where she discusses ignorance

---

[114] Kathleen A. Cahalan and Gordon S. Mikoski, eds., *Opening the Field of Practical Theology: An Introduction* (Lanham: Rowman & Littlefield, 2014). See especially the contributions by Courtney Goto, and Tom Beaudoin and Katherine Turpin. Goto, "Asian American Practical Theologies"; Beaudoin and Turpin, "White Practical Theology."

[115] Goto, "Asian American Practical Theologies," 31–33.

[116] Goto, "Writing in Compliance," 111.

[117] Goto, "Asian American Practical Theologies," 31.

not as a mere lack of knowledge but as an active choice to overlook certain per-spectives.[118] This analysis calls for a deeper self-awareness among white scholars re-garding their positionality and the impact it has on the field of practical theology.

Acknowledging the existence of "unchecked racism, power, and privilege" that not only undermines the efforts of individual scholars of color but also harms mi-norities in the academy, churches, or the public sphere, constitutes a crucial initial step toward change. This recognition involves admitting both to ourselves and to others that we play a part in perpetuating a detrimental and persistent problem. By confronting this reality, we can begin the process of addressing and dismantling systemic issues that distort and damage the contributions and well-being of minor-ities and minoritized groups in academia and religious communities.[119]

As a white, male European possessing a significant degree of societal privilege, my academic influences include scholars and theorists such as Thomas Groome, Jeff Astley, Craig Dykstra, Paul H. Hirst, Gert Biesta, Peter Jarvis, and Malcolm Knowles, all of whom are also white men with similar privileges. This observation extends to Paulo Freire, who, despite his critical contributions to education and pedagogy, reportedly identified with the position of white maleness.[120] This ac-knowledgment highlights the importance of considering the perspectives and po-sitions from which we engage with and contribute to our fields of study.

Recognizing the predominantly white foundation of my perspective serves as an initial, albeit insufficient, step toward fostering greater epistemic responsibility. By explicitly acknowledging my standpoint, I aim to highlight the inherent limita-tions and particularities that accompany my position as a white scholar engaging with a predominantly white audience within the context of a white church. This act of naming aims to open a pathway for more nuanced and responsible scholarly engagement, acknowledging the need for a broader spectrum of voices and per-spectives in the discourse. I return to the effect and the limitation my white per-spective has on my way of understanding our online small groups in section 6.3.3.

To summarize, this chapter has outlined the white theoretical perspectives that inform my examination of online small groups within this dissertation. Later chapters will delve into the insights this perspective yields, particularly concerning my sub-questions: *To what extent and in what ways do group leaders teach in online*

---

[118] Courtney T. Goto, "The Ubiquity of Ignorance: A Practical Theological Challenge of Our Time," *Practical Theology* (2020): 138–49 at 138–39.

[119] Goto, "Writing in Compliance," 118, 23.

[120] bell hooks, *Teaching to Transgress: Education as the Practice of Freedom* (New York: Routledge, 1994), 9.

small groups? and *How can adopting a teaching perspective contribute to the improvement of online small groups?* Before addressing these inquiries, the next chapter will detail and critically evaluate my research design and methodology.

3. Research Design and Methodology

In the *SAGE Encyclopedia of Action Research*'s entry on "Dissertation Writing," action researchers David Coghlan and Patricia Gaya assert:

> While all research demands rigour, action research has to demonstrate its rigour more particularly. This is because action research typically starts out with a fuzzy question, is fuzzy about methods in the initial stages and has fuzzy answers in the early stages. As the research project develops, methods and answers become less fuzzy, and so the questions become less fuzzy. This progression from fuzziness to clarity is the essence of the spirals of action research cycles. Accordingly, the dissertation needs to demonstrate clearly the procedures adopted to achieve rigour and to defend them.[1]

In this chapter, I articulate my "defense of the procedures adopted," detailing the rationale for the methodological choices made in the *Online Small Groups* project. Initially, I assess the overarching research paradigm that frames this dissertation (3.1), subsequently narrowing the focus to action research as a distinctive approach to social inquiry (3.2). Starting with the research design (3.3), I note the exploratory nature of the project and link it to my selection of an emergent design, leading into a discussion on the methods for data collection. Following this, I examine the inductive-abductive approach of the project. I then explore the normative stance from which I engage the *Online Small Groups* project. I consider issues related to the research process itself (3.4). Specifically, I address the quality of the project, research ethics, and reflexivity, before turning to writing (3.5), both as a method of analysis and a means of communication.

3.1 A Participatory and Constructivist Paradigm

In the 1994 edition of the *SAGE Handbook of Qualitative Research*, Yvonna Lincoln and Egon Guba identified and discussed four foundational research

---

[1] Coghlan and Gaya, "Dissertation Writing," 3.

paradigms: positivism, postpositivism, critical theory, and constructivism.[2] Since that time, the landscape of qualitative research has evolved significantly: not only have John Heron and Peter Reason introduced a participatory paradigm as a fifth key perspective, but the use of these paradigms itself has become more flexible.[3] The boundaries among these paradigms have become increasingly fluid, showcasing both confluences and sustained differences.[4]

This dissertation aligns with these contemporary trends by not adhering exclusively to any single paradigm. Nevertheless, it draws heavily on both constructivist and participatory paradigms for its ontological, epistemological, and methodological foundations.

Heron and Reason characterize the participatory paradigm as distinct from both positivism and constructivism, grounding it in a participatory worldview and experiential understanding. This approach posits the cosmos as fundamentally existent, while eschewing claims of absolute knowledge or control. In essence, the participatory paradigm acknowledges an objective reality that is perceived and understood subjectively by humans, positioning the aim of research as the attainment of practical knowledge, including both capacity or skill and the deliberative capacity to act wisely.[5] I align with the participatory paradigm in its view of research's purpose, its recognition of the world's inherent givenness, its admission of knowledge's inherent subjectivity, and its assertion that our understanding of the world is enhanced through active engagement with it.

While I concur with Heron and Reason's criticism of the strong version of social constructivism, which posits that reality does not extend beyond discourse.[6] I also align with Mats Alvesson and Kaj Sköldberg's perspective that social constructivism manifests in varied forms. Leveraging Barlebo Wenneberg's insights, Alvesson and Sköldberg categorize social constructivism into critical, social,

---

[2] Yvonna S. Lincoln, Susan A. Lynham, and Egon G. Guba, "Paradigmatic Controversies, Contradictions, and Emerging Confluences, Revisited," in *The SAGE Handbook of Qualitative Research*, ed. Norman K. Denzin and Yvonna S. Lincoln (Los Angeles: Sage Publications, 2018), 213–63 at 213.

[3] Alan Bryman, "The End of the Paradigm Wars?," in *The SAGE Handbook of Social Research Methods*, ed. Pertti Alasuutari, Leonard Bickman, and Julia Brannen (London: SAGE Publications Ltd, 2012), 13–24.

[4] Lincoln, Lynham, and Guba, "Paradigmatic Controversies," 213–14.

[5] John Heron and Peter Reason, "A Participatory Inquiry Paradigm," *Qualitative Inquiry* 3, no. 3 (1997): 274–94 at 274–88. The participatory worldview thus includes a focus on both *phronesis* and *techne*.

[6] Heron and Reason, "Participatory Inquiry," 278.

epistemological, and ontological branches. These variants exhibit a spectrum of radicalism, from critical social constructivism's assertion that concepts such as "youth" or "race" are not natural but constructed, to ontological social constructivism's more extreme view that reality itself is entirely a social construct.[7]

This differentiation is crucial as it enables the integration of epistemological social constructivism with ontological critical realism.[8] In other words, it supports the simultaneous acknowledgment of knowledge, meaning, and values as socially constructed, and of existence as an objective reality.[9] I specifically explore the social construction of meaning through reflective narrative, which serves as a pivotal method for both analyzing and disseminating research findings, as I elaborate in section 3.5.

3.2 Action Research as an Orientation to Social Inquiry

To date, there is no commonly accepted definition of action research and the field experiences diversification and a proliferation of approaches rather than consolidation.[10] Accordingly, action research should not be seen as a discipline or method

---

[7] Mats Alvesson and Kaj Sköldberg, *Reflexive Methodology: New Vistas for Qualitative Research*, Third ed. (Los Angeles: Sage, 2018), 41–43.

[8] Andrew Root, *Christopraxis: A Practical Theology of the Cross* (Minneapolis: Fortress Press, 2014), 189–242; Pete Ward, *Liquid Ecclesiology: The Gospel and the Church* (Leiden: Brill, 2017), 22–24.

[9] There is no fixed schema for research paradigms and Lincoln and Guba's schema is not the only one. My approach could thus also be understood to fall into a hermeneutic or interpretative paradigm in the sense Charles Taylor, and Harriet Mowat and John Swinton give it. Charles Taylor, *Philosophical Papers: Volume 2: Philosophy and the Human Sciences* (Cambridge: Cambridge University Press, 1985), 15–57; Swinton and Mowat, *Practical Theology*, 33–37.

[10] Hilary Bradbury, ed., introduction to *The SAGE Handbook of Action Research*, 3rd ed. (London: SAGE Publications, 2015), 5.

This is not to suggest that there are no definitions of action research. In her introduction to the third edition of the *SAGE Handbook* editor Hilary Bradbury defines action research as "a democratic and participative orientation to knowledge creation. It brings together action and reflection, theory and practice, in the pursuit of practical solutions to issues of pressing concern. Action research is a pragmatic co-creation of knowing with, not on about, people." Bradbury, introduction to *Handbook of Action Research*, 1.

Many action researchers would surely agree with Bradbury. However, many others would also wish to set the nuances differently. Bridget Somekh, for example, describes action research through eight methodological principles some of which resonate with Bradbury's definition, some of which extend her definition, such as the greater focus on reflexivity in Bridget Somekh,

but rather as a "family of approaches" or an "orientation to knowledge creation," marked by both similarities and significant differences.[11] Indeed, over the past two decades, action research has seen such a growth in approaches that the 2015 *SAGE Handbook of Action Research* lists a broad array, including participatory action research, insider action research, appreciative inquiry, action inquiry, participatory research, action evaluation, action science, systemic intervention, and action learning.[12]

More important than grasping the nuances of these approaches, including their differences and similarities, is recognizing that action research represents not a singular methodology but a spectrum of approaches that share certain "family resemblances."[13] This concept implies that despite observable similarities across various action research methodologies, there exists no definitive criteria to categorically determine what constitutes action research. Nonetheless, I contend that there are three core characteristics commonly shared by most action research approaches.

3.2.1 Core Characteristics of Action Research

First, action research operates on the principle that the most effective knowledge creation occurs at the local level. It embodies a purposeful and structured inquiry

---

Action Research: A Methodology for Change and Development (Berkshire: McGraw-Hill Education, 2005), 6–8.

[11] Reason and Bradbury, *Handbook of Action Research*, 1–7. Acknowledging this range of approaches, I agree with Peter Reason and Hilary Bradbury that there can never be only one right way of doing action research. Reason and Bradbury, *Handbook of Action Research*, 7.

In the first edition of the *SAGE of Action Research*, editors Peter Reason and Hilary Bradbury define action research as "a participatory, democratic process concerned with developing practical knowing in the pursuit of worthwhile human purposes, grounded in a participatory worldview which we believe is emerging at this historical moment." Peter Reason and Hilary Bradbury, "Introduction: Inquiry and Participation in Search of a World Worthy of Human Aspiration," in *Handbook of Action Research: Participative Inquiry and Practice*, ed. Peter Reason and Hilary Bradbury (London: SAGE, 2001), 1–14.

While this definition is helpful, I also find it so broad as to add little substance. The general problem in defining action research is that definitions tend to be either too narrow, excluding approaches that should be included in the action research tradition, or definitions end up being too broad, ending up including too many approaches. I thus agree with Kathryn Herr and Gary Anderson that there is little to be gained by a stable definition of action research. Herr and Anderson, *Action Research Dissertation*, 5.

[12] Hilary Bradbury, ed., *The SAGE Handbook of Action Research*, 3rd ed. (London: SAGE Publications, 2015).

[13] Reason and Bradbury, *Handbook of Action Research*, 7.

conducted *by* or in collaboration *with* individuals deeply acquainted with or having stewardship over a specific context or practice.[14] Furthermore, it posits that the most profound understanding is achieved directly within this context and in the present. Consequently, action research concentrates on analyzing current events in a particular locale to comprehend the circumstances, often from an insider perspective.

This approach is often facilitated through the implementation of action-reflection cycles. An example is the action research cycle (referenced in figure 3.1), which entails iterative phases of planning, acting, observing, and reflecting.[15]

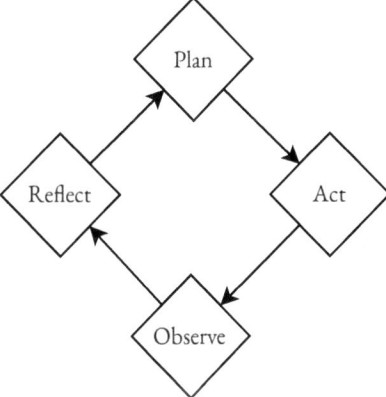

Figure 3.1: The Action Research Cycle

This does not imply that action research disregards history. On the contrary, action research many times acknowledges the significant role of history in molding both the present and the future. The emphasis, however, lies in interpreting the present through its history to shape the future, rather than trying to understand history from the perspective of the present. Consequently, action research predominantly concentrates on current phenomena, striving to comprehend situations as they actively unfold, rather than through retrospective examination.[16]

Second, action research distinguishes itself from other research orientations through its active intervention in the situation under investigation. It is characterized by its immersive, committed, and normative stance, diverging from other

---

[14] Reason and Bradbury, *Handbook of Action Research*, 3–4.
[15] Townsend, *Action Research*, 10–21.
[16] Reason and Bradbury, *Handbook of Action Research*, 6.

approaches that prioritize detachment and objectivity.[17] This emphasis on initiating action or change positions action research alongside efforts toward emancipation and liberation, rendering it inherently engaged and "biased" by design.[18]

Thirdly, a central tenet among action researchers is the importance of collaborative knowledge creation, involving a diverse array of groups and individuals. This collaborative effort typically occurs *in situ* and in the present, through engagement with local participants—those who directly experience or "own" the practices being studied and are, therefore, "insiders" within a particular organization or community. These insiders often join forces with "outsiders," such as academics or consultants, who bring research experience, skills, and organizational resources to the endeavor.[19] This collaboration is particularly crucial in participatory action research, the approach we adopted for the *Online Small Groups* project, emphasizing the synergy between insider knowledge and outsider expertise.

3.2.2 Insider and Outsider Positions

Participatory action research serves as an overarching concept that encompasses itself various approaches to action research, all of which are predicated on collaboration between "insiders" and "outsiders."[20] For academics or consultants operating as "outsiders," this form of research entails engaging with participants not merely as research subjects but as co-researchers possessing similar authority in the generation of knowledge, with important ethical implications, as discussed below. It is critical to note that while insiders may be fully capable of conducting action research independently, research conducted by outsiders *for* or *about* insiders generally falls outside the action research orientation.[21]

---

[17] Brydon-Miller, Greenwood, and Maguire, "Why Action Research?," 13–15.

[18] Ben W. M. Boog, "The Emancipatory Character of Action Research, Its History and the Present State of the Art," *Journal of Community & Applied Social Psychology* 13, no. 6 (2003): 426–38 at 426–27. It is also common to note the links between action research and both liberation theology and Freire's liberation pedagogy, which in turn is closely related to Latin-American theologies of liberation. Brydon-Miller, Greenwood, and Maguire, "Why Action Research?," 11; Gayá Wicks, Reason, and Bradbury, "Living Inquiry," 19.

[19] The "insider" / "outsider" dichotomy as serious disadvantages. Nonetheless, I have opted to use the "insider" / "outsider" distinction here as it is used in the literature on action research and theological action research. Bradbury, *Handbook of Action Research*; Brydon-Miller, Greenwood, and Maguire, "Why Action Research?"; Cameron et al., *Talking*. For a discussion see section 3.2.2.

[20] Chevalier and Buckles, *Participatory Action Research: Theory and Methods for Engaged Inquiry*, 24–30.

[21] Herr and Anderson, *Action Research Dissertation*, 4.

I have employed the terms "insiders" and "outsiders" to distinguish between "local" participants and "academic" contributors. Nonetheless, these terms are not without their complications. Typically, "insiders" and "outsiders" refer to those intimately involved in the context under study and those external to it, respectively. Yet, determining who qualifies as an insider and delineating the boundaries of their insider status presents challenges. The terminology implies a specific social, situational, or communal affiliation for insiders, from which outsiders are excluded. However, individuals categorized as outsiders in one context may well be insiders within similar or broader contexts. For example, while I may have been considered an outsider in the specific online small groups I engaged with, this does not necessarily render me an outsider to the broader parish community, other small groups, or the Church of Sweden at large.

The insider/outsider dichotomy is further troubled by the fluid nature of these roles throughout an action research project. Specifically, it is not uncommon for academics, initially considered "outsiders," to gradually adopt more of an insider's perspective as their engagement in the project deepens—a transformation underscored by Miryam Haarlammert and colleagues.[22] Conversely, once a project concludes, these same academics often transition back towards an outsider status as their connection with the local community diminishes over time. Consequently, Haarlammert and colleagues advocate for describing academics in such scenarios as "partial insiders" rather than outright outsiders, acknowledging the dynamic interplay between these identities.[23]

Reframing the distinction as one between academics and practitioners introduces its own set of challenges, given that academics may also be insiders and practitioners, and local participants might hold academic positions, though they do not operate in this capacity for the project at hand. Consequently, all such terminologies present limitations. Therefore, I continue the use of the insider/outsider terminology, to allow a discussion of our various roles in the project and how these relate to ethical considerations and research quality, while being mindful of the complexities and nuances previously discussed.

---

[22] Miryam Haarlammert et al., "Inside-Out: Representational Ethics and Diverse Communities," *American Journal of Community Psychology* 60, no. 3–4 (2017): 414–23.

[23] Haarlammert et al., "Inside-Out."

3.2.3 Action Research as a Learning Process

Action research is often conceptualized as a learning process.[24] Specifically, it embodies experiential learning, a connection that is unsurprising given the shared foundations of action research and experiential learning in the pioneering work of Kurt Lewin and Paulo Freire.[25]

As previously mentioned, action research often builds on action-reflection cycles, which include planning, acting, observing, and reflecting. These cycles are not linear but rather spiral, with each phase of reflection leading into a new cycle of planning.[26] This concept evolves from Stephen Kemmis and Robin McTaggart's original spiral of self-reflection, further elaborated by Kathryn Herr and Gary L. Anderson. They outline the action research spiral as:

1.   to develop a *plan* of action to improve what is already happening;
2.   to *act* to implement the plan;
3.   to *observe* the effects of action in the context in which it occurs;
4.   to *reflect* on these effects as a basis for further planning, subsequent action, and on, through a succession of cycles.[27]

Andrew Townsend highlights that Kemmis and McTaggart perceive their process not as rigid, sequential steps but as fluid moments within the broader scope of action research.[28]

---

[24] Judi Marshall and Peter Reason, "Adult Learning in Collaborative Action Research: Reflections on the Supervision Process," *Studies in Continuing Education* 15, no. 2 (1993): 117–32; Reason and Torbert, "The Action Turn," 3–6; Stephen Kemmis, Robin McTaggart, and Rhonda Nixon, *The Action Research Planner: Doing Critical Participatory Action Research* (Singapore: Springer, 2014), 10–11; Hilary Bradbury, *How to Do Action Research for Transformations: At a Time of Eco-Social Crisis* (Cheltenham: Edward Elgar Publishing, 2022), 2–4; Brydon-Miller, Greenwood, and Maguire, "Why Action Research?" For a discussion of learning as knowledge generation see also Sami Paavola and Kai Hakkarainen, "The Knowledge Creation Metaphor: An Emergent Epistemological Approach to Learning," *Science & Education* 14 (2005): 535–57.

[25] David A. Kolb, *Experiential Learning: Experience as the Source of Learning and Development*, 2nd ed. (New Jersey: Pearson Education, 2015), 8–9, 28–29, 32–33; Reason and Bradbury, *Handbook of Action Research*, 3; David Coghlan and Mary Brydon-Miller, "Participatory Action Research," in *The SAGE Encyclopedia of Action Research*, ed. David Coghlan and Mary Brydon-Miller (Thousand Oaks: SAGE Publications Ltd, 2014), 583–88 at 583.

[26] Kemmis, McTaggart, and Nixon, *Action Research Planner*, 18.

[27] Herr and Anderson, *Action Research Dissertation*, 5.

[28] Townsend, *Action Research*, 12–14.

Kemmis and McTaggart themselves acknowledge that their model simplifies the complexity of real research endeavors. They advocate for its application primarily as a heuristic tool, aiding in the conceptual planning of action research projects rather than dictating their exact progression.[29] Therefore, the essence lies not in verifying the action research cycles as an exact representation of the research process but in emphasizing action research's role as a distinctive form of experiential learning.

These cycles bear resemblance to David Kolb's experiential learning cycle, depicted in figure 3.2.

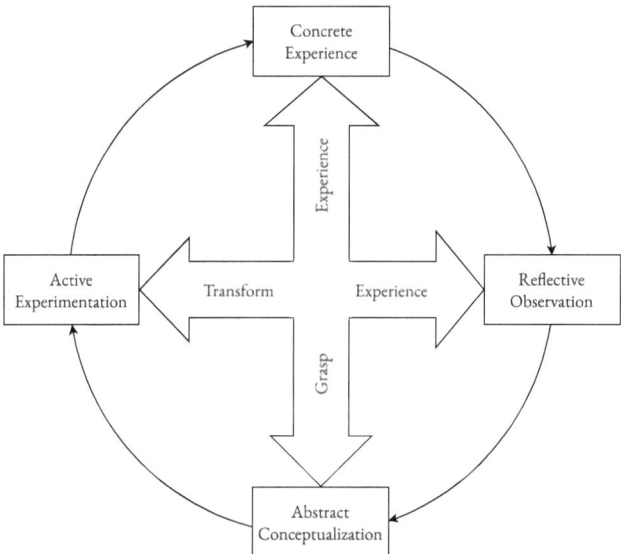

Figure 3.2 Kolb's Experiential Learning Cycle. Reproduced from Kolb (2015).

Kolb's experiential learning cycle also aligns with William Pounds's problem-solving model, Herbert A. Simon's decision-making framework, and Graham Wallas's

---

[29] Kemmis, McTaggart, and Nixon, *Action Research Planner*, 89. One difficulty with the simple model is that it suggests that the moments of planning, acting, observing, and reflecting are sequential and distinct. In practice, it is common to jump back and forth between these moments or to skip moments all together. A plan might not hold upon reflection and might be reformulated without ever being acted out. Action might be unplanned and still lead to significant observations and reflections, and so on.

description of the creative process.[30] Additionally, Kolb's cycle shares parallels with the way in which Don Browning, Richard Osmer, and John Swinton and Harriet Mowat describe research in practical theology.[31]

The essence of these models is their illustration of learning as a fundamental process derived from experience. This paradigm of experiential learning posits that learning equates to the "generation of new knowledge," establishing a profound connection between learning and research.[32] This foundational principle of learning from experience is thus central to both action research and this dissertation.

Yet, for learning to qualify as research, it must transcend the local context, contributing to a broader body of public knowledge. This necessitates connecting local learnings with wider sources of knowledge, a topic I expand upon in section 3.5.2.[33]

Putting all this together, I perceive action research as an orientation towards inquiry aimed at producing public knowledge through systematic reflection on present action at the local level by or with people "owning" the situation in which such action occurs.[34]

3.3 "Designing" an Action Research Project

As my dissertation project was part of the broader action research initiative, *Church in Digital Space*, I inherited two design choices from this larger endeavor. First, *Church in Digital Space* was a participatory action research project, an approach that was extended to the four research and development tracks, including

---

[30] Kolb, *Experiential Learning*, 44–45.

[31] Don S. Browning, *A Fundamental Practical Theology: Descriptive and Strategic Proposals* (Minneapolis: Fortress Press, 1996); Richard Robert Osmer, *Practical Theology: An Introduction* (Grand Rapids: William B. Eerdmans Pub. Co., 2008); Swinton and Mowat, *Practical Theology*.

[32] Kolb, *Experiential Learning*, 41–42. See also Paavola and Hakkarainen, "Knowledge Creation." The generation of new knowledge is a commonly accepted purpose of research.

[33] Reason and Torbert, "The Action Turn," 16–28; Bjørn Gustavsen, Agneta Hansson, and Thoralf U. Qvale, "Action Research and the Challenge of Scope," in *The SAGE Handbook of Action Research: Participative Inquiry and Practice*, ed. Peter Reason and Hilary Bradbury (London: SAGE Publications, 2008), 63–76.

[34] Of course, the concept of ownership is problematic. Recognizing the power imbalances that exist in almost all situations it becomes difficult to know who "owns" a situation. I here merely try to capture the idea of some people having a greater familiarity with and claim to specific situations than others. The distinction becomes especially important in those action research projects that include insiders and outsiders and hence people who can legitimately claim the situation under consideration to very different degrees.

my *Online Small Groups* initiative. Second, the overarching timeline was established in the larger project.

However, as illustrated by Frida Mannerfelt's dissertation, the project's design framework permitted significant flexibility in both the development of the four research and development tracks and the crafting of individual dissertations.[35] Unique to *Online Small Groups* track was, for example, the decision to recruit participants from various parishes, unlike the other tracks that collaborated with two parishes each.

This section outlines the specific design decisions I made within the online small groups project and throughout the composition of this dissertation, offering insights into the evolution of the *Online Small Groups* project. Through this examination, I aim to provide a comprehensive overview of how the project developed, highlighting the iterative process of action research and the adaptability required in response to new challenges and discoveries.

3.3.1 An Explorative Project with an Emergent Design

Action research typically evolves to address problems that become clear only as the research progresses. This dynamic was evident in the *Online Small Groups* project. Instead of initiating the study with a well-developed research question and design, we embarked on the project driven by a collective concern to understand and improve online small groups. Consequently, the nature of the *Online Small Groups* project was inherently exploratory, with an emergent design guiding its progression. Here, *exploratory* signifies the research's aim, while *emergent* pertains to the unfolding process of the research itself.

My decision to embrace an emergent design for the *Online Small Groups* project was driven by two key factors. First, the project was conceived within the broader scope of the *Church in Digital Space* research initiative. As this larger project unfolded, it encompassed various research tracks, the specific outlines of which only began to take shape in the spring of 2021. Consequently, the *Online Small Groups* segment adopted its emergent nature from the overarching *Church*

---

[35] Frida Mannerfelt and Rikard Roitto, "Mellan rit och reklam del 1: Berättelsen om två församlingars utveckling," in *Kyrka i digitala rum: Ett aktionsforskningsprojekt om församlingsliv online i Svenska kyrkan*, ed. Sara Garpe and Jonas Ideström (Uppsala: Church of Sweden, 2022), 46–59; Mannerfelt and Roitto, "Mellan rit och reklam del 2: Interaktion, synkronicitet och integritet i förinspelade digitalt förmedlade andakter"; Frida Mannerfelt, "Co-preaching: The Practice of Preaching in Digital Culture and Space" (PhD, Stockholm School of Theology, 2023).

in Digital Space project, necessitating a design flexible enough to accommodate and respond to the evolving contours of the wider research endeavor.

Second, the *Online Small Groups* project was conceived as participatory action research, fostering a partnership between insider practitioners (the four group leaders) and an outsider academic (myself). This model necessitated an elevated level of openness due to the imperative for collaborative engagement with insiders. Such collaboration, premised on mutuality, precludes either party from imposing a predetermined agenda. Participatory action research thrives on the collective determination of relevant questions and the methodologies to explore them, embracing the inherent complexities, ambiguities, and unpredictabilities of human interaction and cooperation. This approach renders the research process inherently dynamic and occasionally disordered.[36] Herr and Anderson aptly describe this characteristic of participatory action research with the analogy of "designing the plane while flying it," highlighting the adaptive and exploratory essence of this research methodology.[37]

An Explorative Project

In discussing explorative research designs, Richard Swedberg underscores that the essence of most research is to delve into the unknown or to debate contested realms, rendering much of research inherently exploratory. An explorative study, then, is more specifically defined as research that either ventures into new territories, offering preliminary analyses of uncharted topics, or cultivates fresh hypotheses on familiar subjects without immediate empirical testing.[38] The *Online Small Groups* project embodied this exploratory nature in two key ways: it ventured into the relatively uncharted domain of teaching within church-based online small

---

[36] Reason and Bradbury, *Handbook of Action Research*, 4–5; Brydon-Miller, Greenwood, and Maguire, "Why Action Research?," 21; Jill Grant, Geoff Nelson, and Terry Mitchell, "Negotiating the Challenges of Participatory Action Research: Relationships, Power, Participation, Change and Credibility," in *The SAGE Handbook of Action Research: Participative Inquiry and Practice*, ed. Peter Reason and Hilary Bradbury (London: SAGE Publications, 2008), 589–601. In practice the relationship is not necessary one of equals, especially not in relations to the choice of methods. See section 3.4.1.

[37] Kathryn Herr and Gary L. Anderson, "Designing the Plane while Flying it: Proposing and doing the Dissertation," in *The Action Research Dissertation: A Guide for Students and Faculty* (Thousand Oaks: SAGE Publications, 2012), 70–88.

[38] Richard Swedberg, "Exploratory Research," in *The Production of Knowledge: Enhancing Progress in Social Science*, ed. Colin Elman, John Gerring, and James Mahoney (Cambridge: Cambridge University Press), 17–41 at 17–18.

groups for adults, and it developed teaching strategies, as hypotheses, without testing these.

This also meant our approach was not grounded in definitive theory but was guided by sensitizing concepts, providing a directional framework for our inquiry.[39] Sensitizing concepts stand in contrast to definitive concepts by not offering precise definitions of phenomena for empirical study; instead, they provide a general sense of reference and guidance for approaching empirical instances.[40] While definitive concepts dictate what to observe, sensitizing concepts suggest potential directions for examination.[41]

From the outset of the *Online Small Groups* project, our interest gravitated towards understanding learning dynamics, the development of faith, and notions of community within these groups. This focus was reflected in the goals and objectives established prior to initiating our work with the participants.[42] Thus, we embarked on the research with a set of guiding ideas, which provided a direction for our inquiry. However, these were not well-defined and theoretically articulated concepts.

An Emergent Design

Rooted in the principles of explorative action research, the design of our project was inherently emergent, setting it apart from the fixed designs typically seen in quantitative research. Emergent designs commence with broad conceptualizations of the research focus and maintain flexibility to adapt research questions, as well as data collection and analysis procedures in alignment with insights gained during the initial stages of the investigation.[43] Kerstin Given exemplifies emergent designs through ethnography.

> Ethnography is a useful illustration of this process because the ongoing analysis of field-notes leads to a shifting interpretation of both which issues are relatively well understood and which issues require further observations, so that ethnographers make design

---

[39] The notion of sensitizing concepts comes from grounded theory approaches. See Alvesson and Sköldberg, *Reflexive Methodology*, 71.

[40] Herbert Blumer, "What is Wrong with Social Theory?," *American Sociological Review* 19, no. 1 (1954): 3–10 at 7.

[41] Shehr Bano Zaidi, "Situating Sensitizing Concepts in the Constructivist-Critical Grounded Theory Method," *International Journal of Qualitative Methods* 21, no. 1 (2022): 1–6 at 3.

[42] See part 2 and the research plans in appendix B.

[43] Lisa M. Given, "Emergent Design," in *The SAGE Encyclopedia of Qualitative Research Methods*, ed. Lisa M. Given (Thousand Oaks: SAGE Publications, Inc., 2008), 246–48 at 246–47.

decisions—on an almost daily basis—about how to pursue their emerging interpretations.[44]

Emergent designs exhibit variability in the extent of their flexibility, from those
that are adaptive solely in terms of sampling criteria to those where nearly all components of the research—ranging from methodologies to research questions—can
undergo modification. The *Online Small Groups* project was emergent in the evolution of its research question, data collection techniques, researcher positionality,
and theoretical frameworks.

As mentioned, the research questions developed as the project progressed, rather than being predefined. These questions, while guiding the direction of our
exploration, were considered provisional and served more as a compass for our inquiry rather than a strict roadmap.[45]

The project's approach to data collection was similarly adaptive.[46] Initially, we
gathered insights through qualitative feedback forms designed to elicit open-
ended responses on experiences such as the group atmosphere or suggestions for
improvements. Questions like "How did you experience the atmosphere in the
group?" or "Is there anything you think we could do differently or better next
time?" were typical. Some items combined closed-ended and open-ended queries,
prompting participants to expand on new ideas or thoughts stemming from their
conversations. These feedback forms, distributed to both participants and group
leaders immediately following sessions, were typically returned within a week.
While the questions varied between participant and leader forms, the objective was
consistent: to encapsulate the meeting experiences comprehensively.

From the beginning, we planned to augment feedback forms with interviews
of group participants. Invitations for follow-up interviews were extended, yet the
willingness among participants to engage in interviews was notably low during the
fall. Consequently, I conducted only two individual semi-structured interviews,
each via Zoom and lasting approximately thirty-five minutes. To adapt, for the
spring 2022 groups, we integrated an evaluation meeting after the sessions, adopting the format of a semi-structured group interview.[47]

As responses from the feedback forms began to accumulate, I encountered difficulties in interpreting the data, prompting a shift from a mixed methods

---

[44] Given, "Emergent Design," 247.

[45] The research questions thus functioned analogously to sensitizing concepts.

[46] For an overview of the collected data see appendix C.

[47] Anna Davidsson Bremborg, "Interviewing," in *The Routledge Handbook of Research
Methods in the Study of Religion*, ed. Michael Stausberg and Steven Engler (2011), 310–22 at 312–13.

approach to a more ethnographic strategy.[48] In response to this challenge, during the fall of 2021, I attended one meeting for each group to enrich the data gathered from feedback forms and interviews.

My involvement was moderate. I participated in all scheduled activities, it was evident to both myself and the other attendees that my role was primarily observational.[49] I took notes during these sessions and later expanded these into field notes, offering broader reflections on my observations.

Originally, I had envisioned hosting three joint workshops aimed at facilitating a learning exchange among group leaders, focusing on the hurdles and evolving best practices of leading online small groups. The first workshop, conducted in September 2021, centered on the research process, leading to a consensus on the research question and methodology.

However, logistical challenges arose when two groups planned for fall 2021 were postponed to spring 2022, eliminating the overlap between sessions. Specifically, the timing of the second workshop—set immediately after the conclusion of the fall groups and before the commencement of the spring groups—posed difficulties. Given the uncertainties surrounding the start dates of the spring groups, I opted to cancel the second workshop.

By the time of the third and final workshop, only one of the spring groups had begun, leaving the purpose of this workshop to shift towards a discussion on the project's outcomes to date rather than a mutual exchange of learning experiences among leaders.

Rather than facilitating direct peer-to-peer learning among group leaders, the process evolved so that I became the primary conduit through which insights and learning were disseminated. This shift increasingly embedded me within the fabric of the groups under study, culminating in my co-leadership of the groups during the spring of 2022.

Taking on a co-leadership role significantly broadened my participant observation scope. Rather than attending a single session per group, I was actively involved in all meetings, except one meeting in each group for which I was unavailable. This transition also marked a shift in my observational stance from moderate to complete participation.[50]

---

[48] See the entries from Wednesday, September 8, 2021.

[49] Barbara B. Kawulich, "Participant Observation as a Data Collection Method," *Forum Qualitative Sozialforschung / Forum: Qualitative Social Research* 6, no. 2 (2005): 1–28 at 9–10.

[50] Kawulich, "Participant Observation," 10.

Whereas my role in the fall was that of a detached observer, in this new capacity, I immersed myself completely in the group dynamics. This dual role of leader and observer presented challenges, particularly in balancing the responsibilities of guiding the group while simultaneously conducting observational analysis.[51]

Co-leading the spring groups afforded me increased opportunities to directly impact the structure and conduct of the meetings, facilitating the introduction and assessment of potential enhancements. Consequently, my approach to leadership played a substantial role in molding the dynamics of the online small groups. This active involvement underscored the evolving nature of my positionality within the project, highlighting how my role and influence developed alongside the research process.

The theoretical frameworks informing this dissertation have also unfolded in an emergent manner. Initially, my doctoral research was poised to explore traditioning within adult small groups, drawing upon diverse interpretations of tradition and insights from Christian religious education, including Paulo Freire's seminal work, "Pedagogy for the Oppressed."

The unexpected advent of the COVID-19 pandemic, however, led to my inclusion in the action research project, *Church in Digital Space*, necessitating a deep dive into action research literature in spring 2021. Thus, I approached the *Online Small Groups* track with a theoretical understanding of action research principles.

It was only as the project progressed that I began to integrate and apply concepts from Christian religious education. During this period, I delved deeper into educational theories, particularly those proposed by Peter Jarvis and Malcolm S. Knowles, which significantly influenced the dissertation. The exploration of teaching designs emerged as a focal area of interest post-project, as I endeavored to interpret our collective experiences through this lens.

The theoretical perspectives underpinning this dissertation thus evolved dynamically, as insights from my earlier scholarly engagements became pivotal in comprehending the developments within our online small groups. Consequently, the project was not initiated with a predetermined theoretical stance; instead, the theoretical underpinnings unfolded and were refined progressively in response to the project's unfolding narrative and emerging complexities.[52]

---

[51] Michael Agar, *The Professional Stranger: An Informal Introduction to Ethnography*, Second ed. (San Diego: Academic Press, 1996), 241–52; Tim Ingold, "That's Enough about Ethnography," *HAU Journal of Ethnographic Theory* 4, no. 1 (2014): 383–95.

[52] This is an abductive approach to analysis, as I explain below.

Employing an explorative and emergent design meant that many aspects of the research only crystallized with time, which can give the impression that action research is unorderly. Of course, the purported messiness encountered in action research studies is not unique but is often observed across various empirical qualitative research endeavors. The distinctive aspect of action research, however, lies in the partial intentionality of this messiness, rather than it being merely an incidental byproduct of collaborative human endeavors.

Embracing this emergent nature, action research posits that profound insights often originate not from rigid research designs but through dialogues among individuals of diverse experiences and skills, echoing the observations made by Herr and Anderson.[53] Far from being a difficulty to overcome, I, therefore, find that an exploratory and emergent action research approach was well suited as a research design to engage with the learning process during the COVID-19 pandemic.

3.3.2 Working with Action Research Cycles

The *Online Small Groups* project incorporated action research cycles in three distinct ways. First, each group meeting presented the opportunity for one cycle. Before these meetings, we engaged in planning and selecting potential improvements to explore (plan). Subsequently, the meeting itself was conducted (act), during which we gathered data (observe), and this data was later analyzed (reflect). This analysis informed our planning for subsequent meetings, creating a continuous cycle of improvement and adaptation. This process is illustrated in figure 3.3.

---

[53] Herr and Anderson, "Designing the Plane," 3–4. In this sense it is no coincidence that the *Church in Digital Space* action research project started as a series of conversations between different people at the diocesan office and the Stockholm School of Theology.

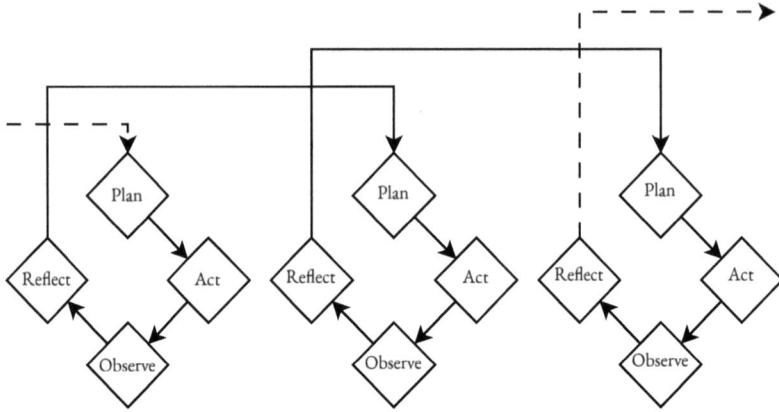

Figure 3.3: The Action Research Spiral

Second, the engagement with each group can be viewed as embodying an action research cycle. This began with the initial planning phase, where we outlined the objectives, data collection methods, and overall aspirations for the research (plan). The implementation phase followed (act), during which we recorded outcomes (observe). The cycle culminated in an analysis of the collected data, reflecting on the implications for future facilitation efforts (reflect). Typically, these cycles started with a collaborative research plan developed by the group leaders and myself.[54] They concluded with an evaluative session, during which we collectively deliberated on each group's outcomes.

Lastly, considering the temporal arrangement of the groups, the entire project can also be conceptualized as a two-cycle action research endeavor. Insights gained from the groups during fall 2021 were integrated into the planning phase for the spring 2022 groups. However, I served as the sole continuous link between these two phases, effectively transferring the learnings and reflections from one cycle to the next. This unique position allowed me to facilitate these broader cycles of action research that spanned the entire duration of the project.

The varied interpretations of action research cycles within the *Online Small Groups* project underscore that these cycles function more as heuristic tools than as rigid structures. The pivotal aspect is not determining the most precise

---

[54] The *Lectio Divina* group that met during the spring of 2022 is an exception to this. Due to the specific circumstances surrounding the group we did not write a research plan, nor was anyone from the parish available for a results meeting.

depiction among these three perspectives, but rather recognizing how each uniquely illustrates the integration of action and reflection throughout different levels and phases of the project.

3.3.3 An Inductive-Abductive Approach

Induction, deduction, and abduction serve as foundational concepts in the realm of inferential reasoning, delineating the processes by which conclusions are drawn from premises. Within the context of qualitative research, these concepts articulate the relationship between theoretical frameworks and empirical evidence.[55] Induction emphasizes the organization of direct experiences into overarching generalizations. Deduction, conversely, starts with theoretical constructs, aiming to classify and scrutinize empirical realities against these pre-established theories. Abduction represents a recursive dialogue between observational data and theoretical perspectives, facilitating the formation of preliminary insights and explanations concerning the studied phenomenon.[56]

Abduction is now recognized as the predominant explanatory framework in numerous case-based research methodologies, having a profound association with hermeneutics and interpretative processes.[57] This iterative movement between empirical observations and theoretical insights mirrors the fundamental dynamics of action research cycles that synergize action with reflection.[58] Consequently, the methodology employed in the *Online Small Groups* project could be characterized as abductive, particularly when considering abduction as an endeavor to "sort out the facts in order to attain an idea of what we find before us, but we fail to immediately achieve a satisfactory understanding and explanation of the phenomenon."[59]

In our efforts to understand the dynamics within the online small groups, our approach was not primarily theoretical; established academic theories did not

---

[55] Alvesson and Sköldberg, *Reflexive Methodology*, 4–8.

[56] Håvard Åsvoll, "Abduction, Deduction and Induction: Can these Concepts Be Used for an Understanding of Methodological Processes in Interpretative Case Studies?," *International Journal of Qualitative Studies in Education* 27, no. 3 (2014): 289–307 at 290–93; Knut Tveitereid, "Making Data Speak: The Shortage of Theory for the Analysis of Qualitative Data in Practical Theology," in *What Really Matters: Scandinavian Perspectives on Ecclesiology and Ethnography*, ed. Jonas Ideström and Tone Stangeland Kaufman (Eugene: Pickwick Publications, 2018), 41–57 at 44–45.

[57] Tveitereid, "Making Data Speak," 44; Alvesson and Sköldberg, *Reflexive Methodology*.

[58] See section 3.2.3.

[59] Åsvoll, "Abduction, Deduction and Induction," 291.

prominently feature until our final joint workshop. Rather, the project utilized an inductive methodology, where understanding and analyzing our collective experiences stemmed from discussions among us, independent of theoretical frameworks. Consequently, this phase of the project leaned more towards induction than abduction. For many of my co-researchers, who were not involved in the deeper layers of interpretation culminating in this dissertation, induction constituted the essence of their analytical approach.

In the process of reflecting on and analyzing the project for this dissertation, I engaged in a more theoretically informed examination, connecting our experiences from the *Online Small Groups* project with the theoretical frameworks outlined in chapter 2. This iterative analysis involved oscillating between empirical evidence and scholarly literature on Christian religious education, small group dynamics, and online learning. Consequently, this later stage of the research project adopted an abductive approach, characterized by a continuous dialogue between theory and data. Therefore, I characterize the research methodology as a two-phased journey, initiating with an inductive approach and culminating in an abductive analysis.

3.3.4 Normativity

Tone Stangeland Kaufman and Jonas Ideström present the perspective that research is always normative, at least if one acknowledges that normativity is embedded in the person of the researcher. However, the discourse among many action researchers extends beyond merely acknowledging this intrinsic "normativity-from-within." They advocate for a proactive ethical commitment to social justice and transformation, or "normativity-from-the-outside," adopting Ideström and Stangeland Kaufman's terminology.[60] A different way to understand this distinction is to distinguish between normativity and prescriptivity, in the way Geir Afdal does.[61]

---

[60] Caroline Lenette, *Participatory Action Research: Ethics and Decolonization* (Oxford: Oxford University Press, 2022); Bradbury, *Action Research for Transformations*; Stephen Kemmis, "Critical Theory and Participatory Action Research," in *The SAGE Handbook of Action Research: Participative Inquiry and Practice*, ed. Peter Reason and Hilary Bradbury (London: SAGE Publications, 2008), 121–38; Boog, "Emancipatory Character"; Jonas Ideström and Tone Stangeland Kaufman, "Whose Voice? Whose Church? Using Action Research in Practical Ecclesiology," in *Mending the world? Possibilities and Obstacles for Religion, Church, and Theology*, ed. Niclas Blåder and Kristina Helgesson Kjellin (Eugene: Pickwick Publications, 2017), 486–502.

[61] Afdal, *Researching*.

Afdal conceptualizes religious education research as a social practice that aims to generate theories about the practice of religious education through empirical engagement. In this context, theory is broadly defined as "a more or less systematic and coherent account of a phenomenon or a system of phenomena," effectively equating theory with the research account.[62] Afdal contents that religious educators and religious education researchers have different ways of conceptualizing the practice of religious education within congregational settings.[63] The development of new knowledge, according to Afdal, emerges from the interplay and negotiation between these differing perspectives. He describes this research strategy of negotiating practitioner and research understandings as "researching religious education as a social practice."[64]

Geir Afdal terms the result of this negotiation in research as an "expressive theory." Such theories elucidate the self-perception and self-interpretation of religious education practitioners, concurrently acknowledging their normative viewpoints.[65] Expressive theories are both "empirically founded and analytically sophisticated," facilitating enhanced comprehension of the practices being studied. [66] Afdal distinguishes expressive theories from prescriptive research methodologies in religious education, which seek to dictate detailed recommendations for improved practice. He expresses considerable skepticism towards these prescriptive approaches, advocating instead for a more interpretative and understanding-driven perspective that values the insights and experiences of practitioners.[67]

Central to Afdal's critique is the perception of prescriptive theories as inherently deductive, essentially prescribing practice directly from theory. His critique can be summarized in two main points. First, prescriptive theories attempt to shape practice solely based on theoretical frameworks, often neglecting the rich tapestry of existing practices and their contextual nuances.[68] Second, researchers, according to Afdal, lack the requisite knowledge, skills, and authority to mandate the application of their findings in practical settings. It is, therefore, incumbent upon religious education practitioners themselves to assess the relevance and applicability of research-derived theories to their work. [69] Afdal's stance is

---

[62] Afdal, *Researching*, 10.
[63] Afdal, *Researching*, 68–73.
[64] Afdal, *Researching*.
[65] Afdal, *Researching*, 74.
[66] Afdal, *Researching*, 75.
[67] Afdal, *Researching*, 16.
[68] Afdal, *Researching*, 15, 73–74.
[69] Afdal, *Researching*, 76–77, 145.

unequivocal: "research in religious education is in no position to prescribe educational practice," advocating for a research approach that respects the autonomy and experiential insights of practitioners in the field.[70]

On many points, I agree with Afdal, though my final assessment diverges significantly from his. Like Afdal, I view religious education fundamentally as a social practice that necessitates deep empirical involvement with both the educational practices and the educators themselves.[71] Additionally, I concur with the challenges associated with researchers providing detailed directives to practitioners, which fail to recognize contextual nuances and undervalue the creativity required to translate theoretical knowledge into practical application.

However, I disagree with Afdal's characterization of prescriptive theories as necessarily being based on a deductive approach that starts with theory and works toward implementation. While I agree with Afdal's criticism of such an application logic, I do not see that this necessarily follows from detailed prescriptions for better practice.

I suggest instead that it is helpful to distinguish between the research process and its outcomes. Regarding the process, I am in accord with Afdal on the importance of mediating between theoretical frameworks and practical application, navigating the dialogues between the "language of research" and the "language of practitioners."[72] To clarify this stance, I introduce the term "prescriptive-constructive" to set apart my methodology from the "prescriptive-deductive" approach critiqued by Afdal. I contend that a prescriptive-constructive approach can be just as grounded in empirical evidence and cognizant of normative considerations as Afdal's descriptive-analytical approach aimed at developing expressive theories.

Moreover, I argue that Afdal's critique of the research methodology does not necessarily extend to a disavowal of prescriptive research outputs.[73] The crux of the matter lies in how one perceives the ultimate goal of research. As previously mentioned, I view the aim of research as contributing to change. Thus, the "mere"

---

[70] Afdal, *Researching*, 71.

[71] Afdal suggests a participatory research strategy that does research *with* practitioners and not *on* them which is very close to the way action researchers frame their approach, even if Afdal, somewhat surprisingly, appears critical of action research. Afdal, *Researching*, 85, 109, 13, 31.

For a discussion of action research see section 3.2. Note also that I use a weak concept of social practice where Afdal probably prefers a strong concept of social practice. Geir Afdal, "Two Concepts of Practice and Theology," *Studia Theologica* 75, no. 1 (2021): 6–29.

[72] Afdal, *Researching*, 117.

[73] Afdal himself appears to make this distinction when he differentiates between research strategies and types of theory. Afdal, *Researching*, 72–75.

generation of knowledge does not suffice; I believe research should aim to produce insights that are both practical and actionable for practitioners.[74] This stance underscores a commitment to not only expanding the knowledge base but also ensuring that such knowledge serves the real-world needs and challenges faced by those in the field.

I concur with Afdal on the point that the practical value and applicability of research findings are ultimately determined by how practitioners utilize them. However, I do not think that this realization exempts researchers from the obligation to anticipate and strive for outputs that could prove most beneficial and applicable.

Where my perspective differs from Afdal's is in the interpretation of the role and impact of research on practice. Afdal appears to posit that research enriches the field by offering novel and improved understandings of religious education practices, thereby facilitating a reexamination of practitioners' self-concepts and methods, potentially catalyzing changes in practice. My skepticism lies in whether purely descriptive-analytical or expressive theoretical accounts are the most effective means for practitioners to do this and to derive actionable insights from research.[75]

The focal point of the discussion, and an area where Afdal and I find common ground, is the inherent complexity of practices. Recognizing religious education as a social practice underscores its intricacy and the diverse avenues through which change is both made possible and resisted.[76] Regardless of whether one frames the process of integrating research findings into practice as application, implementation, translation, or transfer, it is essential to acknowledge that these processes are inherently creative. Practitioners are required to navigate a nuanced landscape, reconciling their individual perspectives and experiences with the contextual dynamics of their operational environment and the insights derived from research. This negotiation is critical for effectively adapting and applying theoretical knowledge to real-world scenarios.

Informed by experiential learning theory, I propose understanding the application of research in practice as a form of "active experimentation."[77] This necessitates identifying concrete implications from research "to make decisions and to

---

[74] See section 3.2 above and chapter 7.

[75] Afdal, *Researching*, 75.

[76] Andreas Reckwitz, "Toward a Theory of Social Practices: A Development in Culturalist Theorizing," *European Journal of Social Theory* 5, no. 2 (2002): 243–63 at 255–56.

[77] See section 3.2.3.

solve problems," as Kolb puts it.[78] However, when researchers focus solely on generating abstract conceptualizations or expressive theories, the entire burden of engaging in active experimentation shifts to practitioners. This shift places undue responsibility on practitioners to bridge the gap between theory and application without any guidance from those who produced the research account.

Given their role in fostering the vital dialogue between practice and research understandings, researchers are uniquely positioned to suggest potential implications from their studies. It is important to clarify that these implications are not intended to be exhaustive or exclusively correct. By presenting both potential implications and an empirical examination of practices, alongside the interplay between practice and theory, researchers equip readers with the means to assess the strength of these implications independently.

By outlining specific examples of implications, researchers can inspire practitioners to undertake their own exploratory applications based on these insights. Consequently, providing detailed guidance not only facilitates learning from research findings but also enhances the likelihood that such research contributes meaningfully to real-world changes.[79]

While I see the value in offering guidance, I concur with Afdal that not all forms of prescriptive advice prove beneficial.[80] Specifically, prescriptions that delve into excessive detail may fail to resonate with or be applicable in practice. This is because the granularity of such prescriptions often narrows their scope of applicability, diminishing their overall utility.[81] Therefore, I argue that the optimal level for prescriptive advice lies in an intermediary zone of abstraction: nuanced enough to provide direction beyond mere theoretical conceptualizations, yet sufficiently grounded to remain relevant and adaptable to the diverse realities of practice.

A last consideration relates back to the connection between normativity and prescriptivity. Based on the preceding discussion I find this relationship more nuanced than a simple binary distinction. In agreement with Tone Stangeland Kaufman, I view these concepts as situated along a continuum of positions, representing varying degrees of normativity rather than wholly separate categories.[82]

---

[78] Kolb, *Experiential Learning*, 42.

[79] I expand on this point in section 3.5.2.

[80] Afdal, *Researching*, 15, 71.

[81] Alvesson and Sköldberg, *Reflexive Methodology*, 26–27.

[82] Afdal, *Researching*, 75; Tone Stangeland Kaufman, "From the Outside, Within, or In Between? Normativity at Work in Empirical Practical Theological Research," in *Conundrums in Practical Theology*, ed. Bonnie J. Miller-McLemore and Joyce Ann Mercer (Leiden: Brill, 2016), 134–62 at 148.

Consequently, my prescriptive-constructive approach should not be perceived as an entirely separate entity from a descriptive-analytical approach. More importantly, it should not be misconstrued as the difference between a normative and a non-normative perspective. Instead, it represents a distinct point along a spectrum that spans from abstract theoretical insights to concrete, actionable recommendations, specifically tailored to the field of religious education practice. This perspective emphasizes a holistic view of research outputs, recognizing the diverse ways they can inform and shape educational practices.

3.4 "Doing" an Action Research Project

While certain elements of the *Online Small Groups* project were "designed" in the planning stages, other aspects emerged only as the project unfolded. Here, I delve into the dynamic nature of the research process, addressing crucial considerations relating to quality, ethics, and reflexivity.

3.4.1 Quality

Every research approach adheres to its unique standards of excellence and benchmarks for quality, and action research is no exception to this rule. Although there's a consensus among action researchers on the significance of maintaining quality, defining what exactly constitutes this quality remains a subject of debate. This challenge partly stems from the dual objectives of action research projects: to effect lasting change within a particular context and to enrich the broader body of knowledge. Additionally, delineating the quality of the research process in relation to the outcomes poses another layer of complexity. Action research places a premium on both the outcomes and the process leading to these results, necessitating that quality assessments encompass the entire research journey.

Despite the diversity in perspectives, discussions about quality in action research often converge on several key attributes. Primarily, quality is deeply intertwined with the research process itself. The principle of conducting research *with* rather than *on* people transcends a mere methodological choice, serving as a hallmark of quality. This encompasses a commitment to methodological rigor and extends to the cultivation of relationships within the research context. Qualities such as openness, transparency, honesty, and truthfulness in these relationships are paramount, as is the researcher's capacity for reflexivity.[83] These elements collectively form a foundational aspect of quality in action research, emphasizing the ethical and relational dimensions of the research endeavor. In discussing the quality of the project, I therefore start by discussing the research process and then move on to an examination of the research outcomes.

Process

Regarding the research process, I more specifically treat the appropriateness of the chosen design, the quality of relationships and my claim to co-produce knowledge with my co-researchers, including how to balance the demands of research and the respect for my co-researcher's limited time resources.

I consider the selection of an explorative and emergent design for this research as a judicious choice regarding the process's quality. The inability to fully pre-plan the groups, coupled with initial uncertainty about our precise research focus, underscored the necessity for a flexible approach capable of responding swiftly to the unfolding dynamics within the groups and emergent data patterns. This adaptability proved crucial for a thorough examination of group interactions.

Moreover, employing an inductive-abductive methodology enabled my co-researchers to significantly influence the project's direction, more so than if we had adhered strictly to pre-existing theoretical frameworks from the outset. This approach facilitated their engagement in making observations directly, without the prerequisite of extensive theoretical grounding, thereby reducing barriers to their active involvement in the research process.[84]

In fostering relationships within the project, I aimed to empower my co-researchers with considerable influence, though the outcome was mixed in success. The dynamics of power posed significant challenges. On one hand, my deeper investment in and reliance on the project occasionally left me feeling exposed and dependent on my co-researchers' decisions, particularly regarding the convening of groups and my level of access to them.

Conversely, I recognized my own authority in shaping the research's direction, suggesting strategies, and overseeing data collection and analysis. This placed me in a position to assess my co-researchers' contributions, even if this appraisal was "only" supposed to contribute to our joint learning. These assessments implied a

---

[83] Bradbury, introduction to *Handbook of Action Research*, 7–8; Coghlan and Brydon-Miller, "Quality," 2–4; Reason and Torbert, "The Action Turn," 9; Herr and Anderson, "Quality Criteria for Action Research: An Ongoing Conversation," 2–9.

[84] On sensitizing and definite concepts see the section 3.3.1.

vulnerability for my co-researchers, as they navigated their roles within the parameters I established. Despite these complexities emerging in some final evaluations, many of these issues went largely unaddressed, highlighting an area for potential growth and reflection in future endeavors.

I am thus ambivalent about the degree of influence my co-researchers had in the project, especially regarding the claim that I was doing research *with* and not *on* or *about* them. Here I see a difference in various stages of the research process. In my assessment, my co-researchers had significant influence over the overall research orientation, even if they were less involved and interested in the precise formulation of our research questions. My co-researchers also controlled how we designed and facilitated online small groups, including which changes to introduce and test. In the action research framework of this dissertation, I would argue that this constitutes more than simply providing material for academic analysis. The way in which we designed and facilitated our groups was the research, it was the process through which new knowledge was created, and in this sense, the project was based on research *with* my co-researchers.

The learning process extended beyond the immediate interactions within the group, however, with the analysis of materials playing a crucial role both during and after the groups' activities. The nature of analysis differed between these two periods. During the project's duration, I regularly shared my analyses with co-researchers through various formats such as individual meetings, the third joint workshop, and final evaluations. Although I primarily conducted the analysis, this framework enabled co-researchers to affirm or question my interpretations, effectively engaging in a collaborative review process.

Following the project's completion, my analysis ventured further, incorporating previous literature and theoretical frameworks, leading to new layers of understanding that were developed independently of my co-researchers. Consequently, this dissertation reflects, to an extent, *on* the research conducted *with* my co-researchers, marking a transition from collaborative exploration to a more individualized scholarly inquiry.

Navigating the delicate balance between maintaining my co-researchers' integrity and adhering to the research design posed a significant challenge in ensuring process quality. Initially, the plan was for groups to operate concurrently, facilitating inter-group learning through joint workshops. However, it soon became apparent that two of the groups slated for fall 2021 might not commence as scheduled. This situation placed me in a dilemma: to honor my co-researchers' broader professional commitments, potentially leading to a delay or cancellation of these groups, or to assert the research design's needs, possibly pushing co-researchers to an uncomfortable extent. Ultimately, I chose to prioritize respecting my co-researchers' situations, although I am not sure how well that succeeded.

Outcomes

Quality in research not only encompasses the process but also the outcomes it yields. In terms of research outcomes, I look at the contribution the project made to various persons and the actionability of findings, discuss the fit between the research project and local needs and the relationship between this initiative and previous literature on methods and Christian religious education.

Participatory action research is characterized by learning at multiple levels: the individual researcher, the group of involved researchers, and the broader community. The extent of learning across these dimensions signifies the project's quality.[85] As detailed in part 2, my personal insights into online small groups and Christian religious education have been considerable (first person). Assessing the learning impact on my co-researchers is more complex, yet feedback from our concluding evaluations suggests they also experienced growth (second person).[86]

Moreover, I posit that the insights shared in this dissertation could extend its relevance and applicability beyond those directly involved in the project (third person). Importantly, our learnings are not merely theoretical but practical, poised to enhance local practices—a hallmark of quality in action research.[87] Thus, I assert that the outcomes of our research align well with the standards of high quality.

Ensuring quality in research moreover requires a strong alignment between the project's outcomes and the local needs it aims to address. This alignment involves both the scope (quantity) and the significance (quality) of the issues tackled by the research. While research inherently focuses on specific questions, participatory action research emphasizes a comprehensive engagement with the broad spectrum of challenges faced by practitioners. This approach obliges academic researchers to work closely with practitioners, not merely selecting issues based on academic interest but collaboratively identifying a relevant set of concerns for investigation.

---

[85] In action research, this is frequently framed as first, second, and third person learning. See, for example, Reason and Torbert, "The Action Turn."

[86] See also Simon Hallonsten and Jonas Ideström, "Kyrka i digitala rum: Reflektioner från ett forskningsprojekt," *Svensk Kyrkotidning* 117, no. 10 (2021).

[87] Herr and Anderson, "Quality Criteria," 5–6; Herr and Anderson, "Designing the Plane," 8–9, 15–17.

The true measure of quality, therefore, lies in the applicability and appropriateness of the research's learnings and interventions for the practitioners involved. This includes choosing suitable methods to effectively address the identified issues. Thus, the third criterion for assessing quality is determined by the extent to which the research's insights resonate with and are actionable within the local context, ensuring that participatory action research serves not only the academic community but, more importantly, the practitioners and their communities.

Evaluating the fit between the project's focus and local needs, I believe the *Online Small Groups* project maintained good quality. Despite setting the four research tracks before engaging potential co-researchers, the project's initial ambiguity and flexibility enabled significant co-researcher influence on the direction and questions pursued. This adaptability was particularly evident as my co-researchers voluntarily chose to join my research track, indicating a genuine local interest in exploring the dynamics of online small groups and Christian religious education. This proactive selection process by co-researchers ensured that the project remained relevant and responsive to the interests and needs within the local context.

Last, akin to all research endeavors, action research must be grounded in a solid methodological foundation. High-quality projects leverage the collective knowledge surrounding their chosen methodologies, ensuring that the research is informed and deliberate. As Kathryn Herr and Gary Anderson articulate, conducting action research may resemble "designing the plane while flying it," yet it is not flying blind.[88]

This final quality criterion emphasizes the importance of connecting the research not only to the local community but also to the broader scholarly dialogue. High-quality action research contributes to the wider body of knowledge within the research field. In my efforts, I have aimed to meet this standard by aligning my methodology with recognized research practices and integrating insights from the *Online Small Groups* project with existing scholarship on Christian religious education, ensuring that this work not only responds to local interests but also enhances the collective understanding of the subject.

3.4.2 Ethics

In action research, the intertwining of research ethics and process quality is profound, as my interactions with co-researchers were imbued with significant ethical

---

[88] Herr and Anderson, "Designing the Plane," 2.

dimensions. In this section, I expand on the discussion of research ethics by considering essential elements such as the necessity of ethical review, the methods employed for data collection, the process of obtaining informed consent, and the measures taken to safeguard the personal integrity of research participants.

Research involving sensitive personal data, such as religious affiliation or religious views, is subject to a mandatory independent ethical review process in Sweden. The *Online Small Groups* project fully complied with this requirement, having undergone the necessary ethical review.[89]

Ethical considerations significantly influenced our data collection methods. Initially, I planned to record meetings to facilitate detailed conversation analysis. However, after discussing the potential impact on the dynamics of the group process, my co-researchers and I eventually determined that the potential adverse effects recordings might have on participant interaction was not outweighed by the benefits of more granular data. Consequently, we decided to use feedback forms, interviews, observations, and field notes as our primary data collection methods, and refrained from recording individual sessions, except for the final evaluations in the spring groups.

The purpose of informed consent is to guarantee that participants are fully aware of what their involvement entails, including any potential risks, how their personal data will be handled, their rights to amend or delete this data, and their right to withdraw from the study at any time. Essentially, informed consent ensures that participants can make knowledgeable decisions about their participation in the research.

To secure informed consent from participants and co-researchers, I prepared standard research information sheets. For the #S:tEskils, #Margareta, and #Djursholm groups, my co-researchers distributed these sheets to the participants. In contrast, I sent out the information sheets to participants in the #Älvsjö group and to the co-researchers themselves. This process ensured clarity and transparency, and provided participants with the opportunity to ask any questions they had about the research before data collection commenced.

I discussed with my co-researchers the timing and method for obtaining signed consent forms. They expressed concerns that requiring participants to sign forms before the groups commenced might discourage participation. Given the evolving nature of our research, this posed additional challenges. Initially, for the #S:tEskils and #Margareta groups, we planned to gather data via feedback forms.[90]

---

[89] See appendix A.
[90] See appendix B.

Recognizing that there is no mandated format for recording informed consent, we opted to integrate a consent query at the beginning of the form. Later, as our data collection method shifted to participant observation, my co-leaders secured verbal consent from the groups before I joined the sessions.

Obtaining signed consent forms was further complicated by the fact that participants never met onsite. For the Älvsjö group, consent was documented at the time of signing up for the group. Participants in Djursholm Parish initially did not sign consent forms. Later efforts to secure consent through emailed and mailed forms met with incomplete responses, as not all participants replied.

Despite challenges with consent form logistics, I am confident that all participants were adequately informed and gave their informed consent. They received all necessary information well in advance, were fully briefed on the nature of the research, and understood the potential implications of their involvement. This confidence is bolstered by instances where participants referenced the information sheets during discussions, particularly concerning the protection of their personal integrity, indicating their awareness and comprehension of the research details.

A crucial ethical issue was how to accurately represent my co-researchers and group participants in the written text. I aimed to strike a balance between protecting them from public exposure and allowing them the opportunity to validate or contest my narrative. This balance was essential for fostering an environment conducive to experimentation, where our exploratory efforts often involved trial and error. It was important not to directly associate individuals with specific failures or learning moments, to avoid undue repercussions. Concurrently, it was necessary to maintain sufficient detail in the narrative to enable co-researchers and participants to credibly challenge or corroborate my descriptions, thereby grounding the research in our collective experience.

It was also significant for me to allow co-researchers the option to claim ownership of the text by using their real names. To accommodate this, I included a provision in the research protocol allowing group leaders to be identified by their actual names, contingent upon their consent and after they had reviewed the text prior to publication. This approach aimed to respect their preferences and ensure their active involvement in how they are represented in the final document.

Only when preparing to send drafts of the dissertation to my co-researchers, together with a list of excerpts specifically pertaining to them, did I consider allowing group participants the option to use their real names as well. Consequently, I emailed both co-researchers and all participants these drafts and excerpts, giving them the opportunity to review the text. This process provided ample time for them to make an informed decision regarding the use of their real names and to offer feedback on how they were represented.

All responses from the co-leaders indicated a preference for using their real names. Many participants also expressed a desire to be identified by their real names in the dissertation. However, some participants had reservations and referred to the information sheet, which outlined commitments to protect their personal integrity by pseudonymizing names. To honor this initial agreement and ensure uniformity in respecting privacy concerns, I decided to pseudonymize the names of all co-researchers, participants, and parishes involved in the study.

My impression was that most of the group leaders and participants focused primarily on the excerpts specifically pertaining to them rather than the complete dissertation draft. The feedback I received was generally positive, though some participants did email critiques concerning how they were portrayed. I made revisions to the manuscript based on their input, as these changes, while important for accuracy and fairness, did not alter the overall narrative of the research.

I invited the group leaders to meet and discuss the dissertation draft. Three of them were able to attend these meetings. During our discussions, they expressed appreciation for the work and provided minor critiques related to factual inaccuracies, such as incorrect times and dates, along with some general comments on the writing. I took their feedback into account and incorporated it into a subsequent revision of the document to ensure accuracy and clarity.

During one of these meetings, a discussion about the inability to use real names led to a creative solution. One co-researcher offered to write a short response detailing her experiences with the project. This response, although published under the pseudonym "Karin Andersson," provided her with an opportunity to share her perspective. Inspired by this, I invited the other group leaders to contribute their reflections, and one more leader took up the offer. These two responses are included in part 2 of the dissertation, enriching the narrative with diverse perspectives from those directly involved.

3.4.3 Reflexivity

Reflexivity is now a recognized standard for quality in social science, action research, and practical theology.[91] To meet this standard, particularly in the United

---

[91] See for example Lincoln, Lynham, and Guba, "Paradigmatic Controversies," 246–24; Bradbury, *Action Research for Transformations*, 55–56; Coghlan and Brydon-Miller, "Quality," 4–6; Judi Marshall and Peter Reason, "Quality in Research as 'Taking an Attitude of Inquiry',"

Kingdom, researchers often include detailed personal prologues or vignettes that explain their intentions and motivations.[92] However, Tone Stangeland Kaufman argues that reflexivity should be viewed not merely as a snapshot of a researcher's social position but as a continuous and integral part of the entire research process.[93] This perspective aligns closely with action researchers like Peter Reason and William Torbert, and David Coghlan, who promote the inclusion of a first-person perspective throughout the research process.[94]

Drawing on Suzanne Collins's *Hunger Games* novels, Stangeland Kaufman likens researchers to gamemakers, who navigate a series of small and large decisions throughout the research design and process. She emphasizes that these decisions have no natural or self-evident outcomes; rather, each choice reflects a normative judgment, influenced by the researcher's subjective preferences for certain results. This framework underscores that research is fundamentally a succession of value-laden decisions. These values, shaped by the researcher's interpretation of the current context and the perceived needs of churches, societies, and academic communities, guide the researcher in crafting a specific piece of research.[95]

While Stangeland Kaufman firmly believes that researchers inevitably act as gamemakers, she advocates for them to be *responsible* in their roles. According to her, this responsibility involves transparency regarding their "assumptions, location,

---

Management Research News 30, no. 5 (2007): 368–80 at 369; Graham, "Action Research," 156; Goto, *Taking on Practical Theology*, 174–79; Jaco S. Dreyer, "Knowledge, Subjectivity, (De)Coloniality, and the Conundrum of Reflexivity," in *Conundrums in Practical Theology*, ed. Bonnie J. Miller-McLemore and Joyce Ann Mercer (Leiden; Boston: Brill, 2016), 90–109.

[92] See for example, Bennett et al., *Invitation to Research*, 12–28; Watkins, *Disclosing Church*, 17–25; Boyd, *The Naked Preacher*, xxiii-xxiv.

[93] Tone Stangeland Kaufman, "Normativity as Pitfall or Ally? Reflexivity as an Interpretive Resource in Ecclesiological and Ethnographic Research," *Ecclesial Practices* 2, no. 1 (2015): 91–107 at 92–93; Stangeland Kaufman, "From the Outside," 136–40; Tone Stangeland Kaufman, "The Researcher as Gamemaker: Teaching Normative Dimensions in Various Phases of Empirical Practical Theological Research," in *Qualitative Research in Theological Education: Pedagogy in Practice*, ed. Mary Clark Moschella and Susan Willhauck (London: SCM Press, 2018), 169–84 at 173–74.

[94] Stangeland Kaufman, "Normativity," 92–93; Stangeland Kaufman, "From the Outside," 136–40; Stangeland Kaufman, "Gamemaker," 173–74; Reason and Torbert, "The Action Turn," 17; David Coghlan, "Authenticity as First Person Practice: An Exploration Based on Bernard Lonergan," *Action Research* 6, no. 3 (2008): 351–66 at 352–53. For a concise discussion about reflexivity and action research see Coghlan and Brydon-Miller, "Quality," 6.

[95] Stangeland Kaufman, "Gamemaker," 173–74.

and pre-understanding." [96] Additionally, responsible researchers should clearly document their choices throughout the research process and provide justifications for these decisions. This approach mirrors Herr and Anderson's emphasis on "a close account of the research process and the reasoning behind the methodological decisions made."[97]

Reflexivity manifests in several forms within research. Initially, it involves a rigorous self-examination and maintaining transparency about how a researcher's assumptions, location, cultural context, and pre-understandings shape the research design and process. Second, reflexivity entails a persistent reflection on the self-in-relation throughout the research process, akin to maintaining an inquisitive focus on both oneself and others. Last, reflexivity includes recognizing first-person learning—acknowledging the transformative effect of research on researchers themselves and the insights gained that may extend beyond the primary research topic.

I have previously explored the first aspect of reflexivity in discussing the emergent design of the *Online Small Groups* project and will revisit this theme in my discussions on writing, aiming to critically reflect on how my assumptions, location, and preunderstanding have influenced the research. The other two aspects of reflexivity is woven throughout my account in part 2 of the dissertation, which consists of a reflexive narrative from our *Online Small Groups* project, where I also detail various learnings.

3.5 "Writing" an Action Research Project

Participatory action research fundamentally emphasizes research conducted *by* or *with* practitioners. [98] This approach inherently fosters the co-creation of knowledge through collaboration, raising significant challenges in terms of representation—specifically, how to reflect the collaborative nature of knowledge creation within a text authored by an individual researcher.[99]

The primary concern here is to balance the authorial authority of the single researcher with the collective authority of all contributors, addressing the risk that collaboratively produced knowledge could be appropriated or disproportionately influenced by the singular perspective of the author, potentially overshadowing the voices of others.

---

[96] Stangeland Kaufman, "Gamemaker," 174.
[97] Herr and Anderson, "Designing the Plane," 8.
[98] Bradbury, introduction to *Handbook of Action Research*.
[99] Lenette, *Ethics and Decolonization*, 2–3.

I thus join the ranks of action researchers who are wary of objectifying individuals by converting their experiences into mere data for academic scrutiny, particularly when it offers no direct benefit to the subjects involved.[100] Consequently, I advocate that the narrative of an action research project should transcend a mere dialogue between the author and the reader *about* practitioner researchers. Instead, it should foster an inclusive conversation *with*—and ideally *among*—all participating researchers.

Fundamentally, questions of representation in participatory action research are grounded in the ethical belief that textual accounts of such projects should mirror their collaborative nature. This involves selecting a writing style that effectively conveys this particular approach to knowledge creation.[101] The ethical imperative to include diverse voices arises from the conviction that the contributions of each researcher in a collaborative endeavor must be acknowledged and not merely appropriated by the report's author.[102] At its core, this requires a commitment to honor and accurately represent the insights of all researchers involved.[103]

In practice, I discovered that honoring the knowledge of all involved researchers was more challenging than anticipated. In an early draft, I attempted to represent our varied perspectives through a collage of quotes, intended as a "chorus of voices." However, critiques quickly emerged that this approach did not adequately address the issue of representation. Despite my intentions, it was still I who selected and arranged the quotes, effectively narrating the story using fragments of others' voices. This realization compelled me to reevaluate and engage with the complexities of writing and representation.

---

[100] Yvonna S. Lincoln, "Ethical Practices in Qualitative Research," in *The Handbook of Social Research Ethics*, ed. Donna M. Mertens and Pauline E. Ginsberg (Thousand Oaks: SAGE Publications, Inc., 2009), 150–69 at 152–53; Mary Brydon-Miller, "Ethics and Action Research: Deepening our Commitment to Principles of Social Justice and Redefining Systems of Democratic Practice," in *The SAGE Handbook of Action Research: Participative Inquiry and Practice*, ed. Peter Reason and Hilary Bradbury (London: SAGE Publications, 2008), 199–210.

[101] Judi Marshall, "Finding Form in Writing for Action Research," in *The SAGE Handbook of Action Research: Participative Inquiry and Practice*, ed. Peter Reason and Hilary Bradbury (London: SAGE Publications, 2008), 682–94 at 685–86.

[102] Miranda Snoeren, Theo Niessen, and Tineke Abma, "Engagement Enacted: Essentials of Initiating an Action Research Project," *Action Research* 10, no. 2 (2012): 189–204 at 201–02.

[103] Grant, Nelson, and Mitchell, "Negotiating the Challenges," 598.

3.5.1 Writing as Analysis

Clifford Geertz highlighted the issue of representation in ethnography in his 1973 work, *The Interpretation of Cultures*, by posing the question, "What does the ethnographer do?" His response, "He writes," emphasized that ethnography is fundamentally the inscription of cultural discourse.[104] For Geertz, the act of writing is inherently an act of interpretation—a process of conjecturing meanings.[105] Consequently, the texts produced by ethnographers are not simply reflections of truth but are "fictions, in the sense that they are 'something made,' 'something fashioned'—the original meaning of *fictiō*."[106]

These ideas were further elaborated in the 1986 landmark volume *Writing Culture*. James Clifford, in the introduction, contends that "ethnographic truths are inherently *partial*—committed and incomplete."[107] He challenges the traditional metaphor that likens reading culture to observing a stable, unchanging fact. Instead, Clifford argues that culture is a dynamic process best understood through interpretation and representation—essentially, through writing.[108] This shift highlights the active role of the ethnographer in constructing cultural representations, rather than merely documenting objective truths. Writing is then more than documentation; it is a process of analysis.

One way to understand writing as a method for analysis is to recognize it as a technology that significantly influences human thought processes. Walter Ong posits that writing detaches language from its author and establishes a "context-free" language, allowing authors to view their own thoughts as external entities.[109] This detachment enables individuals to manage greater volumes of data and complexity and offers a unique means to critically evaluate their thoughts.[110] The act of writing and revising facilitates a specific kind of thinking and analysis, making

---

[104] Clifford Geertz, *The Interpretation of Cultures: Selected Essays*, ed. Robert Darnton, 3rd ed. (New York: Basic Books, 2017), 22.

[105] Geertz, *Interpretation of Cultures*, 17.

[106] Geertz, *Interpretation of Cultures*, 17.

[107] Clifford and Marcus, *Writing Culture*, 7. Emphasis in original.

[108] Clifford and Marcus, *Writing Culture*, 11–12. Geertz made the same point with his concept of "thick description," arguing that any description needs to incorporate cultural interpretation. Geertz, *Interpretation of Cultures*, 18.

[109] Walter J. Ong, *Orality and Literacy: The Technologizing of the Word*, 30th ed. (Abingdon, Oxon: Routledge, 2012), 77–78.

[110] Ong, *Orality and Literacy*, 102–07.

these processes both possible and inevitable. However, Ong notes that the profound impact of writing on thought often goes unrecognized in literate cultures.[111]

One of the important consequences of Geertz's, Clifford's, and Ong's treatment of writing is then the recognition that all ethnographic writing entails analysis. Writing is never the depiction of social reality in language, but always a process of meaning-making, of evaluating the relevance of observations to decide on what should be included and what should be excluded from a text, and the ordering of textual elements to produce a coherent narrative.

As a method of analysis, writing differs from other methods such as coding. Laurel Richardson argues that all writing inherently relies on a narrative structure, which creates meaning by causally and contextually connecting smaller units into a coherent whole.[112] Jack Hart echoes this by defining a story as the deliberate arrangement of material to demonstrate an unfolding causal pattern, allowing larger meanings to surface. Similarly, Janet Burroway differentiates between "story" and "plot."

> A story is a series of events recorded in their chronological order. A plot is a series of events deliberately arranged so as to reveal their dramatic, thematic, and emotional significance. A story gives us only "what happened next," whereas plot's concern is what, how, and why, with scenes ordered to highlight the workings of cause and effect.[113]

Writing transforms a chronicle of events into a plot. This process of contextual meaning-making does not seek to establish universal truths but rather analyzes how events and actions drive the development of specific situations.

Similarly, Hoi F. Cheu understands storytelling as a narrative approach that redefines the depiction of non-repeatable, complex experiences.[114] This deliberate arrangement of events highlights their significance and establishes causal relationships, illustrating how one action precipitates another. Cheu contends that this strategic selection and sequencing of events effectively simplifies complexity, thereby facilitating communication and enhancing our understanding of experiences.[115]

---

[111] Ong, *Orality and Literacy*, 80.

[112] Richardson, *Writing Strategies*, 10–13.

[113] Janet Burroway, Elizabeth Stuckey-French, and Ned Stuckey-French, *Writing Fiction: A Guide to Narrative Craft*, ed. 10th (Chicago: University of Chicago Press, 2019), 142.

[114] Hoi F. Cheu, "Stories as a Scientific Method in Art-Based Health Research," *Journal of Applied Arts & Health* 8, no. 2 (2017): 209–24 at 211. I introduced the concept of rescription in section 3.3.4.

[115] Cheu, "Stories," 212.

Narrative thus transcends mere communication; it is equally about creating meaning. Cheu refers to this as "fictionalization," which he describes as "the extra step from organizing people's stories to theorizing and synthesizing a model for understanding."[116] Fictionalization, therefore, is not about creating fabrications but is a process of abstraction, analysis, and theorization. This process amalgamates disparate elements into a unified whole. In this way, the narrator reconstructs a plot from story elements, communicating real-life events through a fictional lens. Thus, narrative is recognized as a sophisticated method of analysis, not merely an alternative form of presentation.[117]

Laurel Richardson emphasizes that most science writing is inherently engaged in these processes of analysis and meaning-making, crafting coherent narratives that elucidate the dynamics and consequences of observed phenomena.[118] The difference is then not whether or not researchers employ writing as a method of analysis, but in the extent to which it is intentionally employed, which significantly impacts the writing process.

In contrast, Elizabeth Adams St. Pierre asserts that "postmodern" writing, seen as a method of inquiry, diverges from traditional interpretative qualitative inquiry. Drawing on Hubert L. Dreyfus and Paul Rabinow, and Gayatri Chakravorty Spivak, she argues that conventional qualitative research aims to accurately interpret a profound truth existing independently.[119] Success in such research depends on achieving correct interpretations and being reflexive about the researcher's influence on these interpretations.[120] In contrast, postmodern writing focuses on the creation of meaning rather than the discovery of an external truth.[121] This approach has become prominent in ethnography, leading to an extensive discussion among anthropologists and other social scientists about their writing practices.[122]

---

[116] Cheu, "Stories," 215–16.

[117] Cheu, "Stories," 216–17; Richardson and Adams St. Pierre, "Writing."

[118] Richardson, *Writing Strategies*, 11–12.

[119] Richardson and Adams St. Pierre, "Writing," 1425.

[120] Reflexivity denotes the processes through which researchers try to fathom the degree to which their research is influenced by themselves and has become a standard demand in social sciences today. See for example Alvesson and Sköldberg, *Reflexive Methodology*.

[121] Richardson and Adams St. Pierre, "Writing," 1424–26.

[122] Carolyn Ellis and Arthur P. Bochner, eds., *Composing Ethnography: Alternative Forms of Qualitative Writing* (Walnut Creek: AltaMira Press, 1996); Nina Lykke, ed., *Writing Academic Texts Differently: Intersectional Feminist Methodologies and the Playful Art of Writing* (New York: Routledge, 2014); Ghodsee, *From Notes to Narrative*; Helena Wulff, ed., *The*

While there is an apparent contrast between acknowledging that most forms of science writing are indeed employing writing as a method of analysis and postulating that there are two distinct approaches to writing, I understand Richardson and Adams St. Pierre to be largely in agreement with each other.[123] That is, while most writing functions as a form of analysis, it is not always employed so explicitly, which establishes different types of writing, even as authors do not consciously choose a specific style of writing.

The conscious narrative or "postmodern" style is also emerging within practical theology, although it is still relatively undeveloped in Scandinavia. Heather Walton has been a pioneering figure in this area, utilizing diverse genres such as life writing, journals, and autoethnographies, and grounding them in theological, philosophical, and methodological considerations.[124]

Walton anchors theological reflection in the textures of everyday life, crafting a theology that resonates with the altered socioreligious context of contemporary society and addresses the destructive historical uses of theology.[125] Rather than striving to transcend these realities, Walton embraces them, advocating for a theopoetics that scavenges amidst the "ruins" to discover what can nourish life. She envisions the theologian as a poet navigating between beauty and devastation, not through a linear journey but as an existence amidst constant transformation.[126]

Walton is joined by Natalie Wigg-Stevenson in these exploratory efforts. Wigg-Stevenson has effectively connected the crisis of representation found in ethnography with theological discourse.[127] In her scholarship, she increasingly merges

---

Anthropologist as Writer: Genres and Contexts in the Twenty-First Century (New York: Berghahn Books, 2016).

[123] Richardson and Adams St. Pierre, "Writing."

[124] Heather Walton, "Passion and Pain: Conceiving Theology out of Infertility," *Contact* 130, no. 1 (1999): 3–9; Heather Walton, "The Course Outline: Teaching Theology through Creative Writing," *Journal of Adult Theological Education* 9, no. 2 (2012): 210–18; Walton, *Writing Methods*; Walton, *Not Eden*; Heather Walton, "We Have Never Been Theologians: Postsecularism and Practical Theology," *Practical Theology* 11, no. 3 (2018): 218–30; Heather Walton, "Creativity at the Edge of Chaos: Theopoetics in a Blazing World," *Literature & Theology* 33, no. 3 (2019): 336–56; Heather Walton, "A Theopoetics of Practice: Re-forming in Practical Theology," *International Journal of Practical Theology* 23, no. 1 (2019): 3–23.

[125] Heather Walton, "A Theopoetics in Ruins," *Toronto Journal of Theology* 36, no. 2 (2020): 159–69 at 160–61.

[126] Walton, "Theopoetics in Ruins," 168.

[127] Natalie Wigg-Stevenson, "From Proclamation to Conversation: Ethnographic Disruptions to Theological Normativity," *Palgrave Communications* 1, no. 1 (2015): 1–9; Natalie

various genres, incorporating elements of performance art, scholarly prose, and autoethnographic insights.[128] Together with Kristy Nabhan-Warren, Wigg-Stevenson urges ethnographic theologians to deeply consider how to authentically and adequately represent the social and ecclesial realities they document.[129]

Other noteworthy contributions in this vein include Pamela Couture's creative non-fiction exploration of the peacebuilding efforts of the Luba people in the Democratic Republic of Congo from 1996 to 2004, Todd Whitmore's detailed narrative of conflict and post-conflict situations in northern Uganda and South Sudan from 2005 to 2013, Nicola Slee's feminist practical theology, and Maria Liu Wong's examination of theological education.[130] Despite their thematic diversity, each of these works employs literary techniques to delve into, understand, and elucidate their respective subjects.

3.5.2 Writing as Communication

As previously mentioned, action research typically occurs *in situ*, making it inherently local. The knowledge it produces is intended "for me" and "for us."[131] However, the output of this research ultimately becomes public knowledge. Consequently, like all researchers, those conducting action research must consider how to expand the reach of their findings, addressing how local insights can be extended to benefit others in different locations and contexts.

A prevalent method for expanding the scope of qualitative research involves the use of case studies, which explicitly—or implicitly—represent a small segment of a broader class. This approach allows detailed knowledge of the specific cases to inform understanding of the larger class.[132] Crucially, the effectiveness of this

---

Wigg-Stevenson, "Trying to Tell the Truth About a Life: The Problem of Representation for Ethnographic Theology," in *What Really Matters: Scandinavian Perspectives on Ecclesiology and Ethnography*, ed. Jonas Ideström and Tone Stangeland Kaufman (Eugene: Pickwick Publications, 2018), 183–99; Wigg-Stevenson, "Really Going On"; Wigg-Stevenson, *Transgressive Devotion*, 119–25; Nabhan-Warren and Wigg-Stevenson, "Crisis of Representation."

[128] Wigg-Stevenson, *Transgressive Devotion*.

[129] Nabhan-Warren and Wigg-Stevenson, "Crisis of Representation."

[130] Couture, *Not All Victims*; Whitmore, *Imitating Christ*; Slee, *Fragments*; Liu Wong, *Becoming Wise*.

[131] Peter Reason and Judi Marshall argued that action research is for three audiences, "for them," "for us," and "for me." Reason and Marshall, "Research as Personal Process," 112–13.

[132] Bent Flyvbjerg, "Five Misunderstandings about Case Study Research," *Qualitative Inquiry* 12, no. 2 (2006): 219–45 at 220.

generalization depends on the strategic selection of cases, ensuring that the relationship between the specific case and the broader class supports plausible and convincing generalizations.[133]

However, in participatory action research, "cases" are often not selected with strategic consideration for their relevance to a broader class. Indeed, action researchers Bjørn Gustavsen, Agneta Hansson, and Thoralf U. Qvale contend that action research methodologies are generally ill-suited for case study designs.[134] Concurring with Gustavsen, Hansson, and Qvale, I propose that reflective narrative is a more effective method for expanding the scope of action research, an insight I take from Laurel Richardson's reasoning on the functioning of research outputs.

Richardson asserts that the meaning of qualitative research is conveyed throughout the entire text. She believes that research results are delivered through the act of reading, guiding the reader on a mental journey from the first to the last page. According to Richardson, qualitative research findings should not be viewed as mere data to be extracted but rather as a coherent narrative that unfolds. She emphasizes that if the essence of the text emerges through its reading, it is crucial to write in a manner that captivates and engages the reader.[135]

Here, reflective narrative serves as a means to select, organize, and communicate key aspects of experience in a way that entices readers to engage with the developments outlined in the text. As readers journey alongside the author, they participate in the learning process, enabling them to recognize parallels between their circumstances and those depicted in the text. This identification facilitates the application of the text's insights to their contexts, effectively broadening the research's scope.

Richardson refers to this style as CAP (creative analytical processes) ethnographies. CAP accounts typically blend fact and fiction, cross literary genres, and reveal the fusion of the writing process with the written product. Richardson asserts that "CAP ethnographies are not alternative or experimental; they are, in and of themselves, valid and desirable representations of the social," even though they may challenge traditional academic norms.[136]

Mirroring James Clifford's introduction to *Writing Culture,* Richardson underscores that all social scientific writing is a sociohistorical construct and thus

---

[133] Flyvbjerg, "Five Misunderstandings," 221–24.

[134] Gustavsen, Hansson, and Qvale, "Challenge of Scope."

[135] Richardson and Adams St. Pierre, "Writing," 1411.

[136] Richardson and Adams St. Pierre, "Writing," 1412.

subject to change. There is nothing inherently fixed about academic writing styles, including those in practical theology. Embracing a postmodern view on the relativity of truth claims, Richardson contends that alternative writing styles are not less scientific or objective; they simply represent a different approach.[137]

Mirroring Adams St. Pierre's discussion, Richardson argues that one significant distinction between interpretative qualitative writing and creative analytical writing lies in their treatment of author authority. Interpretative qualitative writing aims to establish the author's authority through style, form, the use of references and quotations, and demonstrating reflexivity. This form of writing seeks to persuade the reader that its interpretations are both reliable and accurate.[138]

Conversely, creative analytical writing also attempts to establish author authority but goes further by deconstructing it. It employs creative writing techniques that highlight the text's constructed nature and its inherent partiality, challenging the traditional notion of authoritative narrative.[139]

The intention of the text also varies significantly between interpretative qualitative writing and creative analytical writing. Interpretative qualitative writing aims to communicate specific results, focusing primarily on conveying a particular interpretation of a slice of social reality, and is generally structured like a research report. In contrast, creative analytical writing is less about communicating fixed results and more about facilitating learning and meaning-making through narrative.[140] Thus, the primary concern of CAP ethnographies is not the factual accuracy of the narrative but whether it enhances understanding and stimulates intellectual engagement.[141]

While CAP ethnographies blend elements of both fiction and fact, they do not cross into pure fiction, however. As Richardson delineates, the distinction lies in

---

[137] Richardson and Adams St. Pierre, "Writing," 1411–13.

[138] Richardson and Adams St. Pierre, "Writing," 1412–13.

[139] Richardson and Adams St. Pierre, "Writing," 1413.

[140] Richardson does not use the term "learning" but her request that CAP ethnographies show *impact* goes in the same direction. Richardson and Adams St. Pierre, "Writing," 1418. While not a direct proponent of CAP ethnographies, Bent Flyvbjerg equally argues for storytelling as an effective way to communicate complex social realities. Flyvbjerg notes that in the case of stories told about dense case studies, the "case stories written like this can neither be briefly recounted nor summarized in a few main results. The case story is itself the result. It is a 'virtual reality,' so to speak." Flyvbjerg, "Five Misunderstandings," 238.

[141] Richardson and Adams St. Pierre, "Writing," 1414–17.

the claims made by the author about the text's basis in reality. Creative non-fiction and science writing assert their foundations in actual events.[142]

To communicate research results, I embrace this postmodern approach to research writing, aligning with Richardson's creative analytical writing style. Specifically, I utilize creative non-fiction to "fictionalize" my experiences, in line with Geertz and Cheu's definitions. However, the reflective narrative is fictional only in the sense of "something made" and not in the sense of "something made up."[143] As I claim the narrative as reflective of reality, accuracy is crucial. Events and people are depicted based on real occurrences and the narrative aims to convey these experiences faithfully. The "fictional" account thus contains so much realism that those who experienced the events firsthand can recognize and potentially contest the portrayal, anchoring the narrative firmly within a broader social reality.

This writing style further highlights the partiality of my narrative, not only constructing but also questioning narrator authority, emphasizing that this narrative is just one of many possible interpretations of our collective experiences. Instead of establishing a "chorus of voices" and suggesting that it would be an objective depiction of our experiences, I thus turn to a more subjective account, emphasizing that the reflective narrative is *my* interpretation of events. This approach does not imply that the interpretation is incorrect; rather, it remains inherently partial, engaged, and unfinished—characteristics inherent to all qualitative research. Therefore, my recounting of our journey introduces multiple layers of interpretation, aligning with Clifford Geertz's notion of providing a "thick description."[144]

Narrative is not a cure-all. As Cheu notes, the symbolic presentation of meaning in stories introduces a layer of abstraction that demands more intricate interpretation compared to other forms of research writing. Additionally, Cheu questions the role of aesthetics, noting that while aesthetics can enrich narratives, skilled narrators might use aesthetic elements to overshadow underlying tensions or issues within the story.[145] In other words, narrative does not inherently invite scrutiny or highlight its own biases; instead, it can obscure them, potentially hindering critical engagement with the content. Thus, storytelling, like any other form of research writing, must adhere to ethical standards—it is not inherently

---

[142] Richardson and Adams St. Pierre, "Writing," 1412–13.
[143] Geertz, *Interpretation of Cultures*, 17.
[144] Geertz, *Interpretation of Cultures*, 10–18.
[145] Cheu, "Stories," 216–17.

ethical but requires ethical consideration in its execution.[146] These considerations relate to issues of representation as explored above, but also to the way in which narrative is constructed, as I discuss below.[147]

This being said, I argue that reflective narrative is an effective method to broaden the scope and extrapolate from the local context of the *Online Small Groups* project. First, narrative adeptly handles the project's particularities without necessitating alignment with a broader category. Second, it facilitates the effective communication of research findings by inviting readers to embark on a learning journey alongside me. Third, storytelling can address some of the ethical dilemmas associated with conveying a participatory action research project, allowing me to narrate our experiences as I interpret them, without presenting a definitive or "true" version of events.

3.5.3 How I Tell My Story

There are, of course, many ways to tell a story, and I faced several decisions while crafting the account for part 2. In this section, I explain the rationale behind each decision.

First, I considered the degree of narrativity for the story. Storytelling can range from brief anecdotes to full-fledged fiction.[148] I sought a balance between providing an engaging narrative and the necessity to explain and contextualize this narrative. While an anecdote serves well as an illustration of a broader point, it cannot stand alone. I aimed to present the entire story, allowing readers to form their own judgments.[149] Presenting the *Online Small Groups* as a cohesive story also offered the advantage of analyzing the project as a whole rather than as isolated instances of learning.

This led to the second decision: whether to present the *Online Small Groups* as a single story or as a series of stories. As I said above, each group can be understood as one action research cycle, potentially meriting its own narrative.

---

[146] Heather Walton, "When Love is Not True: Literature and Theology after Romance," in *Literature and Theology: New Interdisciplinary Spaces*, ed. Heather Walton (London: Routledge, 2011), 37–54.

[147] See sections 3.4.2 and 3.5.3.

[148] Jack Hart, *Storycraft: The Complete Guide to Writing Narrative Nonfiction*, Second ed. (Chicago: University of Chicago Press, 2021), 3.

[149] I acknowledge that this is impossible since the story is already an interpretation and thus colored by my reflections. Still, having a larger story piece allows readers to make meaning from that story without me telling them how to do so. In a sense, this is then simply an attempt to "show don't tell."

However, I aimed to explore how insights were transferred between groups, leading me to choose a unified story format, presented chronologically through the structure of a journal. The basic genre and writing conventions are thus those of a reflective research journal.[150]

Choosing to narrate a single, coherent story led me to adopt my own perspective as the lead character. Being the only participant consistently involved in all facets of the project, it was logical for the narrative to follow my experiences. Consequently, I occupy considerable space within our story, reflecting my increasingly prominent role in the project, going from "initiator" of the research to "leader" of online small groups.

However, this approach should not be mistaken for strict autoethnography, which typically centers on the researcher's personal experiences to analyze broader social phenomena.[151] While the *Online Small Groups* project included elements reflective of my personal insights, the primary focus remained on our collective experiences, shared and deliberated through dialogue. Therefore, while the first-person perspective may bear resemblances to autoethnographic methods, it does not constitute an autoethnography in the strict sense.

In composing part 2, I frequently referred to both the collected material—such as feedback form answers, interview and field notes, and research plans—and my theoretical frameworks. Some entries are edited versions of field notes or reflection notes penned during the group meetings. Others are reconstructions of pertinent meetings related to the project. Throughout the drafting process, my decisions on what to include were guided by the anticipated discussions in parts 3 and 4. Therefore, the approach to writing was abductive, building a narrative that intertwined data and theory dynamically as previously discussed.

Throughout the writing of part 2, I endeavored to keep my descriptions closely aligned with the actual material. It was important for me to ensure the narrative remained sufficiently faithful to real events. All events have occurred on the dates given in part 2, as can be seen from appendix C. Descriptions of these events are

---

[150] Walton, *Writing Methods*, 45–50.

[151] Gabrielle Gwyther and Alphia Possamai-Inesedy, "Methodologies à la Carte: An Examination of Emerging Qualitative Methodologies in Social Research," *International Journal of Social Research Methodology* 12, no. 2 (2009): 99–115; Sarah Stahlke Wall, "Toward a Moderate Autoethnography," *International Journal of Qualitative Methods* 15, no. 1 (2016): 1–9; Walton, *Writing Methods*. For an example see Cathy Ross and James Butler, "Encountering Our Own Whiteness: An Autoethnographic Conversation on the Experience of Putting Together a Journal Issue around Mission, Race and Colonialism," *Practical Theology* 15, no. 1–2 (2022): 148–59; Liu Wong, *Becoming Wise*.

kept close to my fieldnotes and recollections, except the description of persons. The latter follows from the need to protect their identities, as explained. However, alterations are small, mainly relating to appearances. I have thus kept gender ratios and the age composition in all groups. Dialogue is generally recreated from notes and material rather than direct quotes. I thus anticipate that individuals who were present during the described events will recognize both themselves and others, thus enabling them to affirm or challenge my account as needed.

One of the ethical dilemmas I faced in composing the narrative was what to include. I found this particularly challenging concerning episodes that had an impact on the research process, but which I judged too personal. Indeed, I included the entries from November 29, 2021, and January 14, 2021, which speak about terrible events in other people's lives, only after being prompted to do so by those affected. I have also excluded episodes that affected the research process and may reflect negatively on involved persons when these effects remained minor in light of the project as a whole.

A related tension surfaced in relation to aesthetics. I have tried to write the reflective narrative in an engaging way, but tried to avoid undue use of tensions to explore our learnings, especially resisting the temptation to create an alliance between the narrator and the reader over and against other research participants. Instead, I attempted to highlight the partiality and incompleteness of my account throughout.

Hashtagging

As previously noted, writing serves both as a method of analysis and as a means of communicating research findings. In part 2, I introduce an additional layer of analysis by assigning hashtags to the journal entries. These hashtags group related entries and provide a convenient means to link discussions back to specific experiences detailed in part 2, functioning similarly to in vitro codes.[152] An index of hashtags is provided in the back matter to list and clarify all tags used.

Hashtags serve multiple purposes. First, they facilitate tracking the narrative within any specific group; by searching for the group or parish hashtag, one can easily trace the developments within each of the four groups. Second, hashtags introduce a preliminary layer of analysis and interpretation by highlighting the themes around which entries are organized. While readers are encouraged to explore meaning beyond what the hashtags suggest, these tags offer initial insights

---

[152] Alvesson and Sköldberg, *Reflexive Methodology*, 79–85.

into the significance I attribute to each entry, providing guidance in navigating the complex themes of online small group research.

Last, I consistently use hashtags to reference the narrative in part 2. In my subsequent analyses and discussions, these hashtags link directly to our experiences, enabling readers to swiftly move between reflective commentary and corresponding narrative segments. I hope that this method enhances the reader's ability to engage with and navigate through the varied dimensions of our project's story.

3.6 Summary and Reflections

In this chapter, I have outlined my rationale for the methodologies adopted and methods implemented both within the *Online Small Groups* project and throughout the writing of this dissertation. While there is a clear linkage between the project execution and the subsequent analytical reflection and writing, I recognize them as distinct processes. Reflection and writing thus transcend mere reporting of findings; they are analytical and, in some respects, creative activities that contribute additional layers of interpretation to the research.

A pivotal aspect of the research project's evolution was my endeavor to conduct research collaboratively with my co-researchers. Although I assess this collaboration as only partially successful, it prompted me to adopt an emergent design where the research questions, data collection methods, researcher positionality, and theoretical frameworks evolved dynamically. This approach facilitated the needed responsiveness to the fluid dynamics of our online small groups, especially in the situation of the COVID-19 pandemic, albeit with the drawback that some decisions were made rather ad-hoc.

Notably, the sequential running of groups—two at a time instead of concurrently—significantly influenced the research design and its quality, as it hindered joint reflective sessions among group leaders. Another consequence was that I became the only person who participated in all parts of the project, which accentuated my role, especially since I co-led the spring groups.

Nevertheless, I consider the quality of our research project fully satisfactory. Although a parallel group design might have been more effective, the sequential format enabled us to incorporate insights from the fall groups into the spring sessions. Although I did not initially intend to place myself at the forefront of the project or this dissertation, this positioning has not, in my view, detrimentally affected the overall research quality. Being centrally involved in all facets of the project provided me with a comprehensive understanding of the various groups and the challenges of group leadership, which has been advantageous in my subsequent reflections on our group interactions. It could be perceived as problematic from a collaborative perspective between academic and practitioner researchers, however.

Moreover, the dissertation's design and its intended purpose warrant mention. I employ a prescriptive-constructive approach to research, which aims to intervene directly in specific situations by offering actionable knowledge. This compelled me to craft my research narrative in a manner that enables others to learn from the experiences that I and my co-researchers made during the *Online Small Groups* project. This dual aim underscores a significant dimension of this dissertation.

Part II:
The Story, which is Already an Interpretation

Initiator

#Djursholm, *Lectio Divina*
Wednesday, May 12, 2021

"That's where we celebrated mass during the pandemic," Eva says pointing to a clearing between some nearby trees. We walk over the lawn and take seats on opposite sides of a white garden table, foldable, painted planks on a metal frame. We are meeting for lunch in the cozy garden behind the Djursholm Parish office, a quaint wooden house painted in Falun red with white trim—like something out of a Swedish postcard. I met Eva through the *Church in Digital Space* project, a participatory action research project initiated by the Diocese of Stockholm last fall. Eva is part of Djursholm's research group, but her primary work is as a deacon in the parish.[1] Much like the garden itself, Eva radiates calm and warmth, and it's easy to imagine that parishioners would have felt at peace here, with her, even in the midst of a pandemic.

I, however, am not at peace. In fact, I am sweating nervously as I try to summon the courage to ask Eva to join my research track on online small groups. Of course, there's no reason to be nervous. In previous meetings, Eva signaled that she might be interested; she has worked with small groups throughout her career, but never online. She needs to keep on her toes, she says. Trying new things keeps your mind agile.

Still, it almost feels like proposing marriage—a promise of commitment tempered by the risk of rejection. Plus, if I am to lead the online small groups research track, I need people to join me, ideally spread across three or four parishes. I thought finding partners would be easy, but most of the seven participating parishes have expressed little enthusiasm for online small groups.

As the conversation hits a lull, I summon my courage and ask: "So, have you thought about whether you would like to join the track on online small groups?" Eva smiles.

---

[1] Garpe and Ideström, *Kyrka i digitala rum*.

"Sure, why not?"

#Margareta, *Lectio Divina*
Tuesday, May 18, 2021

If this were a "marriage," it would be polygamous. Karin Andersson from Margareta Parish got the ok to join the project. Ordained as a pastor in 2010, at the age of twenty-four, Karin brings with her the experience of leading groups online. She's also the first person I have met who seems to like the online format.

In fact, when we met during spring to talk about the online small groups she was running at the time, she reiterated that her online groups worked better than her onsite groups. Where others complain about a lack of connection, Karin points out that she welcomed a larger number of participants in her online group, thus reaching new people and offering them an easy way to get to know the Church. Plus, online meetings take less of her time. That she has enough time—not to mention interest—for the project is wonderful. It will be great to have her onboard.

#Älvsjö, *Bible Study*
Thursday, May 27, 2021

During the last couple of months, I have met with representatives of the seven parishes participating in the *Church in Digital Space* to talk about online communication and digital theology. For the next phase of the project, we are setting up four distinct research tracks, which parishes are welcome to join. Rather than being assigned one or two parishes from the project—which is how the other tracks are set up—I wanted to recruit participants from several parishes. I hoped that this would allow us to learn from and with each other as we each lead an online small group. What's more, I know I need variation across groups if my research is to produce significant findings. After some aggressive lobbying, I was finally given permission by the project's leaders, who were probably tired of my insistent nagging.

In retrospect, maybe they were just trying to save me a lot of anguish. For if the project looked so promising when Eva and Karin joined, it now seems to have hit a wall. I can't seem to recruit any more participants.

Earlier in my graduate studies, I worked, part-time, in debt collection, a miserable job, which entailed cold-calling people who owed money to one entity or another, people who (understandably) either did not answer or, if they did, were immediately annoyed once they understood why I called. I really thought I had left those days behind. Yet here I am, spending my days cold-calling people in the *Church in Digital Space* project to see if there might be someone, anyone, who is remotely interested in joining my research track. I repeat the same pitch over and over, and I know what they are going to say even before I dial their number: "No," or a more polite "Thanks, but, no, thanks," or "We don't know yet," or a "Have you tried that person?" (And yes, I have tried that person.) Over and over, rinse and repeat.

There is someone, however, who *might* be interested to co-lead a group with me. Her name is Camilla Lindström, a newly ordained pastor in Älvsjö Parish. She was a rising star at Ernst & Young before making a career switch / receiving her calling. (Is that the same thing?) Camilla was one of three people attending a Zoom session I hosted on dialogical online communication last month. The other two— Eva and Karin.

#Margareta, *Lectio Divina*
#S:tEskils, *Book Club*
Tuesday, June 1, 2021

Today I met with Karin at Margareta Parish's office. It was the first time we met in person. She is taller than I thought, though I recognize her light blonde hair in tight curls.

"We are in here," she says, ushering me to a meeting room with five large wooden armchairs arranged around a low glass table. "I brought Jessica Bergqvist, deacon in S:t Eskils Parish," Karin announces happily. I look around the empty room before I see her gesturing to the laptop on the table. Unlike Karin, the woman looking out of the screen does not wear a clerical collar but is dressed casually in a bright yellow sweater, which stands out against her black wavy hair.

"Jessica runs an online book club at S:t Eskils. I thought it would be fun if she joined as well." I wave a bit awkwardly at Jessica, who seems to be, like Karin and myself, somewhere in her mid-thirties. I am excited but also a little flustered. I hadn't prepared to pitch this again. But as I launch into the pitch, I find that it's easy, a well-rehearsed routine. Each of us will run an online small group during the fall, and by continuously gathering participants' feedback and reflecting on our groups, we will test how to improve the online format. At three intervals, we will meet with all group leaders to compare notes, providing the opportunity to learn from each other.

While Karin nods affirmatively throughout my explanation, I find it hard to read Jessica's reactions. The laptop stands a good distance from me. I consider scootching my chair closer but decide against it. Best not to appear too eager, though I can feel how tensely I'm sitting. If only they knew how badly I need them to join my project.

I find myself breathing an audible sigh of relief when Karin announces she will include her online *Lectio Divina* group that will meet during the fall. Then she suggests gathering feedback from participants in her spring group to collect any advice or criticism they might have, so we agree to invite participants to an interview.

Somewhat to my surprise, Jessica decides to join with the online book club she is hosting. "During spring, I saw many people experiencing profound social isolation," Jessica explains. "So, I got in touch with an old friend, and we decided to host a book club. It's not focused on Christian readings, but I see it as Christian action in practice."

#Interview1

#Djursholm, *Lectio Divina*
Tuesday, July 6, 2021

Spoke to Eva from Djursholm Parish about the next steps. Time to get concrete and figure out what we are going to do. Eva is swamped right now, however, and the group is only supposed to start at the end of September or the beginning of October, so there is time for planning after summer.

#Älvsjö, *Bible Study*
Tuesday, July 6, 2021 (afternoon)

I'm on a roll! Camilla, the consultant-turned-pastor, is interested in running a group for pastors in the Church of Sweden, a group that will focus on the Christmas readings. She was part of a similar group in seminary, and she thought that worked well. Plus, there is a general dearth of opportunities for pastors to engage in theological reflection with colleagues. The group is also intended to help pastors preach this Christmas season. "The holidays are difficult," Camilla explains. "People expect to hear something fresh and interesting, but everybody knows the readings, and everybody has heard that Christmas sermon a thousand times before."

We decide to lead the group together. It will run under the auspices of Älvsjö Parish, and starting on Wednesday, October 6 we will meet once a week for eight straight weeks.

Planner

#Margareta, *Lectio Divina*
Wednesday, July 7, 2021

I am glad Karin suggested we do the interview with the members of her spring group. Only one person was interested in participating, but that person had a lot of good thoughts.

This morning, over a Zoom call, Niklas told me about his participation in the *Lectio Divina* and online Bible study groups Karin led during spring. Basically, Niklas liked these groups and was surprised by how well they worked. Still, he also highlighted an interesting challenge for online small groups: Onsite meetings usually necessitate traveling somewhere. Going to church or returning home creates a space for mental preparation and reflection that is part of his experience of the group.

Online groups lack these movements. The meeting starts immediately with no preparation time, which makes it more difficult, at least for Niklas, to be really present in the meeting. Niklas suggested playing Taizé songs ten minutes before the actual meeting to allow participants to come early and land, so to speak. These songs would then perform a function like walking to church.

#Interview1, #LandingStrip, #TaizéSongs, #Closing

#Margareta, *Lectio Divina*
Wednesday, July 7, 2021 (afternoon)

It's a twenty-five-minute ride from my apartment to Margareta Parish, which, on a normal day, would be a breeze. But today is not a normal day. Today is a sweltering 31 °C day. I slow down, trying not to get overheated so that I don't arrive a sweaty mess. When that doesn't work, I get off and push my bike the last five hundred meters to give myself time to cool down and dry off. By the time I've climbed the hill up to the church, I'm out of breath.

No matter what Niklas says, online meetings do have clear advantages.

It's a relief when I finally stumble into the cool interior of the art nouveau building with its white walls and verdigris copper roof. The church appears to be empty. Am I early? But then I notice what appears to be a side chapel with glass doors. As I step through those doors, I find myself not in a side chapel but a modern annex. Karin is there, and she has set a table with coffee cups and cinnamon buns. We sit down and chat while she pours coffee.

Then I pull out my laptop, open the draft research plan I have prepared, and start quizzing her.[1] "Can you briefly describe the group, please?" Karin runs through the logistical details of her *Lectio Divina* group. The group will meet via Zoom every other Sunday evening, 6–7 p.m., starting on September 5th. It's an open group that does not require participants to come to every meeting. Information about the group is available on the parish's Facebook page and some people have already made contact. A few days before each session, Karin will send an invitation to those who proclaimed an interest in the group, asking people to sign up for the upcoming meeting. On the day of the meeting, Karin will email participants the meeting link. Readings are taken from the Church of Sweden's lectionary.

"What are your hopes for the group? Do you have any specific goals?" I ask, moving on to the next question in the research template. Karin takes a sip from her coffee, taking her time.

"Well, I guess I hope that the group helps people grow in their faith." I nod and take a note.

"How do you think the group does that?" I probe. It feels a little like an interrogation.

"Well, *Lectio Divina* is basically about setting the scene for an encounter with God. When we read the Bible text people can learn something about who God is and what it means to be human. You know, it's also about finding a language to talk about faith. If you try to put words to your faith and your life, sometimes that helps to understand. It's not always easy. But I think that is why it is so important that people try to share something in the group. Because when we do speak those words then they somehow come to life." She pauses, taking another sip of coffee.

"Listening is also a big part of it. Today there is so much distraction, there is so much noise around us, constantly, but people are not very good at listening. They hear, but they do not listen. So, I think it's also about that. That participants

---

[1] See appendix B.

practice listening, both to themselves, each other, and to God." I nod, typing frantically to catch everything.

"I really think it's important, not only for faith, but also for life in general, you know? That is also why it is so important to create a safe and comfortable atmosphere in the group, so that people dare share things with each other, so that they can both speak and listen." Much later, I will reflect on this conversation and wonder how much of what Karin was telling me was born in that moment and how much she had articulated previously.

When we get to the section about improvement possibilities, the conversation gets more difficult. What exactly is it we—I—want to test? Do I expect Karin to come up with a list? Somehow, I thought she may have a mental list tucked away somewhere. Perhaps we need to wait until we get the first participant feedback to identify improvement possibilities.

I tell Karin about the interview I had this morning, and Niklas's idea of playing Taizé songs ten minutes before the meeting as a kind of landing strip, allowing people to arrive and slow down, easing into the moment. We agree to test that. Karin also wants to test having longer silences after each Bible reading. I wonder if these two strategies are enough, but since we don't have any other ideas, I move on to the section on quality indicators.

Karin walks through each step of the meeting and, in the end, we settle on the following:

1. People sign up for the group.
2. People don't drop out during the meeting (stay the whole hour).
3. Participants return (both within the series of fall meetings and participants who have participated in the May and/or July 2021 *Lectio Divina* groups).
4. People choose to share their thoughts and feelings during the meeting.
5. There is a good meeting atmosphere. Participants seem to be comfortable with silence.
6. People seem to be honest and sincere in their sharing and can say what they think without being afraid that it is "wrong."

Despite the coffee, when we finally get to the section about data gathering, energy is low. Clearly, we are both tired of the process, but we soldier on. I suggest setting up short anonymized online feedback forms to capture participants' feedback after each session. I also propose the creation of a similar form for Karin herself, explaining that it would just function as a prompt to record her observations and reflections. Karin agrees.

Then we talk through the routine: Before each meeting, Karin will send me a list with the email addresses of those who signed up for the meeting. After each group session, I will send out two sets of questions, one for Karin and one for the participants. Once we have some results, Karin and I will meet to discuss her observations and the participant feedback and see in which ways the group could be improved. Then Karin will implement the changes and we will see results in the next round of responses.[2]

As I ride my bike back home, I wonder about our respective roles. Participatory action research frames research participants as co-researchers, but how much agency does Karin have if it is I who decide on the agenda of our conversations, coming with a prepared framework and set of questions? Moreover, if I am the "expert" on carrying out empirical research and on Christian religious education, what is Karin's role and what are reasonable expectations for her?

#ResearchPlan, #Aspirations, #TaizéSongs, #LandingStrip, #MeetingAtmosphere, #FeedbackForms

#Älvsjö, *Bible Study*
Monday, July 12, 2021

It's summer break and I have no more meetings, no teaching, and no grading, which means I finally have some time to write the draft of the research plan I promised to send to Camilla. I had hoped to meet her to brainstorm, but it proved impossible to find a time before summer vacation.

When I put pen to paper—or rather fingers to keyboard—it becomes obvious that I think about these groups from the perspective of Christian religious education. For me, the point is not only to meet other people but also for participants to learn something of value for themselves. So, I try to address online small groups like I would any other kind of learning situation; that is, I start by considering our basic motivation or aspirations, and from there develop the *what* and *how* of each specific meeting.[3]

As I see it, the fundamental purpose of the group that Camilla and I will co-lead is to deepen our common Christian faith. Faith isn't something you have, an

---

[2] See appendix B.
[3] Hedman, *Undervisa*, 11; John Biggs, "Enhancing Teaching through Constructive Alignment," *Higher Education* 32, no. 3 (1996): 347–64; Biggs and Tang, *Teaching*, 7–9. See also chapter 2.

object you can put in a box and cherish. Faith is dynamic and changing—it's something we do—meaning it can flourish and grow, but it can also wither away. As such, there is a need to continuously nurture it, and one way to do this is to talk about faith.

I also realize how strongly influenced I am by Thomas Groome, the Roman Catholic Christian religious education scholar.[4] Or is it simply that he and I happen to think along the same lines? In any case, I agree with Groome that the purpose of Christian religious education is not knowledge, or at least not knowledge alone. Christian teaching addresses our whole being as persons, not only our intellect but also our hearts, identity, and way of life. Faith is not an intellectual position in an abstract theological debate. To believe is living one's life in a particular way. It is trying to love God with all our heart and soul and strength and mind, and to love our neighbor as ourselves. But for Groome, the starting point is not the love of God, which subsequently fosters the love of our neighbor. On the contrary, Groome believes that it is by loving other people that we love God.[5] This resonates with me. The basic task for Christian religious education is therefore to cultivate in ourselves and each other our love of our neighbor.

Here I see a clear parallel to the calling to resist sin. If one believes, as I do, that sin is being curved in on ourselves (*incurvatus in se*), then opening ourselves—to our neighbor, to creation, to God—is a constant process of conversion, of turning away from the destructive powers of sin and towards grace.

The question is how we approach conversion. Again, here I agree with Groome that we need one another to facilitate processes of opening ourselves. Learning happens in community; faith is shared with others. So, the first task in our group is to build community. Second, we need to create space for participants' lives. That is, the group cannot only be about instruction about the Christian story, it needs to enable people to bring their lives into dialogue with each other and the Christian tradition if there is to be any change at all. Third, we need to foster commitment. We should try to create decision points at which participants can make the informed decision to (try to) live according to their faith commitments linking our discussions to their everyday lives. To summarize, we should:

---

[4] Groome, *Christian Religious Education*; Groome, *Sharing Faith*. See also chapter 2.
[5] Groome, *Christian Religious Education*, 23–26.

1. Build a group characterized by openness, honesty, trust, and love.
2. Make space for participants' lives.
3. Encourage concrete decisions.

#ResearchPlan, #GroupBuilding, #DecisionPoint, #Aspirations

#S:tEskils, *Book Club*
Wednesday, August 25, 2021

I am still on vacation, so I meet Jessica via Zoom. She's wearing a bright lime green sweater, which somehow makes the Zoom call feel more vibrant—and makes me wonder how my own clothing choices will affect the online small group I will lead. Jessica's group starts already on Monday, so I am a little stressed about getting a research plan into place. Perhaps it is that stress, or perhaps it's the Zoom format, but the meeting feels a little impersonal and I am not entirely sure how Jessica feels about the research plan.

"What kind of group are you planning?"

"An online book club."

"Who leads the group?"

"I lead the group together with Lotta, an old friend and librarian."

"How often does the group meet?"

"We will meet six times, reading Ann-Helén Laestadius's *Stolen* for the first five sessions and Chimamanda Ngozi Adichie's *Notes on Grief* for the last. *Stolen* deals with the experience of the Sami in Sweden, and *Notes on Grief* is about, well, grief."

As I hear myself reading the questions, I feel as if I was conducting a telephone survey, running through the template I also used with Karin. If it is difficult to establish a connection now, how will we form communities of trust, openness, and honesty in our groups? Need to ponder that more.

Jessica explains again that the book club was a response to COVID-19 restrictions. Being worried about increased isolation and its effect on people's mental health and well-being, she got in touch with Lotta, and they started the group. Jessica went through considerable trouble recruiting people, putting up posts for book club enthusiasts on Facebook, Instagram, and various Swedish websites. On Facebook, she posted her invitation in groups like "We who love to read" and "We who live for reading." Her efforts were rewarded with a group of diverse participants who enjoyed the book club so much that most of them wanted to continue this fall.

For now, there are nine participants registered, the youngest being around twenty and the oldest, eighty-five. I am so busy getting through the questions that

I don't even realize this amazing detail. I mean, where else do people in their twenties and people in their eighties meet to discuss literature?

Most participants are continuing from the spring group, and most live in the parish, though there is one participant from Umeå and another participant from Öregrund. Members are generally not church regulars; many have never participated in any of the parish's other activities.

Besides being a meeting place, the group invites participants into conversations about existential themes. It is important to choose books that challenge participants' perceptions of the world and themselves. Jessica also intends the group as a way for people to get acquainted with the Church of Sweden, even if her intention isn't overtly missional. She does not necessarily expect people to become active parishioners. It's more about showing that the Church of Sweden is many things.

When we get to the question of how to measure whether the group "works," I pull up my notes from the meeting with Karin and so this part becomes something of a copy-paste. Not sure if that is wise, probably better to let Jessica decide for herself what it means that the book club works, but I do think that Karin's quality criteria make a lot of sense.

Jessica says that data gathering is up to me, so I suggest we adopt the same anonymized feedback form setup we use for Karin's group. She agrees, with a slight alteration: we will send participants feedback forms only every other week, lest they get overwhelmed. Leader feedback forms are weekly, however. After participant feedback is collected, we will discuss the results and plan future adjustments.

#ResearchPlan, #Aspiration

Observer

#S:tEskils, *Book Club*
Tuesday, August 31, 2021

Yesterday, Jessica had her first meeting about *Stolen*, after which I sent the leader feedback form. Jessica and Lotta sent them back almost immediately, and it was exciting to read their responses. It made me feel as if I had been there.

What did you think of today's meeting?

"Very positive, participants were happy to meet again, and I felt that they were engaged and wanted to talk about the book. The hour went super-fast."

How did you perceive the meeting atmosphere?

"Good atmosphere, a roundtable of equals. We had different opinions about the book today, that may change as we go along."[1]

Their responses revealed that Jessica and Lotta had split the group in two, which made it easier to talk about the book. They encouraged participants to keep their microphones on to avoid the time-consuming operation of switching microphones on and off, which seems to have improved the flow of the conversation.

Someone made an interesting reflection about encouraging conversation: "Looking back, I reflect on my role as a leader. It's a balancing act. Maybe if I would let it be quiet sometimes [people would be encouraged to pick up the conversation], even if the silence in digital rooms can easily feel a little uncomfortable." So, our basic research design works. Already we are identifying the things we can test to see if they improve the conversation.

Lastly, Jessica and Lotta clearly experienced the book club differently, at least in part. One of them thought that people were "quite happy to share their thoughts about the book," while the other felt that people were "a little reserved

---

[1] In Swedish: "God stämning, högt i tak. Vi hade lite olika åsikter om boken idag, det kan ändras allt eftersom." The expression "högt i tak" is difficult to translate, describing a situation where people can express their opinions freely without regard to formal structures or the expectations of the environment. I try to capture this in the metaphor "a roundtable of equals."

at this first meeting after summer break." It will be interesting to see what the participants say themselves when we get their feedback form next week.

#Microphones, #IndividualDifference

#Djursholm, *Lectio Divina*
Monday, September 6, 2021

Eva from Djursholm Parish decided to postpone her group until November, which means that her group will not run parallel with the others. Not ideal, considering the research design included our learning from one another's experiences. But little I can do about that. After all, "beggars can't be choosers," and I am just happy to have her in the study.

#EmergentDesign

#S:tEskils, *Book Club*
Wednesday, September 8, 2021

We have already received seven participant responses about Monday's meeting. As there were eight participants in total, this is a response rate of 87.5%, which is amazing. That's the good news. The less good news is that I'm not sure how well these forms work.

Asked "How did you experience the atmosphere in the group?" people responded "Good," "Nice and considerate," "Good," "Very good," "Friendly," "Very nice," and "Very good." Of course, this says something, but it is difficult to get a deeper understanding of participants' experiences or of how the atmosphere is created.

The terse responses are also completely unhelpful in determining improvement possibilities. This is a problem, seeing that very few participants have suggestions for improvement. Someone remarked it would be better if Jessica and Lotta posed fewer questions about the book, and someone else commented that it would be easier to have a conversation if everyone read the assigned chapters, but for the most part, participants said they "didn't know," that they "didn't see anything that could be improved," or that they "don't have anything to add."

Still, it surprises me. I always have ideas about how things could be improved. (Which I can imagine some people think is part of my problem....) Is that the occupational hazard of the researcher, being trained to observe and evaluate situations? I don't know.

Still, the forms did yield some insights. For example, answers to the question: "How do you experience the conversation? Does it flow easily?" were mixed. Some were happy with the conversation, while others thought it didn't flow smoothly. I imagine Jessica and Lotta split the participants again, so that conversation flowed in one group, but not in the other. This could point to potential improvement areas, especially since Jessica and Lotta reported experiencing a continued need to moderate the conversation, even as they also note that including longer silences does appear to stimulate reflection.

When I met her on Zoom today, Jessica had some interesting thoughts on why the conversation has been lacking flow. Basically, since people only meet within the framework of the book club, the time they spend together is both quite limited and quite formal. People do not ride the bus home together, nor do they get a drink after the book club. This means that people don't have the same opportunities to get to know each other as they would in an onsite group.

Participant feedback confirms Jessica's suspicion. Group members feel "comfortable with each other and respected" and express that people in the group "care for each other." At the same time, participants do not get personal but relate to each other more "as friends on a superficial level," which is interesting given that most participants continued from the spring group, so that they had a chance to get acquainted. As I read the responses, I find myself thinking of Niklas's comments about online small groups. Indeed, it appears as if some of the things that make onsite groups work lie outside of the group itself, things we get "for free" so to speak.

I told Jessica that some participants expressed that it was difficult to discuss the book if not everyone reads the assigned chapters, and we talked about the meeting structure. Jessica agrees that it would be easier if everyone read the assigned chapters, but also points out that it is difficult to require that of group members. She doesn't want to exclude anyone from the meeting, only because they didn't have the time to read. Improving the group is thus not only about the online format, but also about how to organize and structure the group itself (the "content"). I think the point about moderation also falls into this category. I have seen the same challenges in onsite groups, where conversation does not always flow freely either. So, we face a blend of general difficulties and the more specific challenges that online mediation entails.

We agreed that with the next feedback form, I will invite participants to an interview so I can get a deeper understanding of their responses.

#GroupBuilding, #MeetingAtmosphere, #EmergentDesign

#Margareta, *Lectio Divina*
Wednesday, September 8, 2021 (afternoon)

Karin and I are back to Zoom, which means no coffee and no cinnamon buns, but it does cut down on time—and sweaty bike rides. But since we've already met in person, Zoom works well enough for going over the feedback from her group's first meeting.

People expressed that the meeting was "very rewarding," "interesting, rewarding, and thought-provoking." It was a "warm and intimate meeting even though it was digital." One participant also commented "Karin is a calm, confident, and clear leader," and someone else remarked that they hope the parish continues with its online small groups. Responding to a question about the Taizé songs Karin played before the meeting, participants reported that the songs helped to set the mood and to let them relax.

The Taizé songs weren't the only element designed to set the mood for participants. Before the meeting, Karin emailed them to ask that they find a quiet place to sit, light a candle, and bring a cup of tea.

"You know, I asked everyone to find a cozy spot, and then I sit here at my ugly desk. I felt that I didn't follow my own advice." However, participants did not remark on this, perhaps because they see a clear difference between themselves and Karin. Still, this doesn't mean that her placement is irrelevant, only that it might be in line with participants' expectations.

Karin said that this week's reading, John 17:9–11, was quite difficult, and participants appeared to have a harder time relating to the text than what she remembers from the spring group. Of course, this has nothing to do with the online format, just like in the book club.

When we started the project, there was a strong assumption that digital mediation was the challenge, but I increasingly question that. Having great online small groups is to a significant degree about content, which is obvious now that I think about it. Dah!

Like with Jessica's group, many replies in the feedback form are quite brief, and, again, there are few suggestions for improvement. One participant answered that s/he would like Karin to state more clearly which biblical book, chapter, and verses she reads, but that's it. This could mean that everything is as good as it can be, but somehow, I doubt that. Talking to Karin about her placement and the readings, it is obvious that there are at least some things worthy of further consideration.

Perhaps it is a cultural thing? Perhaps it is culturally expected to express appreciation and gratitude instead of criticism? Perhaps asking participants for improvement possibilities is the wrong way to go here?

So, we agree that I will join the meeting on October 3 to get a first-hand impression of the group. Maybe that will turn up something.

#FeedbackForms, #TaizéSongs #LandingStrip, #EmergentDesign

#Reflection
Friday, September 10, 2021

Somehow, I guess I had hoped for more—increasingly radical insights, transformative experiences, epiphanies. The heavens opening and a voice from above saying: "This is how you have great online small groups!" I have been going around and feeling a little lost and anxious and generally afraid that we might not generate all that many insights. Now I wonder whether my expectations are unrealistic.

I mean, on the face of it, things are going well. Niklas suggested playing Taizé songs, and so we did, we recorded people's feedback, and they generally liked it, and we have one (little) contribution to how to improve online small groups. And there are other examples: Jessica trying out how to get the conversation flowing through longer silences, and Karin reflecting on where to place herself during the meetings. All this is significant, isn't it?

Perhaps this is much more about tweaking these groups, making many small adjustments and improvements, rather than creating something world-changing and astonishing? Perhaps I should celebrate the moments of reflection we are experiencing rather than dismissing them?

#Margareta, *Lectio Divina*
#S:tEskils, *Book Club*
Thursday, September 23, 2021

The feedback forms don't really work. There. I said it.

Karin had her second meeting on Sunday, and Jessica had her fourth on Monday. For both, I sent the leader and the participant forms. Karin answered hers immediately, as did Jessica and Lotta, but one of them is increasingly brief in her responses. I suspect Lotta. She hasn't been all that involved in setting up the research, and I understand that completing these forms over and over is a bother. Still, I had hoped everybody would feel engaged....

For Karin's group, we didn't get any participant responses, which is not strange considering that only two people were attending that week's *Lectio Divina* group.

For the book club, we have received two completed thus far, but the participants' responses are again very terse—and no one is interested in coming to an interview. Most difficult of all, people do not express any criticism or any ideas for improvement.

#EmergentDesign, #FeedbackForms

#Älvsjö, *Bible Study*
Friday, September 24, 2021

I can't seem to win. We received only four registrations for our Christmas readings Bible study group. However, with four participants, the meetings could easily collapse if one or two group members cannot make sessions or decide to drop out. I spoke to Camilla, who shared my apprehension, and we decided to cancel the group. Corporate decision making. Efficient and at times brutal.

We will try again after Christmas with different readings. This of course means that we only have two groups running in parallel with, hopefully, two more groups to follow later.

#EmergentDesign

#S:tEskils, *Book Club*
Friday, October 1, 2021

Ok, perhaps feedback forms aren't totally worthless. I reformulated some of the questions in response to earlier feedback. Specifically, I included the closed question: "Did the conversation give you any new thoughts or ideas?" (yes, no, don't know). This was followed by an open question "If you would, please describe these thoughts or ideas briefly."

Four of five of those who submitted feedback answered the question affirmatively and related how they had started thinking about the relationship between the Swedish majority and the Sami minority, about our modern society's exploitation and conquering of nature, and about the lack of state support for Sami reindeer husbandry.

Participants are still reluctant to express criticism and to suggest improvement possibilities in the feedback form, but these answers demonstrate that there is a potential for learning and for developing new perspectives in the book club. So, the problem might not be with the forms per se, but with what kind of feedback participants are able and comfortable to express.

Perhaps critically assessing these groups requires some previous familiarity with reasoning about learning, teaching, and facilitation. Might be that it is a matter of engagement. After all, providing constructive criticism is often hard work. Or it is tied to the culture governing these groups, so that participants feel that there is little space to express criticism. I wouldn't be surprised if the online format contributed to this. If community and connection are more tenuous in online small groups, perhaps participants find it harder to express critique. Then again, I need to remain open to the possibility that there simply isn't anything to improve. At least on this last point, I will be able to form an opinion when I participate in the groups next week.

#FeedbackForms, #PotentialLearning

Participant Observer

#Margareta, *Lectio Divina*
Sunday, October 3, 2021

I went all in. I lit two candles and placed them on either side of my laptop. The whole configuration sat on our coffee table—a peculiar little altar. I dimmed the lights, put a large, soft pillow on the floor, and made myself a cup of tea. This would never have worked had my wife and kids been home, but they had gone out, leaving me to participate in Karin's *Lectio Divina* group.

Now, as I click the link to open the meeting, Karin is playing Taizé songs. On the screen, I see a Microsoft Word document. "Welcome to today's *Lectio Divina*," it reads in large font over a picture of a tree-rimmed lake in the evening sun. Underneath the picture, Karin has written "We start with a moment of contemplative music."

I close my eyes, trying to center myself. It is difficult. I open my eyes and locate the clock on my screen. 5.57 p.m. Three minutes to go, I still have some time to collect myself. I close my eyes again and listen to the song. "Bless the Lord my soul, and bless God's holy name." I try to relax and to ease into the atmosphere. Breathe. There you go. The song finishes and the next song starts. "In the Lord I'll be ever thankful." I open my eyes for a moment. 6.01 p.m. Not much longer. Any moment now Karin will turn off the song to welcome us. Admittedly, I am not so much in the present as in the near future, when Karen initiates the next movement of this liturgy. But the song keeps playing:

> *In the Lord I'll be ever thankful,*
> *In the Lord I'll rejoice.*
> *Look to God, do not be afraid,*
> *Lift up your voices, the Lord is near;*
> *Lift up your voices the Lord is near.*

6.03 p.m. Has something happened? Perhaps there is some technical issue? Perhaps I should send Karin a text? I feel increasingly anxious. Instead of being closed, my eyes are glued to the screen.

In the Lord I'll be ever thankful,
In the Lord I'll rejoice.
Look to God, do not be . . .

The music stops. Karin's face appears on the screen, and she welcomes us. We are five participants, Karin and myself included.

"We start with a short round of introductions. Please say your name and what God is for you right now." What is God for me right now? I always get nervous when I get these kinds of questions, and while I am still trying to figure out what to say—something deep enough to convey that I am theologically informed, but not so deep or complex that it seems pretentious—I realize that this is low-key. God is a warm feeling, a ray of sunlight, a friendly smile. I relax.

"My name is Simon, and right now God is comfort for me." It feels good to have said something. Somehow that makes me more present in the meeting. I am no longer only a passive observer. I am also a participant.

Karin takes us through a relaxation exercise. It's the perfect landing. I feel my body relaxing and my breath getting slower. At the same time, I wonder whether it would have made sense to explain to us why we do the exercise in the first place. As it is, we have no choice but to trust Karin that the exercise makes sense. But this kind of trust might not always exist in small groups.

"Listen for a word or a phrase that stands out to you," Karin tells us and reads Daniel 6:16–22, the story of Daniel in the lions' den.

"I will read the text again, and after that, we will share a moment of silence," Karin says before rereading the text. As she finishes, she turns off her camera and microphone. We do the same. I close my eyes but find it difficult to concentrate. I feel an urge to constantly check if Karin is back. How will I know when it is time to continue?

I don't even know why I am anxious. Someone I am afraid of being interrupted in the middle of a deep contemplation (not that this usually happens to me) and it feels important to have concluded this moment of introspection before being called back. Perhaps it is related to not feeling in control of the situation.

With an effort, I refocus on the phrase I picked out, "servant of the living God," and to keep my thoughts from wandering. I also feel pretty alone. The connection we had just a moment ago is gone. I remember that Karin and I talked about this in our last meeting. She told me about how she turns off her microphone and her camera. It made sense to me, then: it's the digital equivalent of closing your eyes, a way to focus inward. But now it doesn't feel like closing my eyes, it feels like leaving the room.

Is there a better way to connect participants during the silence? You could play music but then it's not quiet... or show a picture? Hearing the same song or seeing the same image on screen could strengthen the feeling of a shared experience. It would at the very least give me some inkling about what the others are doing right now.

Karin turns her video on, and immediately everyone else follows suit. So, it turns out I wasn't the only one keeping an eye on the screen....

"Does anyone want to share their word or phrase?" Karin asks before instructing not to comment on the sharing. After we have shared, Karin asks us to see how the text touches upon our lives. She reads the passage again, and again cameras and microphones turn off. Now I am alone, kneeling on my living room floor. I close my eyes and try to remember a suitable phrase.

But instead of contemplating the reading, I wonder why the silence is placed after the reading and before the sharing and not after the sharing, in which case there would no longer be any need to try and hold on to one's answer. That might be easier for me. To simply sit and reflect on what was shared. Or is it in the silence I am supposed to hear God's address? Am I jumping to conclusions when I find my "answer" already during the reading? Am I doing this wrong?

Another round of sharing and a final question:

"What does God invite you to do with this text?" More silence. A final round of sharing, which by now feels a little awkward. I have been here for almost forty-five minutes but have not had a conversation with anyone.

It makes sense that we should not comment on each other's sharing. God's address to each of us might be fragile and not open to questioning or scrutiny. Still, not responding to what the others say feels a little impolite. I also want to feel like part of a group. To me, this feels more like every one of us is doing this by him/herself, only that we do it at the same time and in the presence of others. But these others, the other participants, are strangely instrumental in that. As we only switch on our microphones to speak, I cannot hear any affirmative hums. Sharing into the silence feels like dropping a stone into a deep well without hearing a sound or even seeing any ripples on the water. It simply vanishes. It makes me feel a little uneasy.

After the *Lectio Divina* exercise, we have some time left and Karin opens up for a conversation about this Sunday's theme of *Angels*. The conversation flows freely, and only now do I feel that we are doing this together. Being able to exchange ideas with the others becomes an important affirmation of our shared experience, and it bridges the divide that I felt between us. That speaks to how important it is to feel a sense of community and belonging.

It also strikes me that there are things we can improve. It might be that I am simply overly critical and, of course, all this is only my perspective, but setting aside all the usual caveats, I think there are opportunities for improvement, for example keeping cameras on during the moments of silence and placing these moments of silence after the sharing. Then again, whether this constitutes an improvement depends on how the other experienced these moments, which is something I don't actually know yet.

#TaizéSongs, #LandingStrip, #StartingOnTime, #RelaxationExercise, #LossOfControl, #Community, #NeedToUnderstand

#S:tEskils, *Book Club*
Monday, October 4, 2021

We read Chimamanda Ngozi Adichie's *Notes on Grief*. I think Jessica picked that to address experiences of loss and grief that were so widespread during the pandemic—though I didn't get the impression that anyone in the group had directly experienced the COVID-related death of a loved one.

There were nine participants, including me, Jessica, and Lotta. We started with a short round of introductions: "Please, tell us your name and something you did today," Jessica directed us. I found that quite brilliant—a really easy, unpretentious way to get everyone to speak and to land in the situation, much easier than the question of what God means to me right now. It's a nice little landing strip that allows participants to safely arrive in the meeting.

Once we'd introduced ourselves, Lotta started the discussion by asking us what we thought about the book. Even though she pointed out that there were no right or wrong answers, everybody remained silent. Thinking about my own silence, that wasn't so much because I had nothing to say but because I didn't know where to start.

I had somewhat mixed and strong feelings about the book and found it difficult to formulate my thoughts in a way that would not dominate the conversation or that would at least leave sufficient room for different experiences. Later I got the impression others might have experienced a similar difficulty. At the very least, it became clear in the conversation that everyone had opinions about the book.

Is this due to the online format? Perhaps we would have experienced the same kind of half-awkward silence had we met onsite. Then again, had we been seated in the same room it might have been easier to read each other's body language and to pick up on the atmosphere. So, it might have been a combination of how one asks the question and the online situation. Or was that related to my presence, as a researcher? Did I make the others feel uneasy initially?

When no one rose to the challenge, Lotta directed the question to Jessica. After that, the conversation flowed quite freely and needed little moderation.

Observing Jessica and Lotta in their role as group leaders, or more precisely, seeing what they were doing and how it affected the group, was instructive. They were switching between two different "modes" of leadership, especially Lotta.

First, Lotta engaged with participants on equal terms, as when she asked that starting question about the book, pointing out that there are no right or wrong answers. Here she suggests that everyone's opinion is equally valid. However, at other points, Lotta was quite clearly instructing us in an attempt to get us to understand the book more fully, or to nuance a point made by someone.

For example, Lotta explained that Ngozi Adichie has a different cultural background and that we should not put her story into a Swedish context but must understand it based on who Ngozi Adichie is, including her life story, culture, and history. At another point, Lotta explained the difference between an essay and a novel, clarifying that one should have different expectations of the two genres and thus read them differently. But each time Lotta changed into the mode of instruction, the conversation halted and some effort or change in topic was needed to get it going again.

I think this poses a challenge. Moments of instruction appear to risk a temporary interruption in the conversation, as a leader changes from the role of equal conversation partner to the role of expert and instructor. Of course, moments of instruction might be necessary, and at times it is the leader's responsibility to nuance or even rectify, but these interventions come at a cost.

#LandingStrip, #OpeningQuestion, #Instruction

#Margareta, *Lectio Divina*
Monday, October 11, 2021

Martin, one of Karin's participants, agreed to come to a Zoom "interview." I use the quotes somewhat ironically, because I am not sure how much of an "interview" this was. At least it wasn't an interview in which I tried to mine Martin's thoughts. Instead, it was a friendly thirty-five-minute conversation in which we compared our experiences from the *Lectio Divina* session we attended on October 3, 2021. Perhaps the whole call was me trying to see what Martin made of my observations.

Looking at Martin's feedback form, he was quite skeptical about the Taizé songs in the beginning. It was fine as a kind of intermission music, he wrote, but nothing more. When I explained how the Taizé songs came about, he completely changed his mind and thought it was really a wonderful idea. It is as if he couldn't appreciate the songs until he knew what he was supposed to do with them. As it was, the songs were a nuisance. Once he understood their purpose, he perceived them in a new light.

This shows the degree to which participants need to be able to understand not only what is going on, but also why meetings are designed in a particular way. I will take that with me.

We talked about the start of the meeting, and Martin shared my experience of unease when the songs continued playing after the appointed start time. Martin also agreed that it is a bit tricky when Karin turns off her camera during silence as one doesn't know when she is going to call us back. Here he suggested announcing when there is one minute of silent time left. So simple! In any case, I was not alone in experiencing this lack of control as unsettling—another thing to be mindful of in online small groups.

The feedback forms raised another point. Someone commented: "There is trust in the group and we dare to share our reflections. But we do not really know each other so well, so I also feel certain reservations," echoing my unease about sharing into the silence. "Probably all participants would dare to open up more if we had regular meetings for a longer period of time," the comment continued, pinpointing the importance of community and group building. Nonetheless, responses indicated that the group was a space to meet God and that it led them to new insights, even if they did not describe those insights in more detail.

#Interview2, #TaizéSongs, #NeedToUnderstand, #LossOfControl, #Community, #GroupBuilding, #PotentialLearning

#Reflection
Tuesday, October 19, 2021

Time to take stock. Jessica's book club and Karin's *Lectio Divina* groups have finished. What have we learned about online small groups so far? What do I take with me to the other two groups?

1. People need a landing strip to mentally arrive. The Taizé songs were a good example, as were Jessica's opening question about what people had done that day and Karin's relaxation exercise.

2.   Community and group building are important and influence the meeting atmosphere, including participants' willingness to engage in open and honest sharing. Group building is more difficult in online groups, which lack "naturally occurring" forms of socializing.

3.   At times, instruction might be necessary, but it includes the risks of establishing leaders as "experts," which changes the tone and flow of the conversation.

4.   Online meetings can easily lead to a feeling of not being in control of the situation, which is unsettling for participants. Participants further need to understand what is going on and why a certain session element is included to be able to make full "use" of all exercises.

Response from Karin Andersson

#Margareta, *Lectio Divina*

In response to the pandemic's challenges in spring 2021, we decided to transition our Bible study group, "The Life and the Bible," to a digital format. Recognizing how much time people were spending on digital meetings, we decided to shorten our sessions to one hour. At the end of the season, all participants expressed a desire to continue meeting online. In response, we started our online "*Lectio Divina*" group, which was attended during spring 2021 by around eight regular members. We also offered a summer edition in July 2021. However, since it was the holiday season, we had fewer participants.

The parish decided to participate in this dissertation project because the bishop had told our head pastor that it was important to keep offering digital groups.

The *Lectio Divina* group then met three evenings in early autumn. We used the same meeting format we had used in spring and summer, but we opened the group by playing songs from Taizé. Unfortunately, *Lectio Divina* wasn't a suitable format for this research.

Lectio Divina has a set form, and it was difficult to adapt and experiment with the format. I also think that Simon should have taken part in all our sessions as a way of being part of the group and being less distracted by the format. Reading his analysis made me realize that what I took for granted since being familiar with the format was way too distracting for someone just popping in. I also must admit that the theological content of the exercise with reading/listening to the text from the Bible and reflecting on it was always my priority. This was something I realized upon reading Simon's analysis.

So, in this way, I think I made it even more difficult for the *Lectio Divina* to be studied in this dissertation. The format became secondary even though it was what we were supposed to study. The analysis also made me think about how we communicated then (and now) what we are about to do together when we meet. I think that digital gatherings require more verbal explanations than on-site meetings. This is because we lack the common base of each other's presence that being in the same on-site room offers.

In the autumn of 2021, our regular Bible study group started to meet on-site again, gathering the same people who had joined our digital groups in the spring of that year. Some have left and some new have come, and today there are ten members in the group.

But we also have continued to offer online gatherings. In Advent 2021, we launched the "Digital Bible study in Advent" where we read and discussed the text for the coming Sunday. We have continued offering an online group during Advent, and we plan to do this again for Advent 2024. During Lent 2022 and 2023 we also offered an online version of *Lectio Divina* but this year we met on site.

I think that online groups are important in the way that they can complement on-site groups. Groups are easily accessed from home, and you can join in just a minute. But that also makes it more vulnerable since it is easier to skip a session – it takes even less than a minute to decide that "no I won't join tonight." Going forward, I think this is the challenge for online groups. How can we help people prioritize these groups amid every day/evening life taking place at home?

Participant Leader

#Djursholm, *Lectio Divina*
Monday, November 29, 2021

"I understand," I say, clutching the phone to my ear. Eva's voice is as calm as always as she explains that she needs to postpone the group again. It feels like a long time has passed since I met her in the sunny garden in Djursholm Parish, when the weather was getting warm, and I was nervous about whether she would join my research track. Now it's November. It is cold and dark. Eva did join the research track, but her group has not started. Right now, I wonder if it will.

Eva explains that she was supposed to co-lead the group with a colleague, who is unexpectedly and suddenly on long-term leave. Eva doesn't elaborate, but simply clarifies that it is unclear who will take over her responsibilities, both in general and with the group. Despite her calm and apparent good humor, I get the feeling that she is worried. Eva has been appointed supervisor for one of Djursholm Parish's pastoral ministry teams. She has a lot on her hands, and this research project is probably not her most pressing concern.

Still, Eva reiterates that she *will* run a group, which she calls "*Lectio Divina* as Winter Turns to Spring." The group will start on Epiphany and meet every other Thursday until Easter. I'm amazed that Eva pulled this together despite everything that's going on in her work, and with that in mind, I refrain from suggesting we should meet to draw up a research plan.

#Djursholm, *Lectio Divina*
Thursday, January 6, 2022

The invitation said we were welcome to log in fifteen minutes early to socialize. I missed that detail and consequently am the last to arrive when I join the Zoom meeting at 3 p.m. sharp.

There are seven participants, including Eva. She placed herself in a cozy-looking armchair in front of a bookshelf and radiating a warm and reassuring feeling of welcome. Djursholm Parish still has not settled who will take over for Eva's colleague, so, for now, Eva is leading the group by herself.

Stig and Gunilla are maybe in their seventies. They seem to be a couple, sitting next to each other, sharing a screen. Two people appear in one of my little Zoom windows, which makes them a unit: separate yet indivisible. Marianne is about the same age. When I look at her Zoom box, I see an elderly woman sitting at what appears to be a dining table. Something tells me that she lives by herself, but I cannot put my finger on what it is.

Next up in my gallery view is Linda, and then Elin. One of them has a child who has become very interested in church, so she feels she needs to learn about church herself. Both are in their thirties, I would guess.

It strikes me how familiar this all feels. As far as I can see, we are all white, able-bodied, cis-gendered majority Swedes, if I can count myself a majority Swede, seeing that I immigrated from Germany in 2010. The group is comprised of the same kind of people I meet in my parish in central Stockholm on Sunday mornings.

The rooms I peer into do not seem particularly arranged for Bible study—no candles, no drinks, no snacks. No cups of tea or coffee anywhere. No cozy blankets. It feels more like a work meeting. And, at least for me, it is. I am here not primarily to engage in conversation about the biblical text, but to understand how online group leadership works and how it can be improved.

"You probably know about the lectionary," Eva says, and I wonder if we do. I am thinking of Linda, the mother of the child who has taken an interest in church. How well does she know the Church of Sweden, its lectionary, and its calendar? Having grown up Pentecostal, I certainly didn't know about the lectionary before I embarked on my journey towards ordination in the Church of Sweden, a journey that eventually took me elsewhere—here, to this group.

However, later, when we read the Bible text, Linda picks up a Bible she had apparently placed next to her laptop before the meeting. So, she has a Bible at home and is well-prepared to read it. Why shouldn't she know about the Church of Sweden Lectionary? We know so little about others. So little can we see in the small Zoom windows. Dangerous to assume too much.

Eva emphasizes that there is no right or wrong way to understand the reading and encourages us to simply go along. "We will read the text four times," she says, smiling. I feel safe. I wonder whether the others feel safe too. Is there any way to tell?"

Eva talks about the theologian Peter Halldorf. She reads an extract from his work and a prayer he wrote. I do not really understand what is happening and have a hard time keeping up. Why is she reading that text? (Later, I will understand that it was both a way for us to land and a bridge to the reading. But in that moment, it puzzled me, and the prayer had concluded before I realized what was going on.)

Then Eva asks us to simply listen, and she reads the Gospel text for Epiphany 2022, Matthew 2, verses 1–12. Now she wants us to listen for a word or phrase that stands out to us, she says and reads the text a second time.

I feel stressed. All words seem to stand out and I try to find a word that is interesting but not too pious, a word that says something about me, that says something to me. "Jesus"? No. "Star"? No. I don't like this. I decide on the phrase "in a dream." At least it says something about the place where the divine breaks into history. I'm not happy.

The reading is followed by a short moment of silence and then we share our words and phrases. I get caught up in what Gunilla says, "all Jerusalem with him." I had missed that when we read the text. It will be important for how I hear the text the next time around.

Eva asks if anyone else could read the text, but no one volunteers. Eva shrugs, then poses the question:

"Where are you in the text? Where would you place yourself in the story?" Then she reads the text a third time.

I can almost see it in front of me. I'm somewhere in Jerusalem almost 2000 years ago. "All Jerusalem with him." I've never been to Jerusalem so it's a little hard to imagine what it looks like. But I've been to Rome, and I imagine a Jerusalem that looks like ancient Rome. It works.

More important than the city itself is the atmosphere. The city feels overheated. People whisper to each other. Something incredible is about to happen. Or has it already happened? Strange men have been seen walking up to the Royal Palace. Men no one recognized. What did they want? What does this mean? I am part of that city, affected, even as I am not sure this involves me. I am somewhere on the periphery of that story. My everyday life will continue as usual, even as excitement and anxiety stay with me.

Again, everyone shares, with Eva going last. Then follows the fourth and final reading.

"This time I want you to listen for an invitation. What does God invite you to do? Anybody feel like reading?"

"I can read," I say, "if you understand my German accent." They laugh a little to signal that they do understand, and so I begin to read.

Have you noticed that the wise men can only give their gifts once they have arrived where they were supposed to go? They must have carried their gifts with them for a long time. Perhaps they have longed to give them away, yearning that their gifts would be used somewhere, that they might be valued. I want my gifts to be used. I think—I hope—I have something to give. I feel myself carrying this gift, and I feel how it burdens me. I feel like nobody wants it. Maybe I must get where I'm going before my gifts can be used before I can unburden myself? If only I knew where that was....

After some time, I hear Eva saying that it is up to us if we want to share. I consider this for a second and decide to share a slimmed-down version that is a little less personal. Eva goes third this time. It feels good that her words are not going to be the concluding and final statement but simply one of many offerings. It makes her less of an expert charged with being the final arbitrator and more of a participant on equal terms with us. Eva says that she often encounters darkness and evil in her work as a deacon. She says that it has been difficult lately. She tells us that, sometimes, when it feels extra heavy, she takes her deacon's emblem in her hand and prays: "You and I, God! You and I!" and then she throws herself into what lies before her.[1] She talks about the star, about the idea that there is hope. There is a future. It feels strong. Personal.

"We conclude with the Blessing," Eva says, "It's printed on the back cover of the Church of Sweden's hymnal." But wait, does everyone know the Blessing by heart or have a hymnal at home? Apparently not, and so it is a little chaotic as we pray, not least because of the slight time lag you have when videoconferencing. Still, I like praying together more than if Eva had prayed for us. It's a little chaotic—but who says church can't be chaotic?

Eva informs us that the parish can provide participants with Bibles and hymnals, should anyone be interested, quickly reconciling any potential rift caused by absent hymnals.

"See you in two weeks," Eva says, and the meeting ends. My laptop screen turns blank. Everyone is gone.

The phone rings. It's Eva. She wants to know what I thought of today's meeting. She says that online meetings are strange. They end so abruptly, and you have no one to chat with afterward. We talk about my impressions. I say I thought it was good. There was a good balance between silences and conversation. It was nice

---

[1] In the Church of Sweden, each deacon is given a special necklace at their ordination, called a deacon's emblem, which can also be used as a brooch. It is a circle, with a cross centered over the circle. In the center of the cross is a dove with a twig in its beak.

that people related to each other in their sharing. I say that I noticed that she seemed to assume that everyone is quite familiar with the Church and the Bible, and we discuss whether that is a reasonable assumption. Finally, I say that I thought it was good that she chose not to share last in the last round and that it is nice that everyone can get their own hymnal if we are expected to have one.

We talk about the next meeting. Maybe we could stay a little after the actual meeting in case someone wants to debrief, just so that the meeting doesn't end so abruptly. Then we hang up.

As I type up my notes, I reflect on my "Jerusalem experience." I wonder why I place myself outside or on the fringe of Christian stories. It's not that I think they do not concern me, but rather that their effect takes place in my ordinary life and that the effects may not be as strong and transformative as I had expected or hoped. Does that say anything about my relationship with God? And does this mean that the Bible study "worked," if we mean by that that it leads us to reflect on the biblical text and through the text on our relationship with the divine. And why does this insight come now when I write this and not while I was sitting there on Zoom. Could Eva have done something to get me to reflect along these lines already there and then?

#PotentialLearning, #NeedToUnderstand, #Closing

#Djursholm, *Lectio Divina*
Friday, January 14, 2022

I want to mourn with you.
I want to cry when your child dies.
When the world ends—for a moment—an eternity—I want to feel your pain.
I don't want to sit in the apartment next door, watching Netflix.
I want there to be an "us," so I can be with you in the darkness.
That we mean something to each other—whoever you are.
You who lost your child.

Eva's son had an accident. We don't know yet if he'll make it. His partner died in the crash. Things are in an uproar.

#Reflection
January 18, 2022

Fat has soaked through the paper bag. It looks stained. Ugly. I shouldn't have put the bags with pastry on top of the containers of hot soup. Not much to do about that now.

I wanted to show my group leaders my appreciation, make them breakfast, treat them to lunch, bake a cake, something, anything, to show that I am grateful for all the work they have done. Yet, they didn't want to meet in person. I can't say I'm surprised. Every time I attempted to gather the group in person, the closer we got to the date of the meeting, the more people asked whether it wouldn't be possible to join online. I guess it makes sense for a project studying online small groups.

Online meetings are great, but I think we cannot underestimate the importance of eating together. Sharing a meal is so fundamental, it is about hospitality and gift-giving and relationship-building, and probably a thousand other things.

In the end, we decided to have lunch during our online meeting. I considered asking everyone to simply bring lunch. Pragmatic. But there is a difference between eating together and *sharing a meal*. I checked whether I could have food delivered to everyone, but that was prohibitively expensive. So, I made sweet potato soup with chèvre, a family staple.

We eat a lot of Turkish yogurt at home, which comes in white one-liter plastic containers that shut tight—perfect for transporting soup safely. But as I stared at the makeshift containers of soup, I suddenly understood that old adage "presentation matters in cooking." What can I say? They simply didn't look very appetizing. Nor did they feel like gifts. They felt like recycled plastic containers with soup. Not that the fat-stained paper bags with pastry helped matters…

Yesterday, I spent all afternoon biking around Stockholm to deliver plastic containers and greasy bags. I felt more like a delivery guy than a host, especially when I left the soup in front of one door without ever speaking to my "guest," who had COVID.

Today's lunch didn't feel like the shared meal I had wanted. Simply having the same soup on many different plates on many different tables in many different rooms was not enough to establish a sense of connection, at least not for me. Even if the gesture might have been appreciated, I'm not convinced it was worth the effort.

#PreferenceForOnlineMeetings, #SendingSoup

#Djursholm, *Lectio Divina*
Tuesday, January 19, 2022

Eva's son's life is still hanging in the balance. He was in Latin America when it happened, and they are trying to fly him home once his condition allows. I offered to lead the Djursholm group on Thursday, which she accepted.

#Djursholm, *Lectio Divina*
Thursday, January 20, 2022

I was meticulously prepared, and determined to put my learnings to the test. I had informed everyone that I would start playing Taizé songs fifteen minutes before the meeting started and that they were welcome to come and listen if they would like to "land" before the meeting, just as I had learned from Karin in Margareta Parish.

While playing the songs I shared a welcome screen as a visual aid. I used the same image Djursholm Parish used when communicating the group on Facebook. "*Lectio Divina* as Winter Turns to Spring. We start at 3 p.m.," and at least one of the participants did come and listen and expressed appreciation for that after the meeting. I was painstakingly punctual, leaving the welcome screen at exactly 3 p.m. sharp so as not to cause anyone to experience any loss of control.

As an additional "centering exercise," I used Jessica's opening from the book club and asked everyone to tell us about something—anything—that had made them happy during this week. Marianne told us about feeling happy that she picked up her grandchild from school—nice to get to know a little bit more about her life.

Then I explained what was going to happen next, and why I had structured the meeting in this particular way, namely, to address the need to understand that we encountered earlier. I also invited participants to get a pen and piece of paper in case they wanted to jot down words and phrases during the readings or silences.

To help them focus on the here and now, I asked if anyone had any pressing concerns they needed to attend to during the next forty-five minutes. Finally, as a way for them to state their expectations, I gave them a minute to think about whether there was anything particular they hoped to get out of this meeting. With those preparations complete, we were ready for the *Lectio Divina* exercise.

I started with Karin's relaxation exercise. Then I prayed with a slightly adapted passage from the New International Version of Psalm 46:

> *God is our refuge and strength, an ever-present help in trouble.*

Therefore we will not fear, though the earth give way
and the mountains fall into the heart of the sea,
though its waters roar and foam and the mountains quake with their surging.

Nations are in uproar, kingdoms fall; he lifts his voice.
The Lord is with us; the God of Jacob is our refuge.
Come and see what the Lord has done, the desolations he has brought on the earth.

He makes wars cease to the ends of the earth.
He breaks the bow and shatters the spear; he burns the shields with fire.

"Be still, and know that I am God; exalted among the nations, exalted in the earth."
The Lord Almighty is with us; the God of Jacob is our refuge.

We read John 4:27–42. A first reading, a moment of silence. Then a second read-ing, where I prompted everyone to see what, if anything, in the text attracted their attention. A moment of silence, an opportunity to share. The third reading, pre-ceded by the question: "Where do you place yourself in the story?" And again, a moment of silence, an opportunity to share, before the last reading during which participants were asked to see whether there was some kind of appeal in the pas-sage. A final moment of silence, a last round of sharing.

I had also prepared a closing, a moment corresponding to the landing strip, which was supposed to contain a decision point. So, as we drew to a close, I asked people to do the relaxation exercise again and to recall what they had thought about when I asked them about their hopes for this meeting, telling them that this was not something we would share.

"Were your expectations met? How did this meeting turn out? Is there any-thing you can take with you from this meeting into the rest of your week?" We closed with a prayer and the Lord's Blessing, which I screenshared.

As I was saying goodbye, Gunilla spontaneously commented that the meeting had been very valuable. Marianne added that the conversation had been important to her and compared it to the conversation Jesus had with the woman at the well. I thought the meeting went smoothly enough, but it was encouraging to hear that they found the time to be meaningful.

Two things though. One of the participants never turned on his/her camera or microphone. S/he didn't say anything during the entire meeting. That felt a little strange. It's like being watched, but you are not even sure whether the watcher is there. Except I know that this watcher was there, because when I ended the meeting, s/he logged off. At a bare minimum, s/he followed the meeting enough to realize it had concluded. Still, I find myself wondering whether we should require participants to leave their cameras on.

When the meeting was over, I chose to leave the call open, in case anyone wanted to stay and chat. Stig and Gunilla logged out quite quickly, but Marianne lingered. We talked about the research project and about having digital meetings. She enjoys online meetings and has become very accustomed to Zoom. At the same time, she agreed that it's nice to have a little follow-up talk like this. So, I wonder whether there is a better way to end these meetings. Is there a way to include a debrief, of sorts?

When I closed my computer, I felt drained. Not in a bad way, it's just that leading the group while trying to register everything that happened was taxing. I found it hard to be fully present and pay attention to what was happening while keeping one eye on what came next so I could ensure a smooth transition between moments. And actively participating? That was completely out of the question. Unsurprisingly, I did not have any personal moments of insight or revelation as I had in the meeting that Eva led.

Perhaps I don't have the mental capacity to process so much information at the same time. Or perhaps, this is a general aspect of leading? Does leading a group preclude participating on a par with others, and if so, what does that say about the dynamics of leaders and group members? Also, if I wanted to put my learnings to the test, how will I know if any of these exercises "worked"?

Based on my experiences with Karin's *Lectio Divina* group and Jessica's book club, I figured relying on observations would be sufficient. At the very least, we should have some sort of evaluation with the group's participants, to see what they made of the meeting.

#TaizéSongs, #LandingStrip, #OpeningQuestion, #GroupBuilding, #RelaxationExercise, #Closing, #ClearRules, #SeeingEachOther, #BeingFullyPresent, #Debriefing, #DecisionPoints, #PotentialLearning

#Djursholm, *Lectio Divina*
Monday, January 31, 2022

I will keep leading the *Lectio Divina as Winter Turns to Spring* group together with Eva. We will alternate leading sessions, which means that the group will continue and be part of the research project. Knock on wood, this research project may just come together after all.

#EmergentDesign

#Älvsjö, *Bible Study*
Wednesday, February 2, 2022

Camilla, in Älvsjö Parish, and I will try to get an online small group going during Lent. We agreed to adopt the setup we had intended for our Bible study group for Easter. We will meet once a week, starting on Shrove Tuesday, and follow the Church of Sweden's lectionary. Our target group is still pastors in the Church of Sweden, though all are welcome.

We included an invitation for the group in the diocesan newsletter and immediately got a couple of registrations. Some of the people who had expressed an interest during the fall have also signed up. Now there are six participants, so the group is absolutely happening as well!

#EmergentDesign

#Djursholm, *Lectio Divina*
Thursday, February 17, 2022

One of our participants sat in a car, parked somewhere. The camera kept switching on and off and I found it difficult to focus, perhaps because I was leading and keeping an eye out for group dynamics. It was hard to know whether she was able to follow the conversation. It can't have been easy for her either, flipping in and out of the session. Perhaps we should ask people to be either present at meetings or to skip the meeting if they can't fully commit.

Before digital meetings became widespread, people simply missed meetings when they were driving or were sick or had an appointment. And that was ok, wasn't it? This new idea that everyone should be able to participate all the time, no matter what, strikes me as a little odd, especially when this kind of partial participation has negative effects on others in the meeting. But I guess asking people (politely) not to come in case they cannot be fully present somehow goes against the strong notion in the Church of Sweden that one should be as welcoming as possible. And probably the group is important to our participants, otherwise they would not decide to park somewhere for an hour to join. Would it be the right thing to ask people to stay away, only because their schedules are busy? Who knows why she couldn't be at home during the meeting.

To get us started I asked everyone which color represents their current mood. I figured that everyone can easily pick a color and we can say a lot through colors. Even if I registered some skepticism to this unusual opening, the group indulged me and people spoke freely about why they had chosen their respective colors.

I don't think that asking participants to state their expectations landed well, though. Not sure if it is me or if it is based on a subtle reading of the room—but it just didn't feel right. The goal of helping participants to be present is good, but the question felt forced and overly concrete. I am not sure if people really do have any hopes for these meetings, or if everyone has a burning question that needs answering. I will skip that next time.

After the meeting had officially ended, participants stayed for an informal evaluation. We talked about how to start a meeting. Some participants would like to start with a little small talk, while others enjoy the music we play. One participant expressed that she never really knows how to behave when entering a meeting. Should you interrupt an ongoing conversation to say "hi" or just sneak in?

I recognize that difficulty. I have often felt a little uncomfortable when entering a meeting where people were already having a conversation. It is difficult to break into an ongoing conversation in a good way, but if you don't, it feels like eavesdropping, which is also weird. On the other hand, if there are a bunch of people just staring silently at each other, that is almost worse. That's why I opt to play music when I am leading.

Today it was almost a pity that we couldn't engage in small talk, though. I would have enjoyed hearing, briefly, how everyone was doing. Probably it has something to do with how well you know each other. The better you know each other, the more you want to chat. An option would be to start with music at the beginning of a new group and to move on to socializing once people are more comfortable with each other. All this relates to the question of how to build strong community. It also shows how different we are. We will probably never find a form that suits everyone equally well.

We also talked about how online meetings kind of force you to be active, assuming your camera is on. There is no corner in which to hide. Everyone addresses everyone each time they speak. That makes it at times difficult, but it also presents an opportunity. There is no hiding, so people need to be engaged, which our participants appreciate, even if it pushes them out of their comfort zone.

Indeed, people shared my feeling about keeping cameras on during meetings. There was widespread agreement that everyone should have their camera on, otherwise you "think a lot about why that person doesn't have their camera on, what they are doing, and whether they are listening." It takes the focus from the actual conversation.

We also talked about how it might be a good idea to have the opportunity to stay afterward to debrief if you wanted. That shouldn't be mandatory but an open invitation.

Lastly, there was agreement that *Lectio Divina* works well as a method for the group, so we will stick to that.

#TaizéSongs, #GroupBuilding, #IndividualDifferences, #NoHiding, #ClearRules, #SeeingEachOther, #BeingFullyPresent, #Debriefing, #Evaluation

#Reflection
Sunday, February 20, 2022

I had an epiphany about the research while watching the sixth season of *Billions*, a TV show about the intrigues of super-wealthy New York investors. (A strange sentence to read, I can imagine, but hear me out.) Episode five, "Rock of Eye," is about how people are incredibly transactional, and suddenly it clicks: we are dealing with two separate kinds of online meetings—a transactional kind and a relational kind. Many of the people I spoke to in preparation for this research project asserted that online meetings work great. In fact, I have noticed a preference for online meetings also in this research track.

Now, though, I realize that people prefer an online format when the meetings are transactional in nature; that is, the purpose of the meeting is clearly established and the success of the meeting does not (fundamentally) depend on the relationships between participants, but rather on their "function" in the transaction. If I am right, transactional meetings are about exchanges: booking an appointment, consulting a superior, informing about an upcoming event, clarifying the contents of a contract, that sort of thing. These meetings do not depend on establishing strong community. It is the transaction that is foregrounded.

Our online small groups, on the other hand, are relational. It is the developing relationships between participants that make these meetings worthwhile. Truly loving your neighbor, after all, is not transactional. It is fundamentally grounded in a relationship. So, our groups are then above all meeting places. No one is there simply to get information. The groups are about doing something together, about establishing a community that can sustain deep conversations about life and faith. So, online small groups are difficult because they are relational and thus require the building of strong relationships and community, which is arguably more difficult if people remain separated in their disparate places, as group building does not occur "naturally."

Though I could not have articulated it at the time, I suppose much of my wanting to share a meal with my leaders relates to this notion. Meeting online often felt transactional. Sure, it worked, but it lacked the distinctive relational quality I had envisioned and hoped for. Transactional and relational meetings not only have different prerequisites, but they also enable—and limit—different forms of community, collaboration, and conversation.

#PreferenceForOnlineMeetings, #RelationalMeetings, #GroupBuilding, #Community

#Älvsjö, *Bible Study*
Tuesday, March 1, 2022

Today was the first meeting with our Lenten Bible study group. In the end, ten participants signed up. Including Camilla and myself, that makes twelve—almost too many participants, it turns out, at least if everyone is supposed to be given speaking time in the ninety minutes we have allotted. I used a similar setup as I did in the *Lectio Divina as Winter Turns to Spring* group, playing songs before the meeting, and so on.

For introductions, we asked everyone to describe where they are sitting. It gives some more context to the room from which people speak, situating them in a specific place. It is also an easy question everyone can answer and a possibility for people to interact. "What is that nice picture you have on the wall there?" "That is a drawing of Jerusalem I got when we were there with a group of pilgrims in 2006."

As a group-building exercise, we asked participants to write a prayer. We sent them into breakout rooms in groups of three and four for ten minutes.[2] Returning, they had each written a prayer for our group. Camilla and I will combine these into one to use as our opening prayer for each session moving forward. Participants also contribute to the meeting setup by taking turns introducing the week's reading, with Camilla going first.

When Camilla introduced today's reading, it struck me that this instance of instruction didn't disrupt the feeling of the conversation. Perhaps that was because it was so clearly marked as instruction, or because it effectively happened before the conversation, or because we are going to take turns, so that everyone is going to "teach" at some point.

---

[2] Most videoconferencing software has the ability to create small groups, so that the group can be broken up into smaller sections. In these breakout rooms participants only see and hear other participants assigned to the same small group.

Seeing that it is important to establish clear rules, we asked participants whether we could agree on the following:

1. You are either fully present or you skip the meeting. It's fine to miss a few meetings, but it distracts the others if you are here but not really present. If you need to drive or clean during the meeting, it is better to skip that meeting.
2. We all have our cameras on during the entire meeting. It gives security to be able to see each other.
3. Try to find a place where you can sit fairly undisturbed. Use headphones if you are in a room with other people so that our conversation is not over-heard.

Everyone agreed and I even got an email from one of the participants saying that they really appreciated these rules.

#GroupBuilding, #Instruction, #DistributedResponsibility, #ClearRules

#Djursholm, *Lectio Divina*
Thursday, March 3, 2022

Fifth meeting with the *Lectio Divina as Winter Turns to Spring* group.

Eva starts the meeting by telling us about Ash Wednesday, how it disappeared during the Reformation, and how it was reintroduced in the Church of Sweden in the 1980s. She told us about the initial resistance to this "Roman Catholic" custom, and how resistance was slowly overcome so that Ash Wednesday is now an accepted feature in the Church of Sweden, including the tracing the cross of ashes on people's foreheads.

I wonder where she is going with this. It feels like a mini-lecture, and we have entered a specific dynamic of communication; Eva teaches, we listen. Eva tells us that Ash Wednesday marks the beginning of Lent and that fasting in the Old Testament was a way of calling for God's attention, a way of asking God for help. Here she makes the connection to Russia's war on Ukraine. Eva continues to explain how Ash Wednesday mass reminds us of our own mortality, reminds us that we are dust.

"So, now you've had a little church lesson," Eva concludes. She sounds almost surprised herself. I also notice that we have not been involved in any of this. Eva spoke, and we listened.

This introduction reverberated throughout the rest of our meeting. When Eva finished reading Mark 2:18–22 (where Jesus is questioned about fasting) for the second time after having asked us to listen to a word or phrase that draws our attention, Stig wondered why people cannot fast together with the groom. Marianne said she doesn't really get the parable of the wineskins. Linda found the text difficult and didn't "understand." I wondered whether these sudden outbursts of nonunderstanding and demands for explanation were related to the way in which Eva opened the meeting. Perhaps lecturing set the stage for instruction, for a mode in which participants wanted answers and an expert who explained.

It is a testament to Eva's teaching sensibilities that she simply said that some texts are confusing and instead asked us to place ourselves in the text. Eva asks Marianne how she imagines the scene in which Jesus has the conversation with the Pharisees, effectively moving people from a preoccupation with intellectual understanding to embodied knowing. Stig, Marianne, and Linda return to questions of understanding during the rest of the meeting, but there is no more lecturing, even if some of them might have liked some definite answers.

#Instruction

#Älvsjö, *Bible Study*
Tuesday, March 8, 2022

I combined the prayers participants wrote, then printed and laminated them, and sent each participant a prayer card with our group prayer on one side and the Blessing on the other.[3] I also included a high pillar candle around which I had tied a purple silk ribbon. Looked quite nice, actually. But I should probably have been clear on what to do with the candles.

The idea was that we all light our candles together as a kind of ritual gesture when we pray our prayer. However, when we start our second meeting with the Lenten Bible study group, some people have already lit their candles, and the whole "now we light our candles together" moment collapses. But still, it is nice. It doesn't change much on screen; I can't even see most candles in the little windows through which I peak into participants' rooms. But that candle burning on my desk is identical to the candle that every other participant has burning somewhere in their rooms, which generates a feeling of belonging—even if that probably would be stronger if we addressed it explicitly.

To get people to know each other a little better I ask everyone to describe which animal they identify with at the moment. I am a little nervous as the question strikes me as a little odd, but people are indulging me, and it is interesting to

---

[3] See appendix B.

see how much we can express about our current situation by relating that to ani-
mals. It's similar to the question about colors. Sometimes I think it is good to use
these odd questions. The whole purpose is to unsettle us a little, just a little, but
enough that we say something more than the archetypal "I am good, thanks." Not
sure though what people made of this exercise.

One of the participants introduced this week's readings (Matthew 16:21–23),
which was good because it was very different from the way Camilla had chosen to
do that last week, and opened the possibility for others to do it their way in upcoming meetings. It also distributes responsibility, so that leaders and participants
become a little more equal.

Camilla and I had met last week to talk about the group. We talked about ways
to build community and agreed to assign everyone a prayer partner, a person from
the group to keep in your prayers during the week to get people to connect with
each other outside of group meetings.

Lastly, we decided to end the group in breakout rooms. After we had officially
finished, we sent people in groups to their respective rooms to mirror the chit-chat
you would have in onsite meetings when leaving a venue. It's both a chance to
quickly debrief and to talk to people a little more intimately than what is possible
if everyone listens. It is fascinating how much you can use onsite group-building
mechanisms in online small groups if you only think of it. Or so I thought.

#LightingCandles, #OpeningQuestion, #GroupBuilding, #DistributedResponsibility,
#PrayerPartners, #Debriefing, #MimickingOnsiteMeetings, #BreakoutRoomDebrief

#Älvsjö, *Bible Study*
Tuesday, March 15, 2022

The Lenten Bible study works well. Just one observation: Our landing strip and
group building part has gotten much shorter. In the first meeting we spent almost
thirty minutes on introductions and group-building exercises, but now we are
down to eleven minutes. I think that is ok. It's probably more important to spend
a lot of time on group building at the beginning of a new group. Now, people
know each other (at least a little) and so it also makes sense to get to the actual Bible
study more quickly. I also have the feeling that people are quicker in their landings,
as they know by now what is happening in the group.

#LandingStrip, #GroupBuilding

Leader

#Älvsjö, *Bible Study*
Tuesday, April 12, 2022

Today we had the last meeting with our Lenten Bible study group, after which we did an evaluation. No one liked the debriefing in breakout rooms. People reported that closing in breakout rooms worked poorly because they were unsure what was expected of them in that "debriefing." Many felt they had to leave at the appointed time and were uncomfortable being given the responsibility to debrief with someone without having the necessary time to do so.

This disturbed me. I mean, it is ok that they didn't like the debrief, but why didn't anyone tell me before now? We have done that every week and if they didn't like it, why didn't they simply say so? Perhaps there is a cultural thing about not wanting to express criticism after all.

Otherwise, people were quite happy. Those preaching found that the group had helped them in their preparations, either by giving them concrete ideas or by allowing them to reflect on the text from a larger number of perspectives, feeling more grounded in their engagement with the biblical text. Participants also reported how this engagement had frequently been valuable for them personally, a moment of conversation that opened up for theological reflection. They appreciated the candle and the prayer and enjoyed that we took turns introducing the text. Many of them recounted appreciating the open and honest atmosphere in the group and noted how the prayer partners had added to that.

Participants also said that they prioritized the group because it wasn't an ongoing group. Knowing that we would only meet seven times made it more important to attend meetings— something to keep in mind for the future.

#MimickingOnsiteMeetings, #LossOfControl, #LightingCandles, #PrayerPartners, #DistributedResponsibility, #MeetingAtmosphere, #BreakoutRoomDebrief, #PotentialLearning, #Evaluation

#Djursholm, *Lectio Divina*
Thursday, April 28, 2022

I am in high spirits as I make my way back to Djursholm Parish for our final evaluation. Spring is in the air again as we meet in the parish meeting house, just a stone's throw from the little garden where everything started a year ago. As I set the table for coffee and snacks, I contemplate how, in the end, everything worked out. I have come to the end of the line.

As the members of our *Lectio Divina* group arrive, I reflect on the peculiar feeling of seeing them not mediated through cameras and screens. I feel close to them, feel as if I know them, at least a little, and yet, this also feels different. Perhaps because I needed to leave the safety of my own home to get here.

Over coffee and sandwiches, we discuss how the group went. The general feeling is that the group worked well. Being a small group meant that it was easy to get to know each other and to feel that there was a level of trust. Following the same method from week to week meant that it was easy to know what to expect.

It became clear, however, that we also experienced the group differently. Being in the middle of life, balancing small children, work, family, friends, Church, and social activities means that I often feel a little revved up. It's not necessarily a bad feeling, more like the sensation that life is a run, rather than a walk. That makes me appreciate moments when I can be still for a little while. It makes me appreciate landing strips and relaxation exercises and all kinds of maneuvers meant to get me to slow down. I am not alone in this. Linda, too, expressed appreciation for these moments. Her situation seems similar to mine.

But not everybody is experiencing life as a juggling act, especially retired persons, who make up a large part of the Church of Sweden's active parishioners. They might have come to the point where both the general speed of life and their number of commitments and responsibilities have decreased. Stig, Gunilla, and Linda probably do not need to destress as much as I do, and even though they indulged me, they did not necessarily feel that all this landing and relaxing was necessary. Unsurprisingly, you do not need to land if the Bible study group is the only thing on the day's agenda. It might be the other way around, in fact. Perhaps you have been looking forward to this, mentally preparing, so that once the meeting starts you want it to take off, and not "land."

And here I end. It was a good group and we had good conversations, but any kind of setup works on a set of assumptions—assumptions about how busy people are, and how difficult it is to fit these groups into busy schedules. If these assumptions turn out to be wrong, the setup ends up being skewed. Not necessarily useless, but less than ideal.

As I pack up my things, I wonder what to make of all of this. What have I learned about leading online small groups? How far have we traveled on this journey? At least one thing has become painstakingly clear: improving online small groups is not a task one ever finishes. I thought I had it more or less figured out, saw how we'd learned through trial and error how to design and facilitate group sessions.... But it's more complicated than that, isn't it?

This is not to say that we didn't gain valuable insights. I think we did—insights into group and leadership dynamics, the relational nature of online small groups, and the difficulty of continuously assessing how well groups work. And the techniques we developed from landing strips to prayer partners to including decision points are all valuable. But we will have to continue to reflect on these to see how and when they are most appropriate.

My thoughts drift to my dissertation co-supervisor, Heather Walton. I just completed her *Creative Writing as Spiritual Reflection* class. She would conclude every writing exercise with the same words—now ringing true in my ears:

No one ever finishes.

#MeetingAtmosphere, #RelaxationExercise, #IndividualDifferences, #PotentialLearning, #Evaluation

Response from Camilla Lindström

#Älvsjö, *Bible Study*

About one month after my ordination, COVID-19 hit the world. From one week to another, most of the usual weekly activities common in dioceses, parishes, and churches within the Church of Sweden were canceled. That included celebrating mass, as well as church rituals or ecclesial ceremonies such as baptism, confirmation, weddings, and funerals. One can't help but wonder what happens to a church's or a congregation's self-identity when not being able to actually act as a church in terms of evangelization, mission, and not least spread—Christian hope, which is every church's first and foremost task, and the fundament for its being.

The first reaction was shock and paralysis, which after a while grew into some sort of "coping-mentality." As a church, we cannot close our doors, neither literary nor figuratively speaking. So, we started to record shorter devotions through our joint Facebook account to keep contact with the world outside of isolation and hopefully also to reach out to people whom we thought would never participate in a regular service, but who longed for meaning in their lives and also longed to explore if God could be that meaning of life, not least in time of crisis. Not long after that, we started having funerals again, due to the fact that people actually died due to COVID-19. The rules of limitations of participants were at some point down to eight people—hence many funeral homes initiated live cast funerals. That really opened our eyes to what new possibilities the digitalized world could entail in ecclesial contexts.

During my second year as a priest, which was also the second pandemic year, we, who spent our daily lives and work in the Church of Sweden, found more and more new routines in coping with our ecclesial task in a new terrain, seeing the potential in being "church online." I changed diocese from Strängnäs, which is characterized by a rural context, to Stockholm, which is an urban environment where people live, work, and commute closer to one another. In my new parish, "Älvsjö," I immediately became a participant in this new participatory action research project, called *Church in Digital Space*, conducted by the Church of Sweden Diocese of Stockholm.

The aim of the project was to explore and examine what it meant to *be* a church according to the definition "people who meet, gather, and worship in their belief of Jesus Christ as the son of God," but in a digital world. Initially, I held great skepticism towards the project, and towards whether it even was possible to view the church as a *being*, that is, to view "church" as a verb.

I thought that my own points of *if*, and if so, *when* we, who in different ways and roles gather and worship in our belief of Jesus Christ, can actually do that in a digital context, were clear, at least to myself. Was it even possible to bless someone outside of real life? Was there a time limit of when the Blessing started and ceased to "work"? What was the point of recording devotions if we could not celebrate them together with our parish members? Were we producers of some sort of Christian entertainment show that others consumed?

That's when I first met and came to know Simon, which was a Blessing in itself. Being an ordained priest is my second career, my first career was as an economist and behavioral scientist with education as my major. Simon, with his educational and theological background, became the sparring partner I needed to catalyze my doubts of being church (as a verb), and also being church in a digital context. I felt that we spoke the same language in several ways, we shared the same terminology, and I found Simon not at all afraid to confront, challenge, and develop my skeptical thoughts.

When he asked me to co-lead this online small group of pastors, exploring the biblical texts read during the great holy days of the church year with him, I immediately said yes. That was exactly the kind of practical, specific task where I could see that online small groups could work as "*being* church" i.e. "church as a verb"; when the purpose was to deepen our joint Christian faith by actually *doing* something—to discuss the Scripture mirroring our own current life situations. As Simon describes this in his dissertation diary notes:

> Faith isn't something you have, an object you can put in a box and cherish. Faith is dynamic and changing—it's something we do—meaning it can flourish and grow, but it can also wither away. As such, there is a need to continuously nurture it, and one way to do this is to talk about faith.[1]

Faith is a collective action and engagement. That's how Christian faith grows and develops—in community, or, maybe better captured in the Greek word

---

[1] See the entry from Monday, July 12, 2021.

koinonia, which is a transliterated form of the Greek word κοινωνία, which refers to concepts such as fellowship. Simon's suggestion to start an online small group of pastors was a great way to both explore the possibilities and limitations of the digital context, as well as explore different ways of "being church online" in terms of being part of a Christian *koinonia*.

We started to plan the content of our group activity and the purpose of examining lifelong learning in a group of trained priests and academics, all of them well-experienced leaders and also well-educated and very used to both articulate and discuss biblical texts and biblical issues about life and death. We early agreed on rather strict rules for the group, such as always having the camera on, and commitment to be an active part of the group. One other crucial part was that all members of the group should take turns leading the group's initial bible study and moderate the following discussion.

For me, personally, the action research method was challenging and new. My own experience of research methods was in the field of practical theology and qualitative method, but I had never before met qualitative method where the scientist so explicitly was part and a member of the actual research object. That kind of frightened me at first, as well as fascinated me. I was very impressed by Simon, who so bravely and convincingly—and calmly!—took this method on, well aware that it might be considered a risk and also a lot of arguments on the researcher's role and influence on the research object and the consequences of reliability of the whole project.

I am still very impressed by Simon and his pioneer spirit and very thankful for taking me on and challenging me. I have developed in this project, as a Christian, as a priest, and as a human, and I have revalued my own preconceived notions, and it has contributed to my own lifelong learning. And lifelong learning is really a lifeblood needed to keep on momentum.

Part III:
Reflection on the Story in Light of the Experience and the Theory

4. Online Small Groups

In this chapter, I begin a process of reflection on the narrative presented in part 2. I have intentionally composed the story with a surplus of information, not merely as a narrative technique but also in the hope that these specifics might inspire and afford the possibility of learning from my account.[1] The reflection in this part, then, is not meant to exhaustively discuss all elements of the narrative, nor is my objective to dissect the story and deconstruct it into its constituent parts. Instead, reflection connects the narrative account to the theoretical perspectives introduced in chapter 2 and to previous research discussed in section 1.5, to see different aspects of our online small groups.

Seeing differently does not imply seeing better or more clearly. The story's meaning is not concealed, only to be unveiled through my reflections in this part. Instead, the reflective narrative serves as a tool for understanding the multifaceted aspects of online small groups. By highlighting specific elements within the reflective narrative, theoretical perspectives similarly provide certain insights. They enable an exploration of experiences from a different viewpoint, allowing a change in perspective.

In this chapter, I explore how other researchers have conceptualized small groups (4.1) and subsequently employ the didactic relations model to delineate our online small groups as sites of learning and teaching (4.2). I conclude by discussing how my understanding of our online small groups diverges from previous research (4.3).

4.1 Small Groups

Most models of Christian religious education incorporate elements of group discussion or small groups. Thomas Groome's influential shared Christian praxis approach primarily revolves around small group discussions, mirroring the structure

---

[1] See section 3.5.2.

of Peter Balls's model for the Christian initiation of adults.[2] Other religious educators, such as Craig Dykstra, Andrew Root, and Irma Cook Everist, conceptualize Christian religious education as encompassing a variety of forms, allocating space for small groups within the church's broader educational ministry.[3] Consequently, small groups transcend specific models of Christian religious education and span different Christian denominations.[4] Small groups are not so much an independent model of Christian religious education as they are a distinct manifestation of it.

The versatility of small groups partially accounts for their widespread presence. Notably, small groups are a ubiquitous aspect of North American Christianity, with 2019 estimates indicating that sixty percent of U.S. churchgoers regularly participate in small groups.[5] Although this percentage may be smaller in Sweden, seventy percent of parishes in the Church of Sweden Diocese of Stockholm offered some form of small group in February 2020, immediately prior to the extensive outbreak of the COVID-19 virus in Sweden.[6]

The sheer number of small groups suggests that there must be considerable variation among them. Indeed, Harley Atkinson distinguishes between process-oriented groups (affinity groups, home fellowship/share groups), content-oriented groups (Bible study groups, discussion groups), task-oriented groups (committees, work groups, outreach groups, ministry groups), and need-oriented groups (growth groups, support groups, recovery groups, spiritual formation groups).[7] More important than understanding the differences among these types is appreciating the fact that small groups are not a monolithic concept; nor are they necessarily related to churches, parishes, or congregations, even if that is their most common context.[8]

Despite these differences, small groups generally share several characteristics. In his landmark study on small groups in the United States, Robert Wuthnow

---

[2] Groome, *Sharing Faith*; Peter Ball, *Adult Believing: A Guide to the Christian Initiation of Adults* (London: Mowbray, 1988).

[3] Dykstra, *Life of Faith*; Andrew Root, *Faith Formation in a Secular Age: Responding to the Church's Obsession with Youthfulness* (Grand Rapids: Baker Academic, 2017); Cook Everist, *Learning Community*.

[4] Wuthnow, *Sharing the Journey*, 111. See section 2.4 for an introduction to the models of Christian religious education.

[5] Atkinson and Rose, "Small-Group Ministry," 552.

[6] See appendix D.

[7] Atkinson, *Small Groups*, chap. 3.

[8] Wuthnow, *Sharing the Journey*, 64–78.

describes them as voluntary, intentional gatherings, usually with a stated purpose or goal, leaders, and a schedule or agenda.[9] Atkinson, focusing specifically on church-based small groups, identifies six characteristics: (1) Groups are typically small in size, with group membership ranging from three to twelve to fifteen participants as the norm. (2) Participants of small groups are conscious of being part of a specific group, demonstrating group consciousness. (3) Small groups have a shared purpose. (4) This shared purpose can only be achieved by the group as a whole, necessitating interdependence. (5) Small groups are centered around face-to-face interaction. (6) They are cohesive, ensuring that the group persists over time.[10]

4.2 Didactic Relations in Our Online Small Groups

When introducing the didactic relations model, I mentioned that the number of elements has varied between different presentations, as have the namings of the various categories.[11] In my formulation of the didactic relations model in figure 4.1, I parcel out the function of the teacher from Hiim and Hippe's category of frame factors and include both frame factors and teachers as separate elements. Additionally, I expand the category of learners' learning prerequisites to simply "learners."[12] These changes align with the didactic questions, which include the *who* and *whom* of teaching.[13]

---

[9] Wuthnow, *Sharing the Journey*, 135–37.

[10] Atkinson, *Small Groups*, chap. 2.

[11] See section 2.6.

[12] Hiim and Hippe, *Undervisningsplanlegging*, 37–41.

[13] See section 2.6.

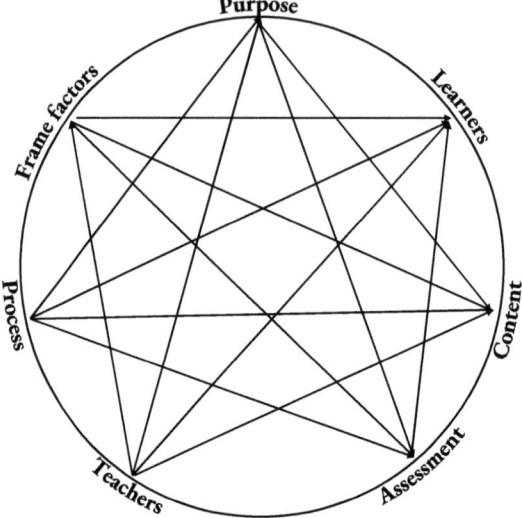

Figure 4.1: The Didactic Relations Model

As all nodes in the didactic relations model are interconnected, an analysis of online small groups can begin with any component, implying no hierarchy in the order of engagement with various elements.[14] My presentation starts with the purpose, content, and process, followed by a reflection on evaluation. I then proceed to examine frame factors, learners, and teachers, respectively.

4.2.1 Purpose

For three of our four groups, we created #ResearchPlans, translations of which are included in appendix B. Part of the #ResearchPlans was a section on the #Aspirations each leader had for their group, including my #Aspirations for the #Älvsjö group.

Examining our #Aspirations, the first critical point is that we indeed had definite #Aspirations for each group.[15] Of course, the formulation of #Aspirations was part of the research process itself, making it impossible to determine whether

---

[14] Hiim and Hippe, *Undervisningsplanlegging*, 41.

[15] It stands to reason that we also had #Aspirations for the #Djursholm group. However, the circumstances of the group were such that we did not produce a comparable research plan and therefore did not speak about our aspirations.

group leaders would have articulated these #Aspirations in writing if not for the research project.

It is also unclear to what extent Jessica and Karin expressed their #Aspirations for the #S:tEskils and #Margareta groups, respectively, only when prompted during our discussion about the #ResearchPlans. Regardless of these circumstances, it is evident that group leaders were able to articulate #Aspirations for each group, demonstrating they had specific intentions, even if these might have been more implicit than explicit at times.

In chapter 7, I examine these intentions in the context of constructive alignment as intended learning outcomes. Here, I simply highlight that each group leader held multiple intentions, including growth in faith (#Margareta and #Älvsjö), the creation of community (#S:tEskils and #Älvsjö), the development of the ability to discuss faith and to listen (#Margareta), fostering a joy of reading and stimulating questions about our place in the world (#S:tEskils), assistance with sermon preparation, and learning about online small groups (#Älvsjö).

The formulation of intentions for each group does not necessarily imply that the purpose preceded the creation of the groups. In other words, the presence of #Aspirations does not mean that the online small groups we led were initially created or designed with those specific purposes in mind. From my view, the process often occurred in reverse; concrete intentions were formulated only after the groups had been convened. Therefore, while it is accurate to say that our online small groups were not explicitly created as sites of teaching, this does not preclude the possibility of these groups being recognized or functioning as sites of teaching once they were established. I revisit this discussion in chapter 6.

4.2.2 Content

In terms of content, there is a clear convergence among the #Margareta, #Djursholm, and #Älvsjö groups. Each of these groups engaged with biblical texts as outlined by the Church of Sweden's lectionary. Additionally, they incorporated traditional Christian practices, including the method of *Lectio Divina*, #PrayerPartners, #LightingCandles, and Christian artifacts like #TaizéSongs. Therefore, the content of these groups can be characterized as embodying the Christian tradition as practiced within the Church of Sweden.

It is crucial to acknowledge, however, that content was not something to be appropriated. A more accurate description would be that for the two *Lectio Divina* groups, the content was God's address, while in the #Älvsjö group, the discussions centered around faith, with Scripture, practices, and artifacts serving as a catalyst.[16] Therefore, the content can be more accurately described as participants' engagement with each other and with the Christian tradition, aligning with the shared praxis approach championed by Thomas Groome.[17]

The #S:tEskils group introduces a complexity to this framework, however. The book club did not incorporate elements traditionally associated with the Christian tradition, instead engaging with works of literary fiction. One might conclude that #S:tEskils represents an exception and should not be considered a form of Christian religious education. This perspective could be based on a definition of Christian religious education that emphasizes direct connections to the Christian tradition and its narratives.

However, I question the usefulness of such a strict delineation. If the Christian tradition is understood as encompassing not only a collection of stories, practices, and artifacts, but also a particular way of being in the world as articulated by the Great Commandment, it becomes challenging to specify which forms Christian religious education should take to cultivate love of God and neighbor.

Caroline Klintborg's work highlights a similar intermingling of Christian and non-Christian perspectives in her analysis of confirmation training in the Church of Sweden. This training explicitly incorporates Christian ethics alongside the knowledge of Christian narratives, practices, and artifacts, suggesting it would be inaccurate to oppose ethics to other components of the tradition.[18] Further, I see no reason to believe that Christian ethics need to be couched in traditional Christian language, with Jesus' parables as an eminent example.

If teaching Christian ethics is a fundamental aspect of Christian religious education, and if such ethics are not solely reliant on traditional Christian language or directly connected to Christian narratives, practices, and artifacts, then the #S:tEskils group can indeed be viewed as participating in Christian religious education. This perspective is especially valid considering the groups' church-based nature, establishing a clear connection to an ecclesial setting, which links the groups to the church's overall message.[19]

---

[16] Jonas Ideström has developed this notion in relation to Gordon Lathrop's concept of juxtaposition, suggesting that the content is theologizing itself, understood as the engagement between Christian stories, practices, and artifacts, on the one hand, and present-day people's life and faith, on the other hand. Ideström, *Ikoniska kartor*, 79–103.

[17] Groome, *Sharing Faith*.

[18] Klintborg, *Var är Jesus?*, 27–33.

[19] McClintock Fulkerson, *Places of Redemption*. McClintock Fulkerson discusses a physical place. Her findings are thus not directly transferrable to online small groups, but I believe the basic mechanisms of place making function analogously.

4.2.3 Process

Above I presented the idea that the content of our online small groups can be framed as "participants' engagement with each other and the Christian tradition," and argued that this perspective holds even when the Christian tradition is not explicitly included, as observed in the #S:tEskils group. Describing the content in such a manner essentially implies that the content of these groups is the process of engagement itself. Indeed, I propose that it is this specific process of interaction and shared exploration that characterizes online small groups as a distinct form of non-formal Christian religious education.

All groups we led centered around dialogue or conversation. The #Margareta group may appear as an outlier since conversation was not actively promoted during the *Lectio Divina* sessions. However, even in this group, there was an element of sharing which facilitated learning from one another and engagement with the biblical text. Furthermore, there was discussion regarding the theme for Sunday towards the end of the sessions, as detailed in my journal entry from Sunday, October 3, 2021.[20] This illustrates that, despite initial appearances, the essence of interactive engagement and shared learning was present across all groups.

While dialogue and conversation are common elements in many settings, I argue that what characterizes our approach in online small groups is what I term "directed dialogue." This approach sits between what John Elias describes as "disciplined learning" and "small group faith sharing."[21] In disciplined learning, the role of teachers is primarily as instructors who guide learners in acquiring specific knowledge. Conversely, small group faith sharing embraces a dialogical approach to education, where teachers act as facilitators of organic group processes rather than as direct sources of knowledge.[22]

The key distinction between instruction and facilitation lies in the authority attributed to the teacher and their contributions, which influences both the perceived purpose of learning and the understanding of knowledge itself.[23] Directed dialogue, therefore, navigates these dynamics by steering the conversation without overshadowing the collaborative exploration of ideas.

In directed dialogue, leaders take on a role that diverges from the traditional roles of instructors or facilitators. They are charged with crafting specific potential learning situations that foster an environment where participants can learn from

---

[20] See chapter Participant Observer in part 2.
[21] Elias, "Models."
[22] Elias, "Models," 182–88.
[23] Astley, "Definitions," 5–9.

and alongside each other through dialogue.[24] This approach necessitates careful planning in how group interactions are orchestrated, including the structuring of meetings, the selection and presentation of topics, and the framing of inquiries. It also involves thoughtful consideration of both the physical and digital contexts in which the group operates, as well as fostering a sense of trust essential for meaningful dialogue.[25]

Consequently, directed dialogue places a significant amount of responsibility on group leaders. The successful functioning of the group does not solely rest on the participants but heavily on how leaders design and manage the online small group dynamics. This design has profound effects on the type of learning that can occur. However, while leaders guide the direction of the conversation, they do not control it. Instead, it is through a collaborative effort with participants that topics are explored, highlighting a cooperative exploration rather than a top-down dissemination of knowledge.

Dialogue is also directed in the sense of being goal-oriented. Discussing Aristotle's epistemology in relation to action research, Norwegian philosopher Olav Eikeland contends that dialogue

> has nothing to do with merely *two* (*dúo*) people talking to each other. Dialogue is a distinctive cognitive, emotional, and practical process – usually unfolded among several participants – that proceeds critically through (*dià*) common ways of speaking and through reasoned speech (*[tou] lógou*).[26]

Eikeland's interpretation emphasizes that dialogue is not about the mere act of talking but about the quality and direction of the conversation. Central to Eikeland's understanding is the claim that dialogue is a means for the generation of knowledge; dialogue is action-based, rather than action-oriented, that is, dialogue is not intended to solve immediate problems but to articulate knowings on the basis of experience.[27] Eikeland thus introduced a nuanced distinction, suggesting that the purpose of dialogue is not to address immediate issues but to cultivate understandings derived from collective experience.

---

[24] See section 6.2.

[25] Norma Cook Everist raised the same point. See Cook Everist, *Learning Community*, 62–68, 81–82.

[26] Olav Eikeland, "Phrónêsis, Aristotle, and Action Research," *International Journal of Action Research* 2, no. 1 (2006): 5–53 at 41. Emphasis in original.

[27] Olav Eikeland, "From Epistemology to Gnoseology: Understanding the Knowledge Claims of Action Research," *Management Research News* 30, no. 5 (2007): 344–58 at 354.

This process of collaborative reflection is central to the dynamics of online small groups. Within these groups, dialogue transforms into joint theological reflection, a cognitive endeavor aimed at weaving together the threads of the Christian tradition and ethics with the fabric of participants' everyday lives. This process of collaborative reflection offers the potential for deep, communal exploration of faith, affording participants the possibility to contextualize and integrate their beliefs within the broader narrative of their personal and communal experiences.

In our online small groups, it was evident how we as leaders had specific learning intentions in mind, as outlined in the #ResearchPlans. These objectives extended beyond the simple act of meeting. This led me to describe online small groups as a form of directed dialogue—dialogue intentionally structured to facilitate specific learning outcomes. This approach ensures that the conversations are not just open-ended or purely social interactions but are guided in a way that makes certain insights and understandings both possible and likely. I explore this further in chapter 6.

4.2.4 Evaluation

The open-ended nature of directed dialogue within the online small groups we examined is further underscored by the general absence of evaluative components. Drawing inspiration from Thomas Groome's praxis model of Christian religious education, I introduced #DecisionPoints into our #Älvsjö group. These #DecisionPoints served as a mechanism for self-evaluation, encouraging learners to contemplate the insights they derived from the discussions. Additionally, the #FeedbackForms we distributed to participants in the #S:tEskils and #Margareta groups were designed to prompt reflection on any learning that occurred within the group. Nonetheless, I speculate that these evaluative elements would not have been incorporated into the groups had it not been for the research project.

As implemented, these components merely prompted participants to reflect on their personal takeaways, rather than assessing whether they had comprehensively grasped specific content. At no point did leaders evaluate participants' learning outcomes, reinforcing the non-prescriptive and participant-centered ethos of these groups.

The lack of formal evaluative measures in the online small groups we observed underscores the notion that the goal of teaching in these settings was not the transmission of specific, pre-defined content for learners to acquire. Instead, these groups offered participants environments in which they were responsible for their own learning process, including monitoring and evaluating any potential "progress." This approach is consistent with the characteristics of non-formal education, where evaluation tends to be less emphasized.[28] In these contexts, the focus shifts from assessing the mastery of content to facilitating experiences and reflections that allow learners to derive personal insights and growth. The minimal presence of evaluative components in our groups aligns with this educational paradigm, emphasizing self-directed learning over traditional measures of achievement.

4.2.5 Frame Factors

The concept of frame factors highlights how any specific potential learning situation is invariably shaped by circumstances beyond the direct control of educators, necessitating adaptive responses from them. Hiim and Hippe categorize these into *material* frame factors, which include aspects like available time, spaces, equipment, and teaching materials, and *organizational* frame factors, encompassing scheduling, distribution of work tasks, established cooperations, and leadership structures, among others.[29]

The relevance of frame factors extends beyond the didactic relations model. U.S.-American educational theorist George J. Posner delineates several categories of frame factors, in the context of curriculum analysis: temporal, physical, political-legal, organizational, personal (or personnel), economic, and cultural.[30]

In this discussion, my focus is on those frame factors that directly impact the social learning situation within online small groups, specifically digital mediation, space and spatiality, and time. I thus abstract from other significant but less directly related frame factors, such as organizational, personnel, and economic factors, which are crucial in determining the feasibility and structure of online small groups but do not directly influence the moment-to-moment dynamics of the learning environment.

Digital mediation stands out as a primary frame factor, distinctly characterizing the online learning environment with its implications for space, spatiality, and timing. Unlike onsite small groups, where interactions unfold within a shared physical space, online small groups rely on videoconferencing technology to

---

[28] Evaluation might however play an important part in Christian religious education as a form of learners' self-assessment. See Roger Walton, "Assessment in Adult Christian Education," in *Learning in the Way: Research and Reflection on Adult Christian Education*, ed. Jeff Astley (Herefordshire: Gracewing, 2000), 90–112.

[29] Hiim and Hippe, *Undervisningsplanlegging*, 56.

[30] George J. Posner, *Analyzing the Curriculum* (Boston: McGraw-Hill, 2004), 193–201.

facilitate communication, generally through software like Zoom and Microsoft Teams in our context. This technology enables participants to visually and audibly connect in real-time, contingent upon the availability and utilization of cameras, microphones, and speakers.

The fundamental distinction between onsite and online small groups, therefore, is not whether participants can engage in face-to-face interaction but rather the physical and geographical location of participants. Onsite gatherings necessitate physical co-presence in a single location, whereas videoconferencing bridges geographical distance, allowing individuals to participate from varied locations. This digital mediation transforms the dynamics of interaction and the experience of communal space and timing, altering the context and dynamics of small group discussions.

In online meetings, the simultaneous visibility of all participants on screen removes the possibility of physically retreating into a corner, both literally and metaphorically speaking (#NoHiding). This constant visibility enforces a form of engagement that might not be as prevalent in onsite settings, where physical space allows for varying degrees of participation visibility.[31] Consequently, this aspect of online communication also fosters a certain democratization, as each participant is given equal visual presence and, ideally, equal opportunity to contribute to the dialogue. This shift can potentially alter the traditional dynamics of conversation, encouraging a more equitable distribution of voice among participants.

Space and spatiality constitute a second critical frame factor. Given that each participant chooses their own physical setting for participation, the group leader's control over the "room" or environment is inherently limited. This contrasts sharply with onsite meetings, where leaders can manipulate the physical space to create a desired atmosphere, including arranging for elements of hospitality.

In the online setting, while group leaders manage the digital meeting space, they can't directly influence the physical surroundings of participants. Attempts to create a shared atmosphere through actions like #LightingCandles or #SendingSoup represent efforts to bridge this gap, yet I experienced these interventions as often having a relatively minor impact compared to the influence of individuals' immediate physical environment and the objects within it. This shift redistributes the responsibility for hospitality, effectively making each participant their own host and shaping the #MeetingAtmosphere in a decentralized manner. This

---

[31] This is of course only true if participants opt to switch on their cameras and the number of participants is small, as it was in all our online small groups. In large meetings some participants will not be visible on the screen and are thus hidden.

distributed responsibility alters the dynamics of hospitality and atmosphere creation, influencing the overall experience of the online small group meetings.

Timing is a third crucial frame factor, shaping the experience of online small groups. The absence of physical travel to a meeting location means transition times between activities can be extremely brief, allowing participants to move swiftly from one task to another without the physical and mental preparation often made possible in commuting. While this immediacy can be seen as an advantage—maximizing the efficiency of participants' schedules—it may also pose challenges, particularly in terms of mental readiness for the meeting. The rapid shift from one context to another, with little to no buffer time, can impact participants' ability to mentally transition into the group's space and focus, as highlighted in #Interview1.

Furthermore, the conclusion of online meetings tends to be markedly abrupt compared to onsite gatherings. The instant a host terminates the session, the digital connection is severed, immediately dispersing the group without the organic, gradual winding down characteristic of physical meetings. This sudden disconnection contrasts sharply with the natural lingering and informal discussions that often follow in-person meetings, affecting the sense of closure and community bonding.

Online small groups are significantly influenced by the characteristics of the *online* learning environment, which encompasses aspects such as digital mediation, a diminished ability for leaders to control the physical space, and alterations in the timing and pacing of interactions. These factors collectively shape the dynamics, engagement, and overall experience of participants within these groups, highlighting the distinct challenges and opportunities presented by online formats compared to traditional onsite settings.

4.2.6 Learners

Just as with frame factors, the characteristics of learners often lie beyond the immediate influence of educators. While it is possible to select learners through various criteria, exerting some degree of control over learner characteristics, educators cannot change the fundamental nature of who a learner is, once they are part of the group. This reality underscores the importance of adaptability in teaching, as educators must respond to the diverse backgrounds, abilities, and perspectives that learners bring to the group.

Describing learner characteristics is a complex endeavor, as evidenced when pondering Natalie Wigg-Stevenson's question: "How do we tell the truth about a life?" in relation to the crisis of representation.[32] Learners do not come to online small groups as blank slates but as individuals whose entire life experiences shape their perspectives, interactions, and responses to the learning environment.[33] Putting aside the more general significance for ethnographic theology here, Wigg-Stevenson's question highlights the challenge inherent in capturing the essence of people and hence of learner characteristics.

Any attempt at outlining the general characteristics of learners is thus by necessity a simplification, focusing on a few salient attributes that, while potentially insightful, cannot encapsulate the full complexity of each individual's life story. Recognizing the uniqueness of each learner, it becomes crucial to approach group settings with sensitivity and attentiveness to the real, lived experiences of the participants present, beyond any generalized profiles.

Still, some more general learner characteristics can be discerned. As previously discussed, participants in our online small groups were all adults, with ages spanning from the early twenties to the seventies. The age distribution varied across the groups. In the #Margareta, S:t Eskils, and Älvsjö groups, the majority of participants were in their thirties, forties, and fifties. Conversely, the #Djursholm group had a higher proportion of participants in late adulthood. There were generally fewer participants in early adulthood.

One crucial difference between individuals in middle and late adulthood lies in their general life circumstances. Participants in middle adulthood were usually economically active and often responsible for children living with them, both factors influencing their daily routines and schedules. Conversely, those in late adulthood were often retired, without children in their household, affording them more time.

Participants were predominantly "majority Swedes," meaning they were white, from the Swedish majority culture, and spoke Swedish as their first language. Observations through videoconferencing software, along with comments about vacations and summer cottage care, suggested that most participants were middle class, and all appeared able-bodied, though some older individuals may

---

[32] Wigg-Stevenson, "Representation," 183.

[33] Jarvis, *Adult Learning*, 63–85; Malcolm S. Knowles, Elwood F. Holton III, and Richard A. Swanson, *The Adult Learner: The Definitive Classic in Adult Education and Human Resource Development*, 6th ed. (London: Elsevier, 2005).

have experienced hearing difficulties.[34] The online small groups were thus largely homogenous in composition, potentially contributing to communication and group formation. This homogeneity also provided a shared cultural understanding upon which group leaders could construct their approach.

The homogeneity of learners is significant as it highlights a limitation in our findings. Specifically, our experiences with homogenous groups leave uncertain the extent to which online small groups can accommodate more diverse learner populations.

4.2.7 Teachers

All group leaders involved in the *Online Small Groups* project were employed by the parishes hosting the groups during the project's duration. Leadership was incorporated into deacons' and pastors' official responsibilities, positioning them as professional rather than lay or volunteer leaders. This detail is significant for at least two reasons. First, it indicates that our online small groups were integrated into the parishes' broader ministry and planned activities. The fact that pastors and deacons conducted groups as part of their formal duties, implies a conscious inclusion of these groups within parishes' overall structure and a certain level of support from parish leadership, ensuring the groups were established and adequately resourced for operation, so that our online small groups should be viewed as part of the parishes' recognized and official educational ministry.

Second, as professionals, group leaders occupied a distinct role relative to group participants, influenced not just by their function within the groups, but also by their professional standing. This difference may have been less pronounced in the #Älvsjö group, with many participants themselves being pastors and deacons. However, in the other groups, a clear distinction existed between ordained leaders and lay participants, influencing the subject positions open to both participants and leaders.[35] For the most part then, group leaders did not engage in our online small groups on par with participants, and their function was more to lead than to engage in personal growth and self-actualization.

---

[34] A participant in the #Djursholm group reported not hearing well. However, it appeared that s/he had most difficulties understanding me, which might have more to do with my German accent then with a general hearing loss.

[35] Osbeck, *Förstå livet*, 26–27.

4.3 Summary and Reflections

This chapter aimed to present an alternative perspective on our online small groups. Based on my examination of the didactic components of the online small group learning situation, I propose that our groups emphasized *directed dialogue*. This involves a process of collective theological reflection, often related to aspects of the Christian tradition (in its broadest sense), guided by a leader who provides clear direction in terms of both content and process. Although this approach is directed, it notably allows participants the freedom to engage in reflection on their own terms. Hence, online small groups create opportunities for reflection without for that reason evaluating participants' learning outcomes. In this regard, online small groups represent a departure from both disciplined learning and small group faith sharing described by John Elias, offering instead a blend of guided discussion and joint exploration.[36]

Online small groups also diverge from the type of directed dialogue observed by Elisabeth Tveito Johnsen in Norwegian Christian religious education for children. Tveito Johnsen identifies a prevalent use of the Initiative-Response-Feedback (IRF) dialogue model among religious educators, where educators ask questions (Initiative), children provide answers (Response), and then educators assess the responses (Feedback).[37] The absence of leader evaluation or feedback in online small groups fosters a more open form of dialogue, encouraging participants to delve into their own reflections rather than assimilating a predetermined set of facts.

Nevertheless, leaders typically had a clear purpose for their groups, evident from the specific #Aspirations leaders articulated. Regardless of whether leaders would have explicitly formulated their goals in writing and whether the establishment of groups occurred before or after goal formulation, most group leaders operated with a set of defined #Aspirations. This indicates a level of intentionality in our online small groups. Below, I build on this to argue for understanding online small groups as sites of teaching.[38]

In examining frame factors, I have particularly concentrated on the impact of the *online* learning situation, which encompasses digital mediation, diminished spatial control for leaders, and variations in timing. Each of these elements influences the learning and teaching dynamics of online small groups.

---

[36] Elias, "Models."
[37] Tveito Johnsen, "Trosopplæring"; Tveito Johnsen, "Læring."
[38] See section 6.2.

The discussion further illustrates that online small groups, as we have experienced them in this project, are characterized by versatility in content, generic applicability, and limited scope. First, the content flexibility of online small groups allows them to cover a broad array of topics, demonstrating their versatility. Although the content in our groups often related to the Christian tradition as practiced in the Church of Sweden, it was not aimed at mere acquisition. Instead, engagement with the Christian tradition was emphasized, with a partial focus on fostering specific attitudes. This approach to content, emphasizing engagement over acquisition, holds true even for the #S:tEskils group, despite it not directly addressing the Christian tradition.

Second, the online small groups in our study were not designed to address specific learning challenges. The participants, being primarily majority Swedes, shared a common cultural background, making the generic format of online small groups effective for them. However, the efficacy of online small groups for diverse types of learners remains uncertain. This includes learners with cognitive variations such as autism spectrum disorders and dementia, individuals facing language barriers, including second language learners, and those from different cultural backgrounds. These factors could potentially complicate communication and conversation in online videoconferencing settings. Currently, online small groups are generic in their applicability and not particularly designed to navigate potential complexities, though there is no indication that the format could not be adapted to accommodate such challenges.

Third, in all parishes, online small groups were integrated into the job responsibilities of employed pastors and deacons. This arrangement placed leaders in a special position vis-à-vis participants, both as salaried employees facilitating groups as part of their professional duties and in terms of their ordination, with the #Älvsjö group being an exception. As church-based groups, our online small groups were part of the parishes' broader educational ministry. Therefore, online small groups were not envisioned as the sole or comprehensive form of Christian religious education. Instead, they represented one facet of Christian religious education and, as such, should be recognized as having a limited scope.

In comparison to previous research on small groups, there are notable similarities between our online small groups and the characteristics outlined by Wuthnow and Atkinson. Similar to Wuthnow's depiction, our online small groups can be described as voluntary, intentional gatherings, each with a defined purpose or goal, leadership, and a planned schedule.[39] Consistent with Atkinson's description, our groups were limited in size, exhibited group consciousness, pursued a common purpose, and necessitated interactive engagement among participants.[40]

Atkinson's fifth characteristic, emphasizing face-to-face interaction in small groups, warrants examination, especially regarding whether online meetings truly embody "face-to-face interaction." Critics may argue that participants in online small groups interact with screens rather than directly with other individuals, suggesting such groups may not fit the strict definition of small groups. This viewpoint stems from a perception of "real" interactions as those occurring onsite.

However, videoconferencing software enables real-time, face-to-face communication, even though it may not allow for traditional eye contact found in onsite meetings. My initial assessment is that online small groups incorporate enough aspects of face-to-face communication to be considered small groups also in Atkinson's sense. Consequently, one insight from comparison with previous research is that online small groups do not fundamentally diverge from onsite small groups. Online small groups are essentially small groups that convene through videoconferencing tools, facilitating real-time oral and visual communication.

While recognizing commonalities between our online small groups and those described by Wuthnow and Atkinson, I also observe several distinctions. As previously mentioned, our online small groups were distinguished by their emphasis on *directed dialogue*, with leader activities extending beyond merely facilitating natural group dynamics.[41] Our online small groups thus encompassed not just the shared purpose identified by Wuthnow and Atkinson but also specific leader intentions, which were often not directly communicated to participants. Wuthnow and Atkinson typically depict group leaders as facilitators; however, below I argue that leaders in our context not only facilitated but taught.[42]

Lastly, our groups may also have diverged from Atkinson's conceptualization of small groups concerning group cohesion and the longevity of the groups. Although both the #S:tEskils and #Älvsjö groups aimed to foster a sense of community, the #S:tEskils group linking the necessity for community to the isolation experienced during COVID-19, both groups were established as temporary configurations, intended to disband after a number of meetings. The same holds for the #Margareta and #Djursholm groups. Consequently, it is uncertain whether the

---

[39] Wuthnow, *Sharing the Journey*, 135–37.

[40] Atkinson, *Small Groups*, chap. 2.

[41] Elias, "Models," 182–88.

[42] Wuthnow, *Sharing the Journey*, 268. Atkinson, *Small Groups*, part 6. See also section 6.1.

dynamics of group cohesion and continuity operated as Atkinson outlines. In the next chapter, I therefore delve deeper into the topic of community.

5. Communities of Faith and/or Learning

Community has emerged as a pivotal concept in academic discussions of both small groups and online learning.[1] The literature on the subject leaves little doubt about its significance, positioning community as a critical, if not paramount, element.[2] Our experiences from the *Online Small Groups* project underscore this significance, as evidenced by our focus on #SeeingEachOther, #GroupBuilding, and #OpeningQuestions. The deliberate aim to foster community was, moreover, an explicit intention for both the #Margareta and #Älvsjö groups.

Nevertheless, this chapter proposes that the notion of community in the small group literature diverges from its portrayal in the online learning discourse. It appears that scholars specializing in small groups and theorists focusing on online learning might imbue community with different meanings.

Consequently, this analysis begins with an examination of the various interpretations of community in these two discourses (5.1). Subsequently, I revisit the *Online Small Groups* project, aligning our observations with these diverse perspectives (5.2). The discussion then shifts to consider community within our online small groups through the lens of the Church of Sweden's folk church ecclesiology,

---

[1] See sections 1.5.2–1.5.3, 4.3.

[2] Wuthnow, *Sharing the Journey*; Latini, *Crisis of Community*; Cook Everist, *Learning Community*; Maddix and Estep, "Spiritual Formation"; Nichols, "Akadameia as Paradigm"; Elisabeth Tveito Johnsen, "Christian Education as a Community of Strangers," in *The Wiley Blackwell Companion to Theology and Qualitative Research*, ed. Pete Ward and Knut Tveitereid (Oxford: Wiley Blackwell, 2022), 340–50; Rena M. Palloff and Keith Pratt, *Collaborating Online: Learning Together in Community* (Hoboken: Jossey-Bass, 2005); Chapman, Ramondt, and Smiley, "Strong Community"; Brindley, Blaschke, and Walti, "Collaborative Learning Groups"; D. Randy Garrison, "From Independence to Collaboration: A Personal Retrospective on Distance Education," in *An Introduction to Distance Education: Understanding Teaching and Learning in a New Era*, ed. Martha F. Cleveland-Innes and D. Randy Garrison (Milton: Taylor and Francis, 2020), 13–24.

offering a potential framework for understanding how community manifested in the *Online Small Groups* project (5.3).

5.1 Community in Small Groups, Online Learning, and Christian Religious Education

An emphasis on community is a defining feature in the literature on small groups, a trend firmly established by Robert Wuthnow's seminal work, *Sharing the Journey*. Wuthnow examines the small group movement in the context of the "crisis of community," a situation of profound shifts in the US-American social landscape, leading to the erosion of traditional forms of community, such as families and villages.[3] Here, community is conceived as enduring social connections that forge bonds of mutual trust and support among people, and thus as the glue holding society together.[4]

Wuthnow's central thesis posits that small groups play a dual role in relation to community: they not only foster the development of communal bonds but also contribute to a broader redefinition of what community means, contributing to a redefinition of community in terms of voluntary associations.[5] However, it is primarily the emphasis on community itself that has left a mark on the literature about small groups, more so than the exploration of its evolving dynamics. For instance, Theresa Latini suggests that small groups have the potential to mitigate feelings of alienation and anomie, thereby aiding individuals in navigating the contemporary crises of community, without attention to the way in which small groups also affect contemporary understandings of community.[6]

The importance of community is similarly underscored by small group practitioners and scholars such as Atkinson, Egli and Marable, and Stetzer and Geiger, highlighting its centrality across various discussions on small group dynamics.[7] These works portray community as pivotal for the effective operation of small groups. It facilitates the development of trustful and supportive relationships,

---

[3] Wuthnow, *Sharing the Journey*, 33–36. Building on Wuthnow's work, Theresa Latini uses the term "crisis of community" to discuss the changes Wuthnow examined. Wuthnow himself does not use the term. Latini, *Crisis of Community*, 11–29.

[4] Wuthnow, *Sharing the Journey*, 11–16.

[5] Wuthnow, *Sharing the Journey*, 21–28.

[6] Latini, *Crisis of Community*, 180–89.

[7] Atkinson, *Small Groups*, chap. 1; Egli and Marable, *Big Impact*, 45–53; Stetzer and Geiger, *Transformational Groups*, chap. 1.

transforming small groups into nurturing environments where God's presence can be felt.

However, community also emerges as an objective for these groups.[8] Thus, community is simultaneously a prerequisite for and an outcome of successful small groups, particularly within church-based groups that infuse community with theological significance.[9] Consequently, in the literature on small groups, community is depicted as consisting of durable and robust social connections that forge permanent collectives.

This perspective contrasts sharply with the notion of community within the online learning discourse. Although community is deemed essential in online learning contexts as well, its interpretation tends to be more instrumental.[10] Drawing from social learning theories and conceptualizing learning as a participatory process, online learning theorists advocate for collaborative learning activities and cooperation.[11]

However, unlike in small group settings, the emphasis here is not on establishing enduring social ties but on creating temporary and goal-oriented relationships to enhance learning through mutual engagement.[12] Community is, hence, linked to the efficacy of learning and learner motivation, rather than the establishment of long-term social networks.[13] Consequently, community serves as a foundation for collaborative learning rather than an end goal, highlighting a fundamental difference in how community is valued and pursued in small groups and online learning environments.[14]

The significance of community has also been highlighted in discussions regarding online formation in theological education.[15] In this, contributions from

---

[8] Wuthnow, *Sharing the Journey*, 11–16; Latini, *Crisis of Community*, 180–89.

[9] Latini, *Crisis of Community*, 180–89; Stetzer and Geiger, *Transformational Groups*, chap. 1.

[10] Chapman, Ramondt, and Smiley, "Strong Community"; Palloff and Pratt, *Collaborating Online*; Brindley, Blaschke, and Walti, "Collaborative Learning Groups."

[11] Michael G. Moore, "Three Types of Interaction," *American Journal of Distance Education* 3, no. 2 (1989): 1–7; Palloff and Pratt, *Collaborating Online*; Michael Grahame Moore, "The Theory of Transactional Distance," in *Handbook of Distance Education*, ed. Michael Grahame Moore (New York: Routledge, 2013), 66–85.

[12] Moore, "Transactional Distance," 75; Palloff and Pratt, *Collaborating Online*, 4–7.

[13] Hill, Song, and West, "Learning Theory," 94–95.

[14] Palloff and Pratt, *Collaborating Online*, 4.

[15] Nichols, "Akadameia as Paradigm"; Maddix, "Online Learning"; Hines et al., "Online Theological Education"; Deulen, "Social Constructivism." For a different take on community in Christian religious education see Tveito Johnsen, "Community of Strangers."

scholars like Mark Nichols and Mark A. Maddix, who explore not only the importance of community but also the characteristics that define online communities, are particularly instructive. Their insights offer valuable perspectives for discerning the distinctions between the concepts of community in the small group and online learning literatures.

Maddix approaches online learning in Christian religious education through the lens of learning communities. He delineates these communities by five criteria: (1) a sense of shared purpose, (2) clear boundaries that identify membership, (3) enforceable rules, (4) interaction among members, and (5) a foundational level of trust, respect, and support.[16]

Comparing Maddix's criteria to Atkinson's characterization of small groups reveals considerable overlap, indicating commonalities between these two models of groups.[17] Both frameworks emphasize a shared purpose and the delineation of the group. Interaction is a crucial element in both, albeit Atkinson envisions it occurring in a face-to-face context, a stipulation Maddix's model does not require. However, Maddix's emphasis on explicit rules represents a departure from Atkinson's description, which instead highlights the importance of group size, the necessity of the group to fulfill its objectives, and cohesion among members.

While Maddix does not explicitly list interdependence as a characteristic of learning communities, the essence of a learning community suggests that interdependence is fundamental. Such communities often facilitate a level of learning that surpasses what can be achieved through individual study, even when conducted alongside others. Neither is size a decisive difference. While Maddix does not give any size limits, it seems reasonable to suggest that learning communities can be small and hence overlap with Atkinson's small groups.[18] This leaves cohesion again as the primary differentiator between small groups and online learning communities.

Mark Nichols's exploration of online theological education introduces a different axis of community conceptualization, the dichotomy of *ekklesia* and *akademeia*. Nichols posits that online education tends to form communities of dialogue akin to academic discourse, rather than communities of fellowship typically found in ecclesial settings.[19] According to Nichols, this distinction arises from the

---

[16] Maddix, "Online Learning," 140.

[17] For Atkinson's characterization of small groups see section 4.1.

[18] Atkinson, *Small Groups*, chap. 2.

[19] Nichols, "Akadameia as Paradigm," 15.

fundamental aim of theological education to encourage learning and scholarly exchange.

In contrast, the essence of the church is framed around the New Testament concept of *allelon*, which embodies ideas of reciprocity, mutuality, and shared responsibility. This biblical notion, Nichols contends, lays the groundwork for Christian fellowship, highlighting a form of community interaction deeply rooted in mutual support and collective growth, distinguishing it from the dialogue-oriented communities formed in online theological education.[20] As Nichols says:

> It must be squarely faced: any form of community based around a highly-structured and temporary membership, particularly where it is based on a transaction (tuition) and artificial distinction between members (faculty, student) is limited in terms of its ability to honestly achieve *allēlon* and therefore represent Christian community. Theological education is not a sound environment for *allēlon* community, and any insistence otherwise has failed to sufficiently nuance just what the term "community" really implies.[21]

The foundational premise here is that online learning does not seek to be the primary milieu for Christian living but serves merely as an arena for academic and theological exploration in eventual support of the *ekklesia*, as the "right and proper context for organic Christian life."[22] Nichols's perspective, thus underscores a clear differentiation between communities of faith and communities of learning, based on their inherent purposes and functions, which significantly influences the type of community each fosters, with reciprocity and mutuality emerging as a potential distinguishing feature, aligning with earlier discussions.

Nichols's differentiation enables a deeper understanding of the varied community concepts presented in the literature on small groups and online learning. According to Nichols's framework, small groups are expressions of *ekklesia* because they are oriented towards establishing enduring, strong communal bonds of reciprocity and mutuality. This contrasts with online Christian religious education, which views community in a more functional light, as a pathway to educational outcomes, and hence represents the ideals of the *akademeia*.

For Nichols, this reasoning supports a case for online theological education. Given that theological education is inherently characterized more by the academic and dialogical nature of the *akademeia* than by the communal and fellowship-oriented nature of the *ekklesia*, one should not see the porous community that online

---

[20] Nichols, "Akadameia as Paradigm," 11.
[21] Nichols, "Akadameia as Paradigm," 14.
[22] Nichols, "Akadameia as Paradigm," 17.

theological education offers as a deficiency, but as simply a different kind of community.[23]

Drawing these discussions together, I find that the difference between the small group literature and the online learning literature hinges on conceptualizations of both the essence of community and its perceived role—whether as a means to an end or an end in itself. Within the context of church-based small groups, community is intertwined with the concept of *ekklesia*, characterized by enduring, robust social bonds that provide mutual care and support.[24] This conceptualization aligns with the vision of community as a collective entity wherein individuals are deeply connected through mutual assistance and emotional bonds, reflecting a commitment to fostering lasting relationships.

Conversely, online learning literature presents community from a functional perspective, viewing it primarily as a facilitator for collaboration and joint learning. Here, the creation of community is not an objective per se but rather a mechanism to enhance individuals' learning. Consequently, communities within online learning environments tend to be more transient, less intimate, and are structured more similarly to the communities found in classroom settings or the academically oriented *akademeia*.[25] These communities are designed to support the educational process, emphasizing the efficiency and effectiveness of learning rather than the development of deep, personal connections among participants. This functional approach to community reflects a different set of priorities, focusing on the instrumental value of communal interactions in achieving specific learning outcomes.

5.2 Community in the *Online Small Groups* Project

One of the "flashes of insight" that struck me during the *Online Small Groups* project was the distinction between transactional meetings and #RelationalMeetings.[26] It became clear to me just how foundational relationships were to our online small groups, underscored by our emphasis on #GroupBuilding and #Community, manifested through various targeted activities designed to enhance these

---

[23] Nichols, "Akadameia as Paradigm," 11–17.

[24] Wuthnow, *Sharing the Journey*, 131–32; Latini, *Crisis of Community*, 57–59.

[25] Palloff and Pratt, *Collaborating Online*, 6–17.

[26] I take the concept of "flashes of insight," "epiphanies," or "disclosures" to mark moments of growing awareness from Theological Action Research. See Cameron et al., *Talking*, 4; Watkins, *Disclosing Church*, 46.

aspects, such as #PrayerPartners, #BeingFullyPresent, and #SeeingEachOther, among others.

However, given the preceding discussion on the nature and purpose of community, a question arises regarding the type of community our online small groups aimed to foster. Were we striving to create a community reflective of the *ekklesia*, rooted in deep, enduring relationships and mutual support or was our goal more aligned with the community of the *akademeia*, characterized by functional, learning-oriented interactions designed to facilitate joint theological exploration? This query invites a deeper reflection on the underlying intentions and outcomes associated with the community-building efforts within our online small groups.

In relation to community, a first observation concerns the longevity of our groups. Both the #S:tEskils and the #Margareta groups had met during the spring of 2021 when we included them in the project in the fall of the same year. These groups thus exhibited some continuity. However, both groups were intentionally designed as temporary configurations, having a predetermined number of sessions before ending, even if Jessica and Karin were open to future iterations of these groups.

The #Djursholm and #Älvsjö groups were perhaps even more temporary, seeing that it was the research project itself that animated the creation of these groups. Even as Eva might have been open to continuing to offer online small groups, there was no explicit intention to do so. Neither was there any such goal in the #Älvsjö group. Indeed, several of our Bible study participants reported that they found it easier to prioritize our meetings precisely because they were numbered. That is, instead of expressing regret that the group disbanded after our seven meetings, participants found that it contributed positively to their experience of the group. There was hence no expectation from group participants either that the group would continue to meet.

A second observation relates to group cohesion. Here, the #Margareta group serves as a prime example, with its open policy not requiring attendees to commit to every meeting. I think Karin imagined a cohesive group with regular attendance by at least some, allowing participants to form connections and to get to know each other over time. However, in a sense, each session was also designed to stand alone, not building on previous meetings, with implications for community.

My journal entry from October 3, 2021, further describes how I experienced community in that session. Participating in the last planned session that fall, I experienced *Lectio Divina* as a largely individual exercise carried out in the presence of others, rather than feeling integrated into a cohesive group. From the way Karin organized the session, it appears that constructing a cohesive group might not have been her primary goal.

Similarly, it is noteworthy that participants in the #Älvsjö group generally disliked the #BreakoutRoomDebrief, in which they were asked to exchange some final observations with each other, intended to imitate the natural chatter that occurs at the end of onsite meetings. This aversion seems partly due to the limitations with #MimickingOnsiteMeetings I recounted in the reflective narrative, so that the debrief format might have been misaligned with expectations. Moreover, participants' discomfort with the #BreakoutRoomDebrief also stems from a reluctance or inability to allocate time for mutual debriefing. The #LossOfControl they reported might be rooted in a fear of being unable to commit the necessary time for a comprehensive debrief with peers. From comments in our final #Evaluation, it appears that participants prioritized control over their schedules over the opportunity to engage with one another through debriefing.

For many participants, practical time constraints rather than a reluctance to engage with others might have contributed to their discomfort. Yet, had the participants placed a higher value on fostering lasting relationships, it seems plausible they would have mentioned this during the final #Evaluation. The absence of such comments suggests that, in general, participants did not anticipate their involvement leading to the creation of enduring bonds. These observations indicate that the pursuit of community was not a primary concern for the #Älvsjö group members.

A final observation pertains to leadership within our groups. Each group was led or co-led by employees of the respective parishes, for whom these groups constituted part of their official duties. In the Church of Sweden, a discussion persists regarding the dynamics between salaried parish personnel, including pastors and deacons, and the laity. Jonas Ideström's research highlights how it is primarily the salaried parish personnel and elected officials[27] who represent the local church, while Sven-Erik Brodd explores how the Church of Sweden currently operates in a manner akin to a service provider.[28] Central to this discussion is the notion that

---

[27] Each Church of Sweden parish has a parish council to which lay persons are elected. The local church thus includes lay persons, but it is the specific group of elected lay persons that constitute the local church, rather than the totality of lay persons in the parish.

[28] Jonas Ideström, *Lokal kyrklig identitet: En studie av implicit ecklesiologi med exemplet Svenska kyrkan i Flemingsberg* (Skellefteå: Artos & Norma, 2009), 247–50; Sven-Erik Brodd, "Pragmatismen som ett kyrkans kännetecken (nota ecclesiae): Om ekonomi, ecklesiologi och kyrkans inre sekularisering," in *Inomkyrklig sekularisering*, ed. Thomas Girmalm and Marie Rosenius (Umeå: Umeå universitet, 2018), 31–55 at 39–40.

a service provider church, centered around salaried staff and elected officials, does not require lay parishioners for its operations. This applies also to our online small groups, whose formation was not finally dependent on the active engagement of their participants.

However, this perspective is somewhat limited, as without participants, there would be no groups at all, as our difficulty with recruiting members to the #Älvsjö group demonstrates. Yet, participants largely act as "consumers" within this framework, choosing from various parish offerings rather than contributing as active creators of the online small groups. Our groups thus depended more on individual leaders than on the group as a collective. This structure likely impacted the sense of community; in our groups, community was secondary, emerging only after the groups' formation by leaders, rather than being the primary focus.

Again, this does not imply that community was deemed irrelevant; on the contrary, the groups' #ResearchPlans emphasize the importance of community for facilitating open and honest exchanges.[29] Still, this suggests that community is perceived instrumentally in similarity to notions in the online learning literature, where community helps foster learning and personal development, but is not necessarily a goal itself.

This analysis suggests a discrepancy in the function of community within our online small groups and the conventional understanding of community presented in the small group literature. #GroupBuilding emerged as a significant process in our groups, but its importance was rooted in facilitating open sharing, vulnerability, and honesty among participants. Thus, the cultivation of strong groups served as a methodological tool rather than the ultimate objective. The nature of community within our online groups was characterized by its functionality and transience, aligning more closely with the community model of the *akademeia*, emphasizing learning and theological explorations, rather than the *ekklesia*, denoting a cohesive community bound by reciprocity, mutuality, shared beliefs, and practices.

5.3 Online Small Groups in the Church of Sweden

If online small groups indeed align more closely with the "academic" and discursive model of the *akademeia* rather than the communal and worship-focused *ekklesia*, it prompts an examination of the reasons behind this alignment and its implications for Christian religious education within the Church of Sweden.

---

[29] See appendix B.

Jonas Ideström and Tone Stangeland Kaufman explore how the theological framing of the Church of Sweden as a folk church influences many parishes' online activities.[30] Their analysis provides a useful lens for understanding the dynamics of community, or its absence, within our online small groups.

Ideström and Stangeland Kaufman delineate three folk church perspectives on the Church of Sweden's engagement with its online presence: "an address in everyday life," "sacramental embodiment," and "visible community."[31] Each view proposes a unique mode through which the gospel's presence and influence in the world can be understood and facilitated. Applying Ideström's and Stangeland Kaufman's simplified model of folk church ecclesiology allows for a critical discussion on how foundational ecclesiological understandings of the Church of Sweden shape the construction and experience of community in online small groups, potentially offering new insights into the engagement and educational strategies in these digital environments.

The three views are all grounded in a non-essentialist view of the Swedish people—defined simply as individuals residing within Sweden as a geographical area, shifting away from traditional, essentialist notions of a "folk" to embrace a broader, inclusive identity.[32] Central to all three perspectives is, moreover, the conviction that the Church is called to proclaim the gospel as a part of its mission to advance the kingdom of God and contribute to the restoration of creation.[33] The distinction among these perspectives lies thus not in their understanding of the Church's mission but in the methodologies and approaches advocated for achieving this calling.

The *address in everyday life* perspective underscores the gospel's integration into the daily lives of individuals, suggesting that its teachings and comforts permeate mundane activities and decisions, thereby affirming its relevance across all aspects of life. In contrast, the *sacramental embodiment* viewpoint emphasizes the tangible expressions of the gospel, particularly through the sacraments and Christian practices such as the Eucharist. This approach focuses on the physical and communal aspects of worship, where divine grace is mediated through specific

---

[30] Jonas Ideström and Tone Stangeland Kaufman, "Hur framträder kyrkan i de digitala rummen? Kommunikation, teologi och folkkyrkotankar," in *Kyrka i digitala rum: Ett aktionsforskningsprojekt om församlingsliv online i Svenska kyrkan*, ed. Jonas Ideström and Sara Garpe (Uppsala: Church of Sweden, 2022), 30–42 at 33–34.

[31] Ideström and Stangeland Kaufman, "Hur framträder kyrkan," 34.

[32] Ideström and Stangeland Kaufman, "Hur framträder kyrkan," 33.

[33] Ideström and Stangeland Kaufman, "Hur framträder kyrkan," 33.

acts. Lastly, the *visible community* perspective brings attention to the church as a local gathering of faith, stressing the importance of communal visibility and the collective assembly of members as a core aspect of the church's identity and mission.[34]

In our online small groups, I see elements from all three perspectives. The #Margareta, #Djursholm, and #Älvsjö groups, for instance, focused on Bible study, echoing the *sacramental embodiment* perspective, particularly if the Word is understood sacramentally. Moreover, the very act of gathering an online small group mirrors the concept of a *visible community*. Yet, as Ideström and Stangeland Kaufman note, both these perspectives have often been linked with liturgical celebrations and local congregational worship, aspects that were less emphasized in our online settings, even as the *visible community* also includes other gatherings than worship.[35]

The *address in everyday life* perspective suggests that the Church's mission centers around the proclamation of the gospel. In this view, it is the proclamation of the Word which constitutes the Church, rather than its reception.[36] Kirsten Donskov Felter, Ninna Edgardh, and Tron Fagermoen expand on this idea by associating it with the concept that God's activity is not confined to the church but operates independently and beyond its bounds. Drawing on Gustaf Wingren's folk church theology, Donskov Felter, Edgardh, and Fagermoen highlight:

> This means on the one hand that the church should not be allowed to understand itself as a distinctive community with fixed boundaries vis-à-vis its surroundings. On the other hand it means that the fellowship of the church is located in the everyday life of its members, as every individual is called to work for the sake of their neighbor.[37]

The Church's mission, therefore, centers on proclaiming the gospel rather than assembling individuals for local worship or gathering them in a visible community. The *address in everyday life* thus stresses the transformative power of the gospel in people's lives as they navigate their daily realities. Ideström and Stangeland Kaufman encapsulate this view succinctly, stating that "proclamation and communication are not a means to get people to church: to reach people in their everyday lives with an appeal that brings the gospel to life is a goal in itself."[38] The Church's role

---

[34] Ideström and Stangeland Kaufman, "Hur framträder kyrkan," 34.
[35] Ideström and Stangeland Kaufman, "Hur framträder kyrkan," 34.
[36] Ideström and Stangeland Kaufman, "Hur framträder kyrkan," 34.
[37] Donskov Felter, Edgardh, and Fagermoen, "Ecclesial Context," 12–13.
[38] Ideström and Stangeland Kaufman, "Hur framträder kyrkan," 34.

is thus not to call people out of their worldly contexts and into the visible community of the Church but to assist them in practicing Christian living where they are.

Following this perspective, our online small groups can be interpreted as a method of linking the proclamation of the gospel with a mode of engaging with the gospel that reaches individuals in their everyday lives, at least if the gospel is understood to encompass Christian ethics and the Christian tradition.[39] In this, I see clear implications for the type of formation our groups offered and that diverged in important ways from prevailing views in the literature on online learning in Christian religious education.

Online Christian education educators routinely regard formation as a process that encourages learners to integrate into a specific community, internalizing and manifesting its beliefs, values, and practices.[40] This prevalent notion of formation inherently assumes that the community shaping the learners stands apart from other communities, the "world," or the "rest of society," embodying a counter-cultural stance. This model of formation suggests a clear demarcation between the community of the Church and the secular outside world, promoting a form of Christian identity that is defined in opposition or distinction to broader societal norms and values.[41]

The folk church concept, as envisioned through the lens of *an address in everyday life*, blurs this distinction. If the essence of the Church revolves around the proclamation of the gospel, then traditional notions of church as community, might not be a necessity according to this perspective. However, revisiting the insights from Donskov Felter, Edgardh, and Fagermoen on Wingren's theology, suggests that the *address in everyday life* does not dispense with community, but rather redefines it as a network of permeable relationships among individuals navigating their lives in the world. Within this framework, the church's community is understood as encompassing all believers scattered across the globe, rather than being confined to a visible, congregational assembly.

Our online small groups thus transcend any simple dichotomy between "academic" communities of learning and "ecclesial" communities of faith. The distinctiveness of these groups, compared to those analyzed by researchers like Wuthnow and Latini, or advocated by Atkinson, Egli and Marable, or Setzer and Geiger, is

---

[39] Cf. section 4.2.2.

[40] Nichols, "Akadameia as Paradigm"; Maddix, "Online Learning"; Hines et al., "Online Theological Education"; Deulen, "Social Constructivism."

[41] Rodney Clapp, *A Peculiar People: The Church as Culture in a Post-Christian Society* (Downers Grove: IVP Academic, 1996).

not that they prioritize learning over fellowship.[42] Instead, the difference lies in the underlying ecclesiological understanding of the community of the Church and the conceptualization of the appropriate setting for Christian living that underpin our engagement.

Therefore, it would be misleading to categorize online small groups as being more or less "ecclesial" based solely on their format or focus. It is essential to acknowledge that online small groups in the Church of Sweden may be guided by a different ecclesiological perspective, leading to an approach to Christian religious education distinct from the models commonly found in the United States. This recognition calls for a broader understanding of how online small groups can serve the mission and ministry of the church in varying cultural and theological contexts.

In the context of the folk church, viewed as an *address in everyday life*, there is no sharp division between fellowship and learning, or between *ekklesia* and *akademeia*. Learning and teaching are integrated into the fabric of Christian living, serving as essential components of continuous formation. Within this framework, online small groups emerge as one among many conduits through which parishes in the Church of Sweden achieve their core mission: to bring individuals to faith in Christ and to nurture that faith. This objective is pursued not through the cultivation of a visible and separate community but through engagement with people as they exist within the broader context of the world.[43]

5.4 Summary and Reflections

Reflecting on how community is understood in the literature on small groups and the literature on online learning reveals a varied understanding of community. A useful framework to parse this diversity is the distinction between communities of learning (*akademeia*) and communities of faith (*ekklesia*). Through this analytical lens, our online small groups seemed to align more with communities of learning than communities of faith, resembling what Nichols describes as extensions of the academy rather than the church.

However, probing the Church of Sweden's folk church ecclesiology, particularly through the notion of an *address in everyday life*, challenges this conclusion. Based on an understanding of the Church as a porous community that connects

---

[42] Wuthnow, *Sharing the Journey*; Latini, *Crisis of Community*; Atkinson, *Small Groups*; Egli and Marable, *Big Impact*; Stetzer and Geiger, *Transformational Groups*.

[43] Svenska kyrkan, *Kyrkoordning*, Introduction to the second section.

individuals navigating their lives in the world, this view highlights that our online small groups do not need to be considered as lacking a communal dimension even if they might not have prioritized the visible community of the groups nor tried to integrate online group participants into the parishes' worshipping community.

Perceived as a vehicle of proclamation, the role of online small groups shifts. Their purpose is not to draw participants out of the world and into the Church but to equip and support them in living out their Christian faith amidst their daily lives. This ecclesiological perspective suggests that portraying our online small groups as somehow lesser manifestations of the Church does a disservice to the complexity and richness of these gatherings. It further underlines that the dichotomy between communities of learning and communities of faith may not be about a distinction between learning and faith, but rather between various ways of conceptualizing the community of the church.

A significant insight from our project is thus that online small groups in the Church of Sweden embody an approach to non-formal Christian religious education that diverges from the focus prevalent in much of the small group literature, which tends towards cultivating lasting, visible communities. Instead, our groups can be understood as facilitating individuals' engagement with Christian living in their daily contexts, which significantly influences the deployment and perceived value of teaching methods, strategies, and techniques.[44] This shift highlights a broader understanding of education and formation within our groups, one that prioritizes equipping individuals for faith practice in the world over and above integrating them into a defined ecclesial community.

Community, as traditionally conceived within ecclesial contexts, thus assumes a different role in the Church of Sweden's online small groups. The absence of a requirement for participants to integrate into a visible worshiping community underscores a shift towards personal growth and formation in the everyday. Our groups can thus be said to reflect an ecclesiological stance that sees the Church's mission as extending beyond the confines of local community boundaries to touch lives in diverse and meaningful ways.

One might add that a challenge with the *address in everyday life* is its neglect of the sender's perspective. Even if it were accepted that the Church is constituted by the proclamation of the gospel rather than its reception or its fruits, there remains the question of who delivers this address. Here I see a risk that the folk church perspective focused on an *address in everyday life* implicitly operates with

---

[44] Wirén, *Undervisning*, 252; Cöster, *bedriva undervisning*, 14–15; Hedman, *Undervisa*, 11; Osbeck, *Förstå livet*, 19; Klintborg, *Vägen är allt.*

a problematic distinction between salaried employees and lay members or a service provider church.

Still, I argue that this perspective makes an important addition to the literature on small groups and online Christian religious education by highlighting how various conceptualizations of the community of the church translate into distinct understandings of formation, especially in relation to community. Varied understandings of church, alongside differing perspectives on the objectives and functions of Christian religious education, thus coalesce to forge diverse educational environments within small groups, highlighting the critical impact of ecclesiological and educational philosophies on the structuring and objectives of such groups.

6. Teaching in Online Small Groups

Christian religious education serves not only as the field in which I place this dissertation but also as my core theoretical perspective, examining online small groups as an *instance* of Christian religious education.[1] Yet, based on the reflective narrative in part 2, some might question the efficacy of Christian religious education as a lens for analyzing and improving online small groups. In essence, the question is how and to what degree group leaders teach in online small groups and hence whether teaching is an adequate theoretical concept for reflection on our story.

In this chapter, I delve into these matters to answer two of my sub-questions: *To what extent and in what ways do group leaders teach in online small groups?* and *How can adopting a teaching perspective contribute to the improvement of online small groups?*

My analysis begins with an exploration of the distinctions between facilitation and teaching (6.1), subsequently leading to an examination of whether our activities as group leaders can be classified as teaching (6.2). I conclude by addressing three potential criticisms regarding the suitability of teaching as a theoretical lens for online small groups (6.3).

6.1 From Facilitation to Teaching

In chapter 2, I described Christian religious education, following Jeff Astley's definition, as an "intentional activity by a teacher or educator."[2] I am not sure, however, whether the group leaders involved in the *Online Small Groups* project would identify as "teachers." I find myself hesitating to use the term "teacher" in the context of leading a small group. This hesitation stems from the observation that many small groups function more as discussion forums, where participants collaboratively explore life and share their faith, as opposed to Sunday school

---

[1] See section 2.2.

[2] Astley, "Aims and Approaches," 3. See section 2.2.

classes, which are more structured around formal teaching and the dissemination of specific content.[3]

Similarly, the small group leaders interviewed by Robert Wuthnow in the 1990s expressed a reluctance towards the concept of teaching.[4] They identified not as teachers, but as facilitators—a persistent distinction, as evidenced by recent literature on small groups that predominantly links group leadership with facilitation and not teaching, suggesting that this sentiment remains unchanged.[5]

From the standpoint of Christian religious education, however, there arises a question of whether facilitation adequately encompasses the essence of group leadership. The Oxford English Dictionary defines "facilitation" as an instance of facilitating, and "to facilitate" as to "make (an action, process, etc.) easy or easier; to promote, help forward; to assist in bringing about (a particular end or result)."[6] Thus, facilitation is characterized more as a support role than an autonomous function. In other words, facilitation inherently presupposes the existence of a goal or objective to be achieved.

When the activities of online group leaders are interpreted as facilitation, the focus typically becomes the group itself or possibly the group's communication dynamics. In the role of facilitators, leaders encourage participants and guide discussions. Yet, this interpretation of facilitation suggests that the process is primarily generated by the group, with leaders acting simply as enablers. It is the act of meeting as a group, along with the community and fellowship it nurtures, that holds transformative potential.[7]

A challenge I perceive with this conceptualization of facilitation is its failure to fully acknowledge how group leaders not only guide meetings but also design them. In our project, we as leaders actively shaped the online small groups we facilitated, both from a broad perspective and in the nuances of each meeting. Thus, our groups were not readily existing entities requiring facilitation, but we deliberately constructed them with specific purposes.

This design process encompassed various dimensions, including the formation of groups, the selection of suitable meeting times, themes or topics for discussion, adherence to certain rules, and the choice of videoconferencing tools. As leaders

---

[3] Elias, "Models," 181–88.

[4] Wuthnow, *Sharing the Journey*, 268.

[5] Latini, *Crisis of Community*, 161–67; Lang and Bochman, "Positive Outcomes," 71; Atkinson, *Small Groups*, 11–12, 105, 42.

[6] Oxford English Dictionary, "facilitate, v., sense 1.a," *Oxford English Dictionary* (2023).

[7] Wuthnow, *Sharing the Journey*, 161–83, 277; Walton, "Disciples Together," 101–11.

we were, consequently, not just enabling spontaneous group processes but implemented the very plans we had devised for our groups.

My concern is that the notion of facilitation might not adequately highlight the critical role of design, potentially limiting the pathways for improving online small groups. In other words, interpreting the duties of group leaders solely within the framework of facilitation could obscure the crucial responsibility they bear in the conceptualization and structuring of online small groups.

This concern is echoed in the critiques by Robert Wuthnow and Roger Walton regarding the transformative capacity of small groups as meeting spaces. Wuthnow highlights that small groups often reinforce existing beliefs among participants rather than challenging them, as the atmosphere in these groups is one of encouragement rather than critique or guidance.[8] Walton similarly points out that in England, small groups tend to emphasize "mutual support and affirmation" over "learning, outreach, challenge or accountability."[9]

Extending this argument to spirituality, Wuthnow suggests that small groups might lead to a "domestication" of the sacred, where God is perceived not as a force that beckons individuals into the wilderness but as a comforting presence within the group's community.[10] Theresa Latini's research supports this view, indicating that in well-developed small groups, the focus on God's immanence is so pronounced that God's transcendence is nearly lost.[11]

These critiques indicate opportunities for improvement, particularly if online small groups are conceptualized within the framework of Christian religious education. The insights from Wuthnow, Walton, and Latini imply that improving these groups involves more than mere facilitation of existing groups. Effective improvement must incorporate design elements capable of injecting new and somewhat divergent dimensions into group sessions, thereby addressing and mitigating some of the inherent limitations identified in small group settings.

Hence, I contend that interpreting online small group leadership solely through the lens of facilitation falls short for two reasons. First, group leaders engage in activities beyond merely facilitating group dynamics. In the context of the *Online Small Groups* project, leaders also played a pivotal role in the design of their groups—a crucial aspect that may be overlooked if their roles are seen as purely facilitative. Second, the concept of facilitation alone does not adequately provide

---

[8] Wuthnow, *Sharing the Journey*, 14.
[9] Walton, "Disciples Together," 112.
[10] Wuthnow, *Sharing the Journey*, 255.
[11] Latini, *Crisis of Community*, 53.

opportunities for the improvement of online small groups as *instances* of Christian religious education. Such improvements are likely to necessitate deliberate design decisions, beyond the mere facilitation of pre-existing group interactions.

6.2 Online Small Groups as Sites of Teaching?

I have characterized teaching as the deliberate creation of specific potential learning situations—contexts where teachers, learners, content, and activities converge in such a manner as to facilitate and enhance the likelihood of learners achieving the desired learning results, given the unique circumstances of each situation.[12] Building on this definition, I propose that the activities undertaken by leaders can indeed be construed as teaching in this manner.

Before advancing my argument, it is critical to address whether teaching necessitates conscious effort. In other words, is it possible for someone to engage in teaching, as defined previously, without being aware of it? My response is affirmative, suggesting that the activities of group leaders can indeed be classified as teaching, regardless of whether the leaders themselves view their actions in this light.

To substantiate my claim, I examine each component of my definition of teaching sequentially. First, I assess whether online small groups constitute specific learning situations. Following this, I explore how these particular learning opportunities were facilitated within our groups, focusing on the potential for learning. Concluding this line of argument, I maintain that the activities conducted by us as group leaders were carried out with deliberate intent—that is, group leaders intentionally established these specific potential learning situations.[13]

---

[12] See section 2.3.

[13] Here I assume that it is possible for the action of a subject to be intentional even if the subject is not unaware of this intentionality. While this claim might seem illogical at first, there is an ongoing philosophical discussion that points to the differentiation of consciousness and intentionality. See for example Charles Siewert, "Consciousness and Intentionality," in *The Stanford Encyclopedia of Philosophy* ed. Edward N. Zalta (Metaphysics Research Lab, Stanford University, 2022); Davide Zottoli, "Intentionality and Inner Awareness," *Phenomenology and Mind* 22 (2022): 68–80.

However, I believe that one does not need to delve into these complex philosophical discussions, but can appreciate the fact from feminist and queer theorists, such as Judith Butler, who have long since argued that human activities should be understood through the notion of performativity, and hence intentionality (a performance having a specific aim it intends to realize), which does not require awareness. See for example Judith Butler, *Gender Trouble: Feminism and the Subversion of Identity* (New York: Routledge, 2006 [1999]).

6.2.1 A *Specific* Learning Situation

I begin my analysis by examining how our online small groups represented specific potential learning situations. These were not merely contexts offering the chance to learn something vague or undefined but were designed to facilitate specific and deliberate learning opportunities. The use of "potential" here underscores that we, as leaders, had limited influence over the actual realization of these potential learnings.

The specificity of potential learning is initially evident from the "materials" utilized in each group. The #Margareta, #Djursholm, and #Älvsjö groups were structured around biblical passages from the Church of Sweden lectionary. Consequently, the learning opportunities for participants were specifically guided by the texts to address themes such as faith (Daniel 6:16–22 on Oct 3, 2021), temptation and sacrifice (Matthew 16:21–23 on Mar 8, 2022), or Jesus and healing (Mark 5:24–34 on Mar 15 & 17, 2022).

These instances are illustrative rather than exhaustive, demonstrating that the groups focused on distinct themes and subjects. This approach was similarly applied in the #S:tEskils group, which fostered specific learning outcomes through its engagement with literature that explored issues of grief and the Sami in Sweden. In the #Margareta group, specificity was also achieved through discussions centered around the chosen theme for the Sunday ("Angels" on Oct 3, 2021). Furthermore, the introduction of specific learning potentials was facilitated by employing elements such as the Church of Sweden lectionary, prayers, #LightingCandles, and the assignment of #PrayerPartners, among others. Consequently, our online small groups were designed to enable *specific* learning experiences.

Certainly, the level of specificity in our groups can be subject to discussion, as can the degree of specificity necessary to classify an activity as teaching. I generally posit that a higher degree of specificity in potential learning correlates with a greater certainty that such activities can be classified as teaching. For instance, teaching differential equations, as mentioned in section 2.3.1, serves as an example where specificity unequivocally indicates teaching.

The crux of the matter rests on whether the topics, themes, and materials presented in our online small groups were sufficiently distinct to facilitate specific learning outcomes. This evaluation is ultimately contingent upon the comparison employed. Our online small groups were not intended to facilitate learning in areas such as cooking, anger management, or mathematics. Similarly, they were not aimed at promoting precise knowledge acquisition, like memorizing the Ten Commandments or comprehending the significance of liturgical vestments.

Nevertheless, I maintain that the learning facilitated by our groups was indeed specific. The groups were structured to enable insights into the Christian faith as practiced and traditioned within the Church of Sweden, through interaction with biblical texts, prayers, and lectionary-based themes. This line of reasoning applies equally to the #S:tEskils group. Therefore, specificity in this context should not be seen as a binary concept but rather as existing on a spectrum.

Determining the precise threshold for what constitutes teaching along the spectrum from general to specific is open to debate and might best be resolved on an individual basis. The level of specificity necessary is influenced by the objectives of teaching and the nature of the learning envisioned. For instance, if the goal of learning is to enable participation in online small groups, the specificity required would be less stringent than if the objective were for learners to memorize the Ten Commandments.

These reflections further aid in differentiating between teaching and instruction, leading me to reference Paulo Freire, a pivotal figure in adult learning theory.[14] At the heart of Freire's educational philosophy is the distinction between the banking concept of education and the concept of liberation education. Briefly, the banking model views knowledge as a commodity that can be transferred from a knowledgeable teacher to a student, whom it views as an empty container to be filled. In essence, this banking concept equates teaching solely with instruction.[15] Contrastingly, Freire's liberation model of education posits that both teachers and students engage in a collaborative exploration, fostering an environment where everyone can gain new understandings.[16]

From Freire, I derive two critical insights. First, teaching is not synonymous with instruction. Although teaching may incorporate elements of instruction, it is overly simplistic to conflate the two concepts. Thus, adopting a teaching perspective for online small groups does not presuppose that these groups function purely as venues for instruction or that learning within them is merely about knowledge acquisition.[17] Second, the role of the teacher remains integral even within a dialogical approach to education. Freire prompts educators to reassess their interactions with "students" but stops short of eliminating the teaching role altogether.

---

[14] Jarvis, *Adult Learning*, 1–6; Jack Mezirow, ed., *Learning as Transformation: Critical Perspectives on a Theory in Progress* (San Francisco: Jossey-Bass, 2000), xiii; Knowles, Holton III, and Swanson, *Adult Learner*, 65.

[15] Freire, *Pedagogy*, 41–48.

[16] Freire, *Pedagogy*, 41–53.

[17] See Sfard, "Two Metaphors."

This insight leads me to recognize that the concept of teaching must be broader than that of instruction, thereby accommodating varying degrees of specificity. To dismiss our online small groups as specific potential learning situations due to an assumed lack of specificity risks constraining the understanding of learning and teaching to the confines of the banking model of education.

Therefore, I maintain that lower levels of specificity are sufficient for teaching to take place, and our online small groups indeed met the necessary level of specificity, though I will later contend that increasing specificity could further improve teaching effectiveness.[18] Consequently, I deem it sufficient for qualifying our online small groups as sites of teaching that they were focused on particular aspects of life and faith, intended to facilitate specific learning experiences, despite the possibly modest degree of specificity.

6.2.2 A Specific *Potential* Learning Situation

The next step in my argument ventures into the somewhat theoretical realm of *potential* learning. The core issue examines whether participants could have learned the specific content presented in our groups, premised on the idea that teaching does not guarantee learning, but should facilitate it at least sporadically.[19] In this context, I transition from viewing *potential* as merely conceivable or speculative to seeing it as both feasible and likely. Additionally, for simplicity's sake, I confine this discussion to intentional learning.[20]

To delve into potential learning, I revisit Gert Biesta's work, who broadly defines learning as "any more or less durable change that is not the result of maturation."[21] This definition implies that learning represents changes arising from an individual's engagement with their surroundings, as opposed to changes driven by biological processes. Additionally, learning denotes changes of at least some

---

[18] See section 7.1.1–7.1.2.

[19] See section 2.3.

[20] As I see it, teaching could also denote the deliberate creation of specific potential learning situations for unintentional learning. For example, the way in which a leader sets up an online small group might be designed to teach participants something about the way in which deacons and pastors relate to lay members of the church, without this ever being raised to the conscious awareness of participants. However, since the #Aspirations we formulated for our small groups usually involved reflective learning, I abstract here from teaching for unintentional learning. For a discussion of different learning types see Jarvis, *Adult Learning*. See also the discussion in section 7.1.7.

[21] Biesta, "Freeing Teaching," 232.

permanence, despite the lack of consensus on the exact duration necessary for a change to be considered learning.[22] Crucially, it is pertinent to underscore that, in this context, learning is characterized as the outcome of an action, rather than the action itself.

To evaluate the potential of learning outcomes materializing, I incorporate Peter Jarvis's theory of the learning process. Jarvis posits that learning commences with a disjuncture—a point where an individual confronts an unfamiliar scenario, prompting the potential for learning. Without such moments of disjuncture, individuals engage with their environment lacking the necessary awareness for intentional learning to occur.[23] Yet, encountering a disjuncture alone does not guarantee learning; individuals must react to this disjuncture with a mindset geared towards learning, rather than a non-learning response.[24] A key aspect of Jarvis's analysis is this emphasis on the fact that not every engagement with potential learning situations results in actual learning, due to the absence of enduring transformation within the learner.[25] For online small groups to serve as effective learning situations, participants must experience a disjuncture, react with a learning response, and undergo a change that is more or less durable as a result of this process.

Demonstrating the *potential* for learning is most straightforward when one can show that learning has indeed taken place. To illustrate this point, I refer to my journal entry from January 6, 2022.

The journal entry describes how Gunilla's comment prompted me to perceive a biblical passage in a new light, and how engaging with the practice of *Lectio Divina* fostered personal reflection regarding my connection with Christian narratives and my desire to share my talents. This scenario encapsulates the essential elements of disjuncture and a subsequent learning response. Admittedly, gauging whether these reflections have resulted in lasting personal transformation is challenging, and any change might be subtle. Nevertheless, I argue this experience adequately demonstrates the potential for learning, intimately linked to the specific

---

[22] Biesta, "Freeing Teaching," 232.

[23] Jarvis, *Adult Learning*, 21–31; Peter Jarvis, "Religious Experience and Experiential Learning," *Religious Education* 103, no. 5 (2008): 553–67 at 551–61. In a later text Jarvis distinguishes between reactive, pro-active, and interactive learning, which appears to include a type of learning that is unconscious and unreflected and which hence would not require the presence of a disjunction. See Peter Jarvis, "Learning to Be a Person: East and West," *Comparative Education* 49, no. 1 (2013): 4–15.

[24] Jarvis, *Adult Learning*, 21–31.

[25] Jarvis, *Adult Learning*, 21–35.

learning situation, Eva established through her intentional meeting organization, leadership style, and selection of texts.

A comparable pattern emerged in both the #Djursholm and #Älvsjö groups, where participants, through their feedback in the #Evaluations, shared how being part of the groups enriched their understanding of biblical texts in nuanced and multifaceted ways. It remains uncertain whether these insights led to enduring transformations, thereby signifying genuine learning within our groups. However, such moments of insight are capable of fostering changes that last, representing *potential* learning. [26] Consequently, I identify instances of #PotentialLearning across all our groups, positioning them as environments ripe with the potential for learning.

6.2.3 A *Deliberately Created* Specific Potential Learning Situation

The final aspect of my argument aims to show that we, as leaders, intentionally structured our online small groups to foster specific potential learning situations. This involves two key elements. First, the deliberate design of online small groups facilitated specific learning opportunities. This acknowledgment comes from the understanding that the selection of texts, the prayers offered, #LightingCandles, and the assignment of #PrayerPartners were all intentional actions. Therefore, online small groups qualify as sites of teaching because leaders crafted them to support specific potential learning experiences.

Furthermore, leaders' responsibilities extend beyond merely designing these groups; they actively facilitate learning within them. The inclusion of elements like #LandingStrips, #ClearRules, #RelaxationExercises, #OpeningQuestions, and emphasizing the significance of #SeeingEachOther are all intentional actions aimed not just at structuring the group, but at guiding the learning process. Each of these components was designed with the intent to not only enable learning but to make it a likely outcome. Hence, online small groups, such as ours, are sites of teaching because leaders consciously engage in both the planning and the facilitation of learning experiences.

In acknowledging facilitation as a component of the learning process, it is crucial to clarify that the facilitation I refer to is directly tied to learning.[27] This means leaders are not just facilitating spontaneous group dynamics or casual discussions. Instead, they deliberately orchestrate and guide potential learning processes. This

---

[26] Jarvis makes a similar point using the concept of disjuncture as a starting point for learning. Jarvis, "Religious Experience," 551–56.

[27] Cf. section 6.1.

distinction highlights the targeted, intentional nature of facilitation in this context—aimed explicitly at achieving specific learning objectives, as opposed to the more general facilitation of group interactions, where the intent to foster learning may not be as pronounced.

In summary, online small groups function as specific potential learning situations. These groups entail the possibility for learning, where the deliberate actions of leaders in designing and facilitating these groups steer learning towards particular outcomes, albeit with varying levels of specificity. Through the lens of teaching applied to the experiences of the *Online Small Groups* project, it is evident that we, as group leaders, purposefully engineered these situations for potential learning, regardless of whether all of us were aware of doing so.[28] Therefore, online small groups can be recognized as sites of teaching, with leaders assuming the roles of educators.

6.2.4 A Broad Understanding of Teaching

Ultimately, the classification of online small groups as sites of teaching hinges on the specific definition of teaching employed. I have defined teaching as the deliberate creation of specific potential learning situations and have argued that, by this definition, group leaders are unequivocally engaged in teaching. Additionally, I have pointed out that teaching encompasses a wider range of activities than mere instruction, linking it to purposeful actions designed to facilitate and enhance the likelihood of specific learning outcomes.

Certainly, there may be critiques of my broad conceptualization of teaching, with some suggesting that its lack of specificity permits an overly wide range of activities to be classified as teaching. However, I maintain that employing a broad definition is not inherently problematic. As previously mentioned, the concept of learning itself is frequently interpreted in broad and general terms, indicating that expansive definitions are not uncommon or necessarily problematic within this domain.[29]

Furthermore, I assert that my conceptualization of teaching is sufficiently precise to contribute meaningfully to both the discussion and improvement of online small groups within the realm of Christian religious education. Specifically, framing teaching as the deliberate creation of specific potential learning situations ensures that only intentional and goal-oriented activities are recognized as teaching. Moreover, the added requirement that such activities occasion learning at least

---

[28] For a brief discussion of intentionality and awareness see footnote 13 in chapter 6.

[29] See section 6.2.1.

every so often allows for a distinction between leader actions that positively influ-ence learning towards predetermined goals and those that do not, and hence nei-ther qualify as teaching. Indeed, one of the strengths of my conceptualization of teaching lies in its breadth, enabling it to encompass a range of activities that might not traditionally be identified as teaching under a narrower interpretation.

Recognizing online small groups as sites of teaching is crucial as it opens path-ways for their improvement as instances of Christian religious education. Viewing these groups as purposeful or goal-directed endeavors elevates teaching as a key concept. This perspective allows for a deeper understanding of how the objectives for these groups are achieved and offers insights into improving the process of achieving these goals.

Before delving into potential improvement, however, I pause to further con-template the concept of teaching from a theoretical standpoint. This reflection goes beyond assessing the compatibility of my teaching definition with our expe-riences from the *Online Small Groups* project. Instead, I explore the utility of teaching as a framework when seeking the improvement of church-based online small groups.

6.3 The Adequacy of a Teaching Perspective

In this section, I address three potential objections to my conceptualization of teaching as a means to characterize and improve online small groups. The first two objections have been raised by readers of earlier dissertation drafts, centering on the applicability of the theoretical framework. The first objection questions the contemporary relevance of the concept of the kingdom of God for Christian reli-gious education within the Church of Sweden. The second objection scrutinizes the appropriateness of adopting formal education theories for discussing and im-proving learning and teaching within the realm of non-formal Christian religious education. The third objection concerns the implications of my white practical theological perspective, specifically how it influences my framing of teaching, es-pecially in relation to power and dominant perspectives.

6.3.1 Objection 1: The Kingdom is Not a Relevant Perspective

My understanding that Christian religious education encompasses teaching as an intentional activity is derived from Anglo-Saxon Christian religious educators. What is more, Thomas Groome's contributions date back to the 1980s and 1990s, Jeff Astley's writings were primarily published in the 1990s and early 2000s, and

Craig Dykstra's works share a similar timeline, among others.[30] Consequently, one might argue that these perspectives, rooted in earlier decades and different cultural, social, and ecclesial contexts, may not directly align with the context of non-formal Christian religious education within the Church of Sweden as of 2024.

Yet, an examination of contemporary literature on learning and teaching within the Church of Sweden reveals that the insights of Groome, Astley, and Dykstra remain pertinent to its educational ministry. To counter the argument of their relevance being outdated, my response is twofold. First, I demonstrate that a consensus exists among Swedish religious educators and scholars regarding education as a deliberate endeavor. Second, I highlight the frequent invocation of the kingdom of God theme, underscoring its ongoing significance in the discourse on religious education within the Church of Sweden.

In his examination of teaching within the Church of Sweden, Henry Cöster articulates a vision of teaching as both intentional and directed towards specific goals. He links this approach to a dual aim: proclamation, which fosters a "courage to live," and general education, which is concerned with the acquisition of factual knowledge.[31] Similarly, Jonas Eek situates his analysis of confirmation training within the Church of Sweden in relation to the distinctive goals of Christian religious education. He observes that:

> teaching can be theoretically defined as structuring. Based on one's aims and intentions, a teacher structures material and teaching opportunities. In all teaching, it is important to clarify the purpose. Only then can you plan and, eventually, evaluate the activity.[32]

Anders Hedman echoes this sentiment, emphasizing the intrinsic link between the rationale and methodology of teaching. He elaborates, "what is most important in teaching is that the *why* of teaching is linked to the *how* of teaching. The purpose must be consistent with, and evident in, the way we work."[33] Lastly, also Caroline Klintborg discusses confirmation training in the Church of Sweden in relation to its goal and purpose, leveraging Gert Biesta's notion that comprehensive education

---

[30] Groome, *Christian Religious Education*; Groome, *Sharing Faith*; Jeff Astley and Leslie J. Francis, eds., *Critical Perspectives on Christian Education: A Reader on the Aims, Principles and Philosophy of Christian Education* (Herefordshire: Gracewing, 1994); Jeff Astley, Leslie J. Francis, and Colin Crowder, eds., *Theological Perspectives on Christian Formation: A Reader on Theology and Christian Education* (Herefordshire: Gracewing, 1996); Astley, *Learning in the Way*; Dykstra, *Life of Faith*. See sections 2.2–2.4.

[31] Cöster, *bedriva undervisning*, 11–23, 44.

[32] Eek, *Stanna i vattnet*, 135.

[33] Hedman, *Undervisa*, 11. Emphasis in original.

encompasses qualification, socialization, and subjectification.[34] Swedish religious educators and scholars thus generally agree with the views of Groome, Astley, and Dykstra, understanding Christian religious education as inherently purpose-driven and teleological.

What is more, the purpose of Christian religious education is often connected to the kingdom of God. To start with, the Church Ordinance identifies the kingdom of God as one of the purposes guiding all primary parish functions, encompassing the educational efforts of the Church.[35] This linkage is further emphasized in relation to baptism and confirmation, illustrating the role of the kingdom of God in the Church of Sweden.[36]

This link may explain why several Swedish religious educators explicitly align the objectives of Christian religious education with the concept of the kingdom of God. Jonas Eek identifies the Kingdom as the ultimate aim of Christian religious education and confirmation training.[37] Similarly, Jakob Wirén ties the Church's mission, the *missio Dei*, to the Kingdom.[38] Anders Hedman also distinctly associates Christian religious education with the kingdom of God, treating it both as a teaching goal and as integral to the curriculum.[39] Finally, Caroline Klintborg shares insights from religious educators in Västerås parish, who perceive their work as contributing to a community that furthers the kingdom of God, showcasing the pervasive influence of this concept across various aspects of religious education in Sweden.[40]

Consequently, the language of the Kingdom is well-integrated and familiar among Swedish religious educators and scholars. While I acknowledge that Swedish authors may not explicitly differentiate between purpose and metapurpose as Groome does, it does not imply that the concept of the kingdom of God lacks relevance in Christian religious education within the Church of Sweden. On the contrary, the Kingdom provides a significant perspective through which Christian religious education is often interpreted and understood. Therefore, I regard the initial objection—that the idea of purpose-driven education aimed at advancing the

---

[34] Klintborg, *Var är Jesus?*, 91–111.

[35] Svenska kyrkan, *Kyrkoordning*, Ch 2 § 1.

[36] Svenska kyrkan, *Kyrkoordning*, Ch 19, 22.

[37] Eek, *Stanna i vattnet*, 71.

[38] Wirén, *Undervisning*, 27, 165.

[39] Hedman, *Undervisa*, 22, 39, 71–75.

[40] Gustavsson [Klintborg], *En process på riktigt*, 41.

kingdom of God is contextually unsuitable for the educational ministry of the Church of Sweden—as without basis.

6.3.2 Objection 2: Concepts from Formal Education Are Inappropriate

The second potential objection to my approach of applying a teaching perspective to online small groups concerns the distinction between formal and non-formal education. Critics might argue that I inaccurately categorize our online small groups as akin to traditional classrooms, overlooking the fact that they represent a fundamentally different type of learning environment where the concept of teaching might not be fitting.

In the field of educational theory and research, it is common to differentiate between formal, non-formal, and informal education.[41] These three educational modalities vary significantly across several dimensions, including the resources available to both educators and learners, the nature of social interactions within the learning context, the extent of adherence to governmental guidelines and regulations, and their overarching objectives.[42] Given these distinctions, it is plausible to surmise that processes of learning and teaching might exhibit notable differences across these settings. This leads to a pertinent inquiry: Is it suitable to apply concepts traditionally associated with formal education in the context of non-formal Christian religious education within congregations, parishes, and churches?

To effectively address this question, I propose starting with an examination of *constructive alignment,* a specific example. I subsequently broaden the discussion to reflect on the more general question of whether it is fitting to incorporate theoretical perspectives from formal education into the context of non-formal Christian religious education.

Constructive alignment is a teaching framework initially devised for use in formal education settings, particularly at universities. It emphasizes the formulation of intended learning outcomes as a cornerstone for organizing teaching and assessing learning effectiveness.[43] Biggs and Tang, proponents of this framework, argue that intended learning outcomes ought to clearly delineate the specific activities learners are expected to perform (such as explain, apply, reflect, evaluate, and so forth), identify the focus of these activities, and establish the standards learners

---

[41] Jarvis, *Adult Learning*, 61–70; Larsson, *Medvandrare*, 31–58.

[42] Friedrich Schweitzer, Wolfgang Ilg, and Peter Schreiner, "Introduction," in *Researching Non-Formal Religious Education in Europe*, ed. Friedrich Schweitzer, Wolfgang Ilg, and Peter Schreiner (Münster: Waxmann, 2019), 7–16 at 1–9.

[43] For an introduction to constructive alignment see section 2.6.

are expected to meet. This approach ensures that the educational process is systematically directed toward achieving clearly defined goals.[44]

The necessity of employing intended learning outcomes, as detailed within the constructive alignment framework, becomes questionable when applied to non-formal religious education. In formal educational contexts, such outcomes are meticulously crafted to not only direct teaching and learning processes but also to facilitate assessment, grading, and the awarding of diplomas.

This level of formality, intrinsic to the assessment and certification processes in formal education, is typically not present in non-formal educational settings. Consequently, it raises the question whether the concept of constructive alignment and the formulation of specific intended learning outcomes is suitable for the sphere of non-formal Christian religious education, given the absence of these formal educational aspects.

However, before dismissing constructive alignment as unsuitable for non-formal education, it is important to consider the benefits this framework provides. Constructive alignment serves as a design framework aimed at enhancing the efficacy of teaching. According to Biggs and Tang, grounding teaching practices in clearly defined intended learning outcomes substantially increases the probability that learners will absorb the knowledge and skills their teachers aim to impart.[45]

From this foundational perspective, constructive alignment is well-suited to educational settings marked by deliberate intent and clearly articulated objectives—qualities that align with how I have approached teaching in online small groups. Moreover, the principle of intentional teaching underlies both formal and non-formal education. In fact, consensus appears to exist among Swedish Christian religious educators and scholars on the significance of explicitly stating educational goals and objectives, underscoring the relevance of constructive alignment's core principles also to the realm of non-formal Christian religious education, as discussed above.[46]

Certainly, skeptics might remain unpersuaded that online small groups function as sites of teaching, leading them to also doubt the suitability of applying theories from formal education to these settings. Yet, my argument hinges on the premise that if online small groups are recognized as sites of teaching, characterized by the deliberate creation of specific potential learning situations, then it logically

---

[44] Biggs and Tang, *Teaching*, 118–24.

[45] Biggs and Tang, *Teaching*, 91–100.

[46] Cöster, *bedriva undervisning*, 11–15; Eek, *Stanna i vattnet*, 135; Hedman, *Undervisa*, 11; Klintborg, *Vägen är allt*, 11–14.

follows that it is appropriate to employ frameworks geared toward such deliberate educational activities.

It is important to clarify, however, that this endorsement does not imply a wholesale applicability of formal educational theories to non-formal settings. Indeed, I believe that the level of formality and precision required for intended learning outcomes in non-formal education does not need to match that of formal education. Indeed, those who have engaged in academic discussions regarding the formulation of intended learning outcomes, as well as the approval of course syllabi and program curricula in higher education institutions, are likely familiar with the extensive debates over verb choice, the exact specification of content for each learning outcome, and the discussions on the nature of knowledge that each outcome aims to impart. This level of meticulousness may not be as necessary or applicable within the framework of non-formal educational settings.

Crafting effective intended learning outcomes is a skill developed by teachers in formal education through both training and practice.[47] It is questionable whether religious educators in non-formal Christian religious education need to attain this specific level of expertise.

Nevertheless, incorporating the concept of intended learning outcomes into non-formal educational contexts can offer a greater degree of specificity to the educational process, moving beyond broad objectives like fostering faith growth through group participation. This approach thus introduces a structured way to articulate and pursue educational goals, enhancing clarity and focus also in non-formal educational settings.[48]

The distinction between the concept of intended learning outcomes and Jeff Astley's enumeration of Christian learning outcomes for adult non-formal religious education illuminates this point further. Astley identifies eight broad outcomes: (1) Christian beliefs-that, understanding, and knowledge; (2) Christian beliefs-in; (3) Christian attitudes and values; (4) Christian emotions and feelings; (5) Christian experiences; (6) Christian moral actions; (7) Christian religious actions; and (8) Christian/theological reflection and criticism.[49]

While comprehensive, Astley's *Christian learning outcomes* lack the specificity and content detail that Biggs and Tang emphasize for intended learning outcomes, such as defining the precise nature of knowledge or the level of understanding to

---

[47] Biggs and Tang, *Teaching*, 301–06.
[48] Cf. section 7.1.1.
[49] Astley, "Aims and Approaches," 1–6.

be achieved.[50] This specificity is crucial for ensuring that teaching activities are effectively aligned with educational objectives, demonstrating the need for more concrete goal-setting in non-formal Christian religious education.

Given these considerations, the development of intended learning outcomes becomes particularly relevant in contexts where they can be effectively integrated with teaching and learning activities through constructive alignment. This is to recognize, that constructive alignment presupposes a considerable degree of control by educators over the potential learning situation, allowing them to tailor teaching processes to increase the likelihood of achieving their learning intentions for participants.

Yet, it is important to acknowledge that congregational practices often adhere to traditional patterns that may not be readily adjustable by leaders. For instance, the structure of learning within liturgical contexts is inherently influenced by the liturgy's ordo, possibly constraining the extent to which religious educators can modify the learning experience to align with specific intended learning outcomes. This reality suggests a nuanced approach to applying the concept of constructive alignment in settings where the flexibility to innovate or deviate from established practices is limited.[51]

In conclusion, I deem concepts from formal education to be suitable for analyzing non-formal Christian education, provided one accepts that formal and non-formal education share the basic characteristic of intentionality and are therefore both sites of teaching. Nonetheless, it is essential to recognize and account for the inherent differences between formal and non-formal educational models. Theories and practices derived from formal education must therefore undergo adaptation and refinement to be fully applicable and effective within non-formal educational contexts. This adaptation process requires a consideration of the unique ways formal education structures learning, ensuring these methodologies are appropriately adjusted for non-formal Christian religious education. Additionally, the diverse nature of non-formal educational environments necessitates that the suitability of any particular educational framework be evaluated on a case-by-case basis. Still, given that non-formal Christian religious education often intersects with both formal and informal educational domains, there exists a valuable opportunity for religious educators to leverage insights and resources from formal education to improve their pedagogical approaches.

---

[50] Biggs and Tang, *Teaching*, 121–24.
[51] Tveito Johnsen, "Gudstjenestelæring"; Gustavsson [Klintborg], *Delaktighetens kris*.

6.3.3 Objection 3: Teaching Builds on and Perpetuates Dominant Perspectives

Tom Beaudoin and Katherine Turpin delineate five key features of white practical theology, many of which resonate with aspects of my dissertation project. The initial trait they identify is an individual-centric approach. This is evident in my project's focus on facilitating personal learning experiences for participants, tailored to their individual lives, rather than integrating them into enduring communal settings. [52] The second characteristic revolves around an aspiration for progress, envisaging a future that transcends present circumstances, closely linked with an emphasis on persons positioned centrally within the socio-ecclesial hierarchy.[53] This perspective is reflected in my interpretation of the kingdom of God as the meta-purpose of Christian religious education and the broader concept of improvement, particularly in relation to teaching efficacy. Moreover, within my framework, the responsibility of achieving teaching effectiveness is placed on group leaders, who wield a degree of power and authority.[54]

The emphasis on teaching effectiveness transitions into the third defining element of white practical theology, as described by Beaudoin and Turpin: a focus on methodical organization and procedural precision, often aimed at increasing efficiency. This emphasis on orderliness is manifest in my efforts to articulate a clear concept of teaching, my examination of learning and teaching in relation to predefined didactic relations, and my advocacy for the deliberate formulation of learning objectives that then inform the structuring and guiding of group sessions.[55]

The fourth characteristic identified is a "preference" given to whiteness, encompassing a preference for white scholars and white scholarship and white theoretical perspectives, which are frequently perceived as foundational to the field and to represent the core areas of academic disciplines, as discussed in section 2.8.[56]

When applying Beaudoin and Turpin's criteria to my dissertation, it becomes evident that the work operates within the realm of white practical theology. This observation reveals that the influence of whiteness extends beyond the theoretical perspectives I employ and my presence as an embodied scholar; it permeates the

---

[52] See section 5.3.

[53] Beaudoin and Turpin, "White Practical Theology," 255–56.

[54] See sections 4.2.7 and 6.2.

[55] See chapter 4, section 6.2 above, and sections 7.1.1–7.1.2.

[56] Beaudoin and Turpin, "White Practical Theology," 259–61.

cultural viewpoints that shape my thinking, thereby influencing most aspects of this study.

The critique of whiteness, as highlighted by Beaudoin and Turpin, unveils its problematic aspects. The preference for whiteness aligns with elements of white supremacy, even if they differ in degree.[57] Moreover, a preference for whiteness entails a form of dominance, as noted by scholars such as Courtney Goto, bell hooks, and Maria Liu Won.[58] White preference is a dominant and dominating outlook when it claims its universality and ascribes particularity only to the racial or ethnic other. The assertion of universality—what Donna Haraway in a different context has called the "god trick"—establishes whites as the norm from which others deviate, obscuring the different conditions under which we live and simultaneously, and erroneously, suggesting that whites have the right to impose their cultural, political, economic, and ecclesial systems onto others.[59] Consequently, an objection can be made that my white perspective builds on and perpetuates the ugly face of whiteness, arguing that my project inadvertently supports and extends these problematic facets.

More concretely, linking the concept of teaching to the necessity for conversion introduces a universalizing claim that may inadvertently perpetuate dominant theological perspectives, particularly concerning sin. Feminist theologians like Rosemary Radford Ruether have critically addressed how traditional interpretations of sin and the call for conversion—central to my depiction of Christian religious education as an endeavor aimed at realizing the kingdom of God—reflect a predominantly male and white viewpoint, portraying the human subject as an individual perpetrator. Ruether contends that, contrary to a narrative focusing on repentance from traits such as anger and pride towards humility and self-abnegation, for women, the journey of conversion is often about a profound self-revelation, a process of "turning around in which [women] literally discover themselves as persons, as centers of being upon which they can stand and build their own identity."[60]

---

[57] Beaudoin and Turpin, "White Practical Theology," 257.

[58] Goto, "Asian American Practical Theologies"; Goto, "Writing in Compliance"; hooks, *Teaching*; Liu Wong, *Becoming Wise*.

[59] Donna Haraway, "Situated Knowledges: The Science Question in Feminism and the Privilege of Partial Perspective," *Feminist Studies* 14, no. 3 (1988): 575–99 at 584; Beaudoin and Turpin, "White Practical Theology," 257–58.

[60] Rosemary Radford Ruether, *Sexism and God-Talk: Toward a Feminist Theology* (Boston: Beacon Press, 1983), 186. While Radford Ruether places her discussion in the context of feminism, I would argue that a similar claim can be made for other subjugated groups.

Moreover, a strong version of this critique might highlight my emphasis on teaching as aligning with a belief in ecclesial hierarchies where individuals wielding power and authority are deemed essential for guiding and educating laypeople, thereby suggesting that the expansion of the kingdom of God hinges crucially on the activities of strong leaders and teachers, rather than all of us.

This critique holds weight regardless of whether teaching targets liberation; even if the kingdom of God as the metapurpose of Christian religious education is acknowledged as a worthy goal, it matters how that Kingdom is understood and who is allowed to define it. The immediate objectives of Christian religious education are similarly scrutinized under this lens.[61] This criticism is especially forceful if considered in the Church of Sweden's historical context, in which teaching has been an important aspect in the colonization of the Sami.[62]

Advocating for an understanding of online small groups as sites of teaching thus risks perpetuating perspectives in which power dynamics are uneven and not all participants are seen as equal contributors to the collective endeavor of advancing the kingdom of God. This approach to teaching may inadvertently solidify the divide between teachers and learners, particularly in situations where group leaders are perceived to have special competence or knowledge due to their formal education or leadership roles, as observed in our groups.[63] This dynamic underscores the potential for teaching perspectives to emphasize hierarchical relationships rather than fostering an inclusive, collaborative learning environment.

Nonetheless, I contend that this perspective does not represent the sole valid interpretation. While teaching inherently involves the exercise of power, it is crucial to recognize that power does not equate domination. Bell hooks compellingly demonstrates that teaching can be both oppressive and emancipatory, heavily influenced by the manner in which it is conducted.[64] In line with this, Courtney Goto and Maria Liu Wong also embrace the concept of teaching within their approaches to Christian religious education, suggesting a nuanced understanding of power dynamics.[65]

---

[61] Cf. section 2.4.

[62] Björn Norlin, "Kyrkan, missionen och skolan," in *Samerna och Svenska kyrkan: Underlag för kyrkligt försoningsarbete*, ed. Daniel Lindmark and Olle Sundström (Möklinta: Gidlunds, 2017), 37–50; Norlin, "Kyrkan och samiska kulturella uttryck."

[63] See section 4.2.7.

[64] hooks, *Teaching*, 35–44. Contrasting oppressive and liberatory education, Paulo Freire has argued the same. Freire, *Pedagogy*, 44–59.

[65] Goto, *Playing*, 91–95, 129–32; Liu Wong, *Becoming Wise*.

For bell hooks, the essence of transformative teaching lies in fostering environments conducive to learning, distinguished by diversity and collective responsibility. This approach mandates that educators cultivate communities of learning anchored in openness and intellectual rigor.[66] Furthermore, hooks emphasizes that any educational approach dedicated to well-being necessitates that teachers engage deeply in their own personal growth and self-actualization to effectively empower their students.[67]. Consequently, the critical question according to hooks is not about the act of teaching itself, but rather the approach and methods employed in teaching.

Courtney Goto, drawing on the insights of psychoanalyst Donald Winnicott, presents the view that religious educators should aim to be "good enough," suggesting a departure from the pursuit of relentless improvement. Goto's description highlights complex qualities of good teaching, such as vulnerability, spontaneity, flexibility, and courage, raising questions about the standards for being "good enough."[68]

While Goto's model places a subdued focus on the act of teaching, it still recognizes the importance of skilled leaders who oversee learning processes. This perspective is evident in her reference to pastor Gary Barbaree's analogy of the church as "a sandbox where designated leaders keep close watch over how playing unfolds so that no one gets hurt while people play with scary issues, including issues of life, death, transformation, justice, and mercy."[69]

Maria Liu Wong's perspective on Christian religious education also resonates with the themes highlighted by Goto, emphasizing a community-centered approach across formal, non-formal, and informal educational settings. Liu Wong's focus is on fostering communities that contribute to the growth and flourishing of God's people and the broader world.[70] This emphasis on communal development parallels Goto's emphasis on leadership qualities over traditional teaching practices.

Liu Wong articulates leadership as a dynamic process of influencing and guiding others toward collective change, mirroring the essence of teaching as I

---

[66] hooks, *Teaching*, 39–40.

[67] hooks, *Teaching*, 15.

[68] Goto, *Playing*, 91–92, 130.

[69] Goto, *Playing*, 92. Gary Barbaree was pastor of the Sacramento Japanese United Methodist Church in California (SJUMC). The SJUMC's engagement with aesthetics in Christian religious education is one of the case studies Goto presents.

[70] Liu Wong, *Becoming Wise*, 8, 132.

understand it. She describes leadership as an interactive and directional activity, sometimes characterized by mutual and reciprocal influence, highlighting the transformative potential inherent in leadership roles. This description underscores the similarity between effective leadership and teaching, where both involve guiding individuals or groups towards new understandings or states of being, emphasizing the fluidity and reciprocal nature of these roles in fostering community and individual development.[71]

Liu Wong's recounting of meticulously planned learning activities further illustrates the connection to teaching. Through these narratives, it becomes evident that individual educators or leaders frequently assume responsibility for the design and execution of educational experiences. This responsibility underscores the teaching aspect of their roles, where careful planning and personal accountability are pivotal in creating effective and impactful learning opportunities.[72]

The similarities between my focus on teaching and the attention Goto and Liu Wong give to leadership within Christian religious education reveal a significant overlap in our approaches. This convergence suggests that the issue may not lie with the act of teaching per se, but rather with the methodologies and attitudes adopted in the teaching process.

Neither the conceptualization of the Kingdom as the metapurpose of Christian religious education nor the recognition of human sinfulness necessitating conversion impose a dominant perspective inherently. While Courtney Goto may not explicitly utilize these terms, there is a discernible alignment between the notions of God's new creation and the kingdom of God.[73] Goto's focus on "leaning into God's new creation" further echoes themes of conversion, particularly in her assertion that the new creation beckons Christians to adopt new forms of being, engaging with others, and behaving in ways that may confront and transform established norms, suggesting an eschatological transition from old to new.[74]

Likewise, Rosemary Radford Ruether's engagement with the concept of conversion illustrates that the notion itself does not inherently necessitate dominance. Ruether explores conversion in a context that emphasizes transformation and renewal without imposing or endorsing structures of domination. Her interpretation suggests that conversion, understood as a profound change in perspective, belief, or behavior, can occur in ways that foster equality, liberation, and

---

[71] Liu Wong, *Becoming Wise*, 115.

[72] Liu Wong, *Becoming Wise*, 44, 75–78, 106.

[73] See section 2.2.

[74] Goto, *Playing*, 12.

empowerment rather than subjugation. This perspective reinforces the idea that the spiritual and ethical dimensions of conversion can contribute to a more inclusive and just community, challenging rather than perpetuating existing power dynamics.[75]

I conclude, then, that teaching does not inherently have to reinforce dominant perspectives. Yet it would be naive to ignore the potential risks it carries in doing so. Recognizing the whiteness of my perspective obliges me to also acknowledge the possibility that it may inadvertently support practices of white dominance, without for that matter categorically labeling all white perspectives as inherently oppressive. Rather than outright dismissing such concerns, I see value in embracing critical perspectives as a needed form of constructive vigilance. This approach compels leaders of online small groups, myself included, to continuously engage with and challenge our assumptions and biases. Similarly, white practical theologians are tasked with confronting and critically examining the implications of our whiteness within our theological explorations and teaching.

In the end, I concur with Tom Beaudoin and Katherine Turpin's assertion that the issue of whiteness cannot be definitively "solved."[76] Rather, whiteness and the process of racialization represent, in Courtney Goto's words, a "harmful, chronic conundrum" that requires a commitment to "taking the same baby steps repeatedly" for its mitigation. This necessitates that white practical theologians reflect critically about their whiteness, interrogating their role in the maintenance of white privilege. For educators, this reflection extends to examining how their teaching practices either reinforce or challenge systems that subjugate specific human beings and their ways of knowing and being in the world. By persistently undertaking these small yet significant steps, there is an opportunity to gradually dismantle the foundation of dominant perspectives, thereby contributing to the creation of academic and ecclesial communities that are more diverse, inclusive, and just.

6.4 Summary and Reflections

I have conceptualized teaching as the deliberate creation of specific potential learning situations and argued that group leader activities in the *Online Small Groups* project can be understood as teaching, group leaders as teachers, and online small groups as sites of teaching, no matter whether group leaders themselves are aware

---

[75] Radford Ruether, *Sexism and God-Talk*, 159–92.
[76] Beaudoin and Turpin, "White Practical Theology," 258.

of this fact or not. Teaching has thus functioned as an etic perspective, viewing it as an observable and definable action external to the subjective experiences and self-identifications of the leaders themselves.

In addressing the sub-question, *to what extent and in what ways do group leaders teach in online small groups?* I conclude that leaders engage in teaching by designing and managing potential specific learning situations. This process involves assembling the groups, choosing relevant subjects, themes, and resources, and guiding prayers, readings, and discussions, which includes posing questions to direct dialogue.[77] In our groups, we, as leaders, also facilitated learning by creating favorable conditions through activities like playing #TaizéSong, implementing #LandingStrips, conducting #RelaxationExercises, and posing #OpeningQuestions. We further emphasized #GroupBuilding and established #ClearRules, embraced #LightingCandles, and incorporated #DecisionPoints. These actions collectively demonstrate the multifaceted role of group leaders in creating specific potential learning situations, highlighting their role as teachers within the context of online small groups.

Of course, it is important to recognize that not all actions undertaken by group leaders in online small groups qualify as teaching. The dynamics within these groups are intricate, and leaders undoubtedly engage in various activities that do not directly contribute to the deliberate creation of specific potential learning situations. For instance, activities like praying might not inherently fall within the scope of teaching. However, I maintain that a substantial portion of the activities performed by leaders aligns closely enough with the conceptualization of teaching to justify the use of the term, especially when considered from an etic perspective.

In addressing the other sub-question, *how can adopting a teaching perspective contribute to the improvement of online small groups?* I assert that recognizing group leaders as teachers, rather than merely facilitators, offers significant benefits. This recognition foregrounds leaders' influence on both structuring and guiding specific potential learning situations within the group setting. Understanding groups as sites of teaching and leaders as teachers, moreover, opens up avenues for their improvement and paves the way for identifying and implementing strategies for the further development of online small groups as an instance of Christian religious education.[78]

I also addressed three potential objections, the first two of which I refuted. I have thus argued that the concept of the kingdom of God remains a pertinent

---

[77] Cf. section 4.3.

[78] See section 7.1.

framework for Christian religious education within the Church of Sweden as of 2024. Additionally, I have reasoned that concepts and insights from formal education can make valuable contributions to our understanding and improvement of non-formal educational activities. However, I acknowledge the validity of the third objection concerning the risk that adopting a teaching perspective may inadvertently reinforce dominant white viewpoints. This acknowledgment serves as a reminder to religious educators of the importance of remaining vigilant about the ways in which educational practices may contribute to the perpetuation of power imbalances and privilege. It underscores the ongoing challenge for scholars and educators alike to keep wrestling with issues of power and marginalization both in the academy and in the church, striving towards a more inclusive and equitable approach to Christian religious education both as a practice and as a scholarly discipline.

Part IV:
Extrapolation to a Broader Context and Articulation of Usable Knowledge

7. Teaching Strategies for Online Small Groups

A distinguishing feature of action research is its focus on "usable knowledge." In this chapter, I formulate usable knowledge by developing eight teaching strategies for online small groups.[1] These strategies represent my clearest response to the first part of my overarching research question: *How can online small groups within the Church of Sweden be improved as instances of Christian religious education?*

Simultaneously, these strategies serve as an extrapolation to a broader context. That is, by formulating these strategies, I transition from the specific experiences of our online small groups to recommendations that I believe are also valuable for other groups and leaders.

Before presenting the strategies, I wish to briefly discuss their epistemic value. Utilizing an emergent and explorative design, I do not regard the strategies below as definitive or final solutions to teaching in online small groups. Indeed, I would be hesitant to label them best practices, considering they were derived from a very limited number of groups. Instead, I find that the most appropriate way to articulate the epistemic value of these strategies is through the lens of David Kolb's model of experiential learning.[2]

Recognizing the considerable resemblance action research bears to experiential learning, I suggest interpreting the narrative in part 2 as an instance of reflective observation, the reflections in part 3 as abstract conceptualizations, and the strategies in this section as active experimentation.[3] Consequently, the aim of this chapter is not to present conclusive results, but rather to propose methods for improving online small groups.[4] The strategies outlined will therefore need to be tested in actual groups, a process likely resulting in their reformulation, adaptation, or

---

[1] For a definition and theoretical discussion of strategies see section 2.7.

[2] See section 3.2.3.

[3] Kolb, *Experiential Learning*, 50–52.

[4] Cf. section 3.3.4.

potentially their dismissal. In summary, I view these strategies as contributions to future cycles of experiential learning about online small groups.

I begin the chapter with a discussion of how the strategies are derived, before presenting the analyses that lead to the formulation of the eight strategies (7.1). I then reflect on these strategies in comparison to other, similar approaches devised for small groups (7.2), and by examining how the strategies might be applied or implemented in specific teaching and learning situations (7.3–7.4).

7.1 Strategies for Online Small Groups

In this section, I employ the theoretical perspective, introduced in chapter 2, to examine our experiences from the *Online Small Groups* project and to develop eight strategies for design and facilitation. Adopting a toolkit approach to theory, I do not adhere to a single theoretical framework but instead utilize multiple theories to explore various facets of teaching in online small groups. Consequently, I will introduce the elements of each theory that I apply directly in the discussion.[5]

In formulating these strategies, I did not adhere to any specific method. Rather, the strategies are derived from areas where I identified potential for improvement—either due to challenges encountered in our online small groups or because certain aspects appeared underdeveloped—and from areas where I believe our experimental approach to online small group leadership has positively impacted our online small groups as instances of Christian religious education.

While this section assesses our online small groups from a teaching standpoint, I want to reemphasize that the essence of the participatory action research project was to introduce and examine new facets of group leadership. Therefore, it would be unjust and misguided to evaluate leaders based on the success of these initiatives. This is particularly true as moments of friction often present the most valuable opportunities for identifying areas for improvement.

Strategies were derived in three different ways. The first set of strategies (3, 4, and 6) originated from empirical observations. I encountered challenges that prompted reflection on our experiences in light of theoretical frameworks, elevating these observations to a broader context. For strategy 3, these were observations related to moments of #Instruction, in both the #S:tEskils and #Djursholm groups. Strategy 4 was initiated by reflections on the challenges of #BeingFully-

---

[5] For a methodological discussion of the advantages and disadvantages of using a toolkit approach see section 2.1.

Present and #SeeingEachOther, while the development of strategy 6 was spurred by experiencing a #LossOfControl.

The development of a second set of strategies (1 and 2), in contrast, was rooted in theory. It was through engaging with learning and teaching theories that I recognized connections to our groups, allowing me to articulate the dynamics within these groups more precisely. This was true for strategies 1 and 2, which linked the teleological nature of Christian religious education to the concept of constructive alignment.[6]

A third and last group of strategies (5, 7, and 8) underwent a more abductive process, oscillating between our experiences and the broader theoretical literature on community, Christian religious education, and online learning for strategy 5, Peter Jarvis's adult learning theory for strategy 7, and research on learning and action research for strategy 8. This iterative process began with observations from the groups, but it was the integration with theoretical insights that clarified my reactions, prompting me to revisit the episodes detailed in part 2 and to reevaluate our experiences through the lens of these theories.

It is also worth noting that all strategies are connected to the teaching and learning process. In chapter 4, I explored online small groups through the lens of the didactic relations model, indicating that learning and teaching emerge from multiple interconnected factors, with process being just one aspect.[7] However, our efforts to improve online small groups primarily concentrated on the process, rather than on the content or the objectives of the groups.[8]

7.1.1 Strategy 1: Formulate Specific Learning Intentions

My experience with the *Online Small Groups* project suggests that it is relatively uncommon for group leaders to explicitly state learning intentions for participants. None of the groups adhered to a specific curriculum or syllabus, and although we defined and clarified goals for each group in the #ResearchPlans,[9] it is

---

[6] See sections 2.2–2.5.

[7] See chapter 4 and especially section 4.2.3.

[8] My dissertation is thus closer to didactic classroom studies which focus attention on the learner-teacher-content interactions in classrooms (broadly understood) then to curriculum analysis, which researches the way in which content and purpose are formulated. Osbeck, Ingerman, and Claesson, "Introduction "; Christina Osbeck and Åke Ingerman, "A Potential Research Direction for Didactic Classroom Studies," in *Didactic Classroom Studies: A Potential Research Direction*, ed. Christina Osbeck, Åke Ingerman, and Silwa Claesson (Lund: Nordic Academic Press, 2018), 193–223; Posner, *Curriculum*, 1–32.

[9] See appendix B.

plausible that group leaders would not have documented these objectives in writing if not for the research project.[10] Moreover, it is unclear whether group leaders formulated goals independently or as a response to our discussion of these #ResearchPlans.[11]

To analyze learning outcomes, I began by converting the goals and ambitions outlined for each group into distinct objectives. This process generally entailed separating individual outcomes from more complex formulations and considering the intentions contained in each formulation. For instance, the #ResearchPlan for the #S:tEskils group includes the goal:

> to raise questions. On Lotta's advice, the circle reads books that arouse emotions, that touch on existential questions and politics, i.e. books that are a little heavier but inspire hope. It is also hoped that the conversations contribute to discovering and learning something new about the world, society, and oneself.

I deconstructed this compound goal into two separate intentions. Furthermore, I rephrased "to raise questions" as "to reflect" and "discovering and learning something new" as "gain new insights," translating the objective from the #S:tEskils #ResearchPlan to mean that participants should: (1) reflect on existential questions and politics, and (2) gain new insights about the world, society, and themselves. My rendering of group objectives is thus an analytical move, marking a shift from an emic to an etic perspective, similar to the process of coding in which interview material is processed and categorized.[12]

In a subsequent step, I juxtaposed each learning intention against the models of Christian religious education.[13] In this, the models provided a structured taxonomy of purpose, content, and method, against which specific educational activities could be analyzed.[14] For example, viewing the #S:tEskils group through the prism of the Christian religious education models reveals parallels between the book club

---

[10] Cf. section 4.2.1

[11] See for example the entries from Wednesday, July 7, 2021, and from Wednesday, August 25, 2021.

[12] Till Mostowlansky and Andrea Rota, "A Matter of Perspective? Disentangling the Emic–Etic Debate in the Scientific Study of Religion\s," *Method & Theory in the Study of Religion* 28, no. 4–5 (2016): 317–36 at 321–21. In Sweden this distinction is usually referred to as the difference between the "object language" (*objektspråk*) and the "analytical language" (*analysspråk*). Carl-Henric Grenholm, *Att förstå religion: metoder för teologisk forskning* (Lund: Studentlitteratur, 2006), 213–14.

[13] See section 2.4.

[14] Tveitereid, "Making Data Speak." See also the introduction to chapter 4.

and the critical, praxis, and practice models, which I elaborate on below. The outcomes are shown in table 7.1.

Learning Intention	Model
#S:tEskils	
Participants should:	
- experience and spread the joy of reading	Community / Practice
- meet each other and break COVID-19 isolation	-
- reflect on existential questions and politics	Critical
- gain new insights about the world, society, and themselves	Critical
- get some understanding of what the Church of Sweden is and know about some of the activities offered by S:t Eskils parish	Schooling
#Margareta	
Participants should:	
- grow in faith	All
- encounter God	Spiritual
- learn about God and what it means to be human	Critical
- be comfortable with sharing their faith with others (in the group)	Practice
- develop good listening skills	Practice
#Älvsjö	
Participants should:	
- deepen their faith	All
- explore their own understanding of faith	Critical
- be able to share both the joys and sorrows of life and faith	Practice
- get inspiration for their sermon preparation	Praxis / Practice
- get first-hand experience with online small groups	Practice

Table 7.1 Intended Learning Outcomes

Additionally, as each model represents a cohesive set of assumptions about Christian religious education, the models serve as an evaluative framework. In other

words, there is agreement within each model between its purpose, content, and method, mirroring the congruency central to constructive alignment.[15]

While the mappings of learning intentions onto the models of Christian religious education in table 7.1 are largely straightforward, some cases warrant further scrutiny. The #S:tEskils goal to "experience and spread the joy of reading" aligns with the practice model, where the aim is for learners to become acquainted with and engage in specific practices—reading, in this case. However, this goal could also be interpreted through the community model lens, emphasizing the joy derived from reading in a community. Similarly, the #Älvsjö goal for participants to "get inspiration for their sermon preparation" links the Christian tradition to the tangible act of preaching, fitting the praxis model. Yet, it also enhances the skill of sermon preparation, aligning with the practice model.

The challenges encountered in aligning intentions and models underscore that each model is an ideal type, somewhat ill-equipped to handle the complexities of real life.[16] However, full accuracy is not crucial for my current aim; the models serve as heuristic tools for understanding and assessment rather than precise theoretical constructs. An approximate alignment is sufficient for illustrating my argument: highlighting that learning intentions intersect with multiple models.

Table 7.1 shows that the learning intentions span the six models of Christian religious education. Table 7.2 lists the frequency of the various models.

Group	Schooling	Critical	Praxis	Spiritual	Practice	Community
#S:tEskils Book Club	1	2	-	-	1	1
#Margareta Lectio Divina	-	1	-	1	2	-
#Älvsjö Bible Study	-	1	1	-	3	-

Table 7.2 Frequency of Mapped Learning Intentions

As can be seen from table 7.2, none of the groups conformed to a single model. The table also highlights the varied focal points among the groups. The #S:tEskils group seems focused on understanding and reflection, while simultaneously

---

[15] See section 2.6.

[16] Richard Swedberg, "How to use Max Weber's ideal type in sociological analysis," Article, *Journal of Classical Sociology* 18, no. 3 (08/01/ 2018): 181–96–96.

fostering the practice of reading. Furthermore, #S:tEskils stands out as the only group with a specific objective related to information dissemination: participants were expected to gain knowledge about the parish's activities. The #ResearchPlan explicitly states that this goal should be achieved by sending informational materials to participants and encouraging them to engage in these activities after the group concludes. Therefore, the emphasis on information is relatively minor and secondary, as it is addressed in only one of the group's six meetings.

The book club also included a goal for participants to meet each other as a means to break COVID-19-induced isolation. However, I do not understand this as an intended learning outcome. The act of meeting was aimed primarily at alleviating isolation and was seen as an objective in its own right, rather than being linked to processes of transformation or change.[17]

The main emphasis of the #Margareta group was on faith development, envisioned through a blend of understanding, trust, and practice. Consequently, the group was structured around three learning outcomes: acquiring knowledge about God and human nature from biblical texts, experiencing God via these readings, and honing listening skills to attune to both God and our fellow human beings.

Additionally, the #Margareta group incorporated an instrumental intended learning outcome focused on the skill of participating in the group. However, the #ResearchPlan clarifies that the aim was not primarily to teach individuals to feel comfortable sharing their faith with others but to establish that sharing as a prerequisite for realizing the other intended learning outcomes.[18] Although this outcome aligns with the practice model, it does not constitute a strong focus for the group. I therefore consider the group to sit between the critical, spiritual, and practice models, rather than exhibiting a clear preference for the latter.

Lastly, also the #Älvsjö group encompassed a variety of objectives, showcasing possibly the broadest range among its goals. This group aimed to deepen faith by critically engaging with participants' understanding of faith, to let participants share the joys and sorrows of life and faith, and to serve as an inspiration for sermon preparation, without there being any apparent connection between the three. Similar to the #Margareta group, an additional objective was included, focusing on enhancing the skill of participating in online small groups.

The discussion above reveals that it is not feasible to categorize the online small groups under any single one of the six models. This difficulty arises partly because

---

[17] Cf. section 6.2.2.

[18] The #ResearchPlans are included in appendix B.

the models represent ideal types, which are not fully equipped to manage the complexity and unpredictability of real life, as stated above. Such a mismatch between the groups and the models may indicate limitations within the theoretical framework itself. Alternatively, it could also reflect that the groups' objectives and #Aspirations exhibit a degree of internal diversity.

Of course, this outcome is not surprising, considering that our groups were not designed to strictly adhere to any of the six models, nor were our #Aspirations intended to align perfectly with the formal criteria for intended learning outcomes. Interpreting this situation as a shortfall or flaw in our groups would thus be misleading.

However, this diversity does highlight a potential area for improvement. Specifically, if online small groups are considered as instances of Christian religious education and thereby as sites of teaching, leaders need to be explicit about their objectives, if they are to intentionally create specific potential learning situations that make it possible and likely that these intentions are realized. The amalgamation of objectives from different models may complicate the design and facilitation of suitable learning and teaching activities.

In this context, the models of Christian religious education could support an evaluative process. Employing the models of Christian religious education offers a means to link metapurpose, purpose, faith dimensions, content, and method in a manner that enables the constructive alignment of teaching activities with leaders' intentions. However, alignment is only possible once these aims are formulated. Consequently, the first strategy is to *formulate specific learning intentions that can guide learning and teaching in online small groups.*

7.1.2 Strategy 2: Constructively Align Teaching and Learning Activities

Paul H. Hirst contends that not all actions performed by a teacher qualify as teaching. He illustrates this point with examples such as opening windows to ventilate a room or sharpening pencils. Hirst argues that the opening of windows or sharpening of pencils does not amount to teaching, as these actions lack the intentional aim of facilitating learners' realizing specific intended learning outcomes.[19]

While I concur that activities like opening windows do not constitute teaching in the strictest sense, I argue that they form part of teaching in a more expansive

---

[19] Admittedly, teachers today might not be sharpening many pencils. That does however not affect Hirst's argument. Hirst, *Knowledge*, 79.

view.[20] Essentially, I believe that effective teaching encompasses a responsibility towards creating a conducive learning environment, including aspects such as the oxygen level in a room. From this wider perspective, any action undertaken to improve the potential learning situation should be regarded as an aspect of teaching. Nevertheless, activities not directly centered on learning intentions are auxiliary or supportive to the principal teaching and learning activities. Consequently, effective teaching should not be solely composed of these auxiliary activities, though it is likely to incorporate some of them.

Admittedly, the distinction between primary and auxiliary teaching and learning activities is meaningful only when learning intentions are considered distinct from the learning situation. In other words, if the goal is for participants to learn about online small groups as such, then all activities are deemed "primary," rendering the distinction irrelevant. Consequently, many sociocultural learning theories, which associate learning with participation, would argue that drawing such a distinction is challenging.[21]

However, upon revisiting the #Aspirations we set for our groups, it becomes evident that several learning intentions are unrelated to participation. It is with respect to these intentions that the distinction between primary and auxiliary activities becomes meaningful.

To examine the relationship between "primary" and "auxiliary" teaching activities, I explore a specific instance: the third meeting of the #Älvsjö Lenten Bible study group on March 15, 2022.

My reason for focusing on a single example is twofold: first, for the #S:tEskils and #Margareta groups, I lack adequate data for a comparable analysis. In both instances, I observed only one meeting, and due to differing priorities at those times, I did not document all leader activities during the observation. Hence, a comparative analysis across all four groups was unfeasible as an analytical approach.

Second, the March 15, 2022, meeting with the #Älvsjö Lenten Bible study group serves as a representative example for the spring groups, as most gatherings with both the #Älvsjö and #Djursholm groups adhered to a similar format, meaning that further analysis of additional sessions would not substantially augment my argument.

---

[20] "Frame factors" are routinely considered part of teaching. See for example Hiim and Hippe, *Undervisningsplanlegging*, 61–62; Posner, *Curriculum*, 91–201.

[21] Sfard, "Two Metaphors."

Table 7.3 outlines the teaching and learning activities for this particular session of the #Älvsjö group.

	Teaching and Learning Activity
9:50 AM	Show the welcome screen and play music
10:00 AM	Welcome
	- Housekeeping
	- How are you right now? Scale 1–5
	- Relaxation exercise
	- Candle, Prayer
10:15 AM	Bible study (Mark 5:21–34)
	- Including break
	- Round after the break
11:10 AM	Closing
	- Relaxation
	- Takeaways from today
	- Reminder: Prayer partners
	- Blessing
11:20 AM	Eval in breakout rooms, 3 and 3

Table 7.3 Planned Teaching and Learning Activities for the Third Meeting of the #Älvsjö Bible Study Group

In reflecting on our planning for the third meeting of the #Älvsjö group, distinguishing between primary and auxiliary teaching and learning activities is not immediately apparent. The session began with the customary #LandingStrip, where I showed a welcome screen and played music, designed to allow participants to arrive at the meeting in an unhurried way. Noticing that few participants utilized this time as intended, we incorporated a #RelaxationExercise directly into the meeting, aiming to achieve the same objective. These actions are unmistakably auxiliary activities.

Similarly, the housekeeping at the start and the reminders at the close of the meeting provide information to participants, yet these do not constitute primary teaching and learning activities in themselves. Taking breaks is also an auxiliary activity. Asking participants how they are, aimed to foster community—a crucial element for enabling participants to share the joys and sorrows of life and faith.

Nonetheless, this endeavor to build community undeniably served a supportive role, as explained in chapter 5.

Determining the nature of other planned activities—whether they are primary or auxiliary—presents more of a challenge. Activities such as #LightingCandles, praying, and Blessing could be considered primary if one adopts, for instance, the spiritual model of Christian religious education. However, the #Älvsjö group did not contain any learning intention focus on spirituality or worship, and based on discussions between Camilla and myself regarding prayer and the lighting of candles, it was evident that we regarded these elements as auxiliary rather than primary.[22]

This narrows down the potential primary teaching and learning activities to three: the Bible study, including the practice of soliciting participants' reflections after the break to stimulate discussion, inquiries regarding key takeaways, and the concluding evaluation. Yet, soliciting reflections is simply a technique to support the Bible study, and the #Evaluation was related to the research project, rather than an integral part of the session as such. I thus conclude that the Bible study, to which we devoted most time during our meeting, was the primary teaching and learning activity. However, the specifics of this primary activity were somewhat ambiguously defined in our planning.

Like all sessions with the group, the meeting on March 15, 2022, commenced with an initial #Instruction about the text. However, instruction is typically aimed at disseminating information, a goal not explicitly listed among our intended learning outcomes.[23] This positions the discussion itself as the teaching and learning activity aligned with the intentions that participants "explore their own understanding of faith" and "get inspiration for their sermon preparation." Nevertheless, how the conversation supports learners in achieving these outcomes remains largely undefined.

The conclusion of the third meeting featured a moment where participants were encouraged to reflect on their takeaways. This was aimed at guiding them to a #DecisionPoint, where the conversation could lead to tangible actions, a concept drawn from the praxis model of Christian religious education. However, this activity does not directly tie into the specific goals and objectives we established for the group. While it could be argued that this exercise is in line with the broader aim of deepening participants' faith, such a general goal ought to be broken down

---

[22] See section 7.1.1 and the entry from Tuesday, March 1, 2022.

[23] See section 7.1.1.

into more specific intended learning outcomes to better inform the planning and execution of teaching and learning activities.

Table 7.4 categorizes the teaching and learning activities, their types, and the learning intentions they address.

	Teaching and Learning Activity	Type	Learning Intention
9:50 AM	Show the welcome screen and play music	Auxiliary	Share joys and sorrows
10:00 AM	Welcome		
	- Housekeeping	Auxiliary	Share joys and sorrows
	- How are you right now? Scale 1–5	Auxiliary	Share joys and sorrows
	- Relaxation exercise	Auxiliary	Share joys and sorrows
	- Candle, Prayer	Auxiliary	Share joys and sorrows
10:15 AM	Bible study (Mark 5:21–34)		
	- Including break	Auxiliary	Share joys and sorrows
	- Conversation, incl. round after the break	Primary	Understanding faith & Sermon Preparation
11:10 AM	Closing		
	- Relaxation	Auxiliary	Share joys and sorrows
	- Takeaways from today	Primary	-
	- Reminder: Prayer partners	Auxiliary	Share joys and sorrows
	- Blessing	Auxiliary	Share joys and sorrows
11:20 AM	Eval in breakout rooms, 3 and 3	Auxiliary	-

Table 7.4 Teaching and Learning Activities, Type, and Learning Intentions for the Third Meeting of the #Älvsjö Bible Study Group

In my analysis, most of the planned activities were auxiliary, designed to bolster the primary ones. Nonetheless, one of the primary activities did not match any intended learning outcome. Significantly, the majority of the meeting time was allocated to the Bible study, a primary activity in sync with two of the intended outcomes. The issue, therefore, is not a misalignment of teaching and learning activities with the learning intentions, nor an inability of participants to learn from the session as conducted. Instead, it suggests that the congruence between activities and outcomes could be enhanced, potentially leading to more effective teaching.

The second strategy builds upon the first: after establishing learning intentions, it is crucial to devise activities that directly aim at achieving these outcomes. This approach likely entails incorporating auxiliary activities into each meeting. However, group leaders must consider how these auxiliary activities can bolster the primary ones and deliberate on how the primary activities are designed to facilitate learners in achieving the intended learning outcomes.

Indeed, as explored in chapter 6, it is beyond the capability of group leaders to guarantee that learners will achieve the learning intentions. Nevertheless, they can intentionally design learning activities that make achieving these outcomes both feasible and likely. Therefore, leaders should investigate which activities most effectively foster the targeted learning. The second strategy, then, is to *constructively align teaching and learning activities with the learning intentions for each group.*

7.1.3 Strategy 3: Instruct with Deliberation and Caution

Among the objectives and #Aspirations of the four groups, only one aligned with the schooling model of Christian religious education, characterized by its focus on information and instruction. The #S:tEskils group had set a goal for participants to gain knowledge about the parish's other activities, which essentially served as a secondary and supporting aim within the group.[24]

During our online small group sessions, I observed instances of #Instruction at two junctures and contemplated their potential implications. Specifically, in our #Djursholm group, I recognized how #Instruction shifted the focus towards factual knowledge and cognitive comprehension, diverging from the experiential and embodied approach that predominantly defined the group's dynamics.

In the #S:tEskils group, I noted the challenges that #Instruction posed for the dynamics between leaders and participants. I observed that #Instruction introduces a distinction between leaders and participants, potentially complicating the sense of equality that typically characterized their relationship. Finally, I reflected on how #DistributedResponsibility in the #Älvsjö group countered the conventional logic of #Instruction.

In *Pedagogy for the Oppressed*, Paulo Freire examines two contrasting perspectives on knowledge and teaching. The "banking" concept of education views knowledge as a commodity that is transferred from a knowledgeable expert to an

---

[24] See section 7.1.1.

ignorant student through instruction. Conversely, the liberation model posits that teachers and students engage in a collaborative journey of discovery, during which both parties can gain new insights.[25] Freire articulates this idea, stating:

> Through dialogue, the teacher-of-the-students and the students-of-the-teacher cease to exist and a new term emerges: teacher-student with students-teachers. The teacher is no longer merely the-one-who-teaches, but one who is himself taught in dialogue with the students, who in turn while being taught also teach. They become jointly responsible for a process in which all grow.[26]

Using Freire's pedagogy to scrutinize our online small groups reveals that the issues I associated with #Instruction stem from divergent educational philosophies and the nuanced dynamics of the teacher-learner relationship. Through Freire's lens, #Instruction is tied to the schooling model of Christian religious education, which relies on the "banking" concept of education. This concept implies a one-way transmission of knowledge: "the teacher teaches and the students are taught; the teacher knows everything and the students know nothing; [...] the teacher talks and the students listen—meekly."[27] This pattern was evident in the instances of #Instruction I described earlier. #Instruction by group leaders carries an underlying presumption of unequal knowledge, with leaders imparting information and participants receiving it in a largely passive manner.

However, most groups do not adhere to a traditional schooling model. Instead, the defined learning intentions lean towards the critical and practice models, suggesting a preference for a more equitable learning environment where everyone is both a learner and a participant. However, instances of #Instruction can disrupt this balance, potentially creating a pronounced divide between those who possess knowledge (the leader) and those who do not (the participants), even as these momentary disruptions do not appear to have enduring impacts on the group's ability to serve as effective learning situations.[28]

This observation offers insight into why the mini-lectures on weekly readings in the #Älvsjö group never truly embodied instances of #Instruction. The shared responsibility for these mini-lectures negated the presumption of privileged knowledge, a perspective that aligns well with the fact that many participants were ordained pastors within the Church of Sweden. By rotating the responsibility for introducing the readings, it was openly acknowledged that everyone could assume

---

[25] Freire, *Pedagogy*, 41–53.
[26] Freire, *Pedagogy*, 53.
[27] Freire, *Pedagogy*, 46.
[28] See entry from Thursday, March 3, 2022.

the "teacher" role. This suggests that it is the conflict between different views of the teacher-learner dynamic that introduces uncertainty into the learning situation, rather than the mere act of disseminating information.

Uncertainties may, however, extend beyond the dynamics between leaders and participants to encompass the very objectives of learning. The banking concept of education predominantly perceives knowledge as factual information that can be transmitted from one individual to another. Observing a shift towards a focus on factual knowledge following a moment of #Instruction in the #Djursholm group indicates that #Instruction may also imply a reshuffling of the perceived intended learning outcomes. Implicitly, #Instruction positions the informational content as a subject matter that learners ought to assimilate. Consequently, #Instruction could also subtly alter the intuited purpose of online small groups.

This observation does not suggest that group leaders should completely avoid instruction. Rather, leaders need to be conscious of the effects that shifting into an instructional mode can have. Leaders should consider the conditions under which #Instruction facilitates participants' achievement of an intended outcome, without disrupting the group's social dynamics or deviating from the implied learning objectives of the online small group. Hence, the third strategy is to *approach instruction with deliberation and caution*.

7.1.4 Strategy 4: Create Favorable Conditions for Dialogue

Transactional distance is a cornerstone concept of online education, emphasizing that distance encompasses more than mere geographical separation; it also pertains to levels of engagement. This perspective opens up the possibility of "closing the distance" in online education by enhancing interaction and connectivity.[29] Although the theory of transactional distance primarily addresses formal education, I propose that its fundamental principles are just as relevant and applicable to non-formal education.

Transactional distance, as a pedagogical construct, gauges the extent to which learners feel either engaged and supported or isolated and disconnected from educators and their peers. The core premise of the theory is not to deem one state preferable over the other but to illustrate that an increase in transactional distance necessitates a higher level of learner autonomy.[30] Nevertheless, with the evolution from traditional distance education to contemporary online education, there is now an acknowledgment of the beneficial impact of peer collaboration.

---

[29] Moore, "Transactional Distance."
[30] Moore, "Transactional Distance," 73.

Consequently, transactional distance is increasingly viewed as a pedagogical hurdle to be surmounted. This perspective is particularly pertinent in educational settings like online small groups, where the learning model is predicated on dialogic and cooperative exploration.[31]

Michael Grahame Moore posits that transactional distance diminishes through dialogue.[32] Yet, within a pedagogical context, dialogue transcends mere discussion. In the setting of small group discussions, dialogue enriches the conversation with distinct attributes like fostering a sense of community, enhancing listening, and encouraging active participation and involvement.[33]

Consequently, effective teaching in online small groups partially hinges on crafting optimal conditions for dialogue to surmount transactional distance and to foster intimacy among participants. Practices like #BeingFullyPresent or #SeeingEachOther are important because they promote dialogue, which, in turn, reduces transactional distance. This underscores the significance of establishing #ClearRules concerning these practices.

Frequently, these guidelines strive to replicate the dynamics of onsite meetings, intended to facilitate participants' presence and mutual visibility. Nonetheless, our experience has highlighted challenges associated with #MimickingOnsite-Meetings. An example is the #Älvsjö group, where we attempted to conclude sessions in breakout rooms to imitate the natural chatter at the end of onsite sessions.

Another significant teaching challenge is the leaders' limited control over participants' physical environments. This issue is illustrated by a reflection of one of the group leaders on an online meeting I hosted during the spring of 2021:

> I'm sitting here and participate in the discussion, but I know that in half an hour someone will ring the doorbell and then I have to accept my grocery delivery because that was the only time available. I'm not really here and now, not one hundred percent. The room you sit in affects you. When you sit at home, there are so many things to think about: the laundry and the food you are going to prepare later and so on. It's different when I sit in church.

#BeingFullyPresent, therefore, is also influenced by the physical environment where participants are situated—an environment over which leaders have little to

---

[31] Shaunna Waltemeyer and Jeff Cranmore, "Closing the Distance in Distance Learning," in *Handbook of Research on Creating Meaningful Experiences in Online Courses*, ed. Lydia Kyei-Blankson, Esther Ntuli, and Joseph Blankson (Hershey: IGI Global, 2020), 14–24 at 16; Palloff and Pratt, *Collaborating Online*, 1–18.

[32] Moore, "Transactional Distance," 71.

[33] Atkinson, *Small Groups*.

no control. We anticipated similar challenges, that participants could not find a quiet place to sit or situations where participants were not alone, potentially leading to group discussions being overheard by others.

Given that group leaders are unable to manage these external factors, participants must assume a portion of the responsibility for facilitating dialogue. The specific methods by which this can be achieved, and the extent of its feasibility, undoubtedly differ across various participants and groups. Nonetheless, it falls upon leaders to motivate participants to embrace this responsibility for dialogue, including the physical settings from which they participate. In this sense, participants need to assume part of the hosting responsibility usually assigned to leaders in onsite meetings. Consequently, the fourth strategy is to *create favorable conditions for dialogue to reduce transactional distance by distributing the host responsibility.*

7.1.5 Strategy 5: Build Strong Groups

In our online small groups, the significance of #Community has been a recurring theme. The #MeetingAtmosphere and the cultivation of trust are crucial for enabling participants to discuss meaningful issues. Various #GroupBuilding practices, such as posing #OpeningQuestions or assigning #PrayerPartners have positively influenced the learning situation. This pattern is echoed when participants emphasized the importance of #SeeingEachOther and of #BeingFullyPresent, underscoring the value of comprehending and engaging in the social context of the group.

I explored the concept of community within online small groups extensively in chapter 5, observing that our online small groups revolved not around the tightly knit community often promoted for small groups in the United States. In our context, the notion of community aligns more closely with its interpretation in online learning—a platform for cooperation among participants. Hence, instead of striving to create closely bonded communities, leaders of online small groups are encouraged to focus on fostering strong, collaborative groups.

Peter Jarvis's learning theory sheds additional light on the significance of group dynamics in learning. Through interviews asking individuals to describe their learning processes, Jarvis developed an adult learning theory that views learning as fundamentally an individual yet inherently social activity.[34] While Jarvis's exploration of the social aspects of learning does not delve deeply into specifics, leaving

----

[34] Jarvis, *Adult Learning*, 1–15.

the "social" somewhat theoretical and abstract, he emphasizes that the value and potential of a learning experience are significantly influenced by the social context.[35] This perspective underlines the critical role that the social environment plays in the learning process.[36]

A further dimension of Jarvis's theory acknowledges that not every experience facilitates learning. Specifically, learning is precipitated by experiences characterized by a disjuncture or mismatch between the individual and the social context of learning.[37] Therefore, a crucial aspect of effective teaching involves crafting social situations that induce this type of disjunctive experience.

Disjunctures, while necessary, do not guarantee learning. Knut Illeris addresses learning obstacles, pointing out that disjunctures often trigger defensiveness, characterized by rejection or misinterpretation, which typically results in a failure to learn.[38] Therefore, it is imperative that disjunctures are introduced in a manner so that the social context prevents the disjuncture from becoming so pronounced that it provokes a defensive reaction.

Through Jarvis's perspective, we understand the critical role of #GroupBuilding, as the learning situation is inherently a social one, particularly evident in #RelationalMeetings. The structure of the social context significantly influences individuals' capacity to learn. The objective is thus not merely to implement specific practices like #PrayerPartners or #OpeningQuestions but to foster social situations that facilitate adult learning. This involves creating contexts where participants find meaningfulness, encountering disjunctures within a safe environment that encourages a learning response. Hence, the fifth strategy is to *build strong groups that support learning.*

7.1.6 Strategy 6: Give Learners Control

Andragogy is an adult learning theory that distinguishes the learning characteristics and needs of adults from those of children and youth.[39] Despite ongoing

---

[35] Jarvis, *Adult Learning*, 31–85.

[36] Jarvis, *Adult Learning*, 71–84.

[37] Jarvis, *Adult Learning*, 81–84. See also the discussion in section 6.2.2.

[38] Knud Illeris, "A Comprehensive Understanding of Human Learning," in *Contemporary Theories of Learning: Learning Theorists... in Their Own Words*, ed. Knud Illeris (Oxon: Routledge, 2018), 1–14 at 1–9.

[39] Andragogy is derived from the Greek *anēr, andr-* "man" to differentiate it from pedagogy, derived from the Greek *paidagōgos,* which in turn comes from *pais, paid-* "boy" and agōgos "leader of." Pedagogy is thus taken to be about the education of children, while andragogy relates to adult education. Knowles, Holton III, and Swanson, *Adult Learner*, 61.

debates about its scientific validity, many practitioners in adult education find andragogy to be a practical and useful framework.[40] Andragogy is based on six foundational assumptions about adult learners, leading to specific pedagogical recommendations. Andragogy posits that:

1. Adult learners need to understand the reason behind their learning.
2. They view themselves as self-responsible for their decisions.
3. Adults bring a richer and more diverse set of experiences to their learning endeavors.
4. They are motivated to learn when they recognize an immediate and applicable need for the knowledge or skills.
5. Adult learning is oriented towards real-life applications, aiming for improvements in life management rather than abstract knowledge acquisition.
6. Internal motivation is the most effective driver for adult learning.[41]

From these assumptions, it follows that adults prefer to be in command of their learning process and situations. This desire for control aligns with the broader perspective that adults aim to manage their lives and learning autonomously, seeking learning environments where this autonomy is respected and facilitated.

In part 2, I described an instance where both I and another participant felt a #LossOfControl, which proved to be quite disconcerting. This sense of losing control was intricately linked to the dynamics of the online small group learning situation, specifically, how online meetings limit the information available to participants about ongoing activities. When a group leader begins a meeting late or disables their camera, participants are left in the dark, unsure of the proceedings, which fosters a sense of #LossOfControl. Additionally, utilizing #BreakoutRoomDebriefs for concluding sessions was ineffective for the #Älvsjö group because participants similarly perceived a #LossOfControl over the situation.[42]

Andragogy sheds light on the discomfort associated with a #LossOfControl, framing it through the lens of adult learners' perception of themselves. Encountering a #LossOfControl compels adult learners to confront a situation where they

---

[40] Elwood F. Holton, Richard A. Swanson, and Sharon S. Naquin, "Andragogy in Practice: Clarifying the Andragogical Model of Adult Learning," *Performance Improvement Quarterly* 14, no. 1 (2001): 118–43 at 119.

[41] Knowles, Holton III, and Swanson, *Adult Learner*, 61–69. For a critical discussion see Jarvis, *Adult Learning*, 1–11.

[42] See entries from Monday, October 11, 2021, and Tuesday, April 12, 2022.

are not self-determined, potentially causing a misalignment between their lived experience and how they view their autonomy.[43]

It is important to acknowledge that not all adult learners may react to a #LossOfControl in the same way or to the same extent, given the #IndividualDifferences among learners in our groups. Furthermore, andragogy posits significant assumptions regarding adult learners' self-conception, assumptions that have yet to be fully substantiated through empirical research.[44] However, observations indicate that a #LossOfControl can have a negative impact on some adult learners, suggesting that efforts should be made to prevent such circumstances.

Andragogy further illuminates the #NeedToUnderstand, rooted in its foundational principle that adult learners must grasp the purpose behind their learning endeavors. This need ties back to adult learners' perception of themselves as autonomous in their learning journey and relates to the discomfort associated with a #LossOfControl. However, the core issue is not merely the lack of control but rather a lack of comprehension of the learning context, hindering learners from steering their own educational experiences. An instance of this, as detailed in part 2, is the playing of #TaizéSongs, where the activity's objective became clear to participants only after its rationale was explicitly communicated.

Providing explanations, while important, does not guarantee learning, however. After recognizing the #NeedToUnderstand in the #Margareta group, I endeavored to clarify the purposes behind our actions in the Djursholm group, which likewise practiced *Lectio Divina*. This included explaining the reasons for incorporating #TaizéSongs and #RelaxationExercises. However, our concluding assessments revealed significant #IndividualDifferences among participants, indicating that not everyone found value in these explanations.

This observation reinforces the idea that andragogical principles serve as broad generalizations about adult learners and may not uniformly apply across the board. [45] Furthermore, it highlights the distinctions between participants at

---

[43] In terms of Jarvis' adult learning theory this disjuncture is however not mitigated by a safe learning environment that would make it possible for adults to learn from the disjuncture, relating rather in a non-learning response. Jarvis, *Adult Learning*, 31.

[44] Holton, Swanson, and Naquin, "Andragogy in Practice," 140.

[45] Andragogy does not claim that the principles are universally applicable. Observing instances in which the principles to not apply does thus not "falsify" the theory, which is intended as a teaching aid based on a number of assumptions, rather than as predictive theory. Knowles, Holton III, and Swanson, *Adult Learner*, 61–70.

different stages of adulthood, underscoring the diversity within adult learning experiences.[46]

Still, teaching strategies do not have to be universally applicable to all learners, provided that the potential benefits for some outweigh any negative implications for others. Throughout our work with small groups, there has not been an instance where participants have expressed dissatisfaction or negative feedback about being informed of the reasons behind certain activities. Consequently, I assess that the risk of adverse effects from such explanations is low, whereas the potential advantages are significant. This assessment supports the promotion of explicitly explaining learning activities to the level of strategy, recognizing its value in enhancing the learning experience.

Informing learners about the rationale behind the various components of the online small groups represents just one of the methods we utilized. In the #Älvsjö group, for instance, we implemented #ClearRules that served a similar purpose. These #ClearRules help manage expectations, enabling adult learners to anticipate what comes next and, ideally, to understand the reasons behind these expectations.

For example, establishing a #ClearRule about taking breaks permits participants to mentally prepare for their engagement. Similarly, #StartingOnTime adheres to a #ClearRule about the commencement of sessions, contributing to a sense of control among participants by ensuring predictability.

Collectively, these practices—mitigating the #LossOfControl, addressing adult learners' #NeedToUnderstand, and setting #ClearRules to manage expectations—comprise a strategy designed to maximize learners' control over their educational engagement. Therefore, the sixth strategy is to *give learners control over the learning situation.*

7.1.7 Strategy 7: Include All Relevant Stops of the Learning Journey

Jarvis conceptualizes learning as both a social process and a complex phenomenon, indicating that learning encompasses various forms, each with its unique structure. He categorizes learning into non-learning, non-reflective, and reflective responses to potential learning situations. The majority of our #Aspirations aligns with reflective learning responses. In this category, learners engage in evaluating both the learning process and its outcomes. This approach to learning emphasizes the active involvement of learners in assessing their educational journey.[47]

---

[46] Cf. section 4.2.6.
[47] Jarvis, *Adult Learning*, 119.

The specific type of learning aimed for in our online small group closely resembles what Jarvis identifies as contemplation, or potentially experimental learning if the learning extends across multiple group meetings. To grasp Jarvis's categorization of learning types more clearly, it is helpful to look at the distinct learning journeys associated with each, as depicted in figure 7.1. This visual aid can illuminate the pathways through which learners might progress in their educational experiences within the group.

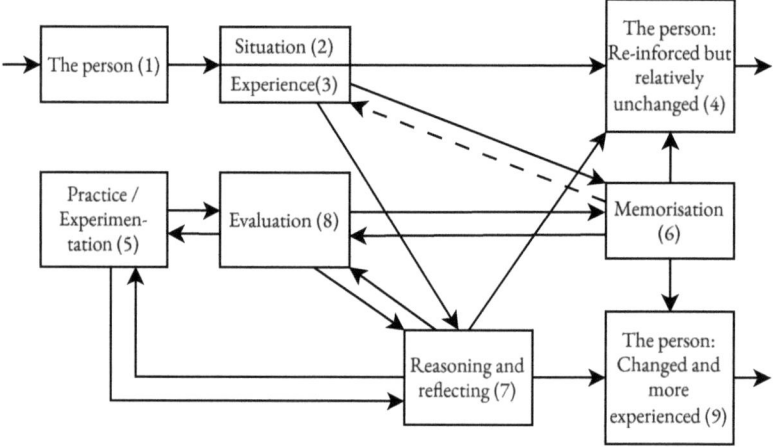

Figure 7.1: A Model of the Learning Process. Reproduced from Jarvis (1987)

In contemplative learning, individuals engage in an experience within a social context (steps 1–3), where they then reason and reflect (step 7), evaluate their reasoning (step 8), commit the outcomes to memory (step 6), and emerge from the situation altered, with enhanced experience (step 9). Therefore, the pathway for contemplative learning follows the sequence from steps 1–3 to 7, then to 8, 6, and finally to 9. Experimental learning introduces an additional phase, moving from reasoning and reflecting (step 7) to engaging in practical application and experimentation (step 5), and then returning to reasoning and reflecting (step 7), making the learning journey extend from steps 1–3 to 7, then to 5, back to 7, followed by 8, 6, and concluding at 9.

Both contemplative and experimental learning may lead to what Jarvis describes as innovation, signifying a transformative change in some aspect of the adult learner's circumstances or life world.[48] The primary distinction lies in the nature of the processes: contemplation involves a purely cognitive exercise, while experimental learning incorporates a phase of empirical testing or validation.[49]

A notable difference between online and onsite small groups is the scope of engagement. In online settings, interaction often remains confined to the designated meeting times, lacking the preparatory and reflective moments that accompany physical gatherings, such as the mental preparation during a walk to the church or the casual group building that occurs as participants arrive and depart. Additionally, the opportunity for reflection while returning home is absent.[50] While #IndividualDifferences mean this is not universally the case, many participants, especially those integrating online small groups into hectic schedules, find their engagement with the group largely limited to the formal session times.

Jarvis's adult learning theory highlights potential challenges associated with the absence of these transitional and reflective moments, particularly when aiming for critical reflection or contemplation. If the contemplative learning journey encompasses all the previously mentioned steps, then the structure of online small group meetings must be adapted to incorporate these elements within the session itself. Our experiences utilizing #TaizéSongs, #OpeningQuestions, #RelaxationExercises, #LandingStrips, #DecisionPoints, and #Closings serve as evidence of the effectiveness of integrating these components directly into online meetings to foster a comprehensive learning experience.

#LandingStrips function as an entryway, guiding individuals into the learning situation (steps 1–3). The dialogues within these meetings act as the medium for reasoning and reflecting (step 7). Prompting participants to identify #DecisionPoints aims to lead them towards evaluation (step 8), and the implementation of a #Closing segment is designed to assist in the memorization of key takeaways (step 6). This structure ensures that participants exit the session (slightly) transformed and with enriched experience (step 9). Thus, incorporating stages of evaluation and memorization directly into the meeting is essential, making them integral components of the learning process.

In practice, the application of Jarvis's model is not as straightforward as it might seem. The model portrays learning as a sequential journey, but our experiences with online small groups reveal a more fluid dynamic. For instance,

---

[48] "Innovation" is thus like transformation in Mezirow. Jarvis, *Adult Learning*, 168; Mezirow, *Learning as Transformation*.

[49] Jarvis, *Adult Learning*, 31–35, 161–69.

[50] See entries from Wednesday, July 7, 2021, and Wednesday, September 8, 2021.

#LandingStrips do not just serve as an entry point; they evolve into a #MeetingAtmosphere that pervades the entire learning journey. This observation challenges the notion of distinct "steps" in learning, suggesting instead that the initial steps (1–3) essentially create the context for subsequent learning activities.

Additionally, Jarvis's model does not account for the roles of mood and mental preparation in learning, aspects we have found critical.[51] The ambiance set by elements like #TaizéSongs is not merely decorative; it fundamentally shapes the learning experience by establishing a particular mood, underscoring the complex interplay between emotional and cognitive elements in the learning process.

It is logical to infer that the learning process encompasses more than just an individual's interaction with the social environment. Jarvis's framework illuminates how the initial steps of the learning journey (1–3) could potentially lead to a non-learning outcome (4), where the learner remains unchanged. Given that contemplative learning necessitates further stages of reasoning and reflecting (7), evaluating (8), and memorizing (6), it becomes crucial for effective teaching to foster conditions where these phases are encouraged, rather than leaving them to chance. This realization emphasizes the critical need for planning by online small group leaders, ensuring that the design of activities supports learners through every stage of their learning journey. Consequently, the seventh strategy is to *include all relevant stops of the learning journey in the meeting*.

7.1.8 Strategy 8: Hone an Attitude of Attentiveness

Incorporating the essential phases of the learning journey is a strategy that highlights the significance of learner self-assessment. Nevertheless, for educators to successfully design situations that effectively foster learning, they must be able to identify moments of learning—to ascertain the efficacy of their teaching approaches. This necessity for educators to gauge learning as it unfolds calls for an alternative strategy.

Evaluating the effectiveness of teaching can be approached through various methods, such as #Evaluations, #FeedbackForms, and #Interviews. However, our experiences have highlighted specific challenges associated with using #FeedbackForms, particularly concerning the rate of response and the interpretation of the data collected. Additionally, conducting formal #Interviews may not always be feasible or appropriate, and while #Evaluations serve as a generally reliable method

---

[51] The importance of moods and mental preparation is recognized by andragogy, which I explore below. Andragogy highlights the need to prepare learners and to set a conducive climate for learning. Knowles, Holton III, and Swanson, *Adult Learner*, 111–22.

for assessing teaching effectiveness, our work with the #Älvsjö group has demonstrated that #Evaluations often yield insights only after a significant delay. This observation does not invalidate these assessment techniques; rather, it suggests that they may not be entirely adequate on their own.

Instead of zeroing in on a particular assessment method, I recommend adopting a broader perspective on evaluation, characterized by attentiveness. This emphasis on being attentive—paying close attention to the present moment, both in terms of interactions with others and self-reflection—is more prominently discussed within the action research literature than in writings on Christian religious education.[52]

Action researchers underscore the critical importance of being present and mindful.[53] Aligning with this viewpoint, Judi Marshall and Peter Reason advocate for adopting an "attitude of inquiry" in action research, viewing it as essential for fostering attentiveness. This approach suggests that quality in research and teaching emerges from a continuous engagement with and curiosity about the learning environment and experiences therein.[54]

At its core, being attentive to both ourselves and others enhances our ability to understand the world around us more deeply.[55] This enhanced perception can lead to reflection, insight, and the development of new behaviors.[56] Although a certain level of attentiveness occurs naturally in interactions among people, it requires deliberate cultivation to fully develop this capacity. Echoing the sentiments of Marshall and Reason, cultivating an attitude of attentiveness is crucial for effectively engaging with and understanding the dynamics of educational environments, especially in the context of online small groups. This focused attention allows educators and participants to capture and respond to the nuanced experiences of learning as they unfold.

The observations underpinning the narrative of our experiences in part 2 emerge from the practice of attentiveness. These observations showcase the intricate relationship between attentiveness, experiential learning, the cycle of action and reflection, and the efforts to enhance teaching within online small groups.

---

[52] The same emphasis is, however, represent in Kolb's experiential learning theory in which attentiveness ensures the quality of concrete experiences. Cf. section 3.2.3.

[53] Peter Reason, "Choice and Quality in Action Research Practice," *Journal of Management Inquiry* 15, no. 2 (2006): 187–203 at 197.

[54] Marshall and Reason, "Quality."

[55] Coghlan, "Authenticity as First Person Practice."

[56] See Kolb's experiential learning cycle in section 3.2.3.

Upon reviewing these entries, it becomes apparent that a meticulous focus on details—pertaining to both personal introspection and the observation of others—provides a framework for evaluating our experiences. Cultivating an attitude of attentiveness aims to make such focused observation a regular practice. Consequently, if evaluating the effectiveness of teaching is to be an integral part of the continuous endeavor to refine and advance teaching methodologies, it necessitates a commitment to these practices of attentiveness.

One can certainly question the need for non-formal education to be in a constant process of improvement and development, especially in the settings of congregations, parishes, and churches, which both generally accept that human beings are necessarily fallible and imperfect, and that growth in faith is ultimately a divine gift.[57] This perspective could foster a laissez-faire approach to the development of Christian religious education, suggesting either a skepticism toward human capacity for achieving excellence or a minimization of the significance of human effort.

Yet, it is widely acknowledged among religious educators that human fallibility is not an obstacle but rather a cause for the need for conversion, discipleship, and growth in faith.[58] Furthermore, there is a consensus that the collaborative effort between the divine and the human in the realm of religious education does not negate the necessity for human endeavor.[59]

Acknowledging this intrinsic need for growth, transformation, and learning highlights the essential role of religious educators in facilitating these processes as effectively as possible. It is this acknowledgment that underscores the significance of continually evaluating the impact of teaching methods. Thus, educators should cultivate an attitude of attentiveness, ensuring that they remain acutely aware of and responsive to the learning needs and progress of those they guide. This approach not only aligns with the foundational principles of Christian education but also enhances the overall educational experience by adapting to and meeting the evolving needs of learners. The final strategy is therefore to *hone an attitude of attentiveness.*

---

[57] Astley and Crowder, "Theological Perspectives," xiv-xvi.

[58] Astley, "Definitions," 3; Groome, *Christian Religious Education*; Dykstra, *Life of Faith*.

[59] Astley and Crowder, "Theological Perspectives," xv; Carol Lakey Hess, "Educating in the Spirit," in *Theological Perspectives on Christian Formation: A Reader on Theology and Christian Education*, ed. Jeff Astley, Leslie J. Francis, and Colin Crowder (Grand Rapids: Eerdmans Publishing Company, 1996), 119–31.

7.2 Discussion

Having outlined strategies I consider beneficial for improving online small groups as instances of Christian religious education, I will now delve into a discussion about these strategies. Initially, I examine what these strategies suggest regarding the similarities and differences between online and onsite small groups. Following this, I compare and contrast these strategies with those proposed by scholars Robert Wuthnow and Theresa Latini, exploring how our approaches align or diverge. Lastly, I explore the practical implementation of these strategies, acknowledging potential challenges and limitations to their broad application.

7.2.1 Online and Onsite Small Groups

At the onset of the *Church in Digital Space* project, we operated under the presumption that the experience of church online would significantly diverge from that of traditional, onsite church gatherings. Interestingly, the strategies I developed for enhancing online small groups do not specifically cater to the online format but appear applicable to both online and onsite settings. This observation might come as a surprise, especially considering our initial assumptions. However, the same reflection is found in the wider online learning literature.

For example, the strategies proposed by Jane E. Brindley, Kerstin M. Blaschke, and Christine Walti for enhancing small conversation-based collaborative learning groups in online education highlight the importance of (1) transparency in expectations, (2) clarity in instructions, (3) task suitability for group work, (4) the relevance and meaning-making of activities, (5) embedding motivational elements within the course design, (6) ensuring learners are prepared for group work, (7) optimal timing for forming groups, (8) upholding learner autonomy, (9) implementing effective monitoring and feedback mechanisms, and (10) allocating ample time for tasks.[60] Similar to the strategies I have outlined, those proposed by Brindley, Blaschke, and Walti do not appear to be exclusively tailored to online settings, suggesting an applicability that transcends the modality of learning environments.

Also Rena M. Palloff and Keith Pratt offer insights into fostering online collaboration, detailing a model for effective online groups.[61] Their model emphasizes essential components such as problem-solving, conflict management, establishing norms, collaborative information processing, and enhancing communication and connections among members. Palloff and Pratt associate these elements with the

---

[60] Brindley, Blaschke, and Walti, "Collaborative Learning Groups."
[61] Palloff and Pratt, *Collaborating Online*.

formation of an online learning community characterized by robust interaction and communication, situated within a social constructivist framework that values presence, reflective and transformative learning experiences, and the strategic utilization of technology.[62]

Comparing the framework provided by Palloff and Pratt with Jane Regan's conceptualization of onsite learning communities and communities of practice in Christian religious education offers valuable insights. Regan, influenced by Peter M. Senge's theories, perceives the parish as a learning community structured around five key disciplines: personal mastery, mental models, shared vision, team learning, and systems thinking.[63] Additionally, in her exploration of communities of practice, Regan highlights three core elements: shared enterprise, mutual engagement, and a common repertoire.[64]

A comparison of the frameworks from Palloff and Pratt and Jane Regan reveals both differences and similarities. However, the focus here is not on their distinctions but rather on the notable absence of any markers that exclusively tie their strategies to either online or onsite settings. Palloff and Pratt's recommendations for effective online groups are just as pertinent to onsite environments, as Regan's insights into onsite learning communities hold value for online contexts. This becomes even clearer with the understanding that "technology" extends beyond digital tools to encompass analog resources like pens, chairs, whiteboards, and books.[65]

This observation suggests a fundamental similarity between online and onsite learning and teaching at the strategic level. This similarity can largely be attributed to the universal human learning processes that underpin both modalities, prompting educators, whether online or onsite, to utilize similar theoretical frameworks. Consequently, the learning and teaching theories employed here are not exclusive to online environments; similarly, the concepts of learning communities and communities of practice are applicable across both settings. This cross-modal applicability of educational strategies underscores the shared foundation of human

---

[62] Palloff and Pratt, *Collaborating Online*, 16.

[63] Regan, *Toward an Adult Church*, 121–30.

[64] Regan, *Two or Three*, 31–39. These are the elements of communities of practice as described by Etienne Wenger, even if Regan does not make the connection explicitly. See Etienne Wenger, *Communities of Practice: Learning, Meaning, and Identity* (Cambridge: Cambridge University Press, 1998).

[65] Ong, *Orality and Literacy*.

learning processes, irrespective of the learning environment's physical or virtual nature.[66]

While it is true that the foundational learning and teaching mechanisms are consistent across online and onsite environments, it does not mean that the strategies developed are not attuned to the nuances of online learning. Indeed, strategies 4–7 are particularly relevant for the online context.

Online small groups exhibit unique characteristics: participants have a limited view of the overall dynamics, interactions are condensed into scheduled meetings, and there is often restricted opportunity for pre- and post-session preparation and reflection. These differences introduce specific challenges and opportunities, necessitating strategies that directly address the constraints and affordances unique to online environments. Consequently, while the core challenges of facilitating effective learning experiences might overlap between online and onsite groups, the extent and nature of these challenges can vary, underscoring the need for adaptable and responsive teaching strategies.

This leads to the conclusion that online small groups within the Church of Sweden should not be seen as a significant departure from earlier forms of education but rather as an extension of traditional, onsite groups, now accessible through digital means. Despite the unique challenges and opportunities presented by digital mediation—requiring leaders to adapt their approaches—the essence of what constitutes small group activities remains consistent. Thus, the transition to online formats does not represent a fundamental shift in the nature of these groups but emphasizes the need for adaptability in leveraging the specific affordances and addressing the constraints of digital environments.

7.2.2 Group and Parish-Level Strategies

The strategies I set out above are designed to improve the dynamics within the group itself, rather than focusing on broader congregational or parish contexts. This approach distinguishes my strategies from those proposed by other small group researchers, such as Robert Wuthnow and Theresa Latini. Their work often extends recommendations to the organizational level, addressing how small groups integrate and function within the larger framework of congregations or parishes.

---

[66] This can be seen since the concepts are used with ease in discussions of both online and onsite education. See Regan, *Toward an Adult Church*, 121–30; Chapman, Ramondt, and Smiley, "Strong Community"; Palloff and Pratt, *Collaborating Online*, 16; Regan, *Two or Three*, 31–39.

In contrast, my focus is on the group-level interactions and practices that directly influence the effectiveness of small group engagement and learning.

Although Robert Wuthnow does not explicitly label them as strategies, his final chapter offers several recommendations that align closely with the strategies I have proposed.[67] Wuthnow's insights include a focus on fostering a cohesive group identity over mere individual participation, the importance of establishing clear goals for the group, the value of undertaking communal projects that extend beyond the group's immediate interests, and the necessity of maintaining connections with members who may not be currently active.[68] He advocates for small groups to serve as bridges connecting members with the broader societal context, suggests that organizational structures within groups should remain unobtrusive, and emphasizes the critical role of understanding and adhering to communication norms.[69]

Indeed, there is a notable convergence between the strategies I have developed and the recommendations made by Wuthnow. For instance, my *Strategy 5: Build Strong Groups* mirrors Wuthnow's advice for groups to operate collectively rather than as mere assemblies of individuals. Similarly, my emphasis on defining clear learning objectives in *Strategy 1* resonates with Wuthnow's emphasis on goal-setting for the group. Furthermore, *Strategy 3: Approach Instruction with Deliberation and Caution* and *Strategy 4: Create Favorable Conditions for Dialogue* align with Wuthnow's guidance for leaders to be cognizant of and responsive to the communication norms within groups.

While there are similarities between my strategies and Wuthnow's recommendations, significant differences also exist. These differences stem, in part, from Wuthnow's particular emphasis on maintaining connections with absent members and minimizing the visibility of structural elements within groups. This approach is indicative of his broader perspective on small groups as related to community building and mutual support. Here I see a clear difference between the way Wuthnow understood small groups in the United States in the 1990s and how our groups worked, as explained in chapters 4 and 5.

---

[67] Wuthnow, *Sharing the Journey*, 361–65. Wuthnow includes observations and recommendations throughout the entire text so that this list is not complete and could be constructed differently. See for example Latini, *Crisis of Community*, 41–44. However, for the present purpose it is not important to establish a complete list of Wuthnow's recommendations as it is to identify some of the salient points for discussion.

[68] Wuthnow, *Sharing the Journey*, 362.

[69] Wuthnow, *Sharing the Journey*, 365.

Wuthnow's concern extends beyond the operational aspects of small groups and addresses their impact on spirituality. He observes a trend within church-based small groups to conceptualize spirituality in overwhelmingly positive terms, which, in his view, risks diluting the deeper, more challenging aspects of spiritual growth demanded by traditional Christian teachings. This redefinition could potentially isolate small group experiences from the broader doctrinal and communal practices of churches, parishes, and congregations. To counteract this tendency, Wuthnow advocates for the integration of small groups into the ministry programs of religious communities. He suggests that such an approach would ensure that small groups complement the wider spiritual and communal objectives, maintaining a connection to the foundational teachings and practices of the Christian faith. As he puts it:

> Small groups should not be the principal activity of the church nor the program that receives greatest emphasis in terms of pastoral time or lay involvement. They should be oriented toward fellowship and caring, but their members should be encouraged to participate in classes and to seek religious instruction in other settings, they should take part in worship services and the sacraments, and they should be encouraged to be of service through their work, in their neighborhoods, and through volunteer activities.[70]

Wuthnow's analysis extends to the social dynamics within small groups, expressing concern over an inward-looking mentality that prioritizes personal benefit and voluntary engagement, often characterized by a "what's in it for me?" attitude. He advocates for small groups to undertake outward-facing activities, such as societal engagement and service projects, and to foster a more robust sense of community—one that is resilient, capable of enduring challenges, and conducive to deep, meaningful interactions. This approach, he argues, would promote a culture of mutual accountability and challenge, essential for the kind of substantive spiritual growth often envisioned by group leaders.[71]

In contrast to Wuthnow's perspective, my reflection on online small groups within the Church of Sweden is rooted in a different ecclesial tradition and a distinct conceptualization of community.[72] This difference is largely informed by the folk church theology, which underpins the approach of these groups. According to this view, participants are considered integral parts of the wider community of the Church by default, situating the online small groups as temporary spaces within the broader tapestry of their daily lives. Rather than aiming to forge long-

---

[70] Wuthnow, *Sharing the Journey*, 364.

[71] Wuthnow, *Sharing the Journey*, 361–66.

[72] See chapter 5.

term communities characterized by deep mutual support and trust, these groups prioritize the individual development of participants.

Theresa Latini takes a congregational approach to her small group strategies, grounded in a thorough analysis of six well-developed small groups. She articulates a theology of small groups centered around the concept of multidimensional *koinonia*, which she translates into four strategies:

1. Integration into the Congregation's Ministry: Small groups should be intentionally woven into the fabric of the congregation's overall ministry design, ensuring they complement and enhance the broader spiritual and community objectives.

2. Clear Mission and Covenant Statements: Each small group should articulate its purpose and operational ethos through mission and covenant statements. These documents should clarify the group's role within the larger congregational context and outline the expectations and commitments of its members.

3. Leadership Training: The effectiveness of small groups is significantly influenced by the quality of their leadership. Hence, providing leaders with appropriate training is crucial for equipping them with the skills necessary to facilitate group dynamics, spiritual growth, and community engagement effectively.

4. Ongoing Evaluation: To ensure that small groups continue to meet their objectives and remain aligned with the congregation's goals, regular assessments are essential. This process allows for continuous improvement and adaptation to the evolving needs of the group and the larger community.[73]

Latini's strategies underscore the importance of integrating small groups into the life of the congregation, emphasizing clear purpose, skilled leadership, and the necessity of regular evaluation to foster a vibrant community life.

Latini's emphasis on establishing clear mission and covenant statements for small groups resonates with my advocacy for setting #ClearRules, illustrating a shared recognition of the need for well-defined frameworks to guide group interactions. Moreover, Latini's concern with trained leadership aligns with the need for effective facilitation but places specific emphasis on competencies that ensure the group's alignment with congregational goals, a theme I revisit in section 8.4.

---

[73] Latini, *Crisis of Community*, 151-79.

However, our approaches diverge in focus and application. My *Strategy 6: Give Learners Control* emphasizes empowering learners by providing them with a clear understanding of expectations and boundaries, thereby facilitating a sense of autonomy and control. In contrast, Latini's approach is more oriented towards defining the small group's identity and operational dynamics in relation to the broader church community, emphasizing communication patterns and the group's integration into the congregational structure. This difference highlights a distinct emphasis: while my strategies are more focused on the internal dynamics and empowerment within the group, Latini's strategies are geared towards strengthening the connective tissue between the group and its wider church context.

The deliberation on whether Christian religious education should be implemented at the congregational or parish level or focused on specific learning situations, like online small groups, reveals the complexity of educational strategy within church contexts. This is not about establishing a hierarchy of approaches but recognizing the diverse ecosystems in which learning occurs. The various levels do not operate in isolation but are deeply interconnected. The larger church body often plays a critical role in supporting small groups through leadership, resources, and space, thereby influencing the effectiveness and character of these smaller units.[74]

In this light, the strategies Latini and I propose can be seen as complementary, addressing different facets of the same multifaceted educational endeavor within the church. By acknowledging the unique contributions and perspectives each approach offers, a more holistic and nuanced understanding of Christian education within contemporary church life emerges, one that appreciates the value of both broad oversight and focused, situational engagement.

7.2.3 Implementing Strategies

Strategies serve as generalized plans of action, offering a guiding framework for approaching various situations. However, the true utility and vitality of these strategies become apparent only in their application. Michel de Certeau's distinction between strategies and tactics provides a valuable lens through which to understand this dynamic.[75]

---

[74] See section 4.2.5.

[75] For an in-depth discussion of de Certeau and an example of how his reasoning can be used in practical theology see Joel Appelfeldt, *Dopet som hantverk: Gudstjänstkreativitet och liturgisk taktik i Svenska kyrkan och Equmeniakyrkan* (Skellefteå: Artos Academic, 2023).

Strategies, in de Certeau's framework, are the overarching principles or systems that individuals or institutions use to establish a sense of place or domain. This "place" then becomes a base from which relationships with others are structured and organized. This "organization" encompasses a broad array of mechanisms—ranging from tangible actions to the application of knowledge—that work together to create a sense of structure and control. In this light, strategies are not just plans or guidelines but foundational elements that define how individuals or groups assert their presence and interact within their environments. They serve as the backdrop against which the more dynamic and opportunistic tactics play out, allowing for the adaptation and negotiation of space within the structured order that strategies provide.[76]

The strategies outlined for improving online small groups in Christian religious education can be understood to serve as mechanisms to establish a "place" within which leaders can operate. This "place" is not geographical but conceptual, a structured space where learning and interaction are intentionally shaped according to the strategies' guiding principles. Strategies such as formulating specific learning intentions and aligning teaching activities, creating good conditions for dialogue, building strong groups, giving learners control, and including relevant stops of the learning journey (strategies 1–2, 4–7) all target the way in which leaders design and plan their groups. Meanwhile, strategies that focus on approaching instruction with deliberation and caution, and fostering an attitude of attentiveness (strategies 3 and 8) contribute to providing general insights on teaching actions that predispose leaders to perform or refrain from specific actions.

In this sense, these strategies do more than merely guide the direction of teaching and interaction; they actively construct the "place" in which leaders of online small groups can "stand" and from which they can engage with participants. Before a participant even joins a session, these strategies have already laid the groundwork for how learning will unfold, dictating the dynamics of interaction and the relational structure between leaders and participants.

Tactics, as Michel de Certeau outlines, are the day-to-day actions and decisions made within the structural framework established by strategies. Unlike strategies that set up a "place" for operations and interactions, tactics operate within this given space, adapting and responding to the immediate context and conditions.[77] In the context of online small groups, tactics are the real-time, adaptive measures

---

[76] Michel de Certeau, *The Practice of Everyday Life*, trans. Steven Rendall (Berkeley: University of California Press, 1984), 31–36.

[77] Certeau, *Everyday Life*, 31–36.

that leaders take to navigate the dynamics of the group, ensuring engagement and addressing the needs and behaviors of participants as they arise.[78]

For example, a tactic such as asking a probing question to stimulate discussion, encouraging a quieter member to share their thoughts, or sensitively responding to someone's vulnerability, are all immediate responses to the unfolding situation. These actions are tactical because they rely on the leader's ability to read the room—virtually, in this case—and make on-the-spot decisions that are informed by and responsive to, but not dictated by, the overarching strategies. They reflect the leader's capacity to dynamically engage with the "place" of learning they established, modifying their approach based on participant interaction, feedback, and the flow of conversation.

This distinction between strategies and tactics highlights the interplay between preparation and presence, between the planning that structures the potential for learning and the spontaneous, situational engagements that bring the learning environment to life. It underscores the necessity of flexibility and adaptiveness in educational leadership, particularly in the fluid and variable context of online groups. De Certeau's framework thus suggests that teaching in online small groups requires a dual focus: a clear understanding of the creation of the specific potential learning situation as a "place" where participants meet (strategy) and a flexible, responsive approach to the unique challenges and opportunities arising in each situation (tactics).

Implementing strategies may then in itself require the application of tactics—those on-the-spot decisions and actions that respond to immediate situations and opportunities for learning. For instance, *Strategy 3: Instruct with Deliberation and Caution* establishes an overarching approach to education, but the tactics involved in delivering #Instruction—such as timing and making connections to the ongoing conversation—are important when actualizing this strategy in practice. Strategies are hence not meant to dictate the specific tactical interactions leaders have with participants. Rather, they set the stage for a variety of potential engagements, acknowledging the need for leaders to adapt to the fluid dynamics of group interaction and individual learning needs. Strategies thus function as guiding principles, focusing on broader educational goals and the overall structure of the learning experience.

---

[78] De Certeau generally attributed strategies and tactics to different actors—like city planners (strategy) and pedestrians (tactics). Applying both strategies and tactics to group leaders is in this sense a departure from de Certeau's original emphasis, even if it is in keeping with his general understanding of strategies and tactics. Certeau, *Everyday Life*.

Moreover, in creating a specific "place," the proposed strategies inherently carry a specific educational and pedagogical perspective, shaping the design and facilitation of these groups.[79] Strategies are hence not neutral or objective; they reflect particular values, assumptions, and intentions regarding what online small groups should achieve and how they should operate. As such, when leaders adopt these strategies, they also, perhaps implicitly, adopt the embedded perspective on the nature and objectives of online small group education. This realization necessitates that leaders of online small groups approach these strategies with a critical awareness of the underlying principles they promote. Leaders must consider how these strategies align with their own educational philosophies and the specific needs of their participants.

7.2.4 The Limited Applicability of Strategies

The strategies designed for leading online small groups, while potentially valuable, inherently reflect the specific contexts from which they were derived, particularly the cultural, social, and economic homogeneity of the participant groups involved. This specificity underscores a critical consideration: strategies are not universally applicable but are shaped by the unique characteristics and dynamics of the groups they are intended to serve, as well as my specific position, as explained in chapter 6.

Concretely, the development of these strategies did not take into account the diverse challenges that might arise in groups with varied cultural, social, or economic backgrounds, as the original groups did not present such diversity.[80] This limitation highlights the necessity for leaders to critically evaluate the relevance and applicability of these strategies to their specific group contexts.

The applicability of strategies might also be limited due to the relatively small empirical material on which they are based. In empirical research, the concept of theoretical saturation helps scholars to establish when an empirical material is sufficiently large to draw valid inferences. Simply put, theoretical saturation occurs at the point at which further data collection does not reveal anything new about the phenomenon in question.[81] Theoretical saturation does not indicate that a phenomenon is completely mapped as new aspects could *theoretically* surface if data

---

[79] See sections 2.2, 4.2.1, and 5.3.

[80] See section 4.2.6.

[81] Steven Engler, "Grounded Theory," in *The Routledge Handbook of Research Methods in the Study of Religion*, ed. Michael Stausberg and Steven Engler (2011), 256–74 at 261–61;

collection would be continued, but it does provide a criterion by which to judge when data collection can be concluded.[82]

In the *Online Small Groups* project, we did not achieve theoretical saturation. This means that engaging with new and different online small groups would likely yield further insights into learning and teaching. Consequently, the strategies presented have limited applicability, as they do not encompass a comprehensive mapping of online small groups.

However, I believe that this limited applicability does not need to be a problem. Given the exploratory research design focused on an area of non-formal Christian religious education with scant prior research, this dissertation does not aim to present a complete depiction of online small groups. Instead, the strategies are intended to aid group leaders in designing and facilitating online small groups, rather than to provide an exhaustive empirical account of teaching in these settings.

Furthermore, these strategies should not be seen as the definitive perspective on online teaching in non-formal Christian religious education, but rather as a contribution to an ongoing conversation. I thus hope that these strategies will inspire Christian educators and scholars to further explore and enhance teaching within non-formal Christian religious education, a process that will surely lead to the revision of the strategies. Still, I believe it is valuable to offer these strategies to connect research in Christian religious education closely with its practice.

7.3 Summary and Reflections

The purpose of this chapter was to articulate usable knowledge in such a manner that it extends from the *Online Small Groups* project to a broader context. More precisely, this chapter offers the most direct response to the first part of my overarching research question: *How can online small groups within the Church of Sweden be improved as instances of Christian religious education?*

In addressing this question, I have developed eight strategies for online small groups, which I hope will be usable when working with online small groups as sites of teaching. I have also noted that these strategies are not exclusively tailored to online environments—they could also potentially benefit onsite groups.

In my discussion of these strategies, I have highlighted that strategies are not simply rules to be applied, but that these strategies should be understood as ways

---

[82] Davidsson Bremborg, "Interviewing," 311–14; Alvesson and Sköldberg, *Reflexive Methodology*, 83.

in which leaders create online small groups as a specific place. Drawing on de Certeau, I have also argued that these strategies need to be combined with tactics to address the fluid dynamics within online groups. Finally, I acknowledged the limited applicability of strategies, positing that leading online groups often necessitates adapting, enhancing, or sometimes abandoning these strategies.

Before moving on to the conclusion, I want to reflect shortly on the relationship between theory and our experiences in the formulation of these strategies. It strikes me that the strategies above could have been formulated in much the same way in a purely theoretical discussion. Similarly, some of the strategies do not appear to require theoretical perspectives at all. Thus, it would be possible to establish strategies 3–8 also solely based on our experiences.

I find it therefore important to notice how I use theory here. Theory functions as a bridge, linking our specific experiences to a wider conceptual landscape. Recognizing alignments between our empirical findings and established theoretical frameworks reinforces the notion that our insights are not merely anecdotal or unique to our context. Instead, they resonate with broader, more universal patterns of learning and teaching. This connection is crucial for positing these strategies as usable knowledge, extending their relevance beyond the four online small groups we directly engaged with to potentially benefit a broader context of similar groups.

Likewise, by connecting theoretical perspectives to our experiences, I hope to demonstrate their relevance and utility within our online small group contexts. Although numerous theories exist, the selection made reflects a deliberate choice to focus on those that significantly inform our understanding and practice of teaching in online settings as conceptualized in this study. This approach not only highlights the applicability of these theories to our specific context but also implicitly argues for their importance in shaping effective teaching strategies. It serves as an endorsement of these selected theoretical frameworks as valuable lenses through which to view, analyze, and improve the pedagogical dynamics of online small group learning.

By synthesizing our experiences with selected theoretical perspectives, the development of the strategies presented transcends mere practical considerations, aiming to embed these strategies within a wider scholarly and practical discourse on Christian religious education in online contexts. This integration serves a dual purpose: first, to demonstrate the relevance of these strategies beyond the specific context of the *Online Small Groups* project, suggesting their potential applicability to similar educational endeavors; and second, to propose theoretical perspectives pertinent when discussing online small groups as instances of Christian religious education.

8. Conclusion: Teaching in the Church of Sweden

The Church of Sweden is confronting profound changes in the socio-cultural and religious landscape: an increase in secularity, a decline in religiosity and Church membership, a reduction in religious literacy, and, perhaps most troubling for the Church, a lack of understanding of its message even among those who participate in the liturgy.[1] While this situation has sparked both scholarly and popular debate, with some questioning the severity of these developments, the concerns remain significant.[2]

These developments have significantly influenced academic and ecclesial examinations of learning and teaching within the Church of Sweden. In this conclusion, I aim to broaden the scope of my discussion, exploring how the *Online Small Groups* project contributes to the ongoing academic dialogue on these subjects.[3] Moving beyond the discussion of online small groups, I turn my attention to more general considerations of teaching practices in the Church of Sweden. In this concluding chapter, I thus address the second part of my research question: *Do these improvement possibilities suggest any implications for Christian religious education within the Church of Sweden more generally?*

I start by discussing the consequences of my understanding of teaching for an assessment of the prevalence and complexity of teaching, as well as considering who is considered the subject of teaching (8.1). I consider the importance of good teaching and relate my teaching perspective to Jonas Ideström's concept of theologizing (8.2), before reflecting on the suitability of online small groups as a

---

[1] Svenska kyrkan, "Svenska kyrkans medlemsutveckling år 1972–2022 (Uppsala); Gustavsson [Klintborg], *Delaktighetens kris*; Straarup and Ekberg, *Försumliga kyrkan*; Eriksson, *Predika*.

[2] See for example Bäckström, Edgardh, and Pettersson, *Religiös förändring i norra Europa: En studie av Sverige*; Thurfjell, *Det gudlösa folket*; Joel Halldorf, *Gud: Återkomsten* (Bromma: Libris, 2018); Thurfjell, *Granskogsfolk: Hur naturen blev svenskarnas religion*.

[3] See section 1.5.1.

teaching method (8.3) and the teaching competences required (8.4). I conclude by noting the role of research in advancing the Church's educational ministry (8.5)

8.1 A Conceptualization of Teaching

Perhaps the main theoretical contribution of this dissertation is the conceptualization of teaching developed in chapter 2. Recognizing that Christian religious education is teleological, I proposed that teaching in the Church is fundamentally aligned with a metapurpose, which I here described with Thomas Groome as the kingdom of God. In terms of the relationship between teaching and learning, I argued that teaching entails the deliberate creation of specific potential learning situations. These are contexts in which teachers, learners, content, and activities are brought together in a manner that facilitates and increases the likelihood of learners achieving the intended outcomes, given the specific conditions of the situation.[4]

In chapter 6, I argued that this conceptualization of teaching is beneficial as it encapsulates the actions of leaders in our online small groups and paves the way for improving these groups as instances of Christian religious education. I also compared my conceptualization of teaching with the approaches taken by other scholars in Christian religious education.

Current discussions on Christian religious education in the Church of Sweden show a notable absence of detailed teaching conceptualizations. Jakob Wirén's *Utmaningsdriven undervisning* (Needs-driven teaching) exemplifies this gap. Wirén anchors his analysis in two primary concepts: teaching and mission, emphasizing their significance in the Church of Sweden's identity as outlined in its Church Ordinance. However, unlike mission, teaching is scarcely elaborated upon conceptually. Instead, Wirén shifts focus to explore education and didactics as research fields, noting how education, is an overarching field focused on learning, and didactics a subfield within education, emphasizing intentional learning in concrete situations.[5] This shift does not imply that *Utmaningsdriven undervisning* neglects teaching; rather, Wirén's theoretical exploration of teaching is limited.

This pattern is also evident in Henry Cöster's *...bedriva undervisning...* (...to teach...). Although Cöster consistently refers to teaching and links it to hermeneutical and didactic competence in the final chapter, the definition of teaching

---

[4] See section 2.3.1.
[5] Wirén, *Undervisning*, 25–30.

remains ambiguous.[6] This trend is not confined to Swedish discourse but is present in the international literature on Christian religious education as well.[7] Therefore, my exploration into conceptualizing teaching addresses a significant gap in the field, particularly when considering the impact that a well-defined concept of teaching can have.

One consequence of this ambiguity is the difficulty in determining where and when teaching occurs. Caroline Klintborg's research highlights the confusion surrounding the concept of teaching among religious educators in the Church of Sweden.[8] This vagueness presents two potential pitfalls. On the one hand, there is a tendency to apply the concept of teaching only to scenarios traditionally recognized as educational, such as confirmation training, possibly due to their similarity to formal educational settings. This narrow application risks overlooking the broader scope of teaching opportunities.

On the other hand, there is a risk to assume that teaching occurs in all church activities. Theologically, it is argued that the church inherently educates through everything it does. Henry Cöster supports this view by stating, "teaching constitutes the unifying designation of the phenomena that are formulated or emphasized in the present situation as *notæ ecclesiæ*, [...] the characteristics of the Church, her universality, the proclamation of the Gospel, the administration of the sacraments, and diakonia."[9] This broad interpretation risks diluting the specificity and intentionality of teaching.

Linking teaching to all church activities complicates identifying those moments that require specific focus from a Christian religious education standpoint. Caroline Klintborg finds that in Västerås Parish, religious educators see teaching mainly as an aspect of other parish activities and that if there is a particular focus on teaching this is usually in connection with children and confirmands.[10] Klintborg underscores the necessity of differentiating between teaching and non-teaching situations and determining which activities are educationally driven. This distinction becomes critical when activities perceived by educators as contributing to a growth in faith lack a defined teaching approach.[11]

---

[6] Cöster, *bedriva undervisning*.
[7] See section 2.3.
[8] Gustavsson [Klintborg], *En process på riktigt*, 37.
[9] Cöster, *bedriva undervisning*, 11.
[10] Gustavsson [Klintborg], *En process på riktigt*, 42–43.
[11] Gustavsson [Klintborg], *En process på riktigt*, 40–41.

Klintborg identifies a third risk: the reduction of teaching to a question of methods. She observes that for many Christian religious educators, teaching primarily addresses the didactic question of *how*, leading to an expectation for educators to be "a living method box that is expected to deliver interesting, exciting and preferably fun methods."[12]

This approach, however, risks an excessive emphasis on methods at the expense of broader educational contemplation, particularly concerning content.[13] Consequently, Klintborg concludes "there is a risk, I believe, that one is expected to contribute to and create a positive feeling without any actual content. [...] In other words, the question of the meaning of teaching presupposes a pedagogically conscious analysis of the other didactic questions as well."[14]

I hope that my conceptualization of teaching circumvents these three risks. I contend that my definition is inclusive enough to encompass situations not traditionally recognized as sites of teaching, like online small groups, while being precise enough to ensure that not all church activities are classified as teaching. By firmly linking teaching to specific intentions, it is clear that teaching extends beyond mere matters of method. Therefore, I maintain that my approach not only addresses a gap in the current discourse on learning and teaching but also offers a way to mitigate the issues arising from overly restrictive or expansive definitions of teaching.

To delve deeper into these matters, I examine three facets of teaching in the Church of Sweden. Initially, I assess how my conceptualization of teaching influences perceptions of its prevalence. Subsequently, I address the complexity of teaching, arguing for a broader understanding than is currently recognized. Following this, I explore who or what constitutes the subject of teaching.

8.1.1 Prevalence

In the context of an impending risk of marginalization, Straarup and Ekberg argue that the Church of Sweden requires an increase in teaching activities or would have needed more teaching activities in any case, suggesting a current shortfall.[15] Their stance relies on an underlying assumption about what constitutes teaching, thereby implying its scarcity.

I have maintained that effective teaching does not hinge on the educator's awareness of their teaching activities. It relies instead on the existence of intentions

---

[12] Gustavsson [Klintborg], *En process på riktigt*, 38–39.
[13] Gustavsson [Klintborg], *En process på riktigt*, 38–39.
[14] Gustavsson [Klintborg], *En process på riktigt*, 39.
[15] Straarup and Ekberg, *Försumliga kyrkan*, 9–11.

and actions explicitly aimed at fulfilling those intentions. This distinction suggests that while being cognizant that one is engaging in teaching can enhance the quality of education, the essence of teaching fundamentally rests on intentionality and purposeful action.[16]

A significant consequence of this perspective is that teaching occurs more widely within the Church of Sweden than commonly recognized. Teaching is not limited to explicitly designated educational settings but is integral to various interactions and gatherings orchestrated by the Church, including online small groups. Consequently, the Church of Sweden encompasses numerous potential venues for teaching, each offering opportunities to facilitate learning.

Acknowledging the widespread occurrence of teaching is crucial in addressing Straarup and Ekberg's assertion that the Church of Sweden has not adequately developed its educational ministry. Their emphasis on explicit teaching contexts obscures the extensive teaching already taking place within the Church. Consequently, it remains uncertain whether the issue lies in the prevalence of teaching. I propose that the focus should instead shift towards enhancing the quality of teaching.

Another consequence of this broader understanding of teaching is the need to redirect scholarly focus toward areas beyond liturgy and confirmation training, which have predominantly captured academic interest in recent years. It advocates for an examination of diverse contexts of learning and teaching within church life, exploring how these various settings contribute uniquely to education aimed at the kingdom of God. This approach underscores the need to appreciate and investigate the full spectrum of teaching environments within the Church of Sweden.

8.1.2 Complexity

I observed how Henry Cöster and Christina Osbeck associate teaching with two tasks, characterized either as proclamation and general education (Cöster) or as a "language of life" and a "language of religion" (Osbeck). These frameworks differentiate between teaching's influence on our lives and the necessity of acquiring knowledge and understanding.[17] I agree with the perspectives of both Cöster and Osbeck, particularly when their delineation of teaching tasks is aligned with Anna

---

[16] See sections 2.2–2.3 and 6.2.

[17] See section 1.5.1. Cöster does not develop the distinction in detail but is clear that teaching encompasses these two dimensions.

Sfard's two metaphors of learning—suggesting that effective teaching encompasses learning as both acquisition and participation.[18]

Yet, there is a risk that the distinctions between life and religion, as well as between proclamation and education, might be overly simplistic to fully encompass the intricacies of Christian religious education aimed at the kingdom of God, as I have outlined.[19] This concern is particularly pertinent considering Osbeck's framing of her argument around learning *about* and learning *from* religion. I associate these approaches with a non-confessional variant of religious education, which notably omits the aspect of learning religion itself, leaving a critical dimension of religious education unaddressed.[20]

In my analysis of various approaches to Christian religious education, I delineated six models, each characterized by a unique blend of dimension, purpose, content, and method, all aimed at the overarching goal of fostering Christian faith, which, in itself, serves the metapurpose of educating for the Kingdom. While Cöster and Osbeck emphasize teaching as a discursive practice and link learning with participation, their frameworks remain strangely singular, concentrating on what I would classify as the critical and spiritual models (Cöster) and the critical and praxis models (Osbeck).

Certainly, I have argued that not every educational endeavor must cover all faith dimensions. From a teaching standpoint, it is instead crucial that the dimensions, content, and method are harmoniously aligned. Yet, in terms of conceptualizing teaching, it proves beneficial to present a framework that more accurately mirrors the complexity of education directed toward the Kingdom. This becomes particularly relevant acknowledging Osbeck's insight that the discourse around learning and teaching within the Church of Sweden influences both the narrative of teaching and the learning process itself.[21]

8.1.3 Subject

This consideration connects to another facet in the conceptualization of teaching, which Osbeck accentuates—the role and function of institutions in education. Osbeck posits that the Church, as an institution, has the responsibility to preserve and pass on specific discourses, including the distinct roles these discourses

---

[18] Sfard, "Two Metaphors."
[19] See section 2.2.
[20] Osbeck, *Förstå livet*, 57. See section 1.4.
[21] Osbeck, *Förstå livet*, 25–31.

afford.[22] I share Osbeck's view in recognizing the significant influence institutions have on particular teaching and learning situations, as well as the importance of being mindful of the subject positions a discourse creates. This aspect is briefly addressed in my discussion on frame factors and more explicitly in *Strategy 3: Approach Instruction with Deliberation and Caution*. Furthermore, I believe it is crucial to examine the dynamics of power within the context of teaching.[23]

Although I thus generally view Osbeck's portrayal of institutional influence on teaching favorably, I perceive challenges in overly associating teaching with the institutional level. This concern becomes apparent, for instance, in Jakob Wirén's examination of how different churches respond to secular and post-Christian contexts.[24]

The central concern here is identifying the subject of teaching. Wirén often appears to view the Church as an institution, as the primary educator, particularly when discussing the development of a national church curriculum, the role of lay volunteers, or the suitability of folk church theology.[25] While Wirén acknowledges that teaching and mission are executed by specific individuals, preventing the institution from dominating, the clarity on who exactly assumes a teaching role and how responsibilities should be distributed across different church levels often remains ambiguous.[26]

Jonas Eek's strategies for enhancing confirmation training similarly exhibit ambiguity regarding the locus of teaching responsibility. Eek advocates for the prioritization, focus, and optimization of confirmation, yet it remains unclear who is responsible for implementing these strategies.[27] Some of Eek's approaches, such as integrating music into confirmation training, are directed at pastors, deacons, and religious educators involved with confirmands. Conversely, other strategies, like extending confirmation training over several years (*flerårskonfirmation*), seem to address policy-making at the parish or diocesan level. Despite Eek underscoring the value of local-level expertise, the distinction between targeting specific activities versus overarching structures is not consistently apparent.[28]

---

[22] Osbeck, *Förstå livet*, 26.

[23] See section 6.3.3.

[24] Wirén, *Undervisning*.

[25] Wirén, *Undervisning*, 203–61.

[26] See for example Wirén, *Undervisning*, 209. The Church of Sweden has three levels: the parish, the diocese, and the national church.

[27] Eek, *Stanna i vattnet*, 157–69.

[28] Eek, *Stanna i vattnet*, 157–69.

Activities, structures, institutions, and actors intertwine in complex ways, yet my conceptualization of teaching contributes valuably to the discourse on Christian religious education in Sweden. By grounding my understanding of teaching in the experiences from our online small groups, I emphasize the roles of specific individuals, thereby spotlighting the importance of teaching within local and tangible contexts. This perspective serves as a crucial counterpart to views of teaching that predominantly consider the institutional backdrop.[29]

8.2 The Importance of Good Teaching

Accepting that teaching occurs more widely within the Church of Sweden than commonly acknowledged raises the question of whether mere prevalence is enough. From my perspective, viewing Christian religious education as a teleological activity, I contend that prevalence alone falls short of what is needed.

Throughout this dissertation, I have presented the argument that my approach to defining teaching not only reveals its presence across various church activities but also suggests that this perspective can enhance those activities, making them more effective as forms of Christian religious education.

This consideration is significant for both our online small groups and the broader conversation. The group leaders I collaborated with did not predominantly view themselves as teachers, making it inappropriate to assess them strictly in teaching terms. Hence, I wish to emphasize that I do not perceive a deficiency in teaching within our online small groups; my assessment of how these groups were led and structured is positive, even as I have noted certain improvement possibilities.

Caroline Klintborg makes comparable remarks regarding Västerås Parish, observing that educators there conduct various activities that do not primarily target traditional Christian religious education. These events are designed to facilitate encounters between people and the Church, with the underlying hope that such interactions will eventually encourage engagement with the Church's teachings.[30]

What is noteworthy for this discussion is that activities in Västerås Parish, which educators do not perceive as sites of teaching, could be perceived as such, akin to online small groups. Particularly, religious educators in Västerås approach these meetings with distinct objectives, viewing them not as ends in themselves but

---

[29] Cf. section 7.2.2.
[30] Gustavsson [Klintborg], *En process på riktigt*, 41–42.

as avenues to spark interest in the Christian faith. This perspective aligns closely with our groups and my understanding of teaching.

Recognizing online small groups and similar gatherings as platforms for teaching enables pastors, deacons, and religious educators to more effectively fulfill their educational goals for these settings. Achieving this, however, necessitates an initial awareness of teaching.

This consideration has been frequently highlighted by scholars in Christian religious education. From Christina Osbeck's assertion that the organization of teaching is a fundamental educational concern to Klintborg and Fransson's exploration of how suitable methods facilitate or limit learning, experts have emphasized the necessity of aligning teaching with intentions, content, and method.[31] This principle is also reflected in the didactic questions, the didactic relations model, and the concept of constructive alignment that I have incorporated into this dissertation.[32]

I also concur with Caroline Klintborg, who addresses the quality of education in the context of the Church of Sweden's confirmation training. Drawing on Gert Biesta's definition of good education, which encompasses qualification, socialization, and subjectification, Klintborg observes that the aspect of qualification is less emphasized compared to the others. This observation prompts a critical inquiry into whether confirmation training adequately equips young people with the necessary qualifications to lead lives as Christians.[33]

Indeed, while I align the notion of good Christian religious education with the kingdom of God rather than with Biesta's framework, both Klintborg's work and mine focus on the critical issue of educational quality. This dissertation thus contributes to the conversation initiated by Klintborg by proposing a different approach to evaluating educational quality. Rather than using Biesta's concept as a benchmark, this work assesses quality through the lens of the purpose and meta-purpose of Christian religious education, employing evaluative criteria rooted in the Christian tradition itself.[34]

8.2.1 Teaching or Theologizing?

Of course, it can be questioned whether good Christian religious education inherently demands high-quality teaching. Notably, there was a subtle shift in focus

---

[31] Osbeck, *Förstå livet*, 55; Klintborg and Fransson, "Metodernas."

[32] See section 2.5–2.6.

[33] Klintborg, *Var är Jesus?*, 106–11.

[34] See section 2.2.

earlier from teaching to the broader concept of education. To delve into the relationship between teaching and education, I explore Jonas Ideström's notion of theologizing.

Ideström characterizes theologizing as a collaborative process of theological reflection, generally in relation to elements from the Christian tradition broadly conceived. This process frequently unfolds in the day-to-day activities of parish life. Theologizing serves as both a means of traditioning and a method for reinterpreting and understanding the Christian tradition anew. In Ideström's words, theologizing acts as the active verb form of theology.[35]

Theologizing shares similarities with my depiction of online small groups as spaces for collective theological reflection and directed dialogue.[36] Moreover, Ideström situates his analysis within the secular and post-Christian context that many scholars in religious education examine.[37] While I emphasize *directed dialogue*, highlighting the significance of teaching, Ideström makes room for conversation. He observes that daily life is filled with intricate, often unexpected interactions among diverse participants and elements. This complexity suggests that fruitful and imaginative discussions are influenced by numerous factors and actors, beyond the control of any single individual or detailed plan. Thus, Ideström suggests:

> what happens in everyday life involves rich, complex and often surprising relationships and connections between a variety of actors and components. This means that there are many factors that interact when good and creative conversations occur, and that no single person or elaborate strategy can command or control them all. Constructive ways of theologizing are therefore not something that can be produced by specific methods or strategies. However, there is a lot that can be done to help create more favorable conditions for this to happen.[38]

Given my focus on strategies and the role of teachers, it is pertinent to explore whether Ideström's concept of theologizing presents an alternative approach to teaching.

Differentiating between intentional and non-intentional learning, as Osbeck does, provides a possible lens through which to examine the distinction between theologizing and teaching.[39] One can argue that I concentrate on deliberate

---

[35] Ideström, *Ikoniska kartor*, 11–12.
[36] See section 4.3.
[37] Ideström, *Ikoniska kartor*, 173–75.
[38] Ideström, *Ikoniska kartor*, 179.
[39] Osbeck, *Förstå livet*, 21–23.

teaching practices, whereas Ideström emphasizes learning that occurs spontaneously through conversation. Thus, teaching and theologizing could be viewed as separate alternatives to the facilitation of learning.

However, I question whether such a neat separation is merited. First, Ideström primarily examines structured group conversations that are similar to the online small groups I have discussed, which align more with intentional learning.[40] Second, his focus appears to be on illustrating the limitations of church leadership in controlling theologizing, rather than critiquing specific methods or strategies. Ideström understands God's self-revelation in Christ to be untamable by the church and its activities, while still acknowledging the church's vital role as a context for encountering this revelation.[41]

Furthermore, in exploring methods to foster and promote creative ways of theologizing, Ideström emphasizes the importance of creating "favorable environments for conversations."[42] This approach resonates with my conceptualization of teaching, which involves crafting distinct potential learning situations, mirroring Ideström's emphasis on conducive settings. Additionally, Ideström's focus on biblical narratives parallels how leaders in online small groups might utilize specific material to direct dialogue.[43] Therefore, I propose that teaching and theologizing are not mutually exclusive but rather intersect frequently within Christian religious education.

There are two significant implications: first, teaching serves as a powerful means to nurture and encourage creative theologizing within the local parish. Second, the act of teaching in no way hinders the process of theologizing; thus, there is no necessity to select one over the other. If theologizing contributes to good Christian religious education, then quality teaching is equally important, serving to bolster theologizing and various other aspects of Christian educational practices.

In conclusion, drawing from our *Online Small Groups* project and my framework for understanding teaching, I contend that the Church of Sweden needs more than to recognize the prevalence of teaching, it needs an awareness of teaching. There is a need for a deeper consciousness about the act of teaching and, more critically, for quality teaching that ultimately connects to the kingdom of God, reflecting the Church's mission and purpose. Consequently, a crucial task for the

---

[40] Ideström, *Ikoniska kartor*, 180.
[41] Ideström, *Ikoniska kartor*, 179.
[42] Ideström, *Ikoniska kartor*, 180.
[43] See section 6.2.1.

Church of Sweden is to raise awareness about the function and responsibility of teaching, particularly in contexts where teaching duties are not inherently recognized.

8.3 Suitability of Online Small Groups as Teaching Method

A critical element of good teaching is the selection of suitable methods. This becomes particularly relevant considering Sara Fransson and Caroline Klintborg's research, which demonstrates that the utilization of appropriate teaching methods significantly enhances learner satisfaction among Church of Sweden confirmands.[44]

A pertinent question arising from this study is identifying the specific contexts in which online small groups serve as an effective "method." Drawing from our experiences with our online small groups, I contend that small groups are particularly well-suited for deepening participants' faith. Essentially, this format is most beneficial for individuals already acquainted with Christian beliefs and traditions.

This observation partly stems from the fact that the majority of participants in our groups possessed pre-existing knowledge and frequently had a prolonged engagement with the Church of Sweden. This insight, hence, reflects the learner demographic we typically encountered. However, I believe that such familiarity also facilitates fuller participation in these groups. Instances of explicit #Instruction were uncommon, and while questions about Christian faith content were generally encouraged, the groups tended to focus more on collaborative involvement and collective theological contemplation.

I thus concur with Anne-Louise Eriksson's viewpoint that engaging meaningfully with the Christian tradition necessitates substantial knowledge, encompassing an understanding of the Bible, Christianity, and familiarity with Christian terminology.[45] When there is a significant disparity in participants' prior knowledge, achieving effective collective theological reflection can become challenging.

In chapter 4, I characterized online small groups as flexible and broadly applicable, suggesting they can be tailored to suit a wide range of learners. The #S:tEskils group serves as a prime example, demanding minimal prior knowledge of books, literature, or the Sami culture. A similar adaptability applies to *Lectio Divina* groups, which did not require prior knowledge either.

---

[44] Klintborg and Fransson, "Metodernas."
[45] Eriksson, *Predika.*

Nonetheless, in both the #Margareta and the #Djursholm groups, I believe participants benefited from previously being acquainted with the Bible and religious terminology. Consequently, it remains ambiguous whether these groups would have been as effective for individuals lacking foundational knowledge of the Christian faith and tradition.

Therefore, I argue that such small groups represent a vital pathway for faith development, continuous conversion, and the practice of Christian living. This holds particular relevance for the Church of Sweden, where small groups tend to prioritize theological reflection over the formation of tightly bonded support communities, serving as platforms for collective theological exploration through directed dialogue.[46]

Online small groups in the Church of Sweden may thus be founded on a folk church theology that acknowledges the Church's crucial role in delivering an address in everyday life. However, this approach might be most effectively directed toward individuals who already have some familiarity with the Church.[47] As a result, I believe that online small groups are not as suitable for missionary efforts aimed at people with limited or no prior understanding of the Christian faith.

This is not to say that online small groups cannot be modified for these contexts. It is feasible to incorporate more instructional content into these groups, akin to the Alpha course approach. Yet, such adjustments would likely shift the groups' dynamics from being centered on directed dialogue to a format closer to that of adult Sunday school.

I also align with Robert Wuthnow and Theresa Latini in their view that such groups should ideally be supplemented with various other educational forms.[48] This notion directly stems from the diverse models of Christian religious education.[49] Considering that faith encompasses the dimensions of believing, trusting, doing, and belonging, a comprehensive educational effort aiming to nurture faith must address each aspect. However, I am skeptical that online small groups can effectively cover all these dimensions. Specifically, I see online small groups as particularly suitable for engaging with beliefs and actions, and they also hold potential for shaping attitudes and developing skills, as demonstrated by the sermon preparation focus in the #Älvsjö group.

---

[46] See section 4.3.

[47] Cf. section 5.3.

[48] See section 7.2.2.

[49] See section 2.4.

Nonetheless, I maintain that there might be more suitable approaches for cultivating attitudes and skills, including various forms of worship and broader participation within the Church community. This consideration also highlights a potential shortcoming of small groups concerning the aspect of belonging, particularly under the premise that integration into the wider parish and Church community is desirable.

Determining the circumstances under which online small groups serve as an effective platform for Christian religious education, and identifying the target audience for these groups, are crucial considerations. Equally important is figuring out how to tailor these groups to meet the needs of specific participants, the nature of the content, and the unique conditions of each group. Addressing these concerns necessitates informed decisions regarding educational strategies and methods, thereby highlighting the need for a certain level of teaching expertise—an issue to which I turn next.

8.4 Building Teaching Competencies

Accepting a given situation as a teaching opportunity enables efforts to improve teaching effectiveness, aiming for activities to more often lead to the realization of intended learning outcomes. My involvement in the *Online Small Groups* project does not allow for a broad assessment of teaching competence within the Church of Sweden. However, Caroline Klintborg's observations regarding Västerås Parish shed light on potential challenges:

> In the encounter with the educators, I perceive expressions of a perceived disempowerment from other professional groups in the Church but also a self-imposed one. [...] At the same time, I wonder if the educators possibly lack the analytical tools that could be expected of them, tools that, for example, enable reflection on the meaning of learning and teaching and a language to clarify this analysis for the other employees in the team. But I also wonder if it is perhaps instead the case that educators too rarely use and thus keep the use of the theoretical tools alive, as a consequence of lack of time, demand or confidence?[50]

From this Klintborg concludes that parishes, including Västerås, should reassess and enrich their continuous education programs for religious educators, ensuring these offerings include comprehensive educational and theological training.[51] This insight underscores the significance of competencies for parish educators and

---

[50] Gustavsson [Klintborg], *En process på riktigt*, 47.
[51] Gustavsson [Klintborg], *En process på riktigt*, 48.

extends to pastors, deacons, church musicians, other parish staff, and lay volunteers. Possessing a diverse array of methods is beneficial, yet inadequate on its own, just as relying solely on policy documents outlining Christian religious education's goals and characteristics falls short of meeting actual needs.[52]

I concur with Klintborg on the necessity for educators to be well-versed in analytical tools that facilitate a deep reflection on the processes of learning and teaching. A critical skill in this domain is the capacity to examine and integrate the objectives of teaching, the content being taught, and the methods employed, along with a broader understanding of didactic relationships and questions.[53] This competency is essential for fostering a reflective and effective teaching practice.

Another widely recognized teaching skill is comprehending the mechanisms of learning. Osbeck and Cöster emphasize the crucial need for individuals in teaching roles to grasp the dynamics of how learning occurs. I contend that it is within this context that Christian religious educators and scholars should explore adjacent areas of research in religious education, particularly studies focused on learning within faith communities. This exploration can offer valuable insights and methodologies applicable to their practice.[54]

The research conducted by Elisabeth Tveito Johnsen and Morten Holmqvist, for instance, examines situations that significantly facilitate religious learning.[55] Their studies, among others, shed light on how learning in faith communities occurs, providing a rich source of insights for those involved in teaching. This research can aid educators in shaping and refining their teaching practices.

Similarly, investigations into teaching within formal religious education contexts, following the didactic approach, offer valuable perspectives and practices that can enhance the effectiveness of teaching in various religious settings.[56]

To take an example, Christina Osbeck's research into language use within two religious education classrooms reveals that the diversity and frequency of question types, the variety of speech genres (such as informative, analytical, interpretative, and narrative forms), and the breadth of content covered by these genres correlate with improved outcomes on religious studies tests. Although Osbeck cautions

---

[52] Gustavsson [Klintborg], *En process på riktigt*, 38–39, 48.

[53] See sections 2.5–2.7, 6.2.1–6.2.3, 7.1.1–7.1.2.

[54] See section 1.4.

[55] Holmqvist, "Material Logics"; Holmqvist, "Learning Religion"; Tveito Johnsen, "Trosopplæring"; Tveito Johnsen, "Læring"; Tveito Johnsen, "Gudstjenestelæring"; Tveito Johnsen, "Religiøs læring."

[56] See section 1.4.

against making sweeping generalizations about the pedagogical implications of her findings, she underscores the significant role teachers play in guiding communication patterns and discourse and the consequences this has on the learning that interaction affords and constraints.[57] Despite her focus on formal educational environments, which differ from the non-formal settings typical of church and parish learning, Osbeck's insights serve as a valuable guide for religious educators. They can apply her observations to better structure interactions in ways that facilitate learning, adapting these strategies to suit the non-formal context of parish-based education.[58]

Therefore, research in adjacent fields presents valuable opportunities for the development of Christian religious education and teaching. However, when delving into these areas, it is essential to consider the distinctions in context (between formal, non-confessional education and informal, confessional education) and approach (prescriptive versus non-prescriptive approaches). Consequently, I agree with Caroline Klintborg's argument that skills and knowledge from these other disciplines require careful adaptation or "translation" to be effectively applied within the realm of Christian religious education, even as I have highlighted how these concepts can be useful.[59]

Moreover, recognizing teaching as involving both strategies and tactics elucidates that its development transcends mere application of research findings; it emerges as a multifaceted activity.[60] Despite this complexity, I maintain that research, such as the strategies I have outlined here remains beneficial. Familiarity with these generalized prescripts of behavior can inspire and direct the attention of small group leaders, thereby supporting teaching efforts and enhancing the efficacy of online small groups as instances of Christian religious education.

However, as I discussed in chapter 7, implementing these strategies is itself a re/creative process, which requires not only the application but also the evaluation and adaptation of the proposed strategies.[61] It is not enough to simply apply these strategies; they must be continually assessed and refined. For teachers and religious educators to develop the competencies necessary for this kind of iterative teaching, they need not only awareness but also the capacity to critically assess and learn from their practices.

---

[57] Osbeck, "Speech Genres," 39–43.
[58] See section 7.1.3.
[59] Gustavsson [Klintborg], *En process på riktigt*, 46. See also section 6.3.2.
[60] See section 7.2.3–7.2.4.
[61] See sections 7.2.3–7.2.4.

Crucially, support mechanisms like peer supervision, ongoing professional development, and access to further training play a vital role in this development process. Therefore, the responsibility for cultivating teaching skills cannot rest on individuals alone. Instead, it should be a collective endeavor supported by the broader ecclesial community, including parishes and dioceses, and should be recognized as a priority deserving of investment to enhance the quality of Christian religious education across the board.

8.5 Final Reflections

The Church of Sweden's *Program for Learning and Teaching* concluded at the close of 2022. As I was finalizing my dissertation, I received a copy of the final report. According to an external evaluation, the program has elevated the significance of learning and teaching within the Church of Sweden, enhancing staff awareness about these critical matters and encouraging more deliberate pedagogical efforts. This indicates progress in promoting an awareness of teaching practices, although the report lacks specifics regarding the church activities where this increased consciousness is most pronounced.[62]

Yet, survey results also indicate that the program's impact on the pedagogical practices of parishes has been relatively small. The report speculates that this limited influence might stem from respondents being unaware that the initiatives they valued were components of the program. However, this situation prompts further inquiry into how extensively parish activities related to learning and teaching have evolved to become more "comprehensive, coherent, and systematic".[63] The external evaluation suggests that there is scant evidence to suggest a shift towards more structured and systematic approaches to learning and teaching as a result of the program.[64]

The limited duration of the program, lasting only four years, and the nature of its impacts—likely to manifest more fully over time—might explain the modest outcomes observed. Nevertheless, this underscores the ongoing necessity to concentrate on issues related to teaching and learning within the Church of Sweden.

In this, I argue that the improvement possibilities identified in the *Online Small Groups* project do suggest implications for Christian religious education

---

[62] Anders Rune, "Slutrapport: Programmet för lärande och undervisning, Church of Sweden, (Uppsala, 2023), 3. Cf. section 8.1.1.

[63] Rune, "Slutrapport," 3.

[64] Westerberg et al., "Slutrapport," 13.

within the Church of Sweden more generally. I maintain that particular emphasis should be placed on refining the conceptualization of teaching, acknowledging that developing a thorough understanding and approach to teaching is crucial for the long-term enhancement of educational practices in the Church. A conceptualization of teaching can then translate into a teaching awareness, and consequently into efforts to improve teaching. Working with various ways to improve online small groups thus demonstrates both the need and the potential to create situations for potential specific learning towards the kingdom of God, a potential that extends far beyond online small groups.

What is more, Christian religious education, aimed at advancing the kingdom of God, must be implemented as a ministerial practice within parishes, transcending the realm of theoretical discussion. Despite this, I am convinced that research in Christian religious education can significantly contribute to the further evolution and enhancement of the Church's teaching ministry, bridging the gap between theory and practice.

Christian religious educators stand to benefit from insights gained through research focused on learning within faith communities as well as didactic studies. However, I see a unique opportunity in the realm of Christian religious education research, particularly through participatory action research projects similar to this one. By engaging directly with practitioners, action research provides academic insights that can significantly influence the continuous improvement of parish activities in ways that other research orientations might not achieve. Therefore, action research represents a viable approach for linking academic knowledge and practical applications within Christian religious education, aiming to enrich both the theoretical and practical aspects of this field.

I have also noted that this kind of research demands different forms of analysis and presentation styles to fulfill its twofold objective: to disseminate practical knowledge and to contribute to academic discourse. I have endeavored to achieve this through the use of creative non-fiction, the narrative shared in part 2, and the subsequent reflections in parts 3 and 4 of this study. The effectiveness of this approach will ultimately be determined by the reception of my work. Echoing the wisdom of my supervisor, the true test of this research's value lies in its application and impact, aptly summarized by the adage, "the proof of the pudding is in the eating."

Epilogue

Writing a dissertation is often a lengthy process; it certainly was in my case. As a result, there is an increasing temporal distance between the period when we explored online small groups together and the final writing phase. For academic researchers, this distance alters one's positionality. While this process of detachment does not necessarily lead to a deeper understanding, such distance can still offer perspective.[1]

Reflecting on our project and subsequent developments, I recognize numerous aspects I would approach differently today. I continue to value action research highly for its capacity to unite academics and practitioners in collaborative inquiry, which ideally fosters the generation of publicly beneficial knowledge— knowledge that influences both the world and the church. However, during the final writing phase, I have come to identify an ethical concern regarding the vulnerability of practitioners who engage in experiments beyond their expertise and comfort. The kind of action research project we have engaged in risks exploiting the experiences of practitioner researchers to identify flaws for improvement. Consequently, an imbalance emerges between my role as an academic researcher— with the authority to assess and represent both my own and my co-researchers' efforts—and the deacons and pastors with whom I collaborated.

I do not believe this issue represents a fundamental flaw in action research itself. Rather, the imbalance stems from the specific manner in which I employed this methodology. For future projects, it is crucial to strengthen the agency of my co-researchers by providing them greater opportunities to influence the process and to express dissent, both throughout the research process and in the published results. Nonetheless, I find some solace in Hilary Bradbury's *How to do Action Research for Transformations*, where she emphasizes that competence in action research is only acquired through experience.[2]

---

[1] Cf. section 3.2.2.

[2] Bradbury, *Action Research for Transformations*, 11–33.

A related concern is determining when "good" is indeed "good enough." Action research, in the context of this dissertation, seeks continuous improvement and transformation. Yet, it was often unclear who desired these changes and for what reasons. Within this work, I associate the imperative for ongoing change with the belief that Christian religious education should aim toward the kingdom of God, viewing teaching as a teleological activity that should perpetually evaluate its contributions to the processes of conversion. This represents a strong normative stance, asserting not only how Christian religious education ought to evolve, but also defining its ultimate goal.

This strong normative position risks dichotomizing the good and righteous against human error and possibly complacency. In essence, adopting such strong normative stances may inadvertently create a narrative of heroes and villains, where those not incessantly striving for "better teaching" are cast in the latter role.

However, it has not always been clear whether the unyielding pursuit of improvement emerged from our collaborative efforts and was genuinely valued, or if it was primarily driven by my expectations placed upon my co-researchers and our groups. Particularly considering recent discussions on the significance of rest, the constant emphasis on improvement merits reevaluation.[3] This presents a dual challenge: personally and professionally, as I plan future projects, and institutionally, for the Church of Sweden. We must find a way to balance "being" and "becoming," striving towards the Kingdom while also resting in the assurance that we are good enough as we are.[4]

This last point gains further momentum when acknowledging the extent of factors beyond our control. To speak candidly, I was initially quite satisfied with my efforts. After extensive reading and reflection, we implemented and tested practices in online small groups during the fall that were later incorporated into our spring sessions. Overall, I was pleased with our leadership approach in these groups. However, this perspective was challenged during our final evaluation in #Djursholm.

In the evaluation, participants did not criticize our leadership of the group per se, but highlighted how their diverse life circumstances led to varied experiences within the group. This revelation was unexpected, though perhaps it should not have been. For a long time, I had been striving to enhance our online small groups under the assumption that a uniform approach to improvement was feasible.

---

[3] Andreas Holmberg, *Gud såg att det var gott: Att vara människa och kyrka i klimatnödens tid* (Stockholm: Verbum, 2023), 91–97.

[4] Goto, *Playing*, 91–92, 130.

However, the responses from our #Djursholm participants made it clear that this was not a realistic expectation.

There is no singular method to improve online small groups or teaching within the Church of Sweden. Each educational approach and group format is perceived differently by participants and learners. Reflecting on this, I now recognize the improbability of discovering any one method that universally suits all. This understanding underscores the need for flexible and adaptive strategies in our educational endeavors.

Where does this leave us? Should we conclude that improvement is subjective and largely beyond our control, and that we should simply persist, accepting that sometimes "good" is indeed "good enough"? I contend otherwise. While recognizing the necessity of rest and reassessing the need for incessant improvement is crucial, we are called to a greater purpose in this time and place. We must refocus our efforts toward expanding the kingdom of God. Andreas Holmberg, the Church of Sweden's Bishop in the Diocese of Stockholm, highlights not only the importance of rest but also the need for conversion and what I term "inner transformation."[5] The absence of a singular, superior method should not discourage us; rather, it should motivate us to continually explore the diverse pathways through which learning and transformation can occur, in online small groups and beyond.

---

[5] Holmberg, *Gud såg*, 31–44.

Appendix A: Ethical Review

This project has been reviewed and approved by the Swedish Ethical Review Authority under registrar id: **2020–02373**.

The ethical review was obtained for an earlier research design titled "Tradering av tro i samtalsgrupper för vuxna i Svenska kyrkan" (Faith Traditioning in Adult Small Groups in the Church of Sweden).

However, the small groups I studied as part of that project were significantly impacted by the COVID-19 pandemic and the corresponding restrictions on meetings. While groups were eventually moved online, the circumstances were so specific that I judged it difficult to use the material I had gathered thus far.

In the fall of 2019, I was offered to be part of the *Church in Digital Space* project, specifically the *Online Small Groups* trajectory, as described in the introduction. The original research design thus changed from a focus on onsite to online groups and through the incorporation of the action research orientation.

In case of significant changes to a research project, these changes need to be reviewed and approved separately by the Swedish Ethical Review Authority for which a separate application is required. However, the Review Authority does not stipulate which changes are considered significant nor does it give advance notice about whether a change application is necessary.

It is thus the responsibility of the individual researchers to determine whether changes are significant and warrant a change application. In consultation with my supervisor, Prof. Tone Stangeland Kaufman, and the academic project leader of the *Church in Digital Space Project*, Prof. Jonas Ideström, I concluded that the changes were not significant in terms of the ethical review.

The shift from onsite to online groups did not include any additional data collection procedures not specified in the original application, nor did it expose participants to any new risks. Likewise, the action research orientation did not in itself change how participant data was recorded, stored, processed, or eventually deleted. If anything, the action research orientation allowed participants a larger degree of control over the research process, which I judged not to require a separate ethical review.

Appendix B: Research Plans

Appendix 2 contains the #ResearchPlans for the #Margareta, #S:tEskils, and #Älvsjö groups. As I explained in part 2, we were never able to complete a #ResearchPlan for the #Djursholm group.[1]

The appendix contains translations of the original documents. The documents show how the research was planned for each group, not how it was carried out. See section 3.3.1 for a discussion about the development of the research design during the project.

Translations were made with the machine translation service Google Translate and I have only made minimal changes where needed to align the translation with the rest of the text. As such, the translation is close to the Swedish original. I judge it more important for this appendix to remain close to the original wording than to improve the flow of the text. The text can therefore feel unpolished at times.

#ResearchPlan #Margareta

Brief description of the group

What kind of group is it? Who leads the group? How often does the group meet? How does the group meet (which tool do you use)?

The *Lectio Divina* group is an open group for spiritual deepening which is aimed primarily at parishioners in Margareta Parish. The group meets three times during the fall; 5 September, 19 September, and 3 October 2021, between 6–7 pm. That is a Sunday every other week. The group meets via Zoom and participants are welcome to attend every meeting or just one.

Later this fall, Margareta Parish will also have a Bible study group called "Life and the Bible," which is a more conversation-based and analytical way of approaching the biblical text. The Life and Bible group will meet onsite.

---

[1] See the entries from Monday, November 29, 2021, and Friday, January 14, 2022.

The group is led by pastor and researcher Karin Andersson and follows the principles of *Lectio Divina*. Sunday's texts are read several times and after each reading, a question is asked. Participants are encouraged to share their thoughts and feelings but are allowed to say pass. No one is allowed to comment on someone else's sharing.

Karin explains the group's structure as follows:

5:50 pm	Zoom opens and participants drop in before 18. The leader makes sure to say hello to each participant.
6 pm	Welcome to tonight's meeting. Presentation round with names and some questions about the Bible. For example, what does the Bible mean to you, do you remember the first time you came into contact with the Bible, and which Bible book do you like best right now?
	Thereafter follows:
	Information about *Lectio Divina*
	Relaxation exercise
	Reading 1: The same Bible text is read twice, and the question is "listen for a word or phrase that catches your eye in the text," silence, round with sharing the answer. No one is allowed to comment on anything anyone else says.
	Reading 2: The same Bible text is read twice, and the question is "listen to how the text touches your life," silence, round with sharing of the answer. No one is allowed to comment on anything anyone else says.
	Reading 3: The same Bible text is read twice, and the question is "Listen if you hear any invitation for the near future, i.e. is there any call to you to do something," silence, round with sharing the answer. No one is allowed to comment on what someone else says.
	Prayer
6.40 pm	18.40 We have left the exercise and talk freely about the coming Sunday's theme. Leaders give some input and may ask a question to get the conversation started.
6.55 pm	Thank you for tonight and the leader prays the Blessing.

Previous experience

What previous experiences are there of similar groups, both physical and digital?

The congregation has long had a Bible study group. But it was in 2019 that the concept of "Life and the Bible" stabilized in its current form.

Lectio Divina is relatively new. Karin Andersson had her first group in May 2021 and another group in July 2021. Each group met three times. So, when we have the group in September and October 2021, Karin has the experience of leading *Lectio Divina* twice before.

The group in May 2021 worked well and the experience is that people tend to be generous in their sharing.

So far, Zoom has worked well as a meeting place for *Lectio Divina*. The exercise itself took about 40 minutes and then we left the exercise and talked about Sunday's theme. I would like the exercise to take a little longer so that it can stand on its own. But it didn't feel right to end 20 minutes earlier and the conversation afterward has also fulfilled its function."

The group's motivation

Why have you chosen to have such a group?

In summer 2021, it looks as if groups can meet onsite again during the fall. The Bible study group "Life and the Bible" is therefore once again onsite. At the same time, Margareta Parish wants to continue its online offerings in and through the research project *Church in Digital Space*. The *Lectio Divina* group was planned for that purpose.

The parish plans to be able to continue to offer digital groups and meetings as a complement to physical groups and meetings.

Practical considerations have been guiding the planning (that the *Lectio Divina* group comes before the Life and Bible group).

The group came about as a result of a training/course in spiritual guidance that Karin Andersson took in January 2021. *Lectio Divina* was part of the course and in May 2021 the parish tried this format for the first time. The aim is to offer a different way of approaching the biblical texts than the more analytical conversation in the "Life and the Bible" group. In that way, *Lectio Divina* complements the conversations in Life and the Bible in the same way that digital meetings complement physical meetings.

At the same time, both groups are independent, and it is fine to be in only one of the groups. The expectation is that there will be partly different participants in the physical and digital groups.

Expectations of the research

What do you hope to get out of the research project?

It is exciting to see what Margareta Parish can contribute to as part of the larger research project.

At the same time, it is a good chance to develop. In every meeting with other people, there is an opportunity to learn something. In *Lectio Divina*, there is thus an opportunity to learn something about faith for the priest as well. In addition, it is important to learn more practical things and tricks to make the group and digital meetings as good as possible.

Ambitions and goals

What hopes do you have for the group? Are there any "goals" you want to achieve?

A basic hope is that people will grow in their faith. The group is part of the work with learning and teaching. The purpose is to prepare a place for the meeting with God. Through the biblical text, an opportunity is given to learn about God and what it means to be human.

The participants must dare to express themselves and talk about their faith and their lives. It is important that participants dare to share.

Another goal is for participants to learn to listen to each other. Today we hear a lot but don't listen. Learning to listen both to other people and to God is a help for faith and for life in general.

For people to dare to share, it is important to create a safe and permissive atmosphere.

Quality indicators

How is a group that works well characterized? How do you know it has been "good"?

The following are quality indicators:

- People sign up for the group.
- People don't drop out (stay the whole hour).
- Participants will return (both within the autumn meetings and participants who have participated in May and/or July 2021).
- People choose to share.
- It's a good atmosphere. Participants seem to be comfortable with the silence.
- The ceiling is high, people seem to be "honest" or "sincere" in their sharing and can say what they think without being afraid that it is "wrong."

Research focus

Is there something, in particular, you want to test, know, learn? Any themes, methods, or techniques?

We want to try the following:

- Playing Taizé songs 10 minutes before the meeting starts so that participants can "land."
- Have a longer silence, maybe 5 minutes?

ATTENTION! This list is continuously updated.

Group Participants' Research Participation

How do you see the participants' participation in the research process? How much should the group's participants be involved in influencing the research?

The participants are informed that the group is part of a research project when they sign up.

Participants can influence the research through the answers they leave in the survey.

Data Collection

How will we collect data and who is responsible for it?

After each meeting, we will send out a survey. There will be three different surveys where the content is adapted to the situation. The first survey will be relatively simple so as not to scare away participants. In the last questionnaire, there will be an invitation to participate in a group interview.

Karin Andersson sends a list of email addresses to Simon Hallonsten when the registration period has expired. Participants have the option to opt out of this when they register.

Simon Hallonsten is responsible for developing the survey and compiling the results. Simon Hallonsten sends out the survey via email after each meeting. The survey is open from Sunday evening to Tuesday.

During or after each meeting, Karin Andersson will write some short reflections. For that, Simon Hallonsten is sending out a special survey. On the Tuesday after the meeting, Karin and Simon have a short reconciliation (approx. 30 min) via Zoom.

Informed Consent

How do we ensure that we get participants' informed consent?

Karin sends out information to research participants as they sign up for the group.

Informed consent is collected in the survey. There is also information about the project for researchers.

Project Plan

Sep 3, 9 am – 12 pm	Joint meeting with Conversations in digital rooms
Sep 5, 6–7 pm	*Lectio Divina* Meeting 1 Feedback form 1 (open until September 7 at 8 am) Write short reflections.
Sep 8, 1 pm	Planning & Reflection Meeting 1
Sep 19, 6–7 pm	*Lectio Divina* Meeting 2 Feedback form 2 (open until September 21 at 8 am) Write short reflections.
Sep 29, 1:30 pm	Planning & Reflection Meeting 2
Oct 3, 6–7 pm	*Lectio Divina* Meeting 3 Feedback form 3 (open until Oct. 5 at 8 a.m.) Write short reflections.
Oct 5	Planning & Reflection Meeting 2
Oct 4–17	Group interview
Oct 18, 1–3 pm	Joint meeting with Conversations in digital rooms (digital meeting)
xx xxx	Evaluation *Lectio Divina*

| Jan 18, 2022, 9 am – 3 pm | Joint meeting with Conversations in digital rooms |

#ResearchPlan #S:tEskils

Brief description of the group

What kind of group is it? Who leads the group? How often does the group meet? How does the group meet (which tool do you use)?

 Online book club – Ann-Helén Laestadius Stöld is an online book club that meets six times in the fall of 2021. The first meeting is planned for August 30, 2021. After that, the group meets every Monday until October 4, 2021. The usual time is between 7–8 pm. The group meets via Zoom.

 The group has currently (25 August 2021) 9 participants and 2 leaders. Participants are between 20/21 and 85 years old and come from different parts of Sweden (Umeå, Öregrund), although the majority come from S:t Eskils Parish. Participants are not used to Church and for the most part, have not participated in the parish's activities before. Most participants have been part of the book club during the spring and will now continue during the fall. Someone has also chosen not to continue and someone has joined, but basically, the same group continues, so it can be assumed that participants have had time to get to know each other a little.

 The group is led by Jessica Bergqvist, a deacon in S:t Eskils Parish, and Lotta Adamsson, a retired librarian.

 At the end of the spring meetings, participants were asked which book they wanted to read during the fall. The group decided to read *Stolen* by Ann-Helén Laestadius at the first five meetings and *Notes on Grief* by Chimamanda Ngozi Adichie at the last meeting. Participants are encouraged to read as much as possible before the meetings, at least a number of chapters.

 At the first meeting, Jessica and Lotta set the rules: what is said here stays here, you get in touch if you can't come, you are present for the whole hour, etc.

 At the meetings, Jessica and Lotta usually begin by welcoming everyone. Then follows a short check-in. After that, they explain the evening's arrangement and repeat that what is said in the group stays in the group. Before each meeting, Lotta writes questions that are discussed by the participants. To have better conversations, the group is divided into two groups according to the wishes of the participants. The groups are based on how much the participants have read. This means that the small groups are usually fairly stable because they tend to be the same people who have read a lot and the same people who haven't had time to read as much. There is a certain mixture, however, within the small groups.

The evening ends with the whole group at 7.50 pm with a round where everyone can share something if they want.

After each meeting, Jessica and Lotta have a short evaluation to see how the evening's meeting went.

Previous experience

What previous experiences are there of similar groups, both physical and digital?

When it became difficult to meet onsite because of the COVID-19 pandemic, Jessica came up with the idea of a book club. She doesn't remember exactly where she got the idea from, but she probably read on Facebook that others had positive experiences with online book clubs. Jessica contacted Lotta, whom she knew from before, and the two decided to invite to an online book club.

It was the first time Jessica had a (digital) book club and the first time one was offered by S:t Eskils Parish.

Jessica made great efforts to invite people to the group. The invitation was primarily sent digitally via Facebook, Instagram, and various web pages for book clubs (https://bokcirklar.se). She shared the information in different groups on Facebook (such as "We who love books" or "We who live to read," etc.). Reaching out widely and spending a lot of time on it was a good strategy because it became a stable group where everyone came to (almost) all the meetings and then chose to continue during the fall. It also shows that the group has functioned well and that it has filled a need. There is also someone who, since the book club, has participated in the congregation's activities with outdoor training.

Although needs will change after corona, Jessica would like to continue the group, especially for people who are used to computers and Zoom. It's nice to see that older people are also in the group.

During the spring meetings, participants seem to have met only at the book club and had no contact beyond that. It does not seem to be common for participants to chat with each other one-on-one during the meetings.

The group's motivation

Why have you chosen to have such a group?

Primarily, the group functions as a meeting place. During the pandemic, many people became lonely and could not have their normal social interaction. The digital book club in S:t Eskils was a way for people to meet and experience community despite the restrictions.

Another purpose of the group was to invite existential conversations or conversations about things that touch through literature. Connected to that is choosing literature that can challenge the reader's perceptions and teach them something new about society and the world they live in.

A third purpose is that people can get to know the Church through various activities. The group's purpose is not primarily missionary in the sense that it is primarily a way to include people in the congregation's other activities. However, it is a different way for people to meet the Church and to reach people other than the already saved.

Ambitions and goals

What hopes do you have for the group? Are there any "goals" you want to achieve?

Ambitions and goals are directly linked to the group's motivation.

One ambition of the group is to create and spread the joy of reading. Then the group wants to give the participants a context and a community during the coronavirus era and thus break isolation and loneliness.

Another goal is to raise questions. On Lotta's advice, the circle reads books that arouse emotions, that touch on existential questions and politics, i.e. books that are a little heavier but inspire hope. It is also hoped that the conversations contribute to discovering and learning something new about the world, society, and oneself.

A third goal is that people can meet the Church. Although many will settle for the group and will not seek out any other of the congregations' activities, they will open their eyes to the Church. It becomes like rings on the water. There is also an ambition to send out other information to the participants about what is happening in the Church to show the possibilities for those who are interested. You should know that it exists.

Expectations of the research

What do you hope to get out of the research project?

In the book club, Jessica has met many people who have no previous connection to the Church of Sweden. It's a whole new group of people that she meets there. Jessica is curious as to whether it is a general trend that online activities reach out to groups other than those usually attending Church.

Quality indicators

How is a group that works well characterized? How do you know it has been "good"?

A sign of quality is that the participants are brave when they share as a whole group. Participants are comfortable expressing their opinions and contradicting each other. It's a good sign that people dare to say what they think.

Another sign of quality is that there are several who want to continue the group now in the autumn. The joints' feeling of fulfillment after the hit is also a sign of quality.

The following are general quality signs:

- People don't drop out (stay the whole hour).
- Participants will return (both during the autumn meetings and participants who have participated in the spring).
- People choose to share.
- It's a good atmosphere. Participants seem to be comfortable with each other.
- The ceiling is high, people seem to be "honest" or "sincere" in their sharing and can say what they think without being afraid that it is "wrong."
- Participants seem to care about each other, there is a sense of community in the group.

Research focus

Is there something, in particular, you want to test, know, learn? Any themes, methods, or techniques?

It is different to lead a digital group compared to a physical group; it requires a different way of leading. You have to be very careful that everyone gets to talk. It becomes more square. You have to spread the word and respond to everyone's posts so that the participants feel validated. It feels awkward when it gets quiet. You can easily feel stupid.

One thing to track is if there is any opportunity to make the conversation flow a little better. Maybe it is easier to talk in small groups if the participants have their microphones on instead of off.

Another track is the issue of community. If the primary purpose of the group is to create a community, then you can think about whether there are more and other things you can do to confirm and build the community.

Group Participants' Research Participation

How do you see the participants' participation in the research process? How much should the group's participants be involved in influencing the research?

It is good if the participants can influence the research. The participants have already been informed that the group is part of a research project. Participants can influence the research through the answers they provide in surveys and possible interviews.

Data Collection

How will we collect data and who is responsible for it?

We collect data through surveys and perhaps through interviews. We plan for three surveys, one after the second, fourth, and last meeting. We can adapt the number and content of the surveys according to the group's response and the mood in the group.

The first questionnaire should be short and fairly general so that the participants feel like answering and participating in the research and do not experience it as tiring right from the start.

Jessica checks with the participants in the group if there is anyone who would like to stand up for an interview and if they prefer to be interviewed individually or in a group.

We collect the leaders' impressions through a special leader survey that is sent after each event. Jessica checks with Lotta whether she also wants to answer the survey.

Informed Consent

How do we ensure that we get participants' informed consent?

Jessica sends out information to research people on Sunday 29 August 2021 when she sends the link to the meeting.

Informed consent is collected in the survey. There is also information about the project for researchers.

Project Plan

Aug 30, 7–8 pm	Online Book Club Meeting 1 Leader feedback form 1
Sep 3, 9 am – 12 pm	Joint meeting with Conversations in digital rooms

Sep 6, 7–8 pm	Online Book Club Meeting 2 Leader feedback form 2 Participant feedback form 1
Sep 8	Planning & Reflection Meeting 1
Sep 13, 7–8 pm	Online Book Club Meeting 3 Leader feedback form 3
Sep 20, 7–8 pm	Online Book Club Meeting 4 Leader feedback form 4 Participant feedback form 2
Sep 23	Planning & Reflection Meeting 2
Sep 27, 7–8 pm	Online Book Club Meeting 5 Leader feedback form 5
Oct 5, 7–8 pm	Online Book Club Meeting 6 Leader feedback form 6 Participant feedback form 3
Oct 18, 1–3 pm	Joint meeting with Conversations in digital rooms (digital meeting)
xx xxx	Evaluation Online Book Club
Jan 18, 2022, 9 am – 3 pm	Joint meeting with Conversations in digital rooms

#ResearchPlan #Älvsjö

Brief description of the group

What kind of group is it? Who leads the group? How often does the group meet? How does the group meet (which tool do you use)?

The online small group "Christmas Readings" is a theological reflection group aimed at pastors in the Church of Sweden. The group meets via Zoom and talks about the texts that are read during Christmas 2021 (1st Advent to and including Boxing Day, 2nd year series). The group meets seven times between 1–3 pm.

Tuesday, September 14, at 1–3 pm First Sunday in Advent

Tuesday, September 21, at 1–3 pm Second Sunday in Advent

Thursday, September 30, at 1–3 pm Third Sunday in Advent

Tuesday, October 12, at 1–3 pm Fourth Sunday in Advent

Thursday, October 28, at 1–3 pm Christmas Eve

Thursday, November 11, at 1–3 pm Christmas Day

Tuesday, November 23, at 1–3 pm Boxing Day

The group is led by Camilla Lindström, a pastor in Älvsjö Parish, and Simon Hallonsten, PhD student at Stockholm University of Theology.

For the group, pre-registration and a willingness to attend all meetings are required. (Things can happen and it doesn't matter if you can't every time, but the idea is to have a reasonably stable group so that there won't be a new group of people at each meeting).

Previous experience

What previous experiences are there of similar groups, both physical and digital?

Camilla Lindström has herself participated in a similar group in Strängnäs diocese during Lent 2021.

Simon Hallonsten has been part of a catechumenate group during 2020/2021. Simon also has some theoretical knowledge of religious pedagogy from his education.

The group's motivation

Why have you chosen to have such a group?

Pastors in the Church of Sweden have the same need for spiritual deepening and theological reflection as everyone else. Perhaps their needs are even greater because they must also lead others in their spiritual development. At the same time, there are limited resources for such deepening and reflection, both in terms of time (it is rarely included in the pastor's work schedule) or opportunity (there are not many small groups that are specifically aimed at pastors).

The purpose of the group is thus twofold: on the one hand to prepare a place for the pastors' own spiritual development and on the other hand to give the pastors resources for their work with learning and teaching in the parishes.

Including pastors in the action research project on online small groups also has the advantage that the pastors learn something about online meetings in and through their participation.

Many pastors will preach during Christmas 2021. Christmas texts can be experienced as particularly challenging because they are well-known, and many people have heard many sermons during the Christmas season. Treating Christmas texts is also intended as an aid in the pastors' sermon preparations.

Ambitions and goals

What hopes do you have for the group? Are there any "goals" you want to achieve?

The first aim is that participating priests have the opportunity to explore and deepen their faith and their understanding of their faith.

Another purpose is to create a community that can bear both what is easy and wonderful about life and faith and what is difficult. One hope is that at least some participants can make contacts that last beyond the group's meetings.

A third purpose is to help the priests with sermon preparation.

A fourth purpose is that participating priests learn something about digital conversations.

Expectations of the research

What do you hope to get out of the research project?

The research project primarily aims to test different methods and techniques when it comes to online small groups so that these groups can be as good as possible.

I expect to learn more about "what works" and what tips and tricks you can use to make the group feel meaningful.

Quality indicators

How is a group that works well characterized? How do you know it has been "good"?

We have thought of the following quality signs:

- The participants prioritize the meetings.
- People arrive on time.

- People don't leave in advance.
- People don't drop out (come to all meetings)
- Everyone gets to speak, and you listen to each other
- It's a good atmosphere. Participants appear to be comfortable and re-laxed.
- There is laughter.
- The ceiling is high, people seem to be "honest" or "sincere" in their sharing and can say what they think without being afraid that it is "wrong."
- Participants get someone/some new thoughts or insights.
- Participants experience the group as keen and rewarding.

Research focus

Is there something, in particular, you want to test, know, learn? Any themes, methods, or techniques?

Lots of things. We will come back to this.

Group Participants' Research Participation

How do you see the participants' participation in the research process? How much should the group's participants be involved in influencing the research?

All participants in the group are co-researchers, i.e. the group is based on the belief that we explore the group and what works well and poorly together.

We make a conscious effort to include everyone's voices.

Data Collection

How will we collect data and who is responsible for it?

I would like to record the Zoom meetings. Recording the meetings makes it possible to study different situations in detail to see what is happening in the group.

In addition to that, I suggest that we collect data through joint reflection, i.e., we ask participants how they have experienced the meeting during the meeting itself. We combine that with feedback forms that we send out from time to time.

I would also suggest that we ask the participants if they would consider being interviewed, either individually or in a group.

In addition, participants can always influence the group and the research by contacting Camilla or Simon and coming up with various inputs and ideas.

After each meeting, Camilla and Simon have a short debriefing to capture reflections and thoughts about the day's meeting.

I think it is good to alternate different ways of collecting data because each way has its pros and cons. This is how it could look:

Meeting 1	Group reflection, 10 last minutes. How has it been, 1–5 plus a short comment. Anything we can do differently?
Meeting 2	Feedback form after the meeting, finish 15 minutes earlier and send out the feedback form via email.
Meeting 3	After meeting 3, we hold a group interview. Before the interview, Simon evaluates the recordings and prepares concrete questions.
Meeting 4	No evaluation. Give the participants time to be more involved in a regular discussion group than in a research project.
Meeting 5	Very short survey. Just type: How was today? Something we can do differently.
Meeting 6	No evaluation. Give the participants time to be more involved in a regular discussion group than in a research project.
Meeting 7	After the last meetings have another group interview to talk about the whole. Before the interview, Simon evaluates the recordings and prepares concrete questions.

ATTENTION! We will need to adapt the data collection in the meantime. Depending on what we want to test and how the group works, we may need to adapt our way of collecting data.

Informed Consent

How do we ensure that we get participants' informed consent?

Yes. Informed consent is collected from all participants as they sign up.

Project Plan

Sep 3, 9 am – 12 pm	Joint meeting with Conversations in digital rooms
Sep 14, 1–3 pm	Meeting 1
Sep 21, 1–3 pm	Meeting 2 Feedback form 1
Sep 30, 1–3 pm	Meeting 3
Oct 1–10	Group Interview 1
Oct, 12 1–3 pm	Meeting 4
Oct 18, 1–3 pm	Joint meeting with Conversations in digital rooms (digital meeting)
Oct 28, 1–3 pm	Meeting 5 Feedback form 2
Nov 11, 1–3 pm	Meeting 6
Nov 24 –Dec 9	Group Interview 2
xx xxx	Evaluation
Jan 18, 2022, 9 am – 3 pm	Joint meeting with Conversations in digital rooms

Lenten Bible Study Prayer

God,

Give us courage to focus on what is important.
Help us find respite, rest, and presence.

Help us to be open to the people and
tasks we face today.
Give us the ability to be present in the moment.

Protect us from division.
Help us to prioritize, to say "No" to be able to say "Yes."
Bring us the calm and peace we cannot create ourselves.

Help us this Lent to see our deepest longing and
to take it seriously,
So that we dare to change and be transformed in your light.

In the name of Jesus,
Amen

Appendix C: Overview of Data Collected

Appendix 3 lists the data collected as part of the *Online Small Groups* project.

Date	Group	Type	Description
Jul 6, 2021	#Älvsjö	Planning & Reflection Meeting	60 min, onsite, Planning Document (written through email correspondence)
Jul 7, 2021	#Margareta	Interview	40 min via Zoom, unrecorded, interview and reflections notes (946 words)
Jul 7, 2021	#Margareta	Planning & Reflection Meeting	60 min, onsite, Planning Document
Aug 25, 2021	#S:tEskils	Planning & Reflection Meeting	60 min, via Zoom, Planning Document
Aug 30, 2021	#S:tEskils	Leader Feedback From	9 open-ended paragraph questions, 2 respondents
Sep 3, 2021	All	Workshop	180 min workshop via Zoom, recorded
Sep 5, 2021	#Margareta	Leader Feedback From	8 open-ended paragraph questions, 5 closed questions, 1 respondent
Sep 5–9, 2021	#Margareta	Participant Feedback From	4 open-ended paragraph questions, 1 closed question, 4 respondents
Sep 6, 2021	#S:tEskils	Leader Feedback From	10 open-ended paragraph questions, 2 respondents
Sep 6–7, 2021	#S:tEskils	Participant Feedback From	7 open-ended paragraph questions, 7 respondents

Sep 9, 2021	#S:tEskils	Planning & Reflection Meeting	60 min meeting via Zoom, recorded
Sep 9, 2021	#Margareta	Planning & Reflection Meeting	60 min meeting via Zoom, recorded
Sep 13, 2021	#S:tEskils	Leader Feedback From	11 open-ended paragraph questions, 2 respondents
Sep 19, 2021	#Margareta	Leader Feedback From	10 open-ended paragraph questions, 4 closed questions, 1 respondent
Sep 20, 2021	#S:tEskils	Leader Feedback From	6 open-ended paragraph questions, 2 respondents
Sep 20–Oct 4, 2021	#S:tEskils	Participant Feedback From	5 open-ended paragraph questions, 7 closed questions with open-ended follow-up questions, 5 respondents
Sep 30, 2021	#Margareta	Planning & Reflection Meeting	60 min meeting via Zoom, conversation notes (593 words)
Oct 3, 2021	#Margareta	Participant Observation	60 min observation, field, and reflection notes (902 words)
Oct 3, 2021	#Margareta	Leader Feedback From	10 open-ended paragraph questions, 4 closed questions, 1 respondent
Oct 3–13, 2021	#Margareta	Participant Feedback From	8 open-ended paragraph questions, 3 closed questions with open-ended follow-up questions, 1 scale, 2 respondents
Oct 4, 2021	#S:tEskils	Participant Observation	60 min observation, field, and reflection notes (1 353 words)
Oct 18, 2021	#Margareta	Planning & Reflection Meeting	120 min presentation and discussion of research results, onsite, voice-recorded
Oct 27, 2021	#Margareta	Interview	30 min via Zoom, unrecorded, interview and reflections notes (784 words)

Oct 29, 2021	#S:tEskils	Planning & Reflection Meeting	90 min presentation and discussion of research results via Zoom
Jan 6, 2022	#Djursholm	Participant Observation	60 min observation via Zoom, field and reflections notes (2 292 words)
Jan 18, 2022	All	Lunch	60 min via Zoom
Jan 19, 2022	#Djursholm	Meeting Plan	Meeting plan (1 296 words)
Jan 20, 2022	#Djursholm	Participant Observation	60 min observation via Zoom, field and reflections notes (1 107 words)
Feb 15, 2022	#Djursholm	Meeting Plan	Meeting plan (1 302 words)
Feb 17, 2022	#Djursholm	Participant Observation	50 min observation via Zoom, field and reflections notes (498 words)
Feb 17, 2022	#Djursholm	Group Evaluation	10 min via Zoom, conversation, and reflection notes (588 words)
Feb 22, 2022	#Älvsjö	Planning & Reflection Meeting	30 min via Zoom, meeting plan (398 words)
Feb 22, 2022	All	Workshop	240 min via Zoom, field and reflections notes (2 760 words)
Mar 1, 2022	#Älvsjö	Participant Observation	90 min observation via Zoom, field, and reflection notes (671 words)
Mar 3, 2022	#Älvsjö	Planning & Reflection Meeting	30 min via Zoom, meeting plan (261 words)
Mar 3, 2022	#Djursholm	Participant Observation	60 min observation via Zoom, field and reflections notes (2 056 words)

Mar 8, 2022	#Älvsjö	Participant Observation	90 min observation via Zoom, field, and reflection notes (818 words)
Mar 14, 2022	#Älvsjö	Planning & Reflection Meeting	30 min via Zoom, meeting plan (171 words)
Mar 15, 2022	#Älvsjö	Participant Observation	90 min observation via Zoom, field, and reflection notes (947 words)
Mar 16, 2022	#Älvsjö	Planning & Reflection Meeting	30 min via Zoom, meeting plan (214 words)
Mar 17, 2022	#Djursholm	Meeting Plan	Meeting plan (1 035 words)
Mar 17, 2022	#Djursholm	Participant Observation	60 min observation via Zoom, field and reflections notes (1 648 words)
Mar 22, 2022	#Älvsjö	Participant Observation	90 min observation via Zoom, field and reflections notes (670 words)
Mar 23–Apr 1, 2022	#Älvsjö	Group Evaluation	Participant feedback per email, 4 respondents (700 words)
Mar 29, 2022	#Älvsjö	Participant Observation	90 min observation via Zoom, field and reflections notes (902 words)
Mar 30, 2022	#Djursholm	Meeting Plan	Meeting plan (1 069 words)
Mar 31, 2022	#Älvsjö	Planning & Reflection Meeting	30 min via Zoom, meeting plan (164 words)
Mar 31, 2022	#Djursholm	Participant Observation	60 min observation via Zoom, field and reflections notes (187 words)
Apr 4, 2022	#Älvsjö	Planning & Reflection Meeting	30 min via Zoom
Apr 7, 2022	#Älvsjö	Planning & Reflection Meeting	30 min via phone, meeting plan (290 words), shared

			observations from meeting April 5, 2022 (287 words)
Apr 12, 2022	#Älvsjö	Participant Observation	90 min observation via Zoom, field and reflections notes (74 words)
Apr 12, 2022	#Älvsjö	Group Evaluation	30 min via Zoom, recorded
Apr 28, 2022	#Djursholm	Group Evaluation	90 min, onsite, recorded, 4 respondents

Appendix D: Mapping of Stockholm Parishes' Educational Activities

Between February 8, 2020, and February 27, 2020, just before the COVID-19 pandemic hit Sweden, I collected data on the various activities conducted by parishes in the Church of Sweden (CoS) Diocese of Stockholm. The data was gathered from the homepages of 50 parishes and 4 vicarages.[1]

The mapping focused exclusively on activities targeted at adults, prioritizing "teaching" activities over other forms of engagement such as special services, music concerts, international development work, and diaconal efforts. This approach was taken to maintain an emphasis on "normal" parish work, thereby excluding activities linked to hospital and prison churches, which often have distinct community roles and outreach strategies.

Several parishes with unique characteristics were identified and excluded from the primary analysis to avoid skewing results towards atypical parish functions. These were:

- Hovförsamlingen (The Royal Palace Parish)
- Finska församlingen/Suomalainen seurakunta (The Finish Parish)
- Tyska församlingen/Deutsche Gemeinde (The German Parish)

The data collection was confined to information directly available on home pages. Material solely mentioned in calendars or print materials was not considered. Additionally, pages that broadly described the parish, such as "About the parish," "Our history," "Cemetery," and "Contact" were not included in the data aggregation process.

This targeted approach has allowed for a concise mapping of adult teaching activities within the CoS Diocese of Stockholm, providing a clear picture of the

---

[1] I translate the Swedish "pastorat" as vicarage. In the Church of Sweden, a vicarage is a larger administrative unit combining a number of parishes, who then share staff and resources.

educational priorities and community engagement strategies employed by its parishes.

The mapping shows that small groups and similar groups are frequent in the CoS Diocese of Stockholm. More than 70% of parishes offer some kind of small group. In addition, more than 50% of parishes also offer other types of groups, such as study circles, and, less frequently, book clubs.

Category Activities	Count	%
Sacred acts Baptism, Confirmation, Weddings, Funerals	54	100%
Music Choirs and Concerts	54	100%
Diaconia Individual Counseling, Grief Groups, Counseling Sessions	52	96,3%
Religious services Mass, Services, Devotions	50	92,6%
Meeting place Open meeting place, often with lunch or coffee, sometimes with a program	49	90,7%
Spirituality Meditation, Retreat, Pilgrimage, Yoga, Sacred Dances, etc.	45	83,3%
Small Groups Bible Study Groups, Theological Discussion, Groups for Men, Life and Faith Groups	38	70,4%
Learning and Teaching Lectures, Study Circles and Courses	30	55,6%
Culture, Society, Politics Film Screenings, Book Clubs, or Theater	21	38,9%
Integration Language Cafés	15	27,8%
Physical Activities Walking Groups, Exercise	8	14,8%
Travel Parish Trips	6	11,1%

Bibliography

Afdal, Geir. *Religion som bevegelse: Læring, kunnskap og mediering.* [Religion as a movement: Learning, knowledge and mediation]. Oslo: Universitetsforlaget, 2013.

—. *Researching Religious Education as Social Practice.* Münster: Waxmann Verlag GmbH, 2010.

—. "Two Concepts of Practice and Theology." *Studia Theologica* 75, no. 1 (2021): 6–29. *https://doi.org/10.1080/0039338X.2021.1914894.*

Agar, Michael. *The Professional Stranger: An Informal Introduction to Ethnography.* Second ed. San Diego: Academic Press, 1996.

Alberg Peters, Rikke, and Hildegunn Juulsgaard Johannesen. "What is Actually True? Approaches to Teaching Conspiracy Theories and Alternative Narratives in History Lessons." *Acta Didactica Norge* 14, no. 4 (2020). *https://doi.org/10.5617/adno.8377.*

Alvesson, Mats, and Kaj Sköldberg. *Reflexive Methodology: New Vistas for Qualitative Research.* Third ed. Los Angeles: Sage, 2018.

"What is Education Research?" American Educational Research Association, 2023, accessed 25 Sep, 2023, *https://www.aera.net/About-AERA/What-is-Education-Research.*

Andersson, Gita. *Bättre än vi trodde: Att förvandlas som människa och kyrka.* [Better than we thought: Transforming as persons and as a church]. Stockholm: Libris, 2022.

Anshori, Isa. "Problem-Based Learning Remodelling Using Islamic Values Integration and Sociological Research in Madrasas." *International Journal of Instruction* 14, no. 2 (2021): 421–42. *https://doi.org/10.29333/iji.2021.14224a.*

Appelfeldt, Joel. *Dopet som hantverk: Gudstjänstkreativitet och liturgisk taktik i Svenska kyrkan och Equmeniakyrkan.* [The craft of baptism: Creative liturgical tactics in the Church of Sweden and the Uniting Church in Sweden]. Skellefteå: Artos Academic, 2023.

Arborelius, Elisabeth. "Finns det en klyfta mellan kyrkan och folket? Intervjuer med församlingsbor och präster i Stockholmsområdet." [Is there a gap between the church and the people? Interviews with parishioners and priests in the Stockholm area.], Acta Universitatis Upsaliensis, 2009.

Astley, Jeff. "Aims and Approaches in Christian Education." In *Learning in the Way: Research and Reflection on Adult Christian Education*, edited by Jeff Astley, 1–32. Herefordshire: Gracewing, 2000.

—. "Definitions, Aims and Approaches: An Overview." In *Critical Perspectives on Christian Education: A Reader on the Aims, Principles and Philosophy of Christian Education*, edited by Jeff Astley and Leslie J. Francis, 3–12. Herefordshire: Gracewing, 1994.

—. "Discipleship Learning." *Rural Theology* 13, no. 1 (2015): 1–3.

—, ed. *Learning in the Way: Research and Reflection on Adult Christian Education.* Herefordshire: Gracewing, 2000.

—. "The Place of Understanding in Christian Education and Education about Christianity." In *Critical Perspectives on Christian Education: A Reader on the Aims, Principles and Philosophy of Christian Education*, edited by Jeff Astley and Leslie J. Francis, 105–17. Herefordshire: Gracewing, 1994.

—. "The Role of Worship in Christian Learning." In *Theological Perspectives on Christian Formation: A Reader on Theology and Christian Education*, edited by Jeff Astley, Leslie J. Francis and Colin Crowder, 244–51. Herefordshire: Gracewing, 1996.

Astley, Jeff, and Colin Crowder. "Theological Perspectives on Christian Education: An Overview." In *Theological Perspectives on Christian Formation: A Reader on Theology and Christian Education*, edited by Jeff Astley, Leslie J. Francis and Colin Crowder, x–xix. Herefordshire: Gracewing, 1996.

Astley, Jeff, and Leslie J. Francis, eds. *Critical Perspectives on Christian Education: A Reader on the Aims, Principles and Philosophy of Christian Education*. Herefordshire: Gracewing, 1994.

Astley, Jeff, Leslie J. Francis, and Colin Crowder, eds. *Theological Perspectives on Christian Formation: A Reader on Theology and Christian Education*. Herefordshire: Gracewing, 1996.

Åsvoll, Håvard. "Abduction, Deduction and Induction: Can these Concepts Be Used for an Understanding of Methodological Processes in Interpretative Case Studies?" *International Journal of Qualitative Studies in Education* 27, no. 3 (2014): 289–307. *https://doi.org/10.1080/09518398.2012.759296*.

Atkinson, Harley. *The Power of Small Groups in Christian Formation*. Eugene: Resource Publications, 2018. EBSCOhost.

Atkinson, Harley, and Joshua Rose. "The Small-Group Ministry Movement of the Last Four Decades." *Christian Education Journal* 17, no. 3 (2020): 547–59. *https://doi.org/10.1177/0739891320942932*.

Babington, Peter. "Ageing Well: Using Action Research in a Parish Church Setting." Doctor of Practical Theology, University of Birmingham, 2017.

Babyak, Andrew T. "A Teaching Strategy for a Christian Virtual Environment." *Journal of Research on Christian Education* 24, no. 1 (2015): 63–77. *https://doi.org/10.1080/10656219.2015.1008080*.

Bäckström, Anders, Ninna Edgardh, and Per Pettersson. *Religiös förändring i norra Europa: En studie av Sverige*. [Religious Change in Northern Europe: A Study of Sweden]. Uppsala: Diakonivetenskapliga institutet, 2004.

Ball, Peter. *Adult Believing: A Guide to the Christian Initiation of Adults*. London: Mowbray, 1988.

Barley, Lynda. "Towards the Development of Priest Researchers in the Church of England." Professional Doctorate in Practical Theology, Anglia Ruskin University, 2014.

Beaudoin, Tom, and Katherine Turpin. "White Practical Theology." In *Opening the Field of Practical Theology: An Introduction*, edited by Kathleen A. Cahalan and Gordon S. Mikoski, 251–69. Lanham: Rowman & Littlefield, 2014.

Bellah, Robert Neelly. *Habits of the Heart: Individualism and Commitment in American Life*. Berkeley: University of California Press, 1996.

Bennett, Zoë, Elaine Graham, Stephen Pattison, and Heather Walton. *Invitation to Research in Practical Theology*. London: Routledge, 2018.

Berglund, Jenny. "State-Funded Faith-Based Schooling for Muslims in the North." *Religion & Education* 46, no. 2 (2019): 210–33. *https://doi.org/10.1080/15507394.2019.1590943*.

Berntsen, John A. "Christian Affections and the Catechumenate." In *Theological Perspectives on Christian Formation: A Reader on Theology and Christian Education*, edited by Jeff Astley, Leslie J. Francis and Colin Crowder, 229–43. Herefordshire: Gracewing, 1996.

Berntson, Martin, Bertil Nilsson, and Cecilia Wejryd. *Kyrka i Sverige: Introduktion till svensk kyrkohistoria*. [Church in Sweden: Introduction to Swedish Church History]. Stockholm: Skellefteå, 2012.

Beverhjelm, Fredrik. *Guide till det strategiska konfirmandarbetet*. [Guide to strategic confirmation work]. Stockholm: Verbum, 2023.

Biesta, Gert. "Freeing Teaching from Learning: Opening Up Existential Possibilities in Educational Relationships." *Studies in Philosophy and Education* 34 (2015): 229–43. *https://doi.org/10.1007/s11217-014-9454-z*.

—. "Interrupting the Politics of Learning." In *Contemporary Theories of Learning: Learning Theorists... in Their Own Words*, edited by Knud Illeris, 243–59. Oxon: Routledge, 2018.

—. *The Rediscovery of Teaching*. New York: Routledge, 2017.

—. "What is Education For? On Good Education, Teacher Judgement, and Educational Professionalism." *European Journal of Education* 50, no. 1 (2015): 75–87. *https://doi.org/10.1111/ejed.12109*.

Biggs, John. "Enhancing Teaching through Constructive Alignment." *Higher Education* 32, no. 3 (1996): 347–64.

Biggs, John, and Catherine Tang. *Teaching for Quality Learning at University: What The Student Does*. 4th ed. Maidenhead: Society for Research into Higher Education, 2011.

Bjørndal, Bjarne, and Sigmund Lieberg. *Nye veier i didaktikken? En innføring i didaktiske emner og begreper*. [New paths in didactics? An introduction to didactic topics and concepts]. Oslo: Aschehoug, 1978.

Blumer, Herbert. "What is Wrong with Social Theory?" *American Sociological Review* 19, no. 1 (1954): 3–10. *https://doi.org/10.2307/2088165*.

Boog, Ben W. M. "The Emancipatory Character of Action Research, Its History and the Present State of the Art." *Journal of Community & Applied Social Psychology* 13, no. 6 (2003): 426–38. *https://doi.org/10.1002/casp.748*.

Boyd, Jason. "Action Research as a Way of Doing Theology (ART): Transforming My Practice of Preaching the Bible with My Congregation." PhD, University of Chester, 2015.

—. *The Naked Preacher: Action Research and a Practice of Preaching*. London: SCM Press, 2018.

Bradbury, Hilary. *How to Do Action Research for Transformations: At a Time of Eco-Social Crisis*. Cheltenham: Edward Elgar Publishing, 2022.

—, ed. Introduction to *The SAGE Handbook of Action Research*. 3rd ed. London: SAGE Publications, 2015.

—, ed. *The SAGE Handbook of Action Research*. 3rd ed. London: SAGE Publications, 2015.

Bradbury, Hilary, Rolla Lewis, and Dusty Columbia Embury. "Education Action Research: With and for the Next Generation." In *The Wiley Handbook of Action Research in Education*, edited by Craig A. Mertler, 7–28. Newark: John Wiley & Sons, 2019.

Bradbury Huang, Hilary. "What is Good Action Research? Why the Resurgent Interest?" *Action Research* 8, no. 1 (2010): 93–109. *https://doi.org/10.1177/1476750310362435*.

Brindley, Jane E., Lisa M. Blaschke, and Christine Walti. "Creating Effective Collaborative Learning Groups in an Online Environment." *International Review of Research in Open and Distance Learning* 10, no. 3 (2009): 1–18. *https://doi.org/10.19173/irrodl.v10i3.675*.

Brodd, Sven-Erik. "Pragmatismen som ett kyrkans kännetecken (nota ecclesiae): Om ekonomi, ecklesiologi och kyrkans inre sekularisering." [Pragmatism as a mark of the church (notae ecclesia): Economics, ecclesiology, and the church's inner secularization]. In *Inomkyrklig sekularisering* [Intra-church secularization], edited by Thomas Girmalm and Marie Rosenius, 31–55. Umeå: Umeå universitet, 2018.

Brouard, Susanna. "Using Theological Action Research to Embed Catholic Social Teaching in a Catholic Development Agency: Abseiling on the Road to Emmaus." Professional Doctorate in Practical Theology, Anglia Ruskin University, 2015.

Browning, Don S. *A Fundamental Practical Theology: Descriptive and Strategic Proposals.* Minneapolis: Fortress Press, 1996.

Brydon-Miller, Mary. "Ethics and Action Research: Deepening our Commitment to Principles of Social Justice and Redefining Systems of Democratic Practice." In *The SAGE Handbook of Action Research: Participative Inquiry and Practice*, edited by Peter Reason and Hilary Bradbury, 199–210. London: SAGE Publications, 2008.

Brydon-Miller, Mary, Davydd Greenwood, and Patricia Maguire. "Why Action Research?" *Action Research* 1, no. 1 (2003): 9–28. *https://doi.org/10.1177/14767503030011002.*

Bryman, Alan. "The End of the Paradigm Wars?" In *The SAGE Handbook of Social Research Methods*, edited by Pertti Alasuutari, Leonard Bickman and Julia Brannen, 13–24. London: SAGE Publications Ltd, 2012.

Burgess, Harold W. *Models of Religious Education: Theory and Practice in Historical and Contemporary Perspective.* Nappanee: Evangel Publishing House, 2001.

Burroway, Janet, Elizabeth Stuckey-French, and Ned Stuckey-French. *Writing Fiction: A Guide to Narrative Craft.* 10th ed. Chicago: University of Chicago Press, 2019.

Burrows, Andrea C. "US Perspectives on Action Research in Education." In *The Wiley Handbook of Action Research in Education*, edited by Craig A. Mertler, 75–96. Newark: John Wiley & Sons, 2019.

Butler, James. "The 'Long and Winding Road' of Faith: Learning about the Christian Life and Discipleship from two Methodist Congregations." *Practical Theology* 13, no. 3 (2020): 277–89. https://doi.org/10.1080/1756073X.2019.1678859.

—. "Prayer as a Research Practice? What Corporate Practices of Prayer Disclose about Theological Action Research." *Ecclesial Practices* 7, no. 2 (2020): 241–57. *https://doi.org/10.1163/22144471-BJA10021.*

Butler, Judith. *Gender Trouble: Feminism and the Subversion of Identity.* New York: Routledge, 2006 [1999].

Cahalan, Kathleen A., and Gordon S. Mikoski, eds. *Opening the Field of Practical Theology: An Introduction.* Lanham: Rowman & Littlefield, 2014.

Cameron, Helen, Deborah Bhatti, Catherine Duce, James Sweeney, and Clare Watkins. *Talking about God in Practice: Theological Action Research and Practical Theology.* London: SCM Press, 2010.

Certeau, Michel de. *The Practice of Everyday Life.* Translated by Steven Rendall. Berkeley: University of California Press, 1984.

Chanthago, Phramaha Jittipong, Phrakrudhammapissamai, and Chayanon Jantaragaroon. "Development of a Learning School in Wat Srichan School, Khon Kaen Province: A Participatory Action Research." *International Journal of Higher Education* 9, no. 1 (2019): 11–21. *https://doi.org/10.5430/ijhe.v9n1p11.*

Chapman, Carole, Leonie Ramondt, and Glenn Smiley. "Strong Community, Deep Learning: Exploring the Link." *Innovations in Education and Teaching International* 42, no. 3 (2005): 217–30. *https://doi.org/10.1080/01587910500167910.*

Chapman, Mark. "Changing the World without Doing Harm: Critical Pedagogy, Participatory Action Research and the Insider Student Researcher." *Religious Studies and Theology* 38, no. 1–2 (2019): 100–16. *https://doi.org/10.1558/rsth.38715.*

Cheu, Hoi F. "Stories as a Scientific Method in Art-Based Health Research." *Journal of Applied Arts & Health* 8, no. 2 (2017): 209–24. *https://doi.org/10.1386/jaah.8.2.209_1.*

Chevalier, Jacques, and Daniel Buckles. *Participatory Action Research: Theory and Methods for Engaged Inquiry.* 2nd ed. Milton: Routledge, 2019.

Christie, Ann. *Ordinary Christology: Who Do You Say I Am? Answers from the Pews.* Farnham: Ashgate, 2012.

Christoffersen, Lisbet, Niels Henrik Gregersen, and Karen Marie Sø Leth-Nissen, eds. *Den praktiske teologi i Danmark 1973–2018: Festskrift til Hans Raun Iversen.* [Practical Theology in Denmark 1973–2018: Festschrift to Hans Raun Iversen.]. Copenhagen: Eksistensen, 2019.

Clapp, Rodney. *A Peculiar People: The Church as Culture in a Post-Christian Society.* Downers Grove: IVP Academic, 1996.

Cleveland-Innes, Martha F., and D. Randy Garrison. "Teaching, Learning, and Beyond." In *An Introduction to Distance Education: Understanding Teaching and Learning in a New Era*, edited by Martha F. Cleveland-Innes and D. Randy Garrison, 191–201. Milton: Taylor and Francis, 2020.

Clifford, James, and George E. Marcus. *Writing Culture: The Poetics and Politics of Ethnography.* Berkeley: University of California Press, 1986.

Coghlan, David. "Authenticity as First Person Practice: An Exploration Based on Bernard Lonergan." *Action Research* 6, no. 3 (2008): 351–66. *https://doi.org/10.1177/1476750308094649.*

Coghlan, David, and Mary Brydon-Miller. "Participatory Action Research." In *The SAGE Encyclopedia of Action Research*, edited by David Coghlan and Mary Brydon-Miller, 583–88. Thousand Oaks: SAGE Publications Ltd, 2014.

—. "Quality." In *The SAGE Encyclopedia of Action Research*, edited by David Coghlan and Mary Brydon-Miller, 667–69. Thousand Oaks: SAGE Publications Ltd, 2014.

Coghlan, David, and Patricia Gaya. "Dissertation Writing." In *The SAGE Encyclopedia of Action Research*, edited by David Coghlan and Mary Brydon-Miller, 281–83. Thousand Oaks: SAGE Publications Ltd, 2014.

Collier, John. "Models of Christian Education." *TEACH Journal of Christian Education* 7, no. 1 (2013): 4–7. *https://doi.org/10.55254/1835-1492.1194.*

Cook Everist, Norma. *The Church as Learning Community: A Comprehensive Guide to Christian Education.* Nashville: Abingdon Press, 2011.

Cornu, Alison Le. "Teaching Practical Theology Using Reusable Electronic Learning Objects: Practical, Educational and Theological Challenges." *Journal of Adult Theological Education* 5, no. 1 (2008): 71–85. *https://doi.org/10.1558/jate2008v5i1.71.*

Cöster, Henry. *"... bedriva undervisning ...": Om kyrkans didaskalia.* ["... to teach ..."]: On the church's didaskalia]. Uppsala: Church of Sweden, 2009.

Couture, Pamela D. *We Are Not All Victims: Local Peacebuilding in the Democratic Republic of Congo.* Zurich: Lit Verlag, 2016.

Curren, Randall, Emily Robertson, and Paul Hager. "The Analytical Movement." In *A Companion to the Philosophy of Education*, edited by Randall Curren, 176–91. Oxford: Blackwell Publishing, 2003.

Dalevi, Sören, and Kristian Niemi. "RE Didactics in Sweden: Defined by the national curriculum? Discussing Didactics of RE in a Swedish context." *Usuteaduslik Ajakiri* 69, no. 1 (2016): 62–78.

Dalevi, Sören, and Christina Osbeck. *Kyrkopedagogik i Munkfors: En utvärdering av ett samarbetsprojekt skola-kyrka.* [Church pedagogy in Munkfors: An evaluation of a school-church collaboration project]. Karlstad: Karlstad University Press, 2012.

Dalziel, James. "Learning Design, Lams, and Christian Education." *Journal of Christian Education* os-54, no. 1 (2011): 39–56. *https://doi.org/10.1177/002196571105400105.*

Davidsson Bremborg, Anna. "Interviewing." In *The Routledge Handbook of Research Methods in the Study of Religion*, edited by Michael Stausberg and Steven Engler, 310–22. Oxon: Routledge, 2011.

Davis, Dent. "Learning our Way: Engaging Laity through Large-scale Participatory Action Research." *Journal of Adult Theological Education* 4, no. 1 (2007): 48–62. *https://doi.org-/10.1558/jate.v4i1.48.*

Deulen, Angela A. "Social Constructivism and Online Learning Environments: Toward a Theological Model for Christian Educators." *Christian Education Journal* 10, no. 1 (2013): 90–98. *https://doi.org/10.1177/073989131301000107.*

Dokecki, Paul R., J. R. Newbrough, and Robert T. O'Gorman. "Toward a Community-Oriented Action Research Framework for Spirituality: Community Psychological and Theological Perspectives." *Journal of Community Psychology* 29, no. 5 (2001): 497–518. *https://doi.org/10.1002/jcop.1033.*

Donskov Felter, Kirsten, Ninna Edgardh, and Tron Fagermoen. "The Scandinavian Ecclesial Context." In *What Really Matters: Scandinavian Perspectives on Ecclesiology and Ethnography*, edited by Jonas Ideström and Tone Stangeland Kaufman, 7–14. Eugene: Pickwick Publications, 2018.

Dreyer, Jaco S. "Knowledge, Subjectivity, (De)Coloniality, and the Conundrum of Reflexivity." In *Conundrums in Practical Theology*, edited by Bonnie J. Miller-McLemore and Joyce Ann Mercer, 90–109. Leiden; Boston: Brill, 2016.

Dunaetz, David R., Diane T. Wong, Alexandria L. Draper, and Jacob P. Salsman. "Barriers to Leading Small Groups among Generation Z and Younger Millennials: An Exploratory Factor Analysis and Implications for Recruitment and Training." *Christian Education Journal* 19, no. 1 (2022): 152–69. *https://doi.org/10.1177/07398913211018482.*

Dykstra, Craig R. *Growing in the Life of Faith: Education and Christian Practices.* Louisville: Geneva Press, 1999.

—. "No Longer Strangers: The Church and its Educational Ministry." In *Theological Perspectives on Christian Formation: A Reader on Theology and Christian Education*, edited by Jeff Astley, Leslie J. Francis and Colin Crowder, 106–18. Herefordshire: Gracewing, 1996.

Eckerdal, Jan. *Kyrka i mission: Att gestalta kristen tro i en efterkristen tid.* [Church in mission: Shaping Christian faith in a post-Christian era]. Stockholm: Verbum, 2017.

Eek, Jonas. *Stanna i vattnet: Kateketikens syfte och sammanhang.* [Staying in the water: Purpose and context of catechetics]. Stockholm: Verbum, 2011.

Egli, Jim, and Joel Comiskey. *Groups that Thrive: 8 Surprising Discoveries About Life-giving Small Groups.* Moreno Valley: CCS Publishing, 2018.

Egli, Jim, and Dwight Marable. *Big Impact: Connecting People to God and One Another in Thriving Groups.* Apple Valley: ChurchSmart Resources, 2011.

Eikeland, Olav. "From Epistemology to Gnoseology: Understanding the Knowledge Claims of Action Research." *Management Research News* 30, no. 5 (2007): 344–58. *https://doi.org-/10.1108/01409170710746346.*

—. "Phrónêsis, Aristotle, and Action Research." *International Journal of Action Research* 2, no. 1 (2006): 5–53.

Elias, John. "Models of Theological Education for the Laity." *Journal of Adult Theological Education* 3, no. 2 (2006): 179–93. *https://doi.org/10.1558/jate.2006.3.2.179.*

Ellis, Carolyn, and Arthur P. Bochner, eds. *Composing Ethnography: Alternative Forms of Qualitative Writing.* Walnut Creek: AltaMira Press, 1996.

Engler, Steven. "Grounded Theory." In *The Routledge Handbook of Research Methods in the Study of Religion*, edited by Michael Stausberg and Steven Engler, 256–74. Oxon: Routledge, 2011.

Eriksson, Anne-Louise. *Att predika en tradition: Om tro och teologisk literacy.* [Preaching a tradition: On faith and theological literacy]. Lund: Arcus, 2012.

Farashahi, Mehdi, and Mahdi Tajeddin. "Effectiveness of Teaching Methods in Business Education: A Comparison Study on the Learning Outcomes of Lectures, Case Studies and Simulations." *The International Journal of Management Education* 16, no. 1 (2018): 131–42. *https://doi.org/10.1016/j.ijme.2018.01.003.*

Feldstein, Lewis M., and Robert D. Putnam. *Better Together: Restoring the American Community.* New York: Simon & Schuster, 2003.

Fenstermacher, Gary D. "Philosophy of Research on Teaching: Three Aspects." In *Handbook of Research on Teaching*, edited by Merlin C. Wittrock, 37–49. New York: MacMillan, 1986.

Flensner, Karin. "Dealing With and Teaching Controversial Issues: Teachers' Pedagogical Approaches to Controversial Issues in Religious Education and Social Studies." *Acta Didactica Norden* 14, no. 4 (2020): 1–21. *https://doi.org/10.5617/adno.8347.*

Flyvbjerg, Bent. "Five Misunderstandings about Case Study Research." *Qualitative Inquiry* 12, no. 2 (2006): 219–45. *https://doi.org/10.1177/1077800405284363.*

Fransson, Sara, ed. *Konfirmation i förändringens tid: En rapport om konfirmander och ledare 2007–2022.* [Confirmation in a time of change: A report on confirmands and leaders 2007–2022.]. Uppsala: Svenska kyrkan, 2023.

Freire, Paulo. "Education, Liberation and the church." In *Theological Perspectives on Christian Formation: A Reader on Theology and Christian Education*, edited by Jeff Astley, Leslie J. Francis and Colin Crowder, 169–86. Herefordshire: Gracewing, 1996.

—. *Pedagogy of the Oppressed.* Translated by Myra Bergman Ramos. New York: Penguin Random House, 2017 [1970].

Garpe, Sara, and Jonas Ideström, eds. *Kyrka i digitala rum: Ett aktionsforskningsprojekt om församlingsliv online i Svenska kyrkan.* [Church in digital space: An action research project on digital parish life in the Church of Sweden.]. Uppsala: Church of Sweden, 2022.

Garrison, D. Randy. "From Independence to Collaboration: A Personal Retrospective on Distance Education." In *An Introduction to Distance Education: Understanding Teaching and Learning in a New Era*, edited by Martha F. Cleveland-Innes and D. Randy Garrison, 13–24. Milton: Taylor and Francis, 2020.

Gayá Wicks, Patricia, Peter Reason, and Hilary Bradbury. "Living Inquiry: Personal, Political and Philosophical Groundings for Action Research Practice." In *The SAGE Handbook of Action Research: Participative Inquiry and Practice*, edited by Peter Reason and Hilary Bradbury, 15–30. London: SAGE Publications, 2008.

Geertz, Clifford. *The Interpretation of Cultures: Selected Essays*. Edited by Robert Darnton. 3rd ed. New York: Basic Books, 2017.

Ghodsee, Kristen Rogheh. *From Notes to Narrative: Writing Ethnographies that Everyone Can Read*. Chicago: The University of Chicago Press, 2016.

Gibbs, Graham, Trevor Habeshaw, and Mantz Yorke. "Institutional Learning and Teaching Strategies in English Higher Education." *Higher Education* 40, no. 3 (2000): 351–72.

Gin, Deborah H. C., Lester G. Brooke, and Barbara Blodgett. "Forum on Seminary Teaching and Formation Online." *Teaching Theology & Religion* 22, no. 1 (2019): 73–87. *https://doi.org/10.1111/teth.12473*.

Given, Lisa M. "Emergent Design." In *The SAGE Encyclopedia of Qualitative Research Methods*, edited by Lisa M. Given, 246–48. Thousand Oaks: SAGE Publications, Inc., 2008.

Goto, Courtney T. "Asian American Practical Theologies." In *Opening the Field of Practical Theology: An Introduction*, edited by Kathleen A. Cahalan and Gordon S. Mikoski, 31–44. Lanham: Rowman & Littlefield, 2014.

—. *The Grace of Playing: Pedagogies for Leaning into God's New Creation*. Eugene: Pickwick, 2016.

—. *Taking on Practical Theology: The Idolization of Context and the Hope of Community*. Leiden; Boston: Brill, 2018.

—. "The Ubiquity of Ignorance: A Practical Theological Challenge of Our Time." *Practical Theology* (2020): 138–49. *https://doi.org/10.1080/1756073X.2020.1728959*.

—. "Writing in Compliance with the Racialized 'Zoo' of Practical Theology." In *Conundrums in Practical Theology*, edited by Bonnie J. Miller-McLemore and Joyce Ann Mercer, 110–33. Leiden; Boston: Brill, 2016.

Graham, Elaine. "Is Practical Theology a Form of 'Action Research'?" *International Journal of Practical Theology* 17, no. 1 (2013): 148–78. *https://doi.org/10.1515/ijpt-2013-0010*.

Grant, Jill, Geoff Nelson, and Terry Mitchell. "Negotiating the Challenges of Participatory Action Research: Relationships, Power, Participation, Change and Credibility." In *The SAGE Handbook of Action Research: Participative Inquiry and Practice*, edited by Peter Reason and Hilary Bradbury, 589–601. London: SAGE Publications, 2008.

Greer, R. Douglas. *Designing Teaching Strategies: An Applied Behavior Analysis Systems Approach*. New York: Academic Press, 2002.

Grenholm, Carl-Henric. *Att förstå religion: metoder för teologisk forskning*. [Understanding religion: methods for theological research]. Lund: Studentlitteratur, 2006.

Groome, Thomas H. *Christian Religious Education: Sharing Our Story and Vision*. San Francisco: Jossey-Bass, 1980.

—. *Sharing Faith: A Comprehensive Approach to Religious Education and Pastoral Ministry: The Way of Shared Praxis*. Eugene: Wipf and Stock, 1998.

Gubi, Peter. "An Exploration of the Impact of Small Reflexive Groups on Personal and Spiritual Development." *Practical Theology* 4, no. 1 (2011): 49–66. *https://doi.org/10.1558/prth.v4i1.49*.

Gustavsen, Bjørn, Agneta Hansson, and Thoralf U. Qvale. "Action Research and the Challenge of Scope." In *The SAGE Handbook of Action Research: Participative Inquiry and Practice*, edited by Peter Reason and Hilary Bradbury, 63–76. London: SAGE Publications, 2008.

Gustavsson [Klintborg], Caroline. *Delaktighetens kris: Gudstjänstens pedagogiska utmaning.* [The crisis of participation: The educational challenge of worship]. Skellefteå: Artos, 2015.

—. *En process på riktigt: Lärande och undervisning i Västerås pastorat 2018: Redovisning av ett forskningsprojekt.* [A real process: Learning and teaching in Västerås Parish 2018: Report of a research project]. Västerås: Västerås pastorat, 2019.

—. "Mellan verklighet och vision: En diskursanalys av Riktlinjer för Svenska kyrkans konfirmandarbete." [Between reality and vision: A discourse analysis of the Guidelines for the Church of Sweden's confirmation work.] *Prismet* 67, no. 3 (2016): 201–14.

—. "Religionspedagogik: Ett forskningsfält i tiden." [Religous Education: Current Review of a Field of Research.] *Nordic Journal of Practical Theology* 37, no. 1 (2020): 78–89.

Gwyther, Gabrielle, and Alphia Possamai-Inesedy. "Methodologies à la Carte: An Examination of Emerging Qualitative Methodologies in Social Research." *International Journal of Social Research Methodology* 12, no. 2 (2009): 99–115. *https://doi.org/10.1080/13645570902727680.*

Haarlammert, Miryam, Dina Birman, Ashmeet Oberoi, and Wendy Jordana Moore. "Inside-Out: Representational Ethics and Diverse Communities." *American Journal of Community Psychology* 60, no. 3–4 (2017): 414–23. *https://doi.org/10.1002/ajcp.12188.*

Hall, Emma, and Bodil Liljefors Persson, eds. *Religionsdidaktik: I teori och praktik.* [Religious Education: In theory and practice.]. Malmö: Föreningen lärare i religionskunskap, 2010.

Halldorf, Joel. *Gud: Återkomsten.* [God: The Return]. Bromma: Libris, 2018.

Hallonsten, Simon. "Digitala samtalsgrupper för vuxna." [Church in Digital Space: An Action Research Project on Digital Parish Life in the Church of Sweden]. In *Kyrka i digitala rum: Ett aktionsforskningsprojekt om församlingsliv online i Svenska kyrkan* [Church in digital space: An action research project on digital parish life in the Church of Sweden], edited by Sara Garpe and Jonas Ideström, 82–98. Uppsala: Svenska kyrkan, 2022.

Hallonsten, Simon, and Jonas Ideström. "Kyrka i digitala rum: Reflektioner från ett forskningsprojekt." [Church in digital space: Reflections from a research project.] *Svensk Kyrkotidning* 117, no. 10 (2021).

Halvarson Britton, Thérèse. "Studiebesök i religionskunskapsundervisningen: Elevers tal om islam före, under och efter ett moskébesök." [Field Visists in Religious Education: Students Expressions about Islam Before, During and After a Visit to a Mosque.], Licentiate thesis, Karlstads universitet, 2014.

Haraway, Donna. "Situated Knowledges: The Science Question in Feminism and the Privilege of Partial Perspective." *Feminist Studies* 14, no. 3 (1988): 575–99. *https://doi.org/10.2307/3178066.*

Harder, Cameron. "Using Participatory Action Research in Seminary Internships." *Theological Education* 42, no. 2 (2007): 127–39.

Hart, Jack. *Storycraft: The Complete Guide to Writing Narrative Nonfiction.* Second ed. Chicago: University of Chicago Press, 2021.

Hartman, Sven, and Tullie Torstenson-Ed. *Barns tankar om livet.* [Children's thoughts about life]. Stockholm: Natur & Kultur, 2007.

Hauerwas, Stanley. "The Gesture of a Truthful Story." In *Theological Perspectives on Christian Formation: A Reader on Theology and Christian Education*, edited by Jeff Astley, Leslie J. Francis and Colin Crowder, 97–105. Herefordshire: Gracewing, 1996.

Hauge, Trond Eiliv. *Å planlegge og designe undervisning.* [To plan and design teaching]. Oslo: Capelen Damm, 2018.

Headley, Selena D. "A Praxis-Based Approach to Theological Training in Cape Town." *HTS Teologiese Studies/Theological Studies* 74, no. 3 (2018): 1–7.

Hedman, Anders. *Undervisa i kristen tro.* [Teaching the christian faith]. Varberg: Argument, 2015.

Helgesson Kjellin, Kristina. *En bra plats att vara på: En antropologisk studie av mångfaldsarbete och identitetsskapande inom Svenska kyrkan.* [A good place to be: An anthropological study of diversity work and identity creation in the Church of Sweden.]. Skellefteå: Artos & Norma, 2016.

Hendricks, Cher C. "History of Action Research in Education." In *The Wiley Handbook of Action Research in Education,* edited by Craig A. Mertler, 29–51. Newark: John Wiley & Sons, 2019.

Heron, John, and Peter Reason. "A Participatory Inquiry Paradigm." *Qualitative Inquiry* 3, no. 3 (1997): 274–94. *https://doi.org/10.1177/107780049700300302.*

Herr, Kathryn, and Gary L. Anderson. *The Action Research Dissertation: A Guide for Students and Faculty.* Thousand Oaks: SAGE Publications, 2012.

—. "Designing the Plane while Flying it: Proposing and doing the Dissertation." In *The Action Research Dissertation: A Guide for Students and Faculty,* 70–88. Thousand Oaks: SAGE Publications, 2012.

—. "Quality Criteria for Action Research: An Ongoing Conversation." In *The Action Research Dissertation: A Guide for Students and Faculty,* 49–68. Thousand Oaks: SAGE Publications, 2012.

Herring, Tina J., and M. Lynn Woolsey. "Three Suggested Teaching Strategies for Students Who are Deaf or Hard of Hearing." *Support for Learning* 35, no. 3 (2020): 346–58. *https://doi.org/10.1111/1467-9604.12314.*

Hess, Carol Lakey. "Educating in the Spirit." In *Theological Perspectives on Christian Formation: A Reader on Theology and Christian Education,* edited by Jeff Astley, Leslie J. Francis and Colin Crowder, 119–31. Grand Rapids: Eerdmans Publishing Company, 1996.

Hiim, Hilde, and Else Marie Hippe. *Undervisningsplanlegging for yrkesfaglærere.* [Teaching design for vocational teachers]. 4th ed. Copenhagen: Gyldendal, 2021.

Hill, Janette R., Liyan Song, and Richard E. West. "Social Learning Theory and Web-Based Learning Environments: A Review of Research and Discussion of Implications." *American Journal of Distance Education* 23, no. 2 (2009): 88–103. *https://doi.org/10.1080-/08923640902857713.*

Hines, Travis S., Thomas R. McGee, Lee "Rusty" Waller, and Sharon Kay Waller. "Online Theological Education: A Case Study of Trinity School for Ministry." *Christian Higher Education* 8, no. 1 (2008): 32–41. *https://doi.org/10.1080/15363750802201284.*

Hirst, Paul H. *Knowledge and the Curriculum: A Collection of Philosophical Papers.* London: Routledge, 1974.

Hockridge, Diane. "What's the Problem? Spiritual Formation in Distance and Online Theological Education." *Journal of Christian Education* os-54, no. 1 (2011): 25–38. *https://-doi.org/10.1177/002196571105400104.*

Hollenweger, Walter J. "Efficiency and Human Values: A Theological Action-Research-Report on Co-Decision in Industry." *Expository Times* 86, no. 8 (1975): 228–32. *https://doi.org-/10.1177/001452467508600803.*

Holley, Raymond. "Learning Religion." In *Critical Perspectives on Christian Education: A Reader on the Aims, Principles and Philosophy of Christian Education*, edited by Jeff Astley and Leslie J. Francis, 76–84. Herefordshire: Gracewing, 1994.

Holmberg, Andreas. *Gud såg att det var gott: Att vara människa och kyrka i klimatnödens tid.* [God saw that it was good: Being human and church in times of climate emergency]. Stockholm: Verbum, 2023.

—. *Kyrka i nytt landskap: En studie av levd ecklesiologi i Svenska kyrkan.* [Church in a new landscape: A study of lived ecclesiology in the Church of Sweden]. Skellefteå: Artos Academic, 2019.

Holmqvist Lidh, Carina. "Representera och bli representerad: Elever med religiös positionering talar om skolans religionskunskapsundervisning." [To Represent and to be represented: Students with religious positioning speak about the school's religious education], Licentiate thesis, Karlstads universitet, 2016.

Holmqvist, Morten. "Learning Religion: Exploring Young People's Participation Through Timespace and Mediation at Confirmation Camp." *Mind, Culture, and Activity* 22, no. 3 (2015): 201–16. *https://doi.org/10.1080/10749039.2015.1026446.*

—. "The Material Logics of Confirmation." *International Journal of Actor-Network Theory and Technological Innovation* 6, no. 4 (2014): 26–37. *https://doi.org/10.4018/ijantti.2014100103.*

Holton, Elwood F., Richard A. Swanson, and Sharon S. Naquin. "Andragogy in Practice: Clarifying the Andragogical Model of Adult Learning." *Performance Improvement Quarterly* 14, no. 1 (2001): 118–43. *https://doi.org/10.1111/j.1937-8327.2001.tb00204.x.*

hooks, bell. *Teaching to Transgress: Education as the Practice of Freedom.* New York: Routledge, 1994.

Hunter-Bowman, Janna L. "Representation and Intersectionality." In *The Wiley Blackwell Companion to Theology and Qualitative Research*, edited by Pete Ward and Knut Tveitereid, 141–50. Oxford: Wiley Blackwell, 2022.

Husebø, Dag, Øystein Lund Johannessen, and Geir Skeie. "Impact of Action Research in Norwegian Religious Education." *British Journal of Religious Education* (2022): 45–56. *https://doi.org/10.1080/01416200.2022.2049207.*

Hussey, Ian. "Investigating High Levels of Small Group Participation in Churches: Case Study Research from Australia." *Practical Theology* (2019): 1–13. *https://doi.org/10.1080/1756073X.2019.1636478.*

Ideström, Jonas. "Action Research and Theology." In *The Wiley Blackwell Companion to Theology and Qualitative Research*, edited by Pete Ward and Knut Tveitereid, 425–34. Oxford: Wiley Blackwell, 2022.

—. *Folkkyrkotanken: Innehåll och utmaningar: En översikt av studier under 2000-talet.* [Folk church: Content and challenges: An overview of studies in the 21st century]. Uppsala: Svenska kyrkan, 2012.

—. *Här får jag vara: En rapport från ett teologiskt forskningsprojekt om konfirmand- och ungdomsverksamheten i Vadstena och Dals församlingar.* [Here I may be: A report from a theological research project on confirmation and youth activities in Vadstena and Dal parishes.]. Linköping: Svenska kyrkan (Linköpings stift), 2019.

—. *Ikoniska kartor: Att göra teologi i kyrkans vardag.* [Iconic maps: Doing theology in everyday church life]. Stockholm: Verbum, 2021.

—. *Lokal kyrklig identitet: En studie av implicit ecklesiologi med exemplet Svenska kyrkan i Flemingsberg.* [Local church identity: A study of implicit ecclesiology with the example of the Church of Sweden in Flemingsberg]. Skellefteå: Artos & Norma, 2009.

Ideström, Jonas, and Stig Linde. "'Att famna komplexiteten': Aktionsforskning, teologi och organisatoriskt lärande." ['Embracing complexity': Action research, theology and organizational learning]. In *Aktionsforskning: Möjligheter, utmaningar och variationer* [Action research: Opportunities, challenges and variations], edited by Hanna Bertilsdotter Rosqvist, Magdalena Elmersjö and Lisa Kings, 171–99. Lund: Studentlitteratur, 2021.

—. "Det här är någonting vi måste göra: Ett teologiskt aktionsforskningsprojekt med Svenska kyrkan i Mölndal." [This is something we must do: A theological action research project with the Church of Sweden in Mölndal.] (Uppsala: Svenska kyrkans forskningsenhet, 2017).

—. "Welfare State Supporter and Civil Society Activist: Church of Sweden in the 'Refugee Crisis' 2015." *Social Inclusion* 7, no. 2 (2019): 4–13. *https://doi.org/10.17645/si.v7i2.1958.*

Ideström, Jonas, and Tone Stangeland Kaufman. "Hur framträder kyrkan i de digitala rummen? Kommunikation, teologi och folkkyrkotankar." [How does the church appear in the digital spaces? Communication, theology and the folk church]. In *Kyrka i digitala rum: Ett aktionsforskningsprojekt om församlingsliv online i Svenska kyrkan* [Church in digital space: An action research project on online parish life in the Church of Sweden], edited by Jonas Ideström and Sara Garpe, 30–42. Uppsala: Church of Sweden, 2022.

—, eds. *What Really Matters: Scandinavian Prspectives on Ecclesiology and Ethnography.* Eugene: Pickwick Publications, 2018.

—. "Whose Voice? Whose Church? Using Action Research in Practical Ecclesiology." In *Mending the world? Possibilities and Obstacles for Religion, Church, and Theology,* edited by Niclas Blåder and Kristina Helgesson Kjellin, 486–502. Eugene: Pickwick Publications, 2017.

Illeris, Knud. "A Comprehensive Understanding of Human Learning." In *Contemporary Theories of Learning: Learning Theorists... in Their Own Words,* edited by Knud Illeris, 1–14. Oxon: Routledge, 2018.

—, ed. *Contemporary Theories of Learning: Learning Theorists... in Their Own Words.* 2nd ed. Oxon: Routledge, 2018.

—. "An Overview of the History of Learning Theory." *European Journal of Education* 53, no. 1 (2018): 86–101. *https://doi.org/10.1111/ejed.12265.*

Ingold, Tim. "That's Enough about Ethnography." *HAU Journal of Ethnographic Theory* 4, no. 1 (2014): 383–95. *https://doi.org/10.14318/hau4.1.021.*

Jarvis, Peter. *Adult Learning in the Social Context.* Oxon: Routledge, 1987.

—. "Learning to Be a Person: East and West." *Comparative Education* 49, no. 1 (2013): 4–15. *https://doi.org/10.1080/03050068.2012.740216.*

—. "Religious Experience and Experiential Learning." *Religious Education* 103, no. 5 (2008): 553–67. *https://doi.org/10.1080/00344080802427200.*

Johannessen, Øystein Lund. "Negotiating and Reshaping Christian Values and Professional Identities through Action Research: Experiential Learning and Professional Development among Christian Religious Education Teachers." *Educational Action Research* 23, no. 3 (2015): 331–49. *https://doi.org/10.1080/09650792.2015.1009141.*

Jones, Serene. *Feminist Theory and Christian Theology: Cartographies of Grace.* Minneapolis: Augsburg Fortress, 2000.

Kappelgaard, Dorte. "Kirke i bevægelse: At understøtte lokal udvikling af kontekstuelle kirkelige praksisser." [Church in motion: Supporting the local development of contextual ecclesial practices.] PhD, Københavns Universitet, 2021.

Kawulich, Barbara B. "Participant Observation as a Data Collection Method." *Forum Qualitative Sozialforschung / Forum: Qualitative Social Research* 6, no. 2 (2005): 1–28. *https://doi.org/https://doi.org/10.17169/fqs-6.2.466.*

Kemmis, Stephen. "Critical Theory and Participatory Action Research." In *The SAGE Handbook of Action Research: Participative Inquiry and Practice*, edited by Peter Reason and Hilary Bradbury, 121–38. London: SAGE Publications, 2008.

Kemmis, Stephen, Robin McTaggart, and Rhonda Nixon. *The Action Research Planner: Doing Critical Participatory Action Research*. Singapore: Springer, 2014.

Kierstin, M. Giunco, Rosen-Reynoso Myra, A. Friedman Audrey, J. Hunter Cristina, and T. Cownie Charles, III. "Lessons From the Field: Catholic School Educators and COVID-19." *Journal of Catholic education* 23, no. 1 (2020): 243–67. *https://doi.org/10.15365/joce.2301172020.*

Killen, Roy. *Teaching Strategies for Quality Teaching and Learning*. Claremont: Juta, 2010.

Klintborg, Caroline. *Vägen är allt: En introduktion till religionspedagogik för den kristna församlingen.* [The way is everything: An Introduction to religious education for the christian congregation]. Varberg: Argument, 2021.

—. *Var är Jesus? Ungas röster om konfirmandundervisning.* [Where is Jesus? Young people's voices about confirmation training]. Stockholm: Verbum, 2023.

Klintborg, Caroline, and Sara Fransson. "Metodernas (icke-) betydelse? Ett religionspedagogiskt perspektiv." [The (Non-)Importance of Methods? A Religious Education Perspective]. In *Konfirmation i förändringens tid* [Confirmation in times of change], edited by Sara Fransson, 77–93. Uppsala: Church of Sweden, 2023.

Knoetze, Johannes J. "Online Theological Education within the South African Context." *HTS Teologiese Studies / Theological Studies* 78, no. 1 (2022): 1–7. *https://doi.org/10.4102/hts.v78i1.7232.*

Knorr Cetina, Karin. "Objectual Practice." In *The Practice Turn in Contemporary Theory*, edited by Karin Knorr Cetina, Theodore R. Schatzki and Eike von Savigny, 175–88. London: Routledge, 2001.

Knowles, Malcolm S., Elwood F. Holton III, and Richard A. Swanson. *The Adult Learner: The Definitive Classic in Adult Education and Human Resource Development.* 6th ed. London: Elsevier, 2005.

Kolb, David A. *Experiential Learning: Experience as the Source of Learning and Development.* 2nd ed. New Jersey: Pearson Education, 2015.

Koukounaras Liagkis, Marios. "The Socio-Pedagogical Dynamics of Religious Knowledge in Religious Education: A Participatory Action-Research in Greek Secondary Schools on Understanding Diversity." *Religions* 13, no. 5 (2022): 395–52. *https://doi.org/10.3390/rel13050395.*

Kullberg, Angelika, and Christina Skodras. "Systematic Variation in Examples in Mathematics Teaching." In *Didactic Classroom Studies: A Potential Research Direction*, edited by Christina Osbeck, Åke Ingerman and Silwa Claesson, 47–65. Lund: Nordic Academic Press, 2018.

Lang, James A., and David J. Bochman. "Positive Outcomes of a Discipleship Process." *Journal of Spiritual Formation and Soul Care* 10, no. 1 (2017): 51–72. *https://doi.org/10.1177/19397909170100005.*

Larsson, Rune. *Församlingspedagogik: en kyrka som undervisar genom hela sitt liv.* [Congregational pedagogy: A church that teaches throughout its life]. Stockholm, Sverige: Books on demand, 2018.

—. *Medvandrare: Vägmärken i religionspedagogiken.* [Fellow travelers: Waymarks in religious pedagogy]. Stockholm: BoD – Books on Demand, 2019.

—. "Modeller för undervisning." [Models for teaching]. In *Livsnära: Teori och praktik kring kyrkans bibelundervisning* [Close to life: Theory and practice of biblical education in the Church], edited by Carl Eber Olivestam, 38–62. Umeå: Umeå University, 1995.

—. *Samtal vid brunnar: Introduktion till religionspedagogikens teori och didaktik.* [Conversations at wells: Introduction to the theory and didactics of religious education]. Lund: Arcus, 2009.

Larsson, Rune, Carl Eber Olivestam, and Björn Wiedel. *Livsnära: Teori och praktik kring kyrkans bibelundervisning.* [Close to life: theory and practice around the church's Bible teaching]. Umeå: Institutionen för religionsvetenskap, 1995.

Larsson, Staffan. *Vuxendidaktik: Fjorton tankelinjer i forskningen om vuxnas lärande.* [Adult education: Fourteen lines of thought in adult learning research]. Stockholm: Natur & Kultur, 2013.

Latini, Theresa F. *The Church and the Crisis of Community: A Practical Theology of Small-Group Ministry.* Grand Rapids: William B. Eerdmans, 2011.

Leganger-Krogstad, Heid. "The Characteristics of Non-Formal Religious Education in a Folk Church: The Norwegian Education Reform." In *Researching Non-Formal Religious Education in Europe*, edited by Friedrich Schweitzer, Wolfgang Ilg and Peter Schreiner, 51–70. Münster: Waxmann, 2019.

Lenette, Caroline. *Participatory Action Research: Ethics and Decolonization.* Oxford: Oxford University Press, 2022.

Lincoln, Yvonna S. "Ethical Practices in Qualitative Research." In *The Handbook of Social Research Ethics*, edited by Donna M. Mertens and Pauline E. Ginsberg, 150–69. Thousand Oaks: SAGE Publications, Inc., 2009.

Lincoln, Yvonna S., Susan A. Lynham, and Egon G. Guba. "Paradigmatic Controversies, Contradictions, and Emerging Confluences, Revisited." In *The SAGE Handbook of Qualitative Research*, edited by Norman K. Denzin and Yvonna S. Lincoln, 213–63. Los Angeles: Sage Publications, 2018.

Liu Wong, Maria. *On Becoming Wise Together: Learning and Leading in the City.* Grand Rapids: William. B. Eerdmans Publishing Company, 2023.

Löfstedt, Malin. *Religionsdidaktik: Mångfald, livsfrågor och etik i skolan.* [Religious didactics: Diversity, life issues and ethics in school]. Lund: Studentlitteratur, 2011.

Löfstedt, Malin, and Katarina Westerlund. "Turning to Practice in Academic Theology and Religious Studies: Research Circles as an Example." *Studia Theologica* 75, no. 1 (2021): 79–98. *https://doi.org/10.1080/0039338X.2021.1917158.*

Löfstedt, Torsten, and Roland Hallgren, eds. *Religionsdidaktiska studier.* [Studies in the didactics of religion.]. Växjö: Linnaeus University Press, 2015.

Lourenço, Orlando. "Piaget, Jean." In *Encyclopedia of Educational Theory and Philosophy*, edited by Denis C. Phillips, 624–28. Thousand Oaks: SAGE Publications, 2014.

Lovat, Terence J. "Action Research and the Praxis Model of Religious Education: A Critique." *British Journal of Religious Education* 11, no. 1 (1988): 30–37. *https://doi.org/10.1080-/0141620880110106.*

Lovell, George. *The Church and Community Development: An Introduction.* Pinner: Grail Publications, 1972.

Lundie, David, Waqaus Ali, Michael Ashton, Sue Billingsley, Hinnah Heydari, Karamat Iqbal, Kate McDowell, and Matthew Thompson. "A Practitioner Action Research Approach to Learning Outside the Classroom in Religious Education: Developing a Dialogical Model Through Reflection by Teachers and Faith Field Visitors." *British Journal of Religious Education* 44, no. 2 (2021): 138–48. *https://doi.org/10.1080/01416200.2021.1969896.*

Lykke, Nina, ed. *Writing Academic Texts Differently: Intersectional Feminist Methodologies and the Playful Art of Writing.* New York: Routledge, 2014.

Maddix, Mark A. "Developing Online Learning Communities." *Christian Education Journal* 10, no. 1 (2013): 139–48. *https://doi.org/10.1177/073989131301000111.*

Maddix, Mark A., and James R. Estep. "Spiritual Formation in Online Higher Education Communities: Nurturing Spirituality in Christian Higher Education Online Degree Programs." *Christian Education Journal* 7, no. 2 (2010): 423–34. *https://doi.org/10.1177/0739-8913100700212.*

Mambo, Alice W. "The Rationale Motive of Adult Christians' Participation in Education Programs among Episcopal Churches in Southern California." *Christian Education Journal* 16, no. 1 (2019): 7–25. *https://doi.org/10.1177/0739891318816105.*

Mannerfelt, Frida. "Co-preaching: The Practice of Preaching in Digital Culture and Space." PhD, Stockholm School of Theology, 2023.

Mannerfelt, Frida, and Rikard Roitto. "Mellan rit och reklam del 1: Berättelsen om två församlingars utveckling." [Between rite and advertising part 1: The story of the development of two parishes]. In *Kyrka i digitala rum: Ett aktionsforskningsprojekt om församlingsliv online i Svenska kyrkan* [Church in digital space: An action research project on online parish life in the Church of Sweden], edited by Sara Garpe and Jonas Ideström, 46–59. Uppsala: Church of Sweden, 2022.

—. "Mellan rit och reklam del 2: Interaktion, synkronicitet och integritet i förinspelade digitalt förmedlade andakter." [Between rite and advertising part 2: Interaction, synchronicity and privacy in pre-recorded digitally mediated devotions]. In *Kyrka i digitala rum: Ett aktionsforskningsprojekt om församlingsliv online i Svenska kyrkan* [Church in digital space: An action research project on online parish life in the Church of Sweden], edited by Sara Garpe and Jonas Ideström, 60–78. Uppsala: Church of Sweden, 2022.

Marshall, Judi. "Finding Form in Writing for Action Research." In *The SAGE Handbook of Action Research: Participative Inquiry and Practice*, edited by Peter Reason and Hilary Bradbury, 682–94. London: SAGE Publications, 2008.

Marshall, Judi, and Peter Reason. "Adult Learning in Collaborative Action Research: Reflections on the Supervision Process." *Studies in Continuing Education* 15, no. 2 (1993): 117–32. *https://doi.org/10.1080/0158037930150204.*

—. "Quality in Research as 'Taking an Attitude of Inquiry'." *Management Research News* 30, no. 5 (2007): 368–80. *https://doi.org/10.1108/01409170710746364.*

Martin, Bruce. "'Living' Education: Action Research as a Practical Approach to Congregational Education." *Religious Education* 95, no. 2 (2000): 151–66. *https://doi.org/10.1080/0034408-000950204.*

—. "Transforming a Local Church Congregation through Action Research." *Educational Action Research* 9, no. 2 (2001): 261–78. *https://doi.org/10.1080/09650790100200152.*

Martin, Dean M. "Learning to Become a Christian." In *Critical Perspectives on Christian Education: A Reader on the Aims, Principles and Philosophy of Christian Education*, edited by Jeff Astley and Leslie J. Francis, 184–201. Herefordshire: Gracewing, 1994.

Martin, Florence, Ting Sun, and Carl D. Westine. "A Systematic Review of Research on Online Teaching and Learning from 2009 to 2018." *Computers & Education* 159 (2020): 1–17. *https://doi.org/10.1016/j.compedu.2020.104009*.

Mawerenga, Jones H., and Johannes J. Knoetze. "Theological Education and the COVID-19 Pandemic in Sub-Saharan Africa: A Malawian Perspective." *In die Skriflig* 56, no. 1 (2022): 1–10. *https://doi.org/10.4102/ids.v56i1.2792*.

McClintock Fulkerson, Mary. *Places of Redemption: Theology for a Worldly Church*. Oxford: Oxford University Press, 2007.

McGuire, Beverley. "Principles for Effective Asynchronous Online Instruction in Religious Studies: Asynchronous Online Instruction." *Teaching Theology and Religion* 20, no. 1 (2017): 28–45. *https://doi.org/10.1111/teth.12363*.

McVey, Mary K., and Susan R. Poyo. "Preparing Catholic Educators to Educate and Evangelize in 21st Century Schools: Action Research of an Analysis of Educator Preparation Program Requirements Including Professional and Pedagogical, Relational, Formational and Evangelistic Education for P-16 Students (PROFEss)." *Catholic Education* 22, no. 2 (2019): 107–18. *https://doi.org/10.15365/joce.2202062019*.

Mezirow, Jack, ed. *Learning as Transformation: Critical Perspectives on a Theory in Progress*. San Francisco: Jossey-Bass, 2000.

Miller-McLemore, Bonnie J. *Also a Mother: Work and Family as Theological Dilemma*. Nashville: Abingdon Press, 1994.

Minor, Cheryl V., and Hannah Sutton-Adams. "Godly Play Went Home: An Exploratory Study of the Experience of Godly Play in Homes during the Covid-19 Pandemic through the Lens of Caregivers." *Religious Education* 117, no. 4 (2022): 313–23. *https://doi.org/10.1080-/00344087.2022.2101814*.

Moisés Peña-Lévano, Luis, and Grace Melo. "Adaptation of Teaching Strategies during the COVID-19 Pandemic." *Applied Economics Teaching Resources* 4, no. 1 (2022): 12–33.

Moore, Michael G. "Three Types of Interaction." *American Journal of Distance Education* 3, no. 2 (1989): 1–7.

Moore, Michael Grahame. "The Theory of Transactional Distance." In *Handbook of Distance Education*, edited by Michael Grahame Moore, 66–85. New York: Routledge, 2013.

Moore, Pamela C. "Instructional Designers and Online Theological Education: May We Help You?" *Theological Education* 52, no. 2 (2019): 13–24.

Mostowlansky, Till, and Andrea Rota. "A Matter of Perspective? Disentangling the Emic–Etic Debate in the Scientific Study of Religion\s." *Method & Theory in the Study of Religion* 28, no. 4–5 (2016): 317–36.

Mudge, Peter. "'In the Land of the Blind, the One-Eyed Is King': Some Pedagogical Foundations for Deep, Practical Online Student Learning." *Journal of Adult Theological Education* 12, no. 2 (2015): 106–20. *https://doi.org/10.1179/1740714115Z.00000000040*.

Müller, Julian, John Eliastam, and Sheila Trahar, eds. *Unfolding Narratives of Ubuntu in Southern Africa*. London: Routledge, 2019.

Mullino Moore, Mary Elizabeth. *Teaching as a Sacramental Act*. Cleveland: The Pilgrim Press, 2004.

Nabhan-Warren, Kristy, and Natalie Wigg-Stevenson. "Situating the 'Crisis of Representation' in Ethnographic Approaches to Theology and Working Toward Community-Centered, Dialogic Approaches." *Ecclesial Practices* 8, no. 2 (2021): 123–28. *https://doi.org/10.1163-/22144471-bja10032*.

Nahnfeldt, Cecilia. "'Tu veux un chewing-gum?' Encounters in Hospitality and Willfulness." In *Contemporary Christian-Cultural Values*, edited by Cecilia Nahnfeldt and Kaia S. Rønsdal, 61–78. London: Routledge, 2021.

"Educational Research Journal." National Foundation for Educational Research, 2023, accessed Sep 25, 2023, *https://www.nfer.ac.uk/publications-research/educational-research-journal/*.

Nichols, Mark. "The Akadameia as Paradigm for Online Community in Theological Distance Education." *Journal of Christian Education* 54, no. 1 (2011): 5–23. *https://doi.org/10.1177-/002196571105400102*.

Nicolini, Davide. *Practice Theory, Work, and Organization: An Introduction.* Oxford: Oxford University Press, 2013.

Noddings, Nel. "Is Teaching a Practice?" *Journal of Philosophy of Education* 37, no. 2 (2003): 241–51. *https://doi.org/10.1111/1467-9752.00323*.

Norlin, Björn. "Kyrkan och samiska kulturella uttryck." [Church and sami cultural expressions]. In *Samerna och Svenska kyrkan: Underlag för kyrkligt försoningsarbete* [The Sami and the Church of Sweden: A basis for church reconciliation work], edited by Daniel Lindmark and Olle Sundström, 51–63. Möklinta: Gidlunds, 2017.

—. "Kyrkan, missionen och skolan." [Church, mission, and school]. In *Samerna och Svenska kyrkan: Underlag för kyrkligt försoningsarbete* [The Sami and the Church of Sweden: A basis for church reconciliation work], edited by Daniel Lindmark and Olle Sundström, 37–50. Möklinta: Gidlunds, 2017.

O'Grady, Kevin. "Researching Religious Education Pedagogy through an Action Research Community of Practice." *British Journal of Religious Education* 32, no. 2 (2010): 119–31. *https://doi.org/10.1080/01416200903537381*.

Olivestam, Carl Eber. *Religionsdidaktik: Om teori, perspektiv och praktik i religionsundervisningen.* [Didactics of religion: Theory, perspectives and practice in religious education]. Stockholm: Remus, 2012.

Ong, Walter J. *Orality and Literacy: The Technologizing of the Word.* 30th ed. Abingdon, Oxon: Routledge, 2012.

Orteza y Miranda, Evelina. "Some Problems with the Expression 'Christian Education'." In *Critical Perspectives on Christian Education: A Reader on the Aims, Principles and Philosophy of Christian Education*, edited by Jeff Astley and Leslie J. Francis, 16–28. Herefordshire: Gracewing, 1994.

Osbeck, Christina. *Att förstå livet: Religionsdidaktik och lärande i diskursiva praktiker.* [Understanding life: Religious education and learning in discursive practices]. Uppsala: Church of Sweden, 2009.

—. "Questions and Speech Genres in Social Studies Classrooms: Comparisons of Communication Patterns." In *Didactic Classroom Studies: A Potential Research Direction*, edited by Christina Osbeck, Åke Ingerman and Silwa Claesson, 23–45. Lund: Nordic Academic Press, 2018.

Osbeck, Christina, and Åke Ingerman. "A Potential Research Direction for Didactic Classroom Studies." In *Didactic Classroom Studies: A Potential Research Direction*, edited by Christina Osbeck, Åke Ingerman and Silwa Claesson, 193–223. Lund: Nordic Academic Press, 2018.

Osbeck, Christina, Åke Ingerman, and Silwa Claesson, eds. *Didactic Classroom Studies: A Potential Research Direction.* Lund: Nordic Academic Press, 2018.

—. "An Introduction to Didactic Classroom Studies." In *Didactic Classroom Studies: A Potential Research Direction,* edited by Christina Osbeck, Åke Ingerman and Silwa Claesson, 9–20. Lund: Nordic Academic Press, 2018.

Osmer, Richard Robert. *Practical Theology: An Introduction.* Grand Rapids: William B. Eerdmans Pub. Co., 2008.

Oxford English Dictionary. Oxford University Press, 2023.

Paavola, Sami, and Kai Hakkarainen. "The Knowledge Creation Metaphor: An Emergent Epistemological Approach to Learning." *Science & Education* 14 (2005): 535–57. *https://-doi.org/10.1007/s11191-004-5157-0.*

Palloff, Rena M., and Keith Pratt. *Collaborating Online: Learning Together in Community.* Hoboken: Jossey-Bass, 2005.

Parker, Stephen G. "Religion and Education: Framing and Mapping the Field." *Religion and Education* 1, no. 1 (2019): 6–16.

Pierce-Friedman, Kathleen, and Laurie Wellner. "Faculty Professional Development in Creating Significant Teaching and Learning Experiences Online." In *Handbook of Research on Creating Meaningful Experiences in Online Courses,* edited by Lydia Kyei-Blankson, Esther Ntuli and Joseph Blankson, 1–13. Hershey: IGI Global, 2020.

Popil, Inna. "Promotion of Critical Thinking by Using Case Studies as Teaching Method." *Nurse Education Today* 31, no. 2 (2011): 204–07. *https://doi.org/10.1016/j.nedt.2010.06.002.*

Porath Sjöö, Elisabeth. "Konfirmandernas bildningsresa: Ungdomars berättelser om sitt deltagande i konfirmandundervisningen." [Confirmands' educational journey: Young people's accounts of their participation in confirmation classes.] PhD, Lunds Universitet, 2008.

Porterfield, Michael, and E. Paulette Isaac-Savage. "The Formation of Online Wisdom Communities amongst Ministerial Students." *Journal of Adult Theological Education* 10, no. 2 (2013): 116–31. *https://doi.org/10.1179/1740714114Z.00000000018.*

Posner, George J. *Analyzing the Curriculum.* Boston: McGraw-Hill, 2004.

Radford Ruether, Rosemary. *Sexism and God-Talk: Toward a Feminist Theology.* Boston: Beacon Press, 1983.

Raider-Roth, Miriam, Amy Rector-Aranda, Tammy Kaiser, Liron Lipinsky, Alison Weikel, Sara Wolkenfeld, and Liat Zaidenberg. "Shared Power, Risk-taking, and Innovation: Participatory Action Research in Jewish Education." *Journal of Jewish Education* 85, no. 2 (2019): 187–208. *https://doi.org/10.1080/15244113.2019.1599234.*

Reason, Peter. "Choice and Quality in Action Research Practice." *Journal of Management Inquiry* 15, no. 2 (2006): 187–203. *https://doi.org/10.1177/1056492606288074.*

Reason, Peter, and Hilary Bradbury. "Introduction: Inquiry and Participation in Search of a World Worthy of Human Aspiration." In *Handbook of Action Research: Participative Inquiry and Practice,* edited by Peter Reason and Hilary Bradbury, 1–14. London: SAGE, 2001.

—, eds. *The SAGE Handbook of Action Research: Participative Inquiry and Practice.* 2nd ed. London: SAGE Publications, 2008.

Reason, Peter, and Judi Marshall. "Research as Personal Process." In *Appreciating Adults Learning: From the Learner's Perspective,* edited by David Boud and Virginia Griffin, 112–26. London: Kogan Page, 1987.

Reason, Peter, and William Torbert. "The Action Turn: Toward a Transformational Social Science." *Concepts and Transformation: International Journal of Action Research and Organizational Renewal* 6, no. 1 (2001): 1–37. *https://doi.org/10.1075/cat.6.1.02rea.*

Reckwitz, Andreas. "Toward a Theory of Social Practices: A Development in Culturalist Theorizing." *European Journal of Social Theory* 5, no. 2 (2002): 243–63.

Regan, Jane E. *Toward an Adult Church: A Vision of Faith Formation.* Chicago: Loyola Press, 2002.

—. *Where Two or Three Are Gathered: Transforming the Parish through Communities of Practice.* New York: Paulist Press, 2016.

Rhodes, Daniel P. "Theology as Social Activity: Theological Action Research and Teaching the Knowledge of Christian Ethics and Practical Ministry." *Scottish Journal of Theology* 73, no. 4 (2020): 340–57. *https://doi.org/10.1017/S0036930620000654.*

Richardson, Laurel. *Writing Strategies: Reaching Diverse Audiences.* Newbury Park, Calif.: Sage Publications, 1990.

Richardson, Laurel, and Elizabeth Adams St. Pierre. "Writing: A Method of Inquiry." In *The SAGE Handbook of Qualitative Research*, edited by Norman K. Denzin and Yvonna S. Lincoln, 1410–44. Los Angeles: Sage Publications, 2018.

Roest, Henk de. *Collaborative Practical Theology: Engaging Practitioners in Research on Christian Practices.* Leiden: Brill, 2020.

Root, Andrew. *Christopraxis: A Practical Theology of the Cross.* Minneapolis: Fortress Press, 2014.

—. *Faith Formation in a Secular Age: Responding to the Church's Obsession with Youthfulness.* Grand Rapids: Baker Academic, 2017.

Rosenius, Marie. *Delaktig i vilken mening? En teologisk analys av delaktighetsstrategier i svenskkyrkligt gudstjänstliv.* [Participation in what sense? A theological analysis of participation strategies in Church of Sweden worship services]. Skellefteå: Artos, 2021.

—. *Svenska kyrkan samma kyrka? Ecklesiologi före och efter relationsförändringen mellan kyrka och stat.* [Church of Sweden the same church? Ecclesiology before and after the change in church-state relations?]. Skellefteå: Artos, 2015.

Rosenius, Marie, and Thomas Girmalm. "Från folkbildning till fortbildning: Synen på lärande och kyrka i Luleå stifts herdabrev." [From Popular Education to Continuing Education: The View of Learning and Church in Luleå Diocese's Pastoral Letters.] *Svensk Teologisk Kvartalskrift* 95, no. 1 (2019): 17–32.

Ross, Cathy, and James Butler. "Encountering Our Own Whiteness: An Autoethnographic Conversation on the Experience of Putting Together a Journal Issue around Mission, Race and Colonialism." *Practical Theology* 15, no. 1–2 (2022): 148–59. *https://doi.org/10.1080/1756073X.2021.2023949.*

Rubenson, Karin. "Karnevalesk gudstjänst: Barns plats i kyrkans liturgi." [Carnival service: Children's place in the liturgy of the church.] PhD, Uppsala University, 2021.

Rune, Anders. "Slutrapport: Programmet för lärande och undervisning." [Final report: Program for learning and teaching.] Uppsala: Svenska kyrkan, 2023.

Säljö, Roger. *Lärande: En introduktion till perspektiv och metaforer.* [Learning: An introduction to perspectives and metaphors]. 2nd ed. Malmö: Gleerups, 2022.

Schuitema, Jaap, Geert ten Dam, and Wiel Veugelers. "Teaching Strategies for Moral Education: A Review." *Journal of Curriculum Studies* 40, no. 1 (2008): 69–89. *https://doi.org/10.1080/00220270701294210.*

Schweitzer, Friedrich, Wolfgang Ilg, and Peter Schreiner. "Introduction." In *Researching Non-Formal Religious Education in Europe*, edited by Friedrich Schweitzer, Wolfgang Ilg and Peter Schreiner, 7–16. Münster: Waxmann, 2019.

—, eds. *Researching Non-Formal Religious Education in Europe*. Münster: Waxmann, 2019.

Selçuk, Mualla, Hasan Sözen, Vahdeddin Şimşek, and Yasemin İpek. "The Online Learning Experience of Theology Students in Turkey during the COVID-19 Pandemic: A New Disposition for RE?" *Religious Education* 116, no. 1 (2021): 74–90. *https://doi.org/10.1080-/00344087.2021.1879987*.

Senthamarai, S. "Interactive Teaching Strategies." 3, no. Suppl. 1 (2018): S36–S38. *https://doi.org-/10.21839/jaar.2018.v3iS1.166*.

Sevensma, Kara, Marj Terpstra, Jack Gibson, Isabella Napitupulu, Elle Quist Nieuwsma, Meri Fuji Siahaan, and Yoolim Song. "Seeking a Scholarship of Pedagogy, Technology, and Faith: A Literature Survey." *International Journal of Christianity & Education* 22, no. 3 (2018): 252–73. *https://doi.org/10.1177/2056997118782514*.

Sfard, Anna. "On Two Metaphors for Learning and the Danger of Choosing Just One." *Educational Researcher* 27, no. 2 (1998): 4–13. *https://doi.org/10.2307/1176193*.

Shepherd, Nick. "Action Research as Professional Development: Educating for Performative Knowledge and Enhancing Theological Capital." *Journal of Adult Theological Education* 9, no. 2 (2012): 121–38. *https://doi.org/10.1179/ate.9.2.q17pq12031207v80*.

Siewert, Charles. "Consciousness and Intentionality." In *The Stanford Encyclopedia of Philosophy* edited by Edward N. Zalta: Metaphysics Research Lab, Stanford University, 2022.

Singh, Europe. "Learning Theory and Online Technologies." *Open Learning* 29, no. 1 (2014): 89–92. *https://doi.org/10.1080/02680513.2013.864550*.

Sjöborg, Anders. "Religious Education and Intercultural Understanding: Examining the Role of Religiosity for Upper Secondary Students' Attitudes Towards RE." *British Journal of Religious Education* 35, no. 1 (2013): 36–54. *https://doi.org/10.1080/01416200.2012.717015*.

Skeie, Geir. "Mangfoldets utfordringer og muligheter sett gjennom religionsdidaktisk forskning. Et nordisk overblikk." [The challenges and opportunities of diversity seen through religious didactic research: A nordic overview.] *Acta Didactica Norden* 11, no. 3 (2017): 1–23.

Slee, Nicola. *Fragments for Fractured Times: What Feminist Practical Theology Brings to the Table*. London: SCM Press, 2020.

Smith, Brian H. "Teaching Religion Online to Nontraditional Adult Learners." *Teaching Theology & Religion* 25, no. 2–3 (2022): 61–71. *https://doi.org/10.1111/teth.12622*.

Smith, Eric C. "Makeshifting the LMS: Strategies and Tactics in the Digital Classroom." *Theological Education* 52, no. 2 (2019): 25–42.

Snoeren, Miranda, Theo Niessen, and Tineke Abma. "Engagement Enacted: Essentials of Initiating an Action Research Project." *Action Research* 10, no. 2 (2012): 189–204. *https://doi.org/10.1177/1476750311426620*.

Somekh, Bridget. *Action Research: A Methodology for Change and Development*. Berkshire: McGraw-Hill Education, 2005.

Stahlke Wall, Sarah. "Toward a Moderate Autoethnography." *International Journal of Qualitative Methods* 15, no. 1 (2016): 1–9. *https://doi.org/10.1177/1609406916674966*.

Stangeland Kaufman, Tone. "From the Outside, Within, or In Between? Normativity at Work in Empirical Practical Theological Research." In *Conundrums in Practical Theology*, edited by Bonnie J. Miller-McLemore and Joyce Ann Mercer, 134–62. Leiden: Brill, 2016.

—. *A New Old Spirituality? A Qualitative Study of Clergy Spirituality in the Nordic Context.* Eugene: Pickwick Publications, 2017.

—. "Normativity as Pitfall or Ally? Reflexivity as an Interpretive Resource in Ecclesiological and Ethnographic Research." *Ecclesial Practices* 2, no. 1 (2015): 91–107. *https://doi.org/10.1163-/22144471-00201006.*

—. "The Researcher as Gamemaker: Teaching Normative Dimensions in Various Phases of Empirical Practical Theological Research." In *Qualitative Research in Theological Education: Pedagogy in Practice,* edited by Mary Clark Moschella and Susan Willhauck, 169–84. London: SCM Press, 2018.

Stark, J. David. "Gaming the System: Online Spiritual Formation in Christian Higher Education." *Theological Education* 52, no. 2 (2019): 43–54.

Stetzer, Ed, and Eric Geiger. *Transformational Groups: Creating a New Scorecard for Groups.* Nashville: B&H Books, 2014. EBSCOhost.

Store, Maria. *Kyrkan lär i förändring.* [The church learns through change]. Stockholm: Verbum, 2017.

Straarup, Jørgen, and Mayvor Ekberg. *Den sorglöst försumliga kyrkan belyst norrifrån.* [The carelessly neglected church illuminated from the north]. Skellefteå: Artos, 2012.

Supriyadi, Tedi, and J. Julia. "The Problem of Students in Reading the Quran: A Reflective-Critical Treatment through Action Research." *International Journal of Instruction* 12, no. 1 (2019): 311–26. *https://doi.org/10.29333/iji.2019.12121a.*

Svenska kyrkan. *Kyrkoordning för Svenska kyrkan.* [Church ordinance of the Church of Sweden]. Uppsala: Svenska kyrkan, 2023.

—. "Svenska kyrkans medlemsutveckling år 1972–2022." [Membership developments in the Church of Sweden 1972–2022.] (Uppsala: 2023). *https://www.svenskakyrkan.se/filer-/1374643/Medlemmar%20i%20Svenska%20kyrkan%201972-2022.pdf?id=2554894.*

Swedberg, Richard. "Exploratory Research." In *The Production of Knowledge: Enhancing Progress in Social Science,* edited by Colin Elman, John Gerring and James Mahoney, 17–41. Cambridge: Cambridge University Press.

—. "How to use Max Weber's ideal type in sociological analysis." *Journal of Classical Sociology* 18, no. 3: 181–96. *https://doi.org/10.1177/1468795X17743643.*

Swinton, John, and Harriet Mowat. *Practical Theology and Qualitative Research.* 2nd ed. London: SCM press, 2016.

Szőke-Milinte, Enikő. "Didactic Teaching Strategies for Successful Learning." *PedActa* 3, no. 2 (2013): 49–58.

Taylor, Charles. *Philosophical Papers: Volume 2: Philosophy and the Human Sciences.* Cambridge: Cambridge University Press, 1985.

Thidevall, Sven, ed. *Mindre folk – mer kyrka? Möjligheter för Svenska kyrkan i en postkristen tid: Rapport 2 från projektet 'Folkkyrka i minoritet'.* [Less folk – more church? Opportunities for the Church of Sweden in a post-christian era: Report 2 from the project 'Folkkyrka i minoritet'.]. Skellefteå: Artos, 2021.

—. *När kartan inte längre stämmer: Svenska kyrkans församlingar i ett samtidshistoriskt perspektiv.* [When the map no longer fits: Parishes of the Church of Sweden in a contemporary historical perspective]. Uppsala: Diakonivetenskapliga institutet, 2003.

Thomason, Steve. "Participatory Action Research as Trinitarian Praxis and a Pedagogical Model for the Suburban Congregation." *Religious Education* 113, no. 1 (2018): 96–108. *https://doi.org/10.1080/00344087.2017.1399851.*

Thurfjell, David. *Det gudlösa folket: De postkristna svenskarna och religionen.* [The godless people: Post-Christian Swedes and religion]. Stockholm: Molin & Sorgenfrei, 2015.

—. *Granskogsfolk: Hur naturen blev svenskarnas religion.* [Fir forest people: How nature became the Swedes' religion]. Stockholm: Norstedts, 2020.

Tobiason, Glory. "Going Small, Going Carefully, With a Friend: Helping Faculty Adopt Lesson-Level Constructive Alignment through Non-Evaluative Peer Observation." *Active Learning in Higher Education* 25, no. 1: 53–66. *https://doi.org/10.1177/14697874221092977.*

Todd, Andrew John. "The Talk, Dynamics and Theological Practice of Bible-Study Groups: A Qualitative Empirical Investigation." PhD, Cardiff University, 2009.

Townsend, Andrew. *Action Research: The Challenges of Understanding and Changing Practice.* New York: Open University Press, 2013.

Tracy, David. *The Analogical Imagination: Christian Theology and the Culture of Pluralism.* New York: Crossroad, 1981.

Trout, John, Paul R. Dokecki, J. R. Newbrough, and Robert T. O'Gorman. "Action Research on Leadership for Community Development in West Africa and North America: A Joining of Liberation Theology and Community Psychology." *Journal of Community Psychology* 31, no. 2 (2003): 129–48. *https://doi.org/10.1002/jcop.10043.*

Tveitereid, Knut. "Making Data Speak: The Shortage of Theory for the Analysis of Qualitative Data in Practical Theology." In *What Really Matters: Scandinavian Perspectives on Ecclesiology and Ethnography,* edited by Jonas Ideström and Tone Stangeland Kaufman, 41–57. Eugene: Pickwick Publications, 2018.

Tveito Johnsen, Elisabeth. "Christian Education as a Community of Strangers." In *The Wiley Blackwell Companion to Theology and Qualitative Research,* edited by Pete Ward and Knut Tveitereid, 340–50. Oxford: Wiley Blackwell, 2022.

—. "Gudstjenestelæring gjennom deltagelse." [Learning worship through participation]. In *Gudstjeneste på ny* [Service all over again], edited by Geir Hellemo, 151–77. Oslo: Universitetsforlaget, 2014.

—. "Hvordan medierer undervisningspreget trosopplæring kristen tro og tradisjon? En Vygotskij-inspirert analyse av læringssituasjoner i Den norske kirkes trosopplæring." [How does teaching-oriented faith education mediate Christian faith and tradition? A Vygotsky-inspired analysis of learning situations in the Church of Norway's faith education.] *Teologisk tidsskrift* 1, no. 2 (2012): 138–65. *https://doi.org/10.18261/ISSN1893-0271-2012-02-03.*

—. "Læring inn i den kristne religionen: Mediering og subjektivering." [Learning into the christian religion: Mediation and subjectivization.] *Prismet* 64, no. 3 (2013): 173–201.

—. "Religiøs læring i sosiale praksiser: En etnografisk studie av mediering, identifisering og forhandlingsprosesser i Den norske kirkes trosopplæring." [Religious learning in social practices: An ethnographic study of mediation, identification and negotiation processes in the Church of Norway's religious education.] PhD, Oslo University, 2014.

Tveito Johnsen, Elisabeth, and Geir Afdal. "Learning and Knowledge Trajectories in Congregations." *Praktische Theologie* 55, no. 2 (2020): 70–75.

—. "Practice Theory in Empirical Practical Theological Research: The Scientific Contribution of LETRA." *Nordic Journal of Practical Theology* 37, no. 2 (2020): 58–76.

Waltemeyer, Shaunna, and Jeff Cranmore. "Closing the Distance in Distance Learning." In *Handbook of Research on Creating Meaningful Experiences in Online Courses,* edited by Lydia Kyei-Blankson, Esther Ntuli and Joseph Blankson, 14–24. Hershey: IGI Global, 2020.

Walton, Heather. "The Course Outline: Teaching Theology through Creative Writing." *Journal of Adult Theological Education* 9, no. 2 (2012): 210–18. *https://doi.org/10.1179-/ate.9.2.pt25581169181731.*

—. "Creativity at the Edge of Chaos: Theopoetics in a Blazing World." *Literature & Theology* 33, no. 3 (2019): 336–56. *https://doi.org/10.1093/litthe/frz029.*

—. *Not Eden: Spiritual Life Writing for this World.* London: SCM Press, 2015.

—. "Passion and Pain: Conceiving Theology out of Infertility." *Contact* 130, no. 1 (1999): 3–9. *https://doi.org/10.1080/13520806.1999.11758874.*

—. "A Theopoetics in Ruins." *Toronto Journal of Theology* 36, no. 2 (2020): 159–69. *https://doi.org/10.3138/tjt-2020-0082.*

—. "A Theopoetics of Practice: Re-forming in Practical Theology." *International Journal of Practical Theology* 23, no. 1 (2019): 3–23. *https://doi.org/10.1515/ijpt-2018-0033.*

—. "We Have Never Been Theologians: Postsecularism and Practical Theology." *Practical Theology* 11, no. 3 (2018): 218–30. *https://doi.org/10.1080/1756073X.2018.1461489.*

—. "When Love is Not True: Literature and Theology after Romance." In *Literature and Theology: New Interdisciplinary Spaces,* edited by Heather Walton, 37–54. London: Routledge, 2011.

—. *Writing Methods in Theological Reflection.* London, England: SCM Press, 2014.

Walton, Roger. "Assessment in Adult Christian Education." In *Learning in the Way: Research and Reflection on Adult Christian Education,* edited by Jeff Astley, 90–112. Herefordshire: Gracewing, 2000.

—. "Disciples Together: The Small Group as a Vehicle for Discipleship Formation." *Journal of Adult Theological Education* 8, no. 2 (2011): 99–114. *https://doi.org/10.1558/JATE.v8i2.99.*

Ward, Pete. *Liquid Ecclesiology: The Gospel and the Church.* Leiden: Brill, 2017.

Warren, Michael. "Religious Formation in the Context of Social Formation." In *Critical Perspectives on Christian Education: A Reader on the Aims, Principles and Philosophy of Christian Education,* edited by Jeff Astley and Leslie J. Francis, 202–14. Herefordshire: Gracewing, 1994.

Watkins, Clare. *Disclosing Church: An Ecclesiology Learned from Conversations in Practice.* Abingdon: Routledge, 2020.

Weekley, David Elias. "Exploring Transgender Spirituality Within a Retreat Setting: Theological Action Research." Doctor of Ministry, Boston University, 2016.

Wenger, Etienne. *Communities of Practice: Learning, Meaning, and Identity.* Cambridge: Cambridge University Press, 1998.

Westerberg, Thomas, Ylva Grauers Berggren, Julius Lybäck, Sophie Karlsson, and Jérôme Gouzou. "Utvärdering av Svenska kyrkans program för lärande och undervisning: Slutrapport." [Evaluation of the Church of Sweden's program for learning and teaching: Final report.] Stockholm: Oxford Research AB, 2023.

Westerhoff, John. "Formation, Education, Instruction." In *Critical Perspectives on Christian Education: A Reader on the Aims, Principles and Philosophy of Christian Education,* edited by Jeff Astley and Leslie J. Francis, 61–72. Herefordshire: Gracewing, 1994.

White, Roger. "Promoting Spiritual Formation in Distance Education." *Christian Education Journal* 3, no. 2 (2006): 303–15. *https://doi.org/10.1177/073989130600300206.*

Whitmore, Todd D. *Imitating Christ in Magwi: An Anthropological Theology.* London: T&T Clark, 2019.

Wiedel, Björn. *Att se är att lära.* [Seeing is learning]. Älvsjö: Studieförbundet Bilda, 2010.

—. *Orden och Jorden: Om trons pedagogik och teologi.* [The words and the earth: On the pedagogy and theology of faith]. Stockholm: Proprius, 2020.

Wigg-Stevenson, Natalie. *Ethnographic Theology: An Inquiry into the Production of Theological Knowledge.* New York: Palgrave Macmillan, 2014.

—. "From Proclamation to Conversation: Ethnographic Disruptions to Theological Normativity." *Palgrave Communications* 1, no. 1 (2015): 1–9. *https://doi.org/10.1057/palcomms.2015.24.*

—. *Transgressive Devotion: Theology as Performance Art.* London: SCM Press, 2021.

—. "Trying to Tell the Truth About a Life: The Problem of Representation for Ethnographic Theology." In *What Really Matters: Scandinavian Perspectives on Ecclesiology and Ethnography,* edited by Jonas Ideström and Tone Stangeland Kaufman, 183–99. Eugene: Pickwick Publications, 2018.

—. "What's Really Going On: Ethnographic Theology and the Production of Theological Knowledge." *Cultural Studies* ↔ *Critical Methodologies* 18, no. 6 (2018): 423–29. *https://doi.org/10.1177/1532708617744576.*

Wingeier, Douglas E. "Christian Education as Faith Translation." In *Critical Perspectives on Christian Education: A Reader on the Aims, Principles and Philosophy of Christian Education,* edited by Jeff Astley and Leslie J. Francis, 238–50. Herefordshire: Gracewing, 1994.

Wirén, Jakob. *Utmaningsdriven undervisning: Hur kyrkan kan dela tro och liv idag.* [Challenge-driven teaching: How the church can share faith and life today]. Stockholm: Verbum, 2017.

Wolfteich, Claire. *Mothering, Public Leadership, and Women's Life Writing: Explorations in Spirituality Studies and Practical Theology* Leiden: Brill, 2017.

Wong, Arch Chee Keen. "Christian Faculty Teaching Reflective Practice: An Action Research Approach to Learning." *Christian Higher Education* 8, no. 3 (2009): 173–86. *https://doi.org/10.1080/15363750902782365.*

—. "Considering Reflection from the Student Perspective in Higher Education." *SAGE Open* 6, no. 1 (2016): 1–9. *https://doi.org/10.1177/2158244016638706.*

—. "How Is the Internship Going Anyways? An Action Research Approach to Understanding the Triad Relationship between Interns, Mentors, and Field Advisors." *Educational Action Research* 19, no. 4 (2011): 517–29. *https://doi.org/10.1080/09650792.2011.625704.*

Wong, Arch Chee Keen, Bill McAlpine, Tim Moore, Dave Brotherton, Ian R. Charter, Emma Emgård, and Fern Buszowski. "Learning Through Shared Christian Praxis: Reflective Practice in the Classroom." *Teaching Theology & Religion* 12, no. 4 (2009): 305–20. *https://doi.org/10.1111/j.1467-9647.2009.00545.x.*

Wulff, Helena, ed. *The Anthropologist as Writer: Genres and Contexts in the Twenty-First Century.* New York: Berghahn Books, 2016.

Wuthnow, Robert. *Sharing the Journey: Support Groups and America's New Quest for Community.* New York: The Free Press, 1994.

Wyman Jr., Jason A. *Constructing Constructive Theology: An Introductory Sketch.* Minneapolis: Fortress Press, 2017.

Yasnitsky, Anton. "Vygotsky, Lev." In *Encyclopedia of Educational Theory and Philosophy,* edited by Denis C. Phillips, 844–46. Thousand Oaks: SAGE Publications, 2014.

Zaidi, Shehr Bano. "Situating Sensitizing Concepts in the Constructivist-Critical Grounded Theory Method." *International Journal of Qualitative Methods* 21, no. 1 (2022): 1–6. *https://doi.org/10.1177/16094069211061957.*

Zottoli, Davide. "Intentionality and Inner Awareness." *Phenomenology and Mind* 22 (2022): 68–80. *https://doi.org/10.17454/pam-2205.*

Index of Hashtags

Dissertationes Theologicae Holmienses

1. Eurell, John-Christian. *Peter's Legacy in Early Christianity: The Appropriation and Use of Peter's Authority in the First Three Centuries.* DTH 1. Stockholm: Enskilda Högskolan Stockholm, 2021.

2. Mannerfelt, Frida. *Co-preaching: The Practice of Preaching in Digital Culture and Spaces.* DTH 2. Stockholm: Enskilda Högskolan Stockholm, 2023.

3. Appelfeldt, Joel. *Dopet som hantverk: Gudstjänstkreativitet och liturgisk taktik i Svenska kyrkan och Equmeniakyrkan.* DTH 3. Skellefteå: Artos Academic, 2023.

4. Gobena, Abate. *Sanctity and Environment in Ethiopian Hagiography: The Case of Gedle Gebre Menfes Qiddus.* DTH 4. Stockholm: Enskilda Högskolan Stockholm, 2023.

5. Lockneus, Elin. *Kyrkbänksteologi.* DTH 5. Skellefteå: Artos Academic, 2023.

6. Asserhed, Björn. *Gardens in the Wasteland: Christian Formation in Three Swedish Church Plants.* DTH 6. Stockholm: Enskilda Högskolan Stockholm, 2024.

7. Hallonsten, Simon. *Online Small Groups as Sites of Teaching: An Action Research Dissertation into Christian Religious Education in the Church of Sweden.* DTH 7. Stockholm: Enskilda Högskolan Stockholm, 2024.